Violence against women's health in international law

MANCHESTER
1824
Manchester University Press

Melland Schill Studies in International Law
Series editors Iain Scobbie and Jean d'Aspremont (Manchester International Law Centre)

MELAND SCHILL STUDIES

Originally associated with the Melland Schill Lectures at the Manchester International Law centre, this prestigious series brings together the very best scholarship, carefully curated by leading experts. Each volume tackles major issues and current developments in the field, and the series has moved beyond its earlier iterations to become a home for exceptional academic work from around the world. Many of the works previously published under the name 'Melland Schill monographs', have become standard references in the field, such as General AVP Rogers' exposition of law on the battlefield; Anthony Carty on the decay of international law; Professors Hilary Charlesworth and Christine Chinkin on feminism and international law; Professors Vaughan Lowe and Robin Churchill on the law of the sea; Nigel White on the law of international organisations; and Professor L.C. Green on the law of armed conflict.
Under the stewardship of new editors and published in a variety of digital editions as well as in print, this venerable series has been given renewed vigour.

Principles of direct and superior responsibility in international humanitarian law
Ilias Bantekas

The treatment and taxation of foreign investment under international law
Fiona Beveridge

War crimes and crimes against humanity in the Rome Statute of the International Criminal Court
Christine Byron

The boundaries of international law
Hilary Charlesworth and Christine Chinkin

The law of the sea
Robin Churchill and Vaughan Lowe

International law and policy of sustainable development
Duncan French

The changing rules on the use of force on international law
Tarcisio Gazzini

Contemporary law of armed conflict
Leslie Green

Child soldiers in international law
Matthew Happold

Human rights in Europe
J.G. Merrills and A.H. Robertson

The rights and duties of neutrals
Stephen Neff

Law on the battlefield
A.P.V. Rogers

Indigenous peoples and human rights
Patrick Thornberry

Jurisprudence of international law
Nicholas Tsagourias

The law of international organisations
Nigel D White

Violence against women's health in international law

SARA DE VIDO

Manchester University Press

Published by Manchester University Press
Altrincham Street, Manchester M1 7JA

www.manchesteruniversitypress.co.uk

British Library Cataloguing-in-Publication Data
A catalogue record for this book is available from the British Library

ISBN 978 1 5261 2497 5 hardback
ISBN 978 1 5261 2498 2 open access

First published 2020

Typeset in 10/12 Times by
Servis Filmsetting Ltd, Stockport, Cheshire

Contents

Acknowledgements

This book started in Manchester, UK, at the Manchester International Law Centre, which I visited in 2015. The original idea I had at that time developed into a much bigger project in the following years. I am grateful to the editors of the Melland Schill Series (MUP) for giving me the opportunity to publish in this prestigious series that hosts one of the books that have been so inspiring for me, *The Boundaries of International Law* by C. Chinkin and H. Charlesworth. My enormous gratitude goes to Jean d'Aspremont and Iain Scobbie for welcoming me to the University of Manchester when I needed to escape from my busy teaching life and for providing invaluable support and advice. The Manchester International Law Centre (MILC), of which they are founders and directors, is an excellent example of what a vibrant academic environment should be. Thanks to the MILC members and to the Women in International Law Network's co-founders and members for making me feel at home every time I am in Manchester.

I owe a lot to the places where the arguments of this research have been elaborated, written and put to the test: I would like to mention in particular Manchester, Tokyo, Boston, Venice, Berlin and the Dolomites. I always take inspiration and energy from working in fascinating libraries, discussions with colleagues and walking surrounded by the enchanting beauty of nature.

This book could never have been completed without the advice, the support, the academic leadership and the friendship of many colleagues around the world. I am grateful to have met amazing feminist scholars over the last few years who have inspired me with their passion and their work. They have guided – and will guide in the future – my teaching and my research.

I would like to thank, in particular, Lourdes Peroni, Sheffield Hallam University, for her valuable feedback; and Laura Candiotto, von Humboldt Senior Research Fellow at the Free University of Berlin, a friend and a great philosopher, for helping me to understand the complexity of the Hippocratic medical paradigm. Particular thanks are due to Professor Riccardo Pisillo Mazzeschi for reading and providing precious comments on chapter 3 of this book. Thanks also to Alexandra David for help with the proofreading and the revision of the bibliography. A particular thanks to the reviewers for their useful comments. All remaining errors are mine.

Acknowledgements

I would like to express my gratitude to the Department of Economics, Ca' Foscari University of Venice, for its financial support and for providing a stimulating environment in which to work, and to all my colleagues in San Giobbe who have always encouraged me. My warm thanks also go to the international students of the course in Gender Studies (Spring 2019) at the Venice International University, who gave me input and ideas (including the translation of a South Korean judgment and some Japanese articles) to conclude the book.

All URLs cited in this book were accessed on 25 July 2019.

Finally, thank you, with boundless love, to my husband Luca for his constant encouragement, for our amazing experiences together, and for always believing in me.

San Vito di Cadore, Italy, July 2019

Abbreviations

African Charter	African Charter on Human and People's Rights
African Commission	African Commission on Human and People's Rights
American Convention	American Convention on Human Rights
American Declaration	American Declaration of the Rights and Duties of Man
Belém do Pará Convention	Inter-American Convention on the Prevention, Punishment, and Eradication of Violence against Women
CAT	UN Committee against Torture
CEDAW	UN Convention on the Elimination of all Forms of Discrimination against Women
CEDAW Committee	UN Committee on the Elimination of Discrimination against Women
CERD	UN Committee on the Elimination of Racial Discrimination
CETS	European Treaty Series [Council of Europe]
CGIL	Confederazione Generale Italiana del Lavoro
CRC	UN Committee on the Rights of the Child
DV	domestic violence
EC	emergency contraception
ECHR	European Convention on Human Rights
ECOSOC	UN Economic and Social Council
ECtHR	European Court of Human Rights
ESCR Committee	UN Economic, Social and Cultural Rights Committee
ETS	European Treaty Series
EU	European Union
FGM/C	female genital mutilation/cutting
FIGO	International Federation of Gynecology and Obstetrics
GC	General Comment

GCS	genital cosmetic surgery
GR	General Recommendation
GREVIO	Council of Europe's Group of Experts on Action against Violence against Women and Domestic Violence
HIV	human immunodeficiency viruses
HRC	Human Rights Committee
IACHR	Inter-American Court of Human Rights
IACommHR	Inter-American Commission on Human Rights
ICC	International Criminal Court
ICCPR	International Covenant on Civil and Political Rights
ICESCR	International Covenant on Economic, Social and Cultural Rights
ICPD	International Convention on Population and Development
ICTR	International Criminal Tribunal for Rwanda
ICTY	International Criminal Tribunal for the former Yugoslavia
ILM	International Legal Materials
Istanbul Convention	Istanbul Convention on Preventing and Combating Violence against Women and Domestic Violence (Council of Europe)
Maputo Protocol	Protocol to the African Charter on Human and Peoples' Rights on the Rights of Women in Africa
NGO	non-governmental organisation
OHCHR	Office of the High Commissioner for Human Rights
OV	obstetric violence
Oviedo Convention	Convention for the Protection of Human Rights and Dignity of the Human Being with regard to the Application of Biology and Medicine
Rome Statute	Rome Statute of the International Criminal Court
SFDI	Société française pour le droit international
SR	Special Rapporteur
TEU	Treaty on the European Union
UN	United Nations
UN GA	UN General Assembly
UNHCR	UN High Commissioner for Refugees
UNTS	UN Treaty Series
VAW	violence against women
VAWH	violence against women's health
WHO	World Health Organization

Introduction: the narrative

Premise and main argument: elaborating the new notion of violence against women's health

Violence against women (VAW) has been the object of hundreds of studies, pertaining to different areas of research. International law has been one of these areas, the analysis focusing on gender-based violence as a violation of human rights, in particular a violation of the principle of non-discrimination, the prohibition of torture, inhuman or degrading treatment, the right to life, the right to respect for private and family life, and on states' obligations in preventing and combating the widespread phenomenon. VAW is characterised by three distinctive elements: its universality, since the phenomenon is not limited to a specific regional, cultural or religious context; the multiplicity of its forms; and the intersectionality of diverse kinds of discrimination against women.[1] The then Secretary-General of the United Nations (UN), Kofi Annan, in an in-depth study published in 2006, considered discrimination against women both as a consequence and as a cause of VAW,[2] in the sense that discrimination against women is at the same time at the very basis of any form of VAW *and* the outcome of VAW, an obstacle to the achievement of gender equality.[3]

In legal analysis great emphasis has been placed over time on discrimination on the basis of sex, which is often intertwined with other bases such as ethnicity, religion, age and sexual orientation. However, in investigating the phenomenon of violence, an aspect has not been explored sufficiently: violence may severely affect women's health, and in particular reproductive health. As pointed out by the UN Committee on the Elimination of Discrimination against Women (CEDAW Committee), 'gender-based violence is a critical health issue for women.'[4]

Yet VAW does not relate solely to the right to health in consequential terms. As affirmed in 1999 by the then Special Rapporteur (SR) on Violence against Women, its Causes and Consequences, Radhika Coomaraswamy, '[v]iolence against women may occur within the context of reproductive health policy. Violence and violations of women's reproductive health may result either from direct State action, via harmful reproductive policies, or from State failure to meet its core obligations to promote the empowerment of women.'[5] Although this argument has not been further developed at the international level, it appears essential in order to build a solid framework for reconceptualising states' obligations in preventing and combating VAW as linked to the right to health and the right to reproductive health.

Using an international law perspective, this book will distil the relationship between violence against women and the right to health, including reproductive health, focusing on the following areas of analysis. Violation of the right to health is a consequence of violence (horizontal dimension), as much as (state) health policies might cause – or create the conditions for – violence against women (vertical dimension). The horizontal dimension aims to consider interpersonal relations, whereas the vertical dimension encompasses state health policies and laws. Both dimensions will be discussed and put to the test throughout the book. The analysis of the relationship will generate one key, innovative idea: violence against women's health (VAWH). This concept is meant to capture the core of the violation of women's rights to health and to reproductive health. Paraphrasing the definition included in the UN General Assembly (UN GA) Declaration on the Elimination of Violence against Women,[6] violence against *women's health* constitutes a violation of *their right to health and reproductive health.*

The idea of VAW is fundamental and well consolidated at the international level; however, despite referring to what I have conceived as the vertical dimension of violence, it mainly focuses on the horizontal, interpersonal dimension. Compared to the concept of VAW, VAWH will be capable of comprehensively grasping the two dimensions of violence affecting women's rights to health and to reproductive health, and will add a new element to the definition: the limitation of women's autonomy, which is absent from the notion of VAW as elaborated at the international level.

The main argument has been built on the paradigm of medicine which has been known since Hippocrates: *anamnesis*, diagnosis, treatment and prognosis.[7] The paradigm is a useful tool for constructing the idea of violence against women's health, describing the state of the law and unearthing states' obligations in countering VAWH. The re-conceptualising of states' obligations will start from the international law of state responsibility and will focus on three types of obligation: obligations of result, due diligence obligations and obligations to progressively take steps. The relationship between VAW and women's right to health is a matter of international human rights law. It allows a legal recognition of the harms to their health suffered by female victims/survivors of violence and, at the same time, it reinforces the justiciability of the right to health at the international, regional and domestic levels.

Background

The relationship between violence against women and the violation of the right to health has not raised as much attention at the international level as has the violation of other rights,[8] in particular civil and political rights. As early as 1980, during the Second World Conference on Women, VAW was considered as a social problem within the ambit of health policies.[9] However, the relationship has never been overtly encapsulated in an international human rights treaty.

VAW emerged as a human rights issue only in the 1990s, as did the concept of reproductive health. Since then, over the years, many commentators, UN bodies, national and international courts have demonstrated that women's health is a human rights issue, and that reproductive rights are a component of women's right to health.[10] The UN Convention on the Elimination of All Forms of Discrimination against Women of 1979 (CEDAW) obliges states 'to eliminate discrimination against women in the field of health care' (Article 12(1)), and the CEDAW Committee has interpreted access to health care, including care of reproductive health, as a basic right.[11] The UN Economic, Social and Cultural Rights Committee (ESCR Committee) acknowledged that the right to the 'highest attainable standard of health' includes 'sexual and reproductive freedoms' in its General Comment (GC) No. 14 (2000), interpreting Article 12 of the International Covenant on Economic, Social and Cultural Rights (ICESCR), and sixteen years later devoted an entire GC, No. 22, to the right to sexual and reproductive health.[12]

Consequences of violence on women's health have been pointed out in communications and concluding observations by the CEDAW Committee, which has also invited states to ensure the adoption of appropriate measures within the health sector.[13] In 2015, UN human rights experts, the Rapporteur on the Rights of Women of the Inter-American Commission on Human Rights (IACommHR) and the SR on the Rights of Women, and Human Rights Defenders of the African Commission on Human and Peoples' Rights presented a joint statement in which they stressed that 'violence against women, harmful gender stereotypes and multiple and intersectional forms of discrimination based on sex and gender lead to the violation of women's sexual and reproductive health rights.'[14]

However, what emerges from existing literature and jurisprudence is that violence affects women's *health*, a concept that is conceived more as a 'status' than a human right.[15] In other words, the right to health has been 'absorbed', and indirectly protected, by invoking civil and political rights, such as the prohibition of discrimination, the prohibition of torture, the right to respect for private and family life, and the right to life. For example, domestic violence (DV) and forced sterilisation have been identified by UN bodies as violations of human rights, in particular the right to life, and the prohibition of torture as clarified by the UN Human Rights Committee (HRC).[16] The reason for what I will call the 'indirect protection' of the right to health is that the HRC, which has been – at least for the time being – one of the most active bodies at UN level in addressing issues of women's health, is not competent to consider alleged violations of the right to health; this right is not enshrined in the International Covenant on Civil and Political Rights (ICCPR), of which the HRC is the guardian.

Similarly, at the regional level, the European Court of Human Rights (ECtHR), for example, has only indirectly promoted and protected the right to health of female victims of violence, by applying articles of the European Convention on Human Rights (ECHR) providing for civil and political rights, namely Articles 3 and 8. Regional human rights courts and UN treaty bodies, by means of interpretation, have easily overcome the absence of an express treaty provision on the right to health by applying 'other' human rights. In other words, international and regional jurisprudence has not directly ensured respect for the right to health; rather, it has indirectly promoted the right's content by applying other, more 'justiciable' rights. This affirmation does not reduce the importance of the right to health. The right to health *is* a human right and so is the right to reproductive health; despite being 'latecomers' among the human rights, that is economic, social, and cultural rights, these rights *are* human rights,[17] which create legal obligations on states that ratified the international treaty in which the same rights are enshrined. Furthermore, at the domestic level, the right to health has found wide recognition; more than two-thirds of the world's constitutions make some reference to the right to health, and 'health-related litigation is now commonly pursued in domestic courts.'[18] The right to reproductive health has recently gained momentum, thanks to an increasing number of cases, in particular on abortion-related issues. For all these reasons, it is time to reconsider the right to health and the right to reproductive health in their relationship with VAW, and put them at the centre of the analysis.

Violence against women: the knowledge so far

The CEDAW, adopted in 1979, which was aimed at drawing attention to women's inequality, did not include provisions on VAW.[19] The UN GA adopted in 1985 a resolution in which it invited states to enact measures in response to DV,[20] and finally, in 1993, it approved a Declaration which addressed VAW as a 'manifestation of historically unequal power relations between men and women' in its preamble.[21] Article 1 of the Declaration defined VAW as 'any act of gender-based violence that results in, or is likely to result in, physical, sexual or psychological harm or suffering to women, including threats of such acts, coercion or arbitrary deprivation of liberty, whether occurring in public or in private life.' The definition is very similar to the one provided in the year preceding the Declaration by the CEDAW Committee in its pivotal GR No. 19. VAW was conceived as 'violence … directed against a woman because she is a woman or that affects women disproportionately,' including 'acts that inflict physical, mental or sexual harm or suffering, threats of such acts, coercion and other deprivations of liberty.'[22] In the Council of Europe Convention on preventing and combating VAW and DV, adopted in 2011 and entering into force in 2014, VAW is defined as 'a violation of human rights and a form of discrimination against women and shall mean all acts of gender-based violence that result in, or are likely to result in, physical, sexual, psychological or economic harm or suffering to women, including threats of such acts, coercion or arbitrary deprivation of liberty, whether occurring in public or in private life' (Article 3).

VAW can be considered from five different perspectives. Firstly, it is a form of discrimination against women, both *de jure* and *de facto*.[23] Secondly, VAW is a form of gender-based violence, and 'gender-based violence against women' was precisely the expression chosen by the CEDAW Committee in its most recent GR No. 35, which replaces GR No. 19 of 1992.[24] Violence against women is based *on gender*, on the fact of women *being women*. Violence does not 'just happen' to occur to women, but it is motivated by 'factors concerned with gender,' such as the need to assert power and control.[25] The philosopher Susan J. Brison pointed out that the reason why

> [i]t is so hard for so many to recognise acts of *gender*-based violence *as* such is that if it is an attack by a stranger, it is viewed as 'a random act of violence,' typically by a psychopath, a monster, 'not one of us,' whereas, if it is an attack by a date/acquaintance/partner/spouse, it is considered to be a crime of passion – motivated by uncontrollable lust or jealous love (that is, if it is considered a crime at all, which, in all too many cases, it is not). That such violence constitutes a violation of women's civil rights is seldom acknowledged.[26]

Thirdly, VAW is a violation of human rights. In GR No. 19, the CEDAW Committee identified the following rights as being infringed by VAW: the right to life; the right not to be subject to torture or to cruel, inhuman or degrading treatment or punishment; the right to equal protection according to humanitarian norms in time of international or internal armed conflict; the right to liberty and security of person; the right to equal protection under the law; the right to equality in the family; the right to the highest attainable standard of physical and mental health; the right to just and favourable conditions of work.[27] Other rights can be considered, such as the right to privacy, including the right of the abused woman to change surname or to eliminate a surname if by virtue of the marriage she has obtained it, and the rights belonging to the so-called 'third generation' of human rights, such as the rights to peace and to a positive cultural context.[28] Fourthly, I conceive VAW as an 'umbrella term,' a cluster of offences and harmful behaviours rather than an offence *per se*.[29] The element of intent, which characterises offences in criminal law, is therefore not necessary to identify VAW and it is indeed absent from international and regional legal instruments on VAW, including the Council of Europe Istanbul Convention on Preventing and Combating Violence against Women and Domestic Violence (Istanbul Convention). The element of intent is relevant only when it comes to assess individual responsibility for the commission of the specific offences (such as stalking, rape, DV) that can be brought within the terms of the more general framework of VAW. States are responsible for VAW when they violate their obligations to protect the human rights of women who are victims/survivors of violence committed by state and non-state actors. Although not intentionally, states cause or create the conditions for VAW, because their systems encourage the perpetuation of patterns of discrimination rooted in the society through policies and laws in the health sector, as I will show, even when these measures are (apparently) adopted for the benefit of women themselves. It has been argued that 'the intention to discriminate may be systematic without being conscious, and thus intentional,' and 'requiring a showing of intent leaves potentially widespread and insidious unconscious discrimination unremedied.'[30] Fifthly, given the widespread recognition of VAW as a violation of human rights at the international, regional and national levels, it sounds reasonable to enquire whether there exists an international custom prohibiting VAW. The CEDAW Committee, in its landmark GR no. 35 on VAW of 2017, answered in the affirmative. The Committee posited that '*opinio juris* and State practice suggest that the prohibition of gender-based violence against women has evolved into a principle of customary international law,' and that 'General recommendation No. 19 has been a key catalyst for this process.'[31] The question is in fact two intertwined questions, as follows: does an international custom prohibiting gender-based VAW exist? If so, what is the content of this norm? The Committee has proved courageous, and the GR will probably spur the consolidation of a custom to that effect in years to come. For the time being, however, I consider this argument with caution, respectfully contending that international custom has embraced the prohibition of *some* forms of VAW, but not all of them, especially when violence is committed by the state through the implementation of laws and policies in the field of health. If we do not consider VAW a distinct crime, but rather a broad term including several offences and harmful behaviours that constitute VAW because they are based on gender, then we can separately analyse whether the prohibition of a specific form of violence has achieved the status of customary international law. In this book, as I will try to demonstrate, I might contend that the prohibition of the forms of violence in the horizontal dimension has gradually consolidated as an international custom, but not all forms of violence identifiable in the vertical dimension.

The reasons underlying the choice of the right to health and the right to reproductive health

In 1994, Mahmoud Fathalla, a professor of obstetrics and gynaecology, and Chair of the World Health Organization (WHO) advisory committee on health research, acknowledged that 'society is not neutral with regard to reproductive rights,' and that in many societies 'the predominant objection against contraceptive use was directed at contraceptive control by women, rather than against contraception itself.'[32] The same year, Rebecca Cook published an innovative paper commissioned by the WHO on *Women's Health and Human Rights*, in which she emphasised the 'pervasive neglect of women's health.'[33] In 1995, Aart Hendriks contended that 'woman's right to sexual and reproductive health is not only threatened by current expressions of deep-rooted, harmful practices – including sexual violence against women and girls, forced marriage, and female genital mutilation – but is also challenged by progress in reproductive medicine.'[34] It is noteworthy that almost twenty years after these outstanding contributions, Erin Nelson, in her remarkable work on the notion of reproductive autonomy, reflected on the fact that the 'history of reproductive regulation is a history of attempting to enforce a traditional view of women as child-rearers.'[35] In 2016, the working group on the issue of discrimination against women in law and in practice, established at UN level, confirmed this view, by stating in its report that 'women's bodies are instrumentalized for cultural, political and economic purposes rooted in patriarchal traditions,' and 'instrumentalization occurs within and beyond the health sector and is deeply embedded in multiple forms of social and political control over women.'[36]

In appreciating the two dimensions at the core of the book – the violation of the right to health is a consequence of violence (horizontal dimension) as much as (state) health policies might be a cause of violence against women (vertical dimension) – which allow me to conceive the new idea of VAWH, the functional relationship existing between VAW and the rights to health and reproductive health should be emphasised. VAW has already been analysed from a human rights perspective, focusing, for example, on non-discrimination and the prohibition of torture, cruel, inhuman or degrading treatment, or punishment.[37] The right to health and the right to reproductive health are also worth exploring in detail, however, for the innovative contribution they can make to the analysis of VAW. First, these human rights – I will conceive them as human rights, and not as mere status – are always impaired by episodes of violence, as much as in all cases VAW is a form of discrimination against women. Secondly, these rights belong to the category of economic, social and cultural rights, which have been deemed less 'justiciable' than other rights. It is time to debunk the myth by demonstrating the justiciability of the right to health and the right to reproductive health as linked to violence against women, and to encourage the inclusion of these rights in international legal instruments.[38] A focus on economic, social and cultural rights would be extremely useful to empower women and to challenge the stereotyped visions of the role women play in society.[39] It is striking indeed that the Council of Europe's pivotal Istanbul Convention, adopted in 2011 and entered into force in 2014, contains just one provision concerning the right of the victim to receive compensation after suffering from a severe impairment of *health*.[40] As correctly pointed out by Cheryl Hanna:

> we legal scholars have been missing something. While our medical colleagues have done tremendous work in documenting the health effects of partner violence, to a large extent, legal scholars have been unsure exactly how physical and reproductive health, in particular, ought to factor into law. But, if we start with the premise that the right to health … is a basic human right, then we can begin to understand how including health in our arguments about affirmative state duties to end gendered violence can provide another perspective and another tool to persuade the powers that be to prioritize eliminating gendered violence.[41]

Thirdly, the focus on these two rights allows me to reflect on the public/private divide. Let us consider population policies. The anti-natalist programmes of many governments have concentrated on the 'excessively' fertile bodies of women belonging for example to ethnic minorities, and accordingly they have 'used language, made recommendations, and provided funds for activities that, in sum, suggest coercion.'[42] Similarly, pro-natalist policies have employed coercive methods. The criminalisation of abortion which has aimed to put 'women, doctors, and other facilitators in danger and sometimes behind bars,' and selective restrictions on contraception, both legal and administrative, 'often in the name of women's health,' are just two examples.[43] Here lies a challenging paradox. States have not traditionally intervened in matters related to DV, since it was considered as pertaining to the 'private' sphere, until the affirmation of VAW as a form of discrimination against women and a violation of human rights in the 1990s. States did however – and do in many cases – interfere with women's 'private' choices concerning their reproductive health in the name of population policies, which have invariably been perceived as more relevant than the individual's autonomy. Population policies also demonstrate the structural nature of discrimination against women, whose rights can be sacrificed for other purposes defined by state (male) authorities. Here this book critically reviews and challenges the traditional distinction private = women, public = men,[44] which is a true picture if we consider the political public sphere as populated by men and the state as male subject, but does not capture in its entirety the complexity of the relationship which is at the core of this book. I will therefore argue that the domestic environment also is *male* and that this view has historically justified the absence of interference by states in cases of domestic violence.[45] Rhonda Copelon interestingly argued that 'patriarchal ideology also constructed the private sphere of family and intimate relations as off-limits to State intervention even where violence was concerned,' and that 'by adopting a hands-off policy, the public sphere supported the violent exercise of power in the so-called private sphere.'[46] This view supports my choice to concentrate on women's rights to health and reproductive health. They have been neglected because the private sphere has been conceived as *male*, and so domestic violence has been excluded from state interference and women's health regarded as not suitable for leaving to women's autonomy only. I contend that the right to health, including sexual and reproductive health, is always at stake in episodes of VAW – in terms of both immediate and lasting consequences – and that an analysis from this perspective is much more gender-sensitive, since, on one hand, it takes into consideration the 'gendered experiences that affect [women's] health,'[47] and on the other hand it implies – in particular with regard to reproductive health – the 'ability' to exercise reproductive autonomy,[48] in other words, women's right to decide. In this book I will use the expression 'right to reproductive health,' as chosen by the Committee on ESCR in its GC No. 22.

Why human rights and why women's rights?

As I explained, I will consider health and reproductive health as human rights, and not as mere status as envisaged by the WHO. It should be stressed at the outset that human rights law is not devoid of criticism. It is not the purpose here to review all the theories existing in the field – this analysis would go well beyond the scope of my research – but to admit that it is impossible not to mention the limits human rights have shown.[49] For the purpose of my book, it is worth spending a few words on the universality issue, which is at the core of the debate on human rights, and in particular of women's rights. Just consider the debate on whether human rights are universal or relative, and the role of culture, while dealing, for example, with female genital mutilation/cutting (FGM/C). Are these practices acceptable because they find their basis in culture? Is the prohibition of these practices at the international level a new form of Western imperialism?[50] The concept of 'Asian values' has been coined for the Asian continent,[51] but does it mean that human rights law is not universal? The debate is too complex to be dealt with in few lines.[52]

Practices that significantly impair a woman's or a girl's bodily integrity have been condemned not only by European countries, but also by countries where FGM/C, for example, is tolerated, and even encouraged, by local communities.[53] One should bear in mind that the victims are usually girls who are too young to express consent to undergo the practice. Even though the practice is transmitted from mother to daughter and is accepted within a community, even if it is perpetrated and supported by women, FGM/C is VAW, as I have argued elsewhere,[54] and it constitutes a violation of human rights, as well as a form of discrimination against women. Moreover, Chinkin and Charlesworth pointed out that what is striking is that 'culture is much more frequently invoked in the context of women's rights than in any other area.'[55] In GC No. 21, the ESCR Committee argued that 'applying limitations to the right of everyone to take part in cultural life may be necessary in certain circumstances, in particular in the case of negative practices, including those attributed to customs and traditions, that infringe upon other human rights.'[56]

Nonetheless, the condemnation of practices such as FGM/C cannot be blind. Other practices widespread in European and American countries, supported by similar stereotyped views of the role of women in society, must be assessed from the perspective of human rights law. Accordingly, this book will explore whether and to what extent genital cosmetic surgery can be compared to FGM/C, in particular in terms of the consent expressed by the girl/woman to the practice.[57]

As I anticipated, VAW is universal, rooted in every society and manifests itself in different forms. In European countries, 'honour' is still a 'mitigating factor' for certain forms of violence – not necessarily under the law but surely within society – and the 'behaviour' of a female victim of rape or sexual abuses determines whether or not she deserves compassion or dishonour.[58]

It can be argued that human rights law has also failed to take into consideration women's specific needs, by 'essentialising the category of women and the attendant privileging of the perspectives of First World women (or some of them) while failing to reflect the multiple factors that interact to constitute violations around the world.'[59] However, the reasoning can go a bit further. In an inspiring book on sex-selective abortions affecting women of Indian origin in India and the United States, Sital Kalantry used the word 'decontextualisation' to contend that universalistic perspectives are limited in evaluating bans on practices that immigrants bring from one country to another.[60] In her view, sex-selective abortion, which is a form of severe discrimination against women and girls in India, cannot be seen in the same way in the USA, where the practice, far from being widespread (as data have shown), has been condemned by anti-abortionist associations for limiting women's autonomy. Context, which is not merely geographical but also social and economic, has therefore a role to play.[61] This book suggests the expression 'contextualised universalism' as appropriate to protect women's rights while taking into account the context in which violence is perpetrated. I argue that the debate shifts from the dichotomy universal–relative to the analysis of different grounds of discrimination. In other words, it is not a matter of *which culture* is at the basis of the violation of women's rights, but rather *across* which grounds – gender, ethnicity, class, social and economic conditions – discrimination is perpetrated. It has been contended that 'neither a claim to universal principles nor a claim to cultural relativism adequately addresses the global aspect of gendered violence.'[62] Considering different grounds for discrimination, as interestingly argued, 'will strengthen our capacity to realise the full humanity and equality of women – and other genders – everywhere.'[63] This perspective permits us to overcome the differences between approaches, by capturing the meaning of discrimination against women, and against other genders as well. It also emphasises the aspect of intersectionality, which I will discuss further in the book. The international community has indeed started, slowly, 'to explore ways to analyse women's human rights that do not represent women as a monolithic category,' meeting the request of feminists from the global South.[64]

So far, I have discussed women's rights. What about those of other genders? Dianne Otto overcomes the duality masculine/feminine by conceiving sex and gender as a fully social and performative category, which implies that international human rights law can reconceive sex/gender as 'a fluid conception that has multiple forms of expression and identification.'[65] By conceiving sex and gender as a dichotomy, women have always been depicted as vulnerable and in need of protection, the object of international treaties which only focus on their weaknesses and therefore reproduce the 'maleness' of the universal subject of international human rights law.[66] The approach has evolved over time, thanks to the work of UN treaty bodies and the increasing focus on women as agents of change; however, one should keep in mind the beginning of the debate before reflecting on its evolution.

Having said that, this book concentrates on women and girls because they are, as data demonstrates worldwide, the majority of victims/survivors of violence. This is a way, not to victimise women but rather to acknowledge the discrimination which is rooted in society. VAW is extremely entrenched in society and in history. This is clear if we consider, for example, the founding myth of Europe: a rape.[67] To acknowledge the structural nature of VAW does not mean excluding episodes of violence committed against other genders, but rather emphasising a dramatic trait of every society. If governments still decide to appoint mostly male ministers, except maybe one or two; if it is still possible to object to women having freedom to choose regarding their body; then there is still room to write and to reflect on the topic. It is a matter of feminist studies, and human rights.

Perspective: the Hippocratic medical paradigm

Existing literature has extensively analysed the phenomenon of VAW and has commented on cases decided by regional and national courts, and by UN treaty bodies, regarding women's health and reproductive rights. This study needed a conceptual model, which I found in the medical paradigm: *anamnesis,* diagnosis, treatment and prognosis. This might seem a simplistic scheme, which only takes into account part of the complexity of 'illness' (there is more than one disease; the patient's reaction can differ according to the circumstances, etc.), but it turns out to be a useful backbone for the main argument. This choice draws heavily on the natural link between health and the field of medicine, but is also dictated by the fact that it has never been explored in these terms. This paradigm is a descriptive one, because it allows a clear systematisation of the different aspects of the research according to a plausible and logical structure. It is also a building paradigm, because through distillation of the relationship between VAW and the rights to health and to reproductive health it conceives a new notion, VAWH, which leads to the reconceptualisation of states' obligations.

The medical paradigm composed of *anamnesis,* diagnosis, treatment and prognosis owes its existence to Hippocrates. Hippocrates of Coen is the name given to the 400BCE author of the Hippocratic *corpus* of writings which defined the school of medicine that bears his name. His life and his works are surrounded in an aura of mystery. As stressed by Edelstein, 'the belief has been current that none of the so-called Hippocratic writings could be ascribed with any certainty to Hippocrates himself.'[68] The *Corpus Hippocraticum* refers to 58 writings which introduced both a theory of disease and a complete description of diagnostics and treatment ('On Fistulas,' 'On Fractures,' 'On Injuries of the Head,' 'The Book of Prognostics,' etc.).[69] Greek medicine differed from previous practices in its search for the true causes of health. Empirical observation was therefore necessary in order to understand the illness and its course.

Anamnesis consists in the act of remembering, in the reconstruction of the medical history of the patient, which goes beyond mere observation of the body. As outlined by Leavy:

> At least as early as Hippocrates' time, it was recognised that human nature is not limited to that which can be observed by the examination of the body. Human nature is historical, and the first part of the examination, then as now, consisted of a history, an *anamnesis* as it is called, which means a calling to mind of a person's past. Nor did Hippocrates make this *anamnesis* just a listing of earlier symptoms or earlier diseases; it is also an account of experiences so far as they are thematically pertinent.[70]

Plato referred to *anamnesis* as 'recollection', although his thought has never been linked to medical history. In his introduction of the theory of recollection in the *Meno*, 81d, it is written that:

> [a]s the whole of nature is akin, and the soul has learned everything, nothing prevents a man, after recalling one thing only – a process men call learning – discovering everything else for himself, if he is brave and does not tire of the search; for searching and learning, are, as a whole, recollection (*anamnesis*).[71]

In other words, *anamnesis* has a technical meaning within Plato's epistemology. It is the process that permits the remembering of Ideas/Forms through the sensible world.

Diagnosis can be defined as the 'identification of the nature of an illness or other problem by examination of the symptoms.'[72] Diagnosis has been considered to provide the 'true state of the patient,' but this affirmation is problematic, since it is 'a construct of medical knowledge and reasoning methodology applied in clinical decision-making.'[73] Accordingly, Sadegh-Zadeh has distinguished between two terms: *diagnostics*, that is the investigation into the patient's health conditions, and diagnosis, which is the outcome of the former.[74] After making a diagnosis, a physician would proceed with treatment, in order to restore the balance that the illness has disrupted, and with prognosis. In Hippocratic medicine, as in every kind of medicine, prognosis is 'the prediction of the outcome of the disease, as well as its fluctuations and transmutations.'[75] If the physician 'knows what course the disease will take, he is also better able to prepare for what is to come.'[76] The 'place of truth' does not reside in the past (*anamnesis*), but rather in the future (prognosis), where it is possible to assess the appropriateness of the treatment and of the interpretative hypothesis from which it originates.[77]

Against this backdrop, it is necessary to ask whether this paradigm can be used in other fields of study. In the book *The Therapy of Desire*, Martha Nussbaum used the paradigm to study the schools of philosophy that developed in the Hellenistic period. Reflecting on Hellenistic ethics, Nussbaum identified three closely related ideas in the therapeutic investigative process.[78] The first two ideas are relevant here, since they concern 'a tentative diagnosis of disease, of factors, especially socially taught beliefs, that are most prominent in preventing people from living well,' and 'a tentative norm of health: a conception (usually general and to some degree open-ended) of the flourishing and complete human life.'[79] Thus the ideas elaborated in Hellenistic thought are well suited to describe all aspects of human life.

In the field of international studies, the sociologist Johan Galtung applied the Hippocratic paradigm to the peaceful resolution of disputes between states in his famous work *Peace by Peaceful Means*.[80] He argued that peace studies 'have much to learn from the paradigm,' and that 'much thought, speech and action in the field of violence/peace diagnoses violence, but then only as direct and physical, and mainly the acute case.'[81] He interestingly contended that the prognosis is that 'unless treated, violence will be repeated.' With regard to therapies, the 'so what, what are you going to do about it?', Galtung was convinced that 'we need maps of the social reality in which violence and peace can unfold.'[82] The question was therefore the following: how can peace researchers do peace work (therapy)? Accordingly, he elaborated different peace research paradigms.

The challenge this book faces is to build the new concept of VAWH. The book will not consider the woman as unique patient, because I believe that depicting women as vulnerable subjects does not help in eradicating VAW. Women are agents of change as much as they are victims when, for example, they bring their cases before domestic or regional courts, or before international bodies. Therefore, I contend in the diagnosis that VAWH is an illness that, by personally affecting individuals, affects the entire society. VAW is indeed a 'public health' concern, as stressed by the WHO;[83] so is VAWH. The *anamnesis* will not consider the personal experiences and the emotions of women, but it will be conducted from an international law perspective. *Mutatis mutandis*, empirical observation and the act of remembering entail, from an international legal point of view, the analysis of state practice and of international, regional and domestic jurisprudence in order to find common trends and critically discuss the interpretation given to legal instruments in force.

The framework built in the first part of this book will pave the way for a reconceptualising of states' obligations under international law, which constitutes the treatment. As recently posited by the ESCR Committee in its GC on the right to sexual and reproductive health, 'States parties have a core obligation to ensure, at the very least, minimum essential levels of satisfaction of the right to sexual and reproductive health. In this regard, States parties should be guided by contemporary human rights instruments and jurisprudence, as well as the most current international guidelines and protocols established by United Nations agencies, in particular WHO and the United Nations Population Fund.'[84]

The strength of my reasoning lies in the fact that both dimensions, the horizontal and the vertical as conceived in this book, can be unified while discussing the reconceptualising of states' obligations. In both dimensions, I will contend that – and provide examples of how – states bear legal obligations of result, due diligence and to progressively take steps. I will show that the difference between the two dimensions does not concern the 'type' of the obligations, but rather the fact that obligations 'specialise' along one or other of the two explored dimensions.

Structure of the book

The first chapter contains the *anamnesis* and is based on the analysis of selected jurisprudence of regional human rights and domestic courts, and of the quasi-jurisprudence of UN treaty bodies, related to both dimensions, focusing on the applicants, the direct or indirect application of the rights to health and reproductive health, the relevance of women's health in the analysis and reparations. The second chapter, the diagnosis, draws on the precedent and conceptualises the notion of VAWH, a new socio-legal notion, which will prove capable of encompassing both the horizontal and the vertical dimensions of violence. In this chapter I will construct the notion of VAWH as a form of discrimination against women, and a violation of the rights to health and to reproductive health. I will then reflect on autonomy and consent, and I will elaborate a human rights-based notion of autonomy as related to VAWH. In the third chapter, I will delve into treatment, which, in my view, is the reconceptualising of states' obligations. I will start from basic notions of international law, before finding the most suitable category to apply to VAWH. I will provide examples of states' obligations of result, due diligence and to progressively take steps putting both dimensions under the same umbrella. Finally, as prognosis I will provide some concluding remarks, challenging, for the last time, my paradigm, and wondering whether it is not international law itself that is the ultimate cause of VAWH.

Notes

1 United Nations (UN) Economic and Social Council (ECOSOC), *Integration of the Human Rights of Women and the Gender Perspective: Violence against Women towards an Effective Implementation of International Norms to End Violence against Women*, Report of the Special Rapporteur (SR) on Violence against Women (VAW), its causes and consequences, Yakin Ertürk, E/CN.4/2004/66, 26 December 2003, pp. 16–17. For a discussion of intersectionality, see chapter 1, 'Involuntary sterilisation: Context and legal background'.

2 UN General Assembly (UN GA), Sixty-first session, Advancement of women. In-depth study on all forms of violence against women. Report of the Secretary-General, 6 July 2006, para. 377.

3 See C. Chinkin, 'Violence against women', in M.A. Freeman, C. Chinkin and B. Rudolf (eds), *The UN Convention on the Elimination of All Forms of Discrimination against Women* (Oxford: Oxford University Press, 2012) 443, p. 446. See also C. Bunch, 'Transforming human rights from a feminist perspective', in J. Peters and A. Wolper (eds), *Women's Rights, Human Rights, International Feminist Perspectives* (New York, London: Routledge, 1995) 11, p. 15.

4 Views of 27 November 2012, *S.V.P. v. Bulgaria*, Communication No. 31/2011, para. 9.10.

5 'Integration of the Human Rights of Women and the Gender Perspective Violence against Women', E/CN.4/1999/68/Add.4, 21 January 1999, para. 44.

6 A/RES/48/104, 20 December 1993.

7 On Hippocrates and his method, see J. Jouanna, *Hippocrate: Pour une archéologie de l'école de Cnide* (Paris: Les Belles Lettres, 1974), and P. Van der Eijk, *Medicine and Philosophy in Classical Antiquity: Doctors and Philosophers on Nature, Soul, Health and Disease* (Cambridge: Cambridge University Press, 2005), p. 45*ff.*

8 On VAW, hundreds of articles and books have been written. A complete bibliography on women's rights (including violence against women) until 1995 is given in R. Cook and V. Oosterveld, 'A selected bibliography of women's human rights', *The American University Law Review* 44 (1995) 1429, and, until 2012 with specific regard to the UN Convention, M. Freeman, C. Chinkin and B. Rudolf (eds), *The UN Convention on the Elimination of All Forms of Discrimination against Women* (Oxford: Oxford University Press, 2012), p. 689 (Convention henceforth referred to as CEDAW). As reference articles and books, *inter alia*: S. Brownmiller, *Against our Will. Men, Women and Rape* (New York: Fawcett Columbine, 1975); H. Charlesworth and C. Chinkin, 'Violence against women: a global issue', in J. Stubbs (ed.), *Women, Male, Violence and the Law* (Sydney: Institute of Criminology, 1994) 13; R.J. Cook (ed.), *Human Rights of Women: National and International Perspectives* (Philadelphia: University of Pennsylvania Press, 1994); R. Copelon, 'Recognizing the egregious in the everyday: domestic violence as torture', *Columbia Human Rights Law Review* 25 (1994) 291; C. MacKinnon, 'On torture: a feminist perspective on human rights', in K.E. and Paul Mahoney (eds), *Human Rights in the Twenty-First Century: A Global Challenge* (The Hague: Martinus Nijhoff, 1993) 21; K. Dawn Askin and D.M. Koenig, *Women and International Human Rights Law,* vol. 1 (New York: Transnational Publishers, Inc., 1999); C. Chinkin and H. Charlesworth, *The Boundaries of International Law: A Feminist Analysis* (Manchester: Manchester University Press, 2000); S. Engle Merry, 'Constructing a global law – violence against women and the human rights system', *Law and Social Inquiry* 28 (2003) 941; S. Engle Merry, *Human Rights and Gender Violence* (Chicago: University of Chicago Press, 2006); C. Benninger-Budel (ed.), *Due Diligence and its Application to Protect Women from Violence* (The Hague: Brill, Nijhoff, 2008); A. Byrnes and E. Bath, 'Violence against women, the obligation of due diligence, and the optional protocol to the Convention on the Elimination of All Forms of Discrimination against Women – recent developments', *Human Rights Law Review* 8 (2008) 517; B. Meyersfeld, *Domestic Violence and International Law* (Oxford: Hart Publishing, 2012); Chinkin, 'Violence against women'; A. Edwards, *Violence against Women under International Human Rights Law* (Cambridge: Cambridge University Press, 2010).

9 Report of the World Conference of the UN Decade for Women, Copenhagen, 1980, A/CONF.94/35, Resolution 5, para. 141(f). A comment appears in Chinkin, 'Violence against women', p. 445.

10 On reproductive and sexual rights, see the outstanding book by R.J. Cook, B.M. Dickens and M.F. Fathalla (eds), *Reproductive Health and Human Rights: Integrating Medicine, Ethics, and Law* (Oxford: Oxford University Press, 2003). See also, among others, for a general overview regarding legal issues, Cook, *Human Rights of Women*; R. Cook, 'International human rights and women's reproductive health', *Studies in Family Planning* 24 (1993) 73; M. Scheinin, 'Sexual rights as human rights – protected under existing human rights treaties?', *Nordic Journal of International Law* 67 (1998) 17; I.L.

Feitshans, 'Is there a human right to reproductive health?', *Texas Journal of Women and the Law* 8 (1998–9) 93; D. Bogecho, 'Putting it to good use: the international Covenant on Civil and Political Rights and Women's Rights to Reproductive Health', *Review of Law and Women's Studies* 13 (2003–4) 229; J.M. Joachim, *Gender Violence and Reproductive Rights* (Washington DC: Georgetown University Press, 2007); S. Correa, R. Petchesky and R. Parker (eds), *Sexuality, Health and Human Rights* (Abingdon: Routledge, 2008); S. Deller Ross, *Women's Human Rights: The International and Comparative Law Casebook* (Philadelphia: University of Pennsylvania Press, 2008); L. Reichenbach and M.J. Roseman (eds), *Reproductive Health and Human Rights* (Philadelphia: University of Pennsylvania Press, 2009); A. Kulczycki (ed.), *Critical Issues in Reproductive Health* (Dordrecht, Heidelberg, New York, London: Springer, 2014). Also relevant are the articles published in *Health and Human Rights Journal* (among others, see D. Uberoi and M. De Bruyn, 'Human rights *versus* control over women's reproductive self-determination', *Health and Human Rights* 15 (2013) 161), and the World Health Organization (WHO) report on *Global and regional estimates of violence against women: prevalence and health effects of intimate partner violence and non-partner sexual violence*, Geneva, 2013.

Also relevant are the articles published in *Health and Human Rights Journal* (among others, see D. Uberoi and M. De Bruyn, 'Human rights *versus* control over women's reproductive self-determination', *Health and Human Rights* 15 (2013), p. 161), and the World Health Organization (WHO) report on *Global and regional estimates of violence against women: prevalence and health effects of intimate partner violence and non-partner sexual violence*, Geneva, 2013.

11 General Recommendation (GR) No. 24 (1999) on Article 12 of the Convention, Women and Health (CEDAW Committee). See also R.J. Cook and V. Undurraga, 'Article 12', in Freeman *et al.*, *The UN Convention*, 311, p. 317.

12 General Comment (GC) No. 14 (2000) on the Right to the Highest Attainable Standard of Health and GC No. 22 (2016) on Sexual and Reproductive Health (UN Economic, Social and Cultural Rights (ESCR) Committee). See also, although it is not my purpose to provide an analysis here, GC No. 36 (2018) on the Right to Life (Human Rights Committee – HRC) which reflects on abortion at para. 8.

13 See, for the cases before 2010, Cook and Undurraga, 'Article 12', and, among recent examples, the concluding observations of the CEDAW Committee on Slovenia, 23 November 2015, p. 11, where the Committee found that cuts in the health budget and the new requirement for women to cover 20 per cent of the cost of sexual and reproductive health services have negative consequences for women's health.

14 Joint Statement of 24 September 2015, available at www.ohchr.org/SP/NewsEvents/Pages/DisplayNews.aspx?NewsID=16490&LangID=E (accessed 15 October 2019).

15 On the right to health see J. Tobin, *The Right to Health in International Law* (Oxford: Oxford University Press, 2012) and bibliography there included. See also M. Bèlanger, 'Réflexions sur la réalité du droit international de la santé', *Revue québécoise de droit international* II (1985) 19; A. Hendriks, 'The right to health', *European Journal of Health Law* 1 (1994) 187; B. Toebes, 'Towards an improved understanding of the international human right to health', *Human Rights Quarterly* 21 (1999) 661; A. Hendriks, 'The close connection between classical rights and the right to health, with special reference to the right to sexual and reproductive health', *Medicine and Law* 18 (1999) 225; B. Toebes, R. Ferguson, M.M. Markovic and O. Nnamuchi (eds),

The Right to Health: A Multi-Country Study of Law, Policy and Practice (The Hague: Asser Press, 2014); P. Hunt (author of numerous publications and reports while he was UN SR on the right to health), 'Interpreting the international right to health in a human rights-based approach to health', *Health and Human Rights* 18 (2016) 109; T. Murphy, *Health and Human Rights* (Oxford and Portland, OR: Hart Publishing, 2013); M.A. Grodin, D. Tarantola, G.J. Annas and S. Gruskin (eds), *Health and Human Rights in a Changing World* (New York, London: Routledge, 2013); L. Forman, L. Caraoshi, A.R. Chapman and E. Lamprea, 'Conceptualizing minimum core obligations under the right to health: how should we define and implement the "morality of the depths"', *International Journal of Human Rights* (2016) 531; C. Napoli, 'Le droit des femmes à la santé', in M. Jänterä-Jareborg and H. Tignoudja (eds), *Women's Rights and the Elimination of Discrimination* (The Hague: Brill Nijhoff, 2016) 555; J. Tasioulas, *The Minimum Core of the Human Right to Health* (Washington DC: World Bank, 2017), available at https://openknowledge.worldbank.org/handle/10986/29143.

16 Bogecho, 'Putting it to good use', p. 247*ff*. Among the views adopted by UN committees, see for example the case *K.L. v. Peru*, of 22 November 2005, Communication No. 1153/2003. On forced and involuntary sterilisation, see the comprehensive report of the WHO, *Eliminating Forced, Coercive and Otherwise Involuntary Sterilization. An Interagency Statement* (Geneva, 2014).

17 On the importance of distinguishing the right to health from the 'interest in health' see the recent article by J. Tasioulas, 'Saving human rights from human rights law', *Vanderbilt Journal of Transnational Law* 52 (2019) 1167. See also the previous work by J. Tasioulas and E. Vayena, 'The place of human rights and the common good in global health policy', *Theoretical Medicine and Bioethics* 37 (2016) 365, p. 370.

18 B. Saul, D. Kinley and J. Mowbray, *The International Covenant on Economic, Social and Cultural Rights. Commentary, Cases and Materials* (Oxford: Oxford University Press, 2014), pp. 1061–2.

19 D. Otto, 'Women's rights', in D. Moeckli, S. Shah and S. Sivakumaran (eds), *International Human Rights Law* (Oxford: Oxford University Press, 3rd edn, 2018) 317. The author identifies four limits of the Convention: the comparison between men and women, the lack of reference to VAW, the assumption of normative married heterosexuality and 'the very limited acknowledgement of multiple and intersectional forms of discrimination.'

20 A/RES/40/36 (1985).

21 A/RES/48/104, preamble.

22 GR No. 19, A/47/38 (1992), CEDAW Committee, para. 6.

23 The 2011 (Council of Europe) Istanbul Convention on Preventing and Combating Violence against Women and Domestic Violence (Istanbul Convention) promotes the 'realisation of *de jure* and *de facto* equality between women and men' as 'a key element in the prevention of violence against women' (preamble).

24 GR No. 35 on gender-based violence against women, updating GR No. 19, 14 July 2017, CEDAW/C/GC/35.

25 Chinkin, 'Violence against women', p. 452.

26 S.J. Brison, 'Justice and gender-based violence', *Revue international de philosophie* 67:3 (2013) 263.

27 GR No. 19, para. 7.

28 See the Protocol to the African Charter on Human and People's Rights on the Rights of Women in Africa (Maputo Protocol), 11 July 2003, Articles 16 and 17.

29 See, in more detail, S. De Vido, *Donne, violenza e diritto internazionale. La Convenzione di Istanbul del Consiglio d'Europa del 2011* (Udine, Milan: Mimesis, 2016).

30 A.X. Fellmeth, *Paradigms of International Human Rights Law* (Oxford: Oxford University Press, 2016), p. 162 and p. 178. *Contra,* R. Sifris, *Reproductive Freedom, Torture and International Human Rights* (London and New York: Routledge, 2014), p. 128, contending that when 'harms are clearly foreseeable,' it is difficult to argue 'that they are not intended.'

31 GR No. 35, para. 2. See a comment in S. De Vido, 'The prohibition of violence against women as customary international law? Remarks on the CEDAW General Recommendation No. 35', *Diritti umani diritto internazionale* 2 (2018) 379.

32 M.F. Fathalla, 'The impact of reproductive subordination on women's health family planning services', *American University Law Review* 44 (1994–5) 1179, pp. 1181–2.

33 R. Cook, *Women's Health and Human Rights* (Geneva: WHO, 1994), p. 5.

34 A. Hendriks, 'Promotion and protection of women's right to sexual and reproductive health under international law: the economic Covenant and the women's Convention conference on the interventional protection of reproductive rights: the right to health', *American University Law Review* 44 (1995) 1123, p. 1127.

35 E. Nelson, *Law, Policy, and Reproductive Autonomy* (Oxford, Portland, OR: Hart Publishing, 2013), p. 66.

36 Report of the working group on the issue of discrimination against women in law and in practice, A/HRC/32/44, 8 April 2016, para. 18.

37 See, for example, the analysis in A. Edwards, *Violence against Women under International Human Rights Law* (Cambridge: Cambridge University Press, 2011).

38 On justiciability, see M.K. Addo, 'The justiciability of economic, social and cultural rights', *Commonwealth Law Bulletin* 14 (1988) 1425; M.K. Addo, 'Justiciability re-examined', in R. Beddard and D.M. Hill (eds), *Economic, Social and Cultural Rights: Progress and Achievement* (London: Macmillan, 1992) 93. See also K. Tomasevski, 'Justiciability of economic, social and cultural rights', *ICJ Review* (1995) 203; J.K. Mapulanga-Hulston, 'Examining the justiciability of economic, social and cultural rights', *The International Journal of Human Rights* 6 (2002) 29, p. 36; M.J. Dennis and D. P. Steward, 'Justiciability of economic, social and cultural rights: should there be an international complaints mechanism to adjudicate the rights to food, water, housing and health?', *American Journal of International Law* 98 (2004) 462; C. Chinkin, *The Protection of Economic, Social and Cultural Rights Post-Conflict*, paper of 2007, p. 33 available at www2.ohchr.org/english/issues/women/docs/Paper_Protection_ESCR.pdf; L. Forman, 'Justice and justiciability: advancing solidarity and justice through South Africans' right to health jurisprudence', *Medicine and Law* 27 (2008) 661.

39 See C. Chinkin and S. Wright, 'The hunger trap: women, food and self-determination', *Michigan Journal of International Law* 14 (1992–3) 262, p. 312.

40 I am referring to Article 30 of the Convention. On the Istanbul Convention, see De Vido, *Donne, Violenza,* and R. McQuigg, *The Istanbul Convention, Domestic Violence and Human Rights* (Abingdon: Routledge, 2017).

41 C. Hanna, 'Health, human rights, and violence against women and girls: broadly redefining affirmative state duties after *Opuz v. Turkey*', *Hastings International & Comparative Law Review* 34 (2011) 127, p. 136. She was referring to the thoughts of Virginia A. Leary, 'The right to health in international human rights law', *Health and Human Rights* 1:1 (1994) 24.

42 R. Solinger and M. Nakachi, 'Introduction', in R. Solinger and M. Nakachi (eds), *Reproductive States* (Oxford: Oxford University Press, 2016) 1, p. 21.

43 Solinger, Nakachi, 'Introduction', pp. 21–2.

44 See C. Pateman, 'Critiques of the public private dichotomy', in S.I. Benn and G.F. Gaus (eds), *Public and Private in Social Life* (New York: St Martin's Press, 1983) 281; C. Pateman, *The Sexual Contract* (Stanford, CA: Stanford University Press, 1988); S. Moller Okin, *Women in Western Political Thought* (Princeton, NJ: Princeton University Press, 1988). See also Meyersfeld, *Domestic Violence*, p. 100; H. Charlesworth, C. Chinkin and S. Wright, 'Feminist approaches to international law', *American Journal of International Law* 85 (1991) 613, p. 615; R. Gavison, 'Feminism and the public/private distinction', *Stanford Law Review* 45 (1992) 1; C. Romany, 'State responsibility goes private: a feminist critique of the public/private distinction in international human rights law', in Cook, *Human Rights of Women*, 85; K. Engle, 'International human rights and feminism: when discourses meet', *Michigan Journal of International Law* 13 (1991–2) 5, p. 17; D. Sullivan, 'The public/private distinction in international human rights law', in J. Peters and A. Wolper (eds), *Women's Rights, Human Rights: International Feminist Perspectives* (New York, Routledge, 1995) 103, E. Wicks, *The State and the Body* (Oxford and Portland, OR: Hart, 2016), p. 16*ff.*

45 S. Wright, 'Women and the global economic order: a feminist perspective', *American University International Law Review* 10 (1995) 861, p. 867.

46 R. Copelon, 'Gender violence as torture: the contribution of CAT General Comment no. 2', *New York City Law Review* 11 (2008) 229, p. 237.

47 R.C. Cook, 'Gender, health and human rights', in M. Grodin, D. Tarantola, G. Annas and S. Gruskin (eds), *Health and Human Rights in a Changing World* (Abingdon: Routledge, 2013) 341, p. 345.

48 Nelson, *Law, Policy,* p. 52.

49 An overview of the theories on human rights is given in F. Mégret, 'International human rights law theory', in A. Orakhelashvili, *Research Handbook on the Theory and History of International Law* (Cheltenham: Elgar, 2011) 199. See also (non-exhaustive list), between law, philosophy and history, B. Bourgeois, *Philosophie et droits de l'homme: de Kant à Marx* (Paris: Presses Universitaires de France, 1990); C. Corradetti (ed.), *Philosophical Dimensions of Human Rights* (Dordrecht: Springer, 2012); M. Boylan, *Natural Human Rights* (Cambridge: Cambridge University Press, 2014); O. De Schutter, *International Human Rights Law* (Cambridge: Cambridge University Press, 2nd edn, 2014); C. Focarelli, *La persona umana nel diritto internazionale* (Bologna: Mulino, 2013); R. Cruft, S.M. Liao and M. Renzo, *Philosophical Foundations of Human Rights* (Oxford: Oxford University Press, 2015); D. and E. Lee, *Human Rights and the Ethics of Globalization* (Cambridge: Cambridge University Press, 2010); J. Donnelly, *Universal Human Rights in Theory and Practice* (Ithaca, NY and London: Cornell University Press, 2013); A. Cassese, *I diritti umani oggi* (Roma: Laterza, 6th edn, 2019); S. Besson, 'Legal human rights theory', in K. Lippert-Rasmussen, K. Brownlee and D. Coady (eds), *A Companion to Applied Philosophy*

(Hoboken, NJ: Wiley-Blackwell, 2017) 328; S. Fredman, *Comparative Human Rights Law* (Oxford: Oxford University Press, 2018); S. Besson, 'Justifications', in Moeckli *et al.*, *International Human Rights Law*, 22. See the critical perspective of E. Posner, *The Twilight of Human Rights Law* (Oxford: Oxford University Press, 2014).

50 See also A. Cassese, *I diritti umani oggi* (Roma: Laterza, 1st edn, 2005), p. 70, who argues that it is necessary to reconcile universalism with cultural pluralism, and M.B. Dembour, 'Critiques', in Moeckli *et al.*, *International Human Rights Law,* 41, p. 50.

51 A. Sen, 'Human rights and Asian values', 1997 lecture, available at www.carnegiecouncil.org/publications/archive/morgenthau/254.

52 See, *inter alia*, J. Donnelly, 'The relative universality of human rights', *Human Rights Quarterly* 29 (2007) 281, E. Brems, 'Reconciling universality and diversity in international human rights law', in A. Sajó, *Human Rights with Modesty: The Problem of Universalism* (The Hague: Brill, 2004) 213; F. Lenzerini, *The Culturalization of Human Rights Law* (Oxford: Oxford University Press, 2014), chap. 1, and Oxford bibliography on the topic, www.oxfordbibliographies.com/view/document/obo-9780199796953/obo-9780199796953–0153.xml (last update 27 June 2017).

53 See, for example, Article 5(b) of the Maputo Protocol. Examples of national legislation are given at www.npwj.org/FGM/Status-african-legislations-FGM.html.

54 S. De Vido, 'Culturally motivated crimes against women in a multicultural Europe. The case of criminalization of FGM in the 2011 CoE Istanbul Convention', in L. Zagato and M. Vecco (eds), *Citizens of Europe: Cultures and Rights* (Venice: Edizioni Ca' Foscari, 2015) 93.

55 Chinkin and Charlesworth, *The Boundaries of International Law*, p. 222.

56 GC No. 21, Right of everyone to take part in cultural life (art. 15, para. 1 (a), International Covenant on Economic, Social and Cultural Rights (ICESCR)), 21 December 2009 (ESCR Committee), E/C.12/GC/21, para. 19.

57 See below, in Chapter 1, 'The horizontal, 'interpersonal' dimension: Female genital mutilation/cutting'.

58 See the judgment by the Italian Court of Appeal in Florence, No. 858 of 3 June 2015, which acquitted six defendants who were charged with mass rape of a young woman. The argument supporting the acquittal was based on the contradictory declarations of the woman and on the fact that 'it was a moment of weakness and fragility, which a non-coherent *[sic!]* life [such] as hers wanted to remove and censor.'

59 A. Byrne, 'Gender challenges for international human rights', in S. Sheeran and Sir Nigel Rodley (eds), *Routledge Handbook of International Human Rights Law* (London, New York: Routledge, 2013) 615, p. 619.

60 S. Kalantry, *Women's Human Rights and Migration: Sex-Selective Abortion Laws in the United States and India* (Philadelphia: Pennsylvania University Press, 2017).

61 With regard to marital rape, see K. Yllö and M.G. Torres (eds), *Marital Rape: Consent, Marriage and Social Change in Global Context* (Oxford: Oxford University Press, 2016).

62 J. Hua, *Trafficking Women's Human Rights* (Minneapolis: University of Minnesota Press, 2011), p. 11.

63 D. Otto, 'Gender and sexual diversity: a question of humanity?' *Melbourne Journal of International Law* 17 (2016) 477, p. 484.

64 J.E. Bond, 'International intersectionality: a theoretical and pragmatic exploration of women's international human rights law', *Emory Law Journal* 52 (2003) 71, p. 72.

65 D. Otto, 'International human rights law: towards rethinking sex/gender. Dualism and asymmetry', in M. Davies and V. Munzo (eds), *A Research Companion in Feminist Legal Theory* (London: Ashgate, 2013), p. 211. See also D. Otto (ed.), *Queering International Law. Possibilities, Alliances, Complicities, Risks* (London: Routledge, 2017).
66 Otto, 'Women's rights', p. 311.
67 Zeus felt in love with Europa, and transformed himself into a bull in order to approach the woman and abduct her. The story is taken from Ovid's *Metamorphoses* and has been depicted by Rubens in his famous oil on panel *The Rape of Europa* (1636–7).
68 L. Edelstein, 'The genuine works of Hippocrates', *Bulletin of the History of Medicine* 7 (1939), reproduced in O. and C.L. Temkin (eds), *Ancient Medicine: Selected Papers of Ludwig Edelstein* (Baltimore, MD: The Johns Hopkins Press, 1967), p. 133.
69 T. Koch, 'The Hippocratic thorn in bioethics' hide: cults, sects, and strangeness', *Journal of Medicine and Philosophy* 39 (2014) 75, p. 77.
70 S.A. Leavy, *The Psychoanalytic Dialogue* (New Haven, CT: Yale University Press, 1980), p. 8.
71 See 'Plato's ethics: an overview', in *Stanford Encyclopedia of Philosophy* available at http://plato.stanford.edu/entries/plato-ethics/ (last accessed on 1 October 2019).
72 Oxford Dictionaries, available at https://en.oxforddictionaries.com/definition/diagnosis (last accessed on 1 June 2019).
73 K. Sadegh-Zadeh, 'The logic of diagnosis', in F. Gifford (ed.), *Philosophy of Medicine* (Oxford: Elsevier, 2011), p. 357.
74 Sadegh-Zadeh, 'Logic of diagnosis'.
75 L. Edelstein, 'Hippocratic prognosis', chap. 11 of *Peri aeron und die Sammlung der hippokratischen Schriften* (Berlin: Weidmannsche Buchhandlung, 1931), reproduced in Temkin and Temkin, *Ancient Medicine*, p. 69.
76 Edelstein, 'Hippocratic prognosis'.
77 U. Galimberti, *Psiche e techne* (Milan: Feltrinelli, 2004), p. 259.
78 M. Nussbaum, *The Therapy of Desire* (Princeton, NJ: Princeton University Press, 2009), p. 28.
79 Nussbaum, *Therapy of Desire*, pp. 28–9.
80 J. Galtung, *Peace by Peaceful Means* (London: Sage, 1996).
81 Galtung, *Peace by Peaceful Means*, p. 26.
82 Galtung, *Peace by Peaceful Means*, p. 27.
83 WHO, 'Violence against women: an urgent public health priority', *Bulletin of the World Health Organization* 89 (2011) 2.
84 GC No. 22, para. 49.

1

The *anamnesis*: 'case history' on violence against women, and against women's rights to health and to reproductive health

The *anamnesis*, a two-dimensional approach

The *anamnesis* mainly consists in case history. However, Hippocrates went beyond the mere identification of 'symptoms' or 'earlier diseases,' and included in the *anamnesis* his own experience, as far as it was pertinent.[1] Hippocrates also 'listened' to patients, to discover their 'personalities, dream, daily habits,' in a process that resembled the modern 'psycho-therapeutic interaction between the doctor and the patient.'[2] *Mutatis mutandis,* the role of a lawyer is to investigate case law, and his/her analysis is inevitably influenced by his/her own experience as a scholar. I am using this metaphor to introduce the analysis of the relationship between VAW and human rights to health and to reproductive health, distinguishing the two dimensions of the relationship that constitute the backbone of my argument, and that will frame the notion of VAWH in chapter 2 (the diagnosis).

Violence against women's health does not constitute simply a process of putting together ideas that are completely separate, but grasps the complexity of the relationship at the core of this book and constitutes a solid structure on which states' obligations may be reconceived. The first dimension is characterised by violations of women's rights to health and to reproductive health as a consequence of VAW; the second includes health policies or laws which might impact on women's health and constitute a form of gender-based violence. The first dimension pertains to inter-individual relationships, and is 'horizontal' in the structure of my analysis.[3] The second refers to behaviours of the state in the health sector – mainly through policies and laws – that produce, or create the conditions of, violence as defined in the introduction. It is 'vertical' and encompasses, as I will demonstrate through the *anamnesis* and the diagnosis, actions and behaviours of health personnel who exercise a public function, namely the provision of health services. I found a partial match with my understanding of the two dimensions of violence in the definitions provided by the WHO, according to which the horizontal dimension consists in 'interpersonal violence': violence between individuals, including 'family and intimate partner violence and community violence,' the former committed within the context of the family, 'community' referring to 'acquaintance and stranger violence,' violence in workplaces and other institutions.[4] The WHO categorisation does not precisely match my vertical dimension, although we can regard the WHO notion of 'collective violence,' meaning social, political and economic violence, as also referring to violence committed through state laws and policies.

The bi-dimensional relationship will be explored using the jurisprudence of regional human rights courts and the activity of international human rights bodies, along with some relevant national judgments and state practice. I will study the decisions following three axes, which correspond to specific questions:

1. Who are the applicants?
2. Has the right to health been applied directly? In which ways was women's health relevant in the decision?
3. What reparations, if any, have been granted to the person(s) whose rights have been violated?

I will propose cases which have been decided after the affirmation of the notion of reproductive health at the international level, hence after the mid-1990s. The purpose of this book is not to elaborate a database of jurisprudence but to reflect on legal issues arising from selected decisions and judgments to support my paradigm or put it to the test. A comparative analysis is beyond the scope of my research. I will integrate regional jurisprudence and international quasi-jurisprudence with national judgments that are particularly significant and contribute to the definition of VAWH.

With regard to the first dimension, the rights to health and to reproductive health emerge as the main rights affected by episodes of violence. Violence against women 'puts women's lives and their health at risk.'[5] I have selected three main areas to examine: domestic violence, rape committed in times of peace, including marital rape, and female genital mutilation/cutting. The analysis will allow me to cover different, and often interrelated, 'contexts of violence,' namely the family environment, the community context and the state.[6]

Turning to the other dimension of the relationship, I argue that health policies or laws affecting women's health might be a cause of violence. This affirmation might seem quite strong at first sight. It is not. As I discussed in the introduction, the notion of violence can be conceived as an 'umbrella term' beneath which many forms of gender-based violence can be referred, including ones originating from and/or 'provoked by' state laws and policies. This book will concentrate on some forms of violence that relate to the 'vertical dimension' of violence: abortion, involuntary sterilisation,[7] maternal health and access to emergency contraception.[8] On abortion, the form that will open the second part of the *anamnesis*, feminists and feminist lawyers have written extensively.[9] In this book I will demonstrate, referring to several judgments, decisions and reports, that restrictive abortion laws cause violence to women, who suffer from depression, stress and physical injuries as a consequence of denial or limits to access to the practice by the authorities. This violence is gender-based and rooted in the consideration of women as weak and ill-suited to making (what society perceives as) 'appropriate' decisions. As posited by a scholar, 'laws that question the moral agency of women perpetuate stereotypes that women lack the capacity for rational decision-making.'[10] Law and health policies can constitute a 'barrier to women's access to services.'[11] I found maternal health another area well worth the investigating, and I will also focus on the underexplored issue of 'obstetric violence,' defined by the WHO as 'disrespectful and abusive treatment during childbirth.'[12]

Both dimensions will demonstrate that when the state, acting as a 'male' actor, does not prevent interpersonal violence, or hinders access to health services, it perpetuates discrimination against women, and tolerates, contributes and causes VAWH.[13]

The horizontal, 'interpersonal' dimension

Domestic violence

Context and legal background

Domestic violence (DV) violates women's fundamental rights, including the right to health and the right to reproductive health.

The term 'intimate partner violence' (IPV) is often used as a synonym of DV. However, the former is meant to include physical, sexual and emotional abuse and controlling behaviours by a current or former intimate partner, whereas DV is a broader concept that also encompasses violence between people that are not intimately related. Michelle Madden Dempsey, in her philosophical analysis, elaborated thirteen conceptual categories relating to the concept of DV. In particular, she represented DV in its strong sense as violence that occurs in domestic contexts and that tends to sustain or perpetuate patriarchy (wife battering, in Madden Dempsey's example), and in its weak sense as not perpetuating patriarchy (Madden Dempsey cites the violent retaliation of the victim of DV against her abuser).[14] The author further distinguished DV in its strong sense from 'domestic abuse,' the latter being meant to include actions which perpetuate patriarchy but are non-violent, such as refusing to allow the abused person to work outside the home or access to money.[15] The map of conceptual categories she offered is interesting, although it does not grasp how psychological and economic pressure can be as severe as battering, even without evident physical harm, and affect women's right to health. Arguing that 'the right to be free from domestic violence is an international human right for which States can be held liable,'[16] Bonita Meyersfeld identified a specific subset of DV that she calls 'systemic intimate violence,' having the following 'internationalising elements':

a) severe emotional or physical harm, including threat of such harm;
b) a continuum of violence;
c) a male perpetrator;

d) the victim is part of a group which is discriminated against or is vulnerable;
e) violence is part of a system.[17]

The adjective 'systemic' clearly captures the essence of a behaviour which is rooted in society. In this section, I will use DV or IPV interchangeably, respecting the choice made by the court /UN body whose decision is under investigation, and I will stress the impact of this form of violence on women's health.

DV was not recognised until as late as the 1990s in international legal instruments. In the 1993 Declaration on the elimination of violence against women, the UN GA emphasised that VAW can be committed 'in public or in private life.'[18] In 2004, the GA specifically addressed domestic violence in a landmark resolution, No. 58/147, which defined DV as 'violence that occurs within the private sphere, generally between individuals who are related through blood or intimacy,' and 'one of the most common and least visible forms of violence against women and [having] consequences [that] affect many areas of the lives of victims.'[19] It also described the different forms of DV, including physical, psychological and sexual violence, and – disrupting the public/private divide – pointed out that 'domestic violence is of public concern and requires States to take serious action to protect victims and prevent domestic violence.'[20] The GA also recognised one of the most hidden forms of DV, economic deprivation and isolation, and that 'such conduct may cause imminent harm to the safety, health or well-being of women.'[21] The Resolution went on to express the Assembly's concern that DV is still present in all regions of the world, and that such violence, including sexual violence in marriage, continued to be treated by some countries as a private matter.[22] Then in 2017, 24 years after its 1993 Declaration, the GA confirmed the unchanged situation of DV in the world, despite measures adopted at the international, regional and national levels. In Resolution No. 71/170, it stressed that DV 'remains the most prevalent and least visible form of violence against women of all social strata across the world,' and that 'such violence is a violation, abuse or impairment of the enjoyment of [women's] human rights and fundamental freedoms [which] is unacceptable.'[23]

At the regional level, the Inter-American Convention on the Prevention, Punishment, and Eradication of Violence against Women (Belém do Pará Convention) of 1994 elaborates the notion of violence in the different contexts where it occurs, including 'within the family or domestic unit or within any other interpersonal relationship, whether or not the perpetrator shares or has shared the same residence with the woman,' and considers it as encompassing different forms of violence, such as 'among others, rape, battery and sexual abuse' (Article 2). The 2011 Council of Europe Istanbul Convention defines 'domestic violence' as 'all acts of physical, sexual, psychological or economic violence that occur within the family or domestic unit or between former or current spouses or partners, whether or not the perpetrator shares or has shared the same residence with the victim' (Article 3(b)). It is interesting to note first that DV is considered under the Convention as one form of VAW; second, that DV is an open definition, which does not openly refer to women as victims of violence. Despite being clear that DV affects all genders, the Convention fails to capture 'the very particular wrong of domestic abuse as a crime against women, which perpetuates patriarchy.'[24]

Judgments and decisions

Judgments regarding DV, especially at the national level, are often drenched in stereotypes and lack a gender-sensitive approach to the cases.[25] Stereotypes may affect judges' perceptions of whether DV occurs in same-sex relationships, or their views about witness credibility, for example.[26] Stereotypes can also lead the judge to impose a lesser sentence on the perpetrators of violence. In a study on the practice of the Tribunal in Milan, Italy, which examined 96 proceedings for ill-treatment (*maltrattamenti*)[27] in the household, judges considered as mitigating circumstances, among other things, difficult conditions at work, a high level of conflict existing in the relationship and the fact that the defendant's behaviour was 'irreprehensible … outside the household.'[28] With regard to the latter, in particular, the absence of violence towards other people has been seen by judges as evidence that violence within the family was caused by an unexpected reaction to specific, difficult circumstances or by 'emotional turmoil.' The missing point in the legal reasoning of these judges is the fact that DV is a form of discrimination against women *on the basis of gender,* and is not necessarily the expression of a borderline violent personality.

The jurisprudence of regional human rights courts and the quasi-jurisprudence of UN treaty bodies have sometimes been responses to judicial stereotypes at the domestic level.[29] My analysis will follow the three axes outlined in the introduction to this chapter – in a first section I will outline the applicant's identity and the background to the case, in a second I will consider whether the right to health or health considerations featured in the legal reasoning and in a third I will describe reparations made. I will investigate cases involving severe violations of the woman's right to health, such as permanent disablement, or of her right to life (femicide);[30] cases involving physical, psychological and/or economic violence; and cases of DV leading to the death of one of the woman's relatives.

Who is the applicant?

In cases concerning DV, the applicant is usually the woman who endured/survived the violence, or one of her relatives, and they may be represented, when the system allows this, by an association protecting women's rights.

Starting with cases of femicide or attempted femicide, the CEDAW Committee presented two related views in 2007.[31] The first case concerned Fatma Yildirim, an Austrian national of Turkish origin. She had been repeatedly abused by her husband, who also threatened to kill her. In 2003, the police had issued an expulsion and prohibition order against the husband, and requested the Vienna Public Prosecutor to detain the man on account of the dangerous threats he addressed to the woman. The Prosecutor rejected the request. Yildirim was also stalked and threatened by her husband at her workplace. One night, while returning home after work, she was stabbed to death in the street. Her husband was arrested, convicted and sentenced to life imprisonment. A complaint was filed with the CEDAW Committee by the Vienna Intervention Centre against Domestic Violence and the Association for Women's Access to Justice on behalf of Banu Akbak, Gülen Khan and Melissa Özdemir (descendants of Ms Yildirim). The second similar case, decided on the same day by the CEDAW Committee, also concerned an Austrian national of Turkish origin, Şahide Goekce, who was killed by her husband after being repeatedly threatened by him.

At regional level, two cases are worth mentioning here. The first, decided by the IACommHR, involved Maria da Penha Maia Fernandes, who had been abused by her husband for many years. The applicant and her family lived in Fortaleza, in the state of Ceard, Brazil. The violence culminated in two attempted murders. In the first, 1983, attempt, her husband shot her. She survived, but suffered irreversible paraplegia and psychological trauma. A criminal proceeding started against the husband but no final judgment had been achieved after more than fifteen years and the perpetrator had been free for the entire period, despite all the charges against him. Ms Fernandes filed a complaint with the Commission, citing the inaction of the authorities which had condoned the violence for years. In the Commission's report of 16 April 2001 the complaint was considered admissible,[32] even though the applicant had not exhausted all domestic remedies, because of the length of the proceedings and the related risk that the delay could have led to application of the statute of limitations.

More recently, the ECtHR handed down judgment in a case of femicide occurring in Turkey.[33] The applicants were the daughters and the son of the victim, Selma Civek. She had been abused by her husband for many years. One day, the man abducted her and injured her arm with a knife. Civek reported the case to the police. The authorities issued a protection order, which was not respected. Civek reported several times that her husband was threatening her with death. On 14 January 2011, she was killed in the street by her husband, who stabbed her twenty-two times. The man explained the act as a consequence of his wife's infidelity. He was convicted of murder and sentenced to life imprisonment. The application was filed with the ECtHR some months after the murder, the applicants claiming that the authorities had failed to protect their mother.

Dozens of cases of physical, psychological and/or economic violence have been investigated by international and regional judicial or quasi-judicial bodies. I have chosen examples that best stress the impact of DV on women's health. Starting with the UN system, in *A.T. v. Hungary* the CEDAW Committee analysed the case of a woman who had been subjected to severe domestic abuse by her husband.[34] Despite having been threatened by him, A.T. could not leave her house and move to a shelter, because none was equipped to welcome her and her disabled child. Even after she did manage to leave the apartment where they lived, her husband continued to stalk and beat her, as ten medical certificates demonstrated. She claimed that her physical integrity, physical and mental health, and life were at serious risk and that she lived in constant fear. Criminal and civil proceedings started against the husband, without success. A.T. complained that the state had failed to provide her with effective remedies.

Three years later, the CEDAW Committee adopted pivotal views in *V.K. v. Bulgaria*,[35] a case involving multiple forms of DV, including economic violence. The applicant, of Bulgarian nationality, lived in Poland with her husband and her children. She was not allowed to work or given access to the family's income, except a small allowance to cover basic needs. In winter 2006–7, the family returned to Bulgaria for a holiday. During an argument, V.K.'s husband became violent and hit her. Her parents immediately reported the case to the police in Sofia. She was visited at the local hospital, where the doctors certified bruises on her forehead and hands. After several episodes of violence once back in Poland, she filed a request for protective measures with the Polish courts, without success. Despite support given by a centre in Warsaw, she could not escape her violent husband and stay in Poland, so decided to move to Bulgaria, where she applied for an immediate protection order, which she obtained. Notwithstanding all the evidence presented in court, her request for a permanent protection order was dismissed. Her husband, his friends and her mother-in-law were heard as witnesses. V.K.'s appeal was rejected and she remained without any support, while her husband started divorce proceedings, asking for custody of their children. She claimed that the state was not able to provide her with effective protection against DV.

The psychological impact of DV significantly mattered in one of many cases heard by the ECtHR, *Loreta Valiulienė v. Lithuania*, decided in 2013.[36] The applicant, a Lithuanian national, had been beaten by her partner, a Belgian national, sustaining minor bodily harm. After an episode of violence in 2001, she filed an application with the District Court to start a private prosecution. However, the next year, the Court transferred the case to a public prosecutor after suspending the pre-trial investigation twice. In the meantime, a new law entered into force, providing that a prosecution for minor bodily harm should be brought by the victim in a private capacity. Accordingly, Valiulienė decided to start a private prosecution. Nonetheless, the Court refused to hear it, citing the statute of limitations. The regional court upheld this decision in 2007. Valiulienė then filed a complaint with the ECtHR. In *Angelica Camelia Bălşan v. Romania*,[37] the applicant suffered from multiple physical assaults by her husband, often in front of their children. She reported the episodes of violence to the police and used all the available legal measures to get protection from her husband. However, her applications were never successful. The Hunedoara County Court, for example, dismissed her appeal against the decision to dismiss her claim for damages as ill-founded, arguing that she had provoked the acts of violence by her behaviour and that the acts had not reached the level of severity to justify damages. A letter she sent to the police asking for protective measures was not taken into consideration. She eventually filed a complaint with the ECtHR complaining about the lack of protection by the authorities.

In many cases of DV, a relative of the woman dies as a consequence of the violence. Killing a relative is a form of VAW, along with the clear violation of the victim's right to life. The IACommHR issued a historic decision against the United States in 2011. The claim was presented by the American Civil Liberties Union on behalf of *Jessica Gonzáles (then Lenahan)* and her three daughters, who had been murdered by their father (Lenahan's former husband) in 1999.[38] After the divorce, Lenahan obtained a – first temporary then permanent – restraining order from the authorities, which her former husband constantly violated. The night of the murder, she went to the police station claiming that her ex-husband had run off with their daughters. The police officer issued a missing person's report, but then it took several hours to proceed with the 'attempts to locate'. Later that night, the husband reached the police station, fired shots through the window and was wounded (fatally) by the officers, who then discovered the bodies of the three girls in his truck. Lenahan's substantive and procedural due process claims, based on the lack of adequate investigation of the murders, were dismissed by the US Supreme Court.[39] She then filed a complaint with the IACommHR, which considered her claim admissible because she had exhausted all domestic remedies.

A similar case was examined by the CEDAW Committee in its *Angela González Carreño v. Spain* views of 15 August 2014.[40] The applicant, represented by Counsel Women's Link Worldwide, was Angela González Carreño, whose daughter, Andrea Rascón González, was murdered by her father, the applicant's former husband. After several episodes of violence and threats, González Carreño left the marital residence in 1999. Following a trial separation, she continued to be subjected to harassment and intimidation by her former husband, including death threats in the street and by telephone. Her daughter was frightened. González Carreño asked for protective orders to keep her former husband away from both her and her daughter. Despite several reports to the police, he was convicted for harassment only. On 24 April 2003, González Carreño took her daughter to social services to meet her father. Andrea never came back. She was found dead at her father's house a few hours later: he had killed her and then committed suicide. González Carreño tried several administrative and judicial appeals alleging miscarriage of justice on the part of the state, without success. On 30 November 2010, she appealed *in amparo* to the Constitutional Court, alleging violation of her constitutional rights, but the Court dismissed the appeal. She eventually sent her complaint to the CEDAW Committee, which considered the case admissible.

The landmark case in Europe is *Opuz v. Turkey*, decided in 2009. The applicant, Nahide Opuz, and her mother were victims of Opuz's husband, H.O., over many years. Both women had filed several complaints to the public authorities and then withdrawn them, because they were under threat of death. No prosecution was brought against the husband, who eventually shot and killed his mother-in-law. After the murder, he was convicted and sentenced to life imprisonment, but released for good conduct pending appeal before the Court of Cassation. Following a domestic court's decision, the police authorities took some measures to protect Opuz, who then filed a complaint with the ECtHR complaining about the violation of several ECHR rights. The Court declared the case admissible and decided to examine in the merits stage the question of the effectiveness of the domestic remedies in providing protection to the applicant and her mother. Eight years later, the ECtHR rendered another pivotal judgment on DV, in the *Elisaveta Talpis v. Italy* case.[41]

Has the right to health been applied directly? In which ways was women's health relevant in the judgment?

Application of the rights to health and to reproductive health depends to a great extent on the legal instruments on which the competence of the judicial or quasi-judicial body is based. I will examine my example cases in the order in which they were presented in the previous section.

In *Fatma Yildirim,* the applicants complained that Fatma had been the victim of a violation of Articles 1, 2, 3 and 5 CEDAW (principle of non-discrimination and related state obligations) by Austria. The Committee pointed out that the Austrian authorities 'knew or should have known' the risk she was facing,[42] and that the Public Prosecutor should not have turned down her requests to the police to arrest her husband. In response to the Austrian government, which contended that at that time an arrest was disproportionate, the Committee argued that 'the perpetrator's rights cannot supersede women's human rights to life and to physical and mental integrity,' and found the state responsible for violating the deceased Fatma Yildirim's rights to life and to physical and mental integrity.[43] The responsibility of the state arose even though her husband was subsequently prosecuted 'to the full extent of the law' for killing his wife. In *Şahide Goekce*, the reasoning of the Committee in the merits was quite similar to that in *Yildirim*, so will not be reported here. In both cases, the right to health was not directly mentioned, although the Committee recognised a violation of both women's right to physical and mental integrity, which was relevant in order to establish the violation of the rights protected by the ECHR, in particular the right to life.

Shifting my focus to the regional level, in *Maria da Penha Maia Fernandes*, the IACommHR found Brazil in violation of Articles 8 (right to a fair trial) and 25 (right to judicial protection) of the American Convention on Human Rights (American Convention) in relation to Article 1(1), and the corresponding Articles of the American Declaration of the Rights and Duties of Man (American Declaration). Brazil was also considered responsible for violating the principle of equality before the law (Article 24 of the American Convention), along with Articles II (right to equality before the law) and XVIII (right to a fair trial) of the American Declaration. In particular, the Commission stressed the biased approach of the authorities towards DV: the courts had proved to be reluctant to prosecute and punish the perpetrator of DV, and the practices of some defence lawyers 'sustained in turn by some courts – have the effect of requiring the victim to demonstrate the sanctity of her reputation and her moral blamelessness.'[44] The Commission concluded that this had been a case of DV and that the state had tolerated the violence involved,[45] and that several rights of the American Convention had been violated, along with Article 7 of the Belém do Pará Convention, which was applied for the first time. The right to health was not explicitly mentioned, even though the Commission referred to the damage to da Penha's physical and mental integrity.

In the ECtHR judgment in *Selma Civek,* the immediacy of the risk to her right to life played a pivotal role in the legal reasoning. The Court applied in this case, as well as in the *Talpis* judgment, the '*Osman* test'.[46] This provides that, in order to avoid an excessive burden on the authorities, the positive obligation to protect the right to life requires that the authorities 'knew or ought to have known at the time of the existence of a real and immediate risk to the life of an identified individual or individuals from the criminal acts of a third party,' and that 'they failed to take measures within the scope of their powers which, judged reasonably, might have been expected to avoid that risk.'[47] Where a third party poses a real and immediate threat to the life of an individual, the positive obligation consists in adopting all reasonable measures to protect against the risk.[48] Even though the Turkish authorities had adopted some measures to prevent violence against Selma Civek, the Court highlighted that DV was a general problem, not just in Turkey, but also in all the other Member States of the Council of Europe.[49] Saying that DV 'does not concern women only,'[50] however, the Strasbourg judges failed to capture the gendered roots of violence. The Court acknowledged that the victim and several witnesses had reported the threats made by the husband and that, despite taking several measures, the authorities had not reacted in a sufficient and concrete manner to prevent the killing of Selma Civek.[51] The right to health had no role to play, even though more than once Civek had reported to the authorities her poor state of psychological health as a consequence of the repeated episodes of violence.[52] The Court only referred to 'different forms of violence,' including physical aggressions and verbal abuses.[53]

In *A.T. v. Hungary*, the CEDAW Committee acknowledged that the state had not been able to provide immediate protection to A.T. and her children, and that domestic courts had not considered DV cases a priority. Owing to the absence of specific legislation on DV and sexual harassment, and the lack of provisions on protection orders, the Committee found that the state had violated Article 2(a), (b) and (e) CEDAW, and infringed A.T.'s human rights, in particular her right to security.[54] An interesting aspect is that the Committee addressed the general attitude of the authorities towards women. A.T. had never succeeded, temporarily or permanently, in preventing her husband from entering the apartment in which she lived. This demonstrated to the Committee that the authorities had a stereotyped view of the role of women in society. Hungary was also found in violation of Article 5 CEDAW.[55] In *V.K. v. Bulgaria*, the complaint concerned Articles 2(c), 2(e)–(g) and 5 on the obligation to eradicate stereotypes of women, and Article 16 CEDAW on non-discrimination in all matters relating to marriage. In the merits, the Committee took into account that one reason presented by the domestic court for refusing permanent protection for the applicant was that no episode of violence had occurred during the one-month period required under national law to justify a protection order. However, the Committee recalled that gender-based violence does not require 'a direct and immediate threat to the life or health of the victim,' and that 'such violence … also covers acts that inflict mental or sexual harm or suffering, threats of any such acts, coercion and other deprivations of liberty.'[56] The domestic courts had only focused on the direct and immediate threat to life or health, 'neglecting' V.K.'s emotional and psychological suffering. The Committee stressed that psychological and economic violence constitute forms of violence as severe as physical harm. In its decision, the Committee also addressed the issue of gender stereotypes. The decision of the national court was considered to have lacked 'gender sensitivity, in that it reflect[ed] the preconceived notion that domestic violence is to a large extent a private matter falling within the private sphere which, in principle, should not be subject to State control.'[57] Even though, during the month preceding the request for a protection order, V.K. had not suffered any physical harm, she 'nevertheless suffered from considerable fear and anguish.'[58] That was enough for the Committee to conclude that the state had violated her human rights. In this way, V.K.'s right to health entered legal reasoning through the back door and played a pivotal role in determining the responsibility of the state for violations of the rights enshrined in CEDAW.

Turning to the ECtHR jurisprudence, in *Valiulienė v. Lithuania* the judges in Strasbourg applied Article 3 ECHR, even though the applicant had suffered minor bodily injuries, acknowledging in this way the psychological consequences of DV.[59] The Court found that Lithuania had infringed Article 3 ECHR because it had not provided adequate protection to Loreta Valiulienė. The judgment paved the way for other judgments on DV in which analysis of the 'level of intensity' necessary to trigger Article 3 on the prohibition of torture, inhuman or degrading treatment or punishment was reduced to a mere assessment of the relevance of the provision to the complaint.[60] Furthermore, even though the right to health is not included in the ECHR, and therefore could not be directly invoked, the ECtHR jurisprudence has shown that VAW affects women's health even where physical injuries are minor.[61] As contended by Judge De Albuquerque in his concurring opinion, physical pain is only one of the effects of domestic violence, 'which has an inherent humiliating and debasing character for the victim.'[62] In *Bălşan v. Romania*, the Court analysed the issue of exhaustion of domestic remedies in the merits, under Article 3 ECHR, being relevant to the question of whether sufficient, effective safeguards against DV had been provided for Angelica Camelia Bălşan. In order to apply Article 3 ECHR, the Court stressed that physical injuries, 'combined with her feelings of fear and hopelessness,' had been 'sufficiently serious to reach the required level of severity under Article 3 of the Convention and thus impose a positive obligation on the Government under this provision.'[63] As in previous cases, the European Court stressed that a state's obligations arise when 'the authorities knew or ought to have known at the time of the existence of a real and immediate risk of ill-treatment of an identified individual from the criminal acts of a third party,' and they failed to take measures.[64] It was convinced that the Romanian jurisdictional authorities had not granted any protection to Bălşan, and that the measure decided by the courts – an administrative fine – had no deterrent effect.[65] The Court concluded that Romania had violated Article 3 ECHR. With regard to Article 14, in conjunction with Article 3, the ECtHR investigated the behaviour of national authorities and courts, which, owing to the length of the proceedings and the repeated denial of any forms of protection, clearly demonstrated 'a discriminatory attitude towards the applicant as a woman.'[66] Again, Bălşan's health was relevant in addressing violations of other articles of the European Convention.

Jessica Gonzáles (then Lenahan) pointed out in her complaint before the IACommHR that she and her daughters had been in imminent danger of 'harm to [her/their] emotional health or welfare' because the defendant had not been excluded by the authorities from the family home.[67] Even though its analysis was not based on Jessica Lenahan's right to health, the Commission investigated the element of *risk of harm* when discussing state obligations under Article II of the American Declaration, and the duty of protection relating to the right to life, which is particularly rigorous in the case of children.[68] In that sense, the Inter-American Commission considered that 'the issuance of a restraining order signals a State's recognition of risk that the beneficiaries would suffer harm from domestic violence on the part of the restrained party, and need State protection.'[69] The fact that the authorities 'should have known' the risk is combined with the element of discrimination linked to the enforcement of protection orders, 'a problem that has disproportionately affected women,' especially those belonging to ethnic and racial minorities.[70] The Commission, relying on previous Inter-American and European jurisprudence, and on UN treaty bodies' quasi-jurisprudence, based its reasoning on the concept of due diligence obligations.[71] Having considered the facts of the case, it concluded that the state had failed to act with due diligence to protect Lenahan and her daughters from domestic violence, and that it had violated the principle of non-discrimination and the right to equal protection before the law. Moreover, it had failed to undertake reasonable measures to prevent the murders of the girls, in violation of Lenahan's daughters' right to life under Article I of the American Declaration.[72]

In a similar case, *Angela González Carreño v. Spain*, the CEDAW Committee considered that the authorities and the social services had not showed any interest in evaluating all aspects of the benefits or the harms procured to the child as a consequence of the regime of unsupervised visits by her father. The element of discrimination is pivotal here: according to the Committee, it was the 'stereotyped conception of visiting rights based on formal equality which, in the present case, gave clear advantages to the father despite his abusive conduct and minimized the situation of mother and daughter as victims of violence, placing them in a vulnerable position.'[73] The best interest of the child, *combined with* the existence of a context of DV, must be taken into account in any judicial decision.[74] In terms of the applicant's right to health, the only reference is the passage in which the Committee noted that 'the author ... has suffered harm of the utmost seriousness and an irreparable injury,'[75] the loss of her daughter and the violations suffered.

Hence it concluded that the absence of reparations constituted a violation of Article 2(b) and (c) – prohibition of all discrimination against women, and legal protection of the rights of women on an equal basis with men – and 16 CEDAW (elimination of discrimination against women in all matters relating to marriage and family relations).[76]

As stated in the previous section, *Opuz v. Turkey* is the leading case on DV in the ECtHR jurisprudence, even though the analysis chiefly focused on the procedural aspects of the investigations at national level rather than on the effects of violence on Opuz's health. The ECtHR found violations by Turkey of the right to life (protected in Article 2 ECHR), and of the prohibition of torture, inhuman or degrading treatment (Article 3) because the state had failed to protect Opuz and her mother. The Court also found that the state had breached the prohibition of discrimination (Article 14), in conjunction with the previous articles. The judges clearly acknowledged that 'while a decision not to prosecute in a particular case would not necessarily be in breach of due diligence obligations, a law or practice which automatically paralyzed a domestic violence investigation or prosecution where a victim withdrew her complaint would be.'[77] In the last example considered in this section, *Talpis v. Italy,* the ECtHR found, by a majority of six votes to one, that Italy had violated Article 2 ECHR, as a consequence of the death of Elisaveta Talpis's son and the attempted murder of Talpis herself, and, by unanimity, that the state had infringed Article 3 ECHR because the authorities had failed to protect Talpis against violence. There was no reference to her right to health, even though the Court affirmed that national authorities 'have a duty to examine the victim's situation of extreme psychological, physical and material insecurity and vulnerability and, with the utmost expedition, to assess the situation accordingly.'[78] With regard to Article 2 ECHR, the Court applied the '*Osman* test'. Given the circumstances of the case, it considered that her husband had constituted a real threat to Talpis (and her right to health in the sense of physical and mental integrity), and that the state has an obligation to adopt concrete measures in order to protect an individual whose life is threatened. The Court also found that Italy had violated the prohibition of torture, inhuman or degrading treatment or punishment, and the prohibition of discrimination on the basis of gender.[79]

Reparations

Reparations can take different forms.[80] In GR No. 33 on access to justice, the CEDAW Committee asserted that 'remedies should include as appropriate, restitution (reinstatement); compensation (whether provided in the form of money, goods or services); and rehabilitation (medical and psychological care and other social services).'[81] For my analysis, I will mainly focus on monetary compensation and on the decision to recommend general measures the state must adopt in order to redress violations of women's human rights. Given the fact that each system for protecting human rights has its own peculiarities, the analysis that follows will assemble the cases judged by a particular jurisdictional or quasi-jurisdictional body.

Starting from the UN level, the CEDAW Committee elaborated several general recommendations to Austria in *Yildirim* and *Goekce,* including to act 'with due diligence to prevent and respond to such violence against women and adequately provid[e] for sanctions for the failure to do so;' to prosecute perpetrators of domestic violence in a speedy manner; to ensure that criminal and civil remedies are utilised in cases where the perpetrator of domestic violence poses 'a dangerous threat to the victim;' to ensure enhanced coordination among law enforcement and judicial officers; and 'to strengthen training programmes and education on domestic violence for judges, lawyers and law enforcement officials.'[82] Due consideration – added the Committee – must be given to women's safety.[83] The Committee did not mention any specific reparation for the claimant's relatives. In *A.T.*, a case that was decided two years before *Yildirim* and *Goekce*, the Committee recommended the state take 'immediate and effective measures to guarantee the physical and mental integrity of A.T. and her family,' ensure a safe home for A.T. and her children, and grant child support and legal assistance. The right to health enters the determination of reparations where the Committee stressed that they must be 'proportionate to the physical and mental harm undergone and to the gravity of the violations of her rights.'[84] The Committee also recommended the state adopt a series of measures aimed at ensuring the law's 'maximum' protection of victims of violence, including training for law enforcement authorities, lawyers and judges, and rehabilitation programmes for offenders.[85] Similarly, in the most recent case (*González Carreño*), the Committee called upon the state to grant the applicant appropriate reparation and comprehensive compensation, and to conduct exhaustive and impartial investigation; and, in general, to ensure that acts of domestic violence are taken into consideration when determining custody and visitation rights regarding children so that 'the exercise of custody or visiting rights will not endanger the safety of the victims of violence, including the children.'[86] The Tribunal Supremo de España considered the recommendations in *Carreño* as 'binding,' despite their notoriously 'soft' character, because of the international treaties Spain has ratified and in order to make rights and liberties 'reales y concretos.'[87]

Moving to the regional legal systems, in *da Penha* the IACommHR recommended the state complete the proceedings against the perpetrator of the crimes against Maria da Penha, conduct serious and impartial investigation of the case, adopt measures to grant the victim actual compensation and continue reforms aimed at putting an end to the condoning by the state of DV against women in Brazil.[88] In terms of general reforms, Brazil adopted a law, named after Maria da Penha, which came into force in 2006, to improve its system of protection of victims of DV.[89] The IACommHR, in *Lenahan*, recommended the United States, *inter alia*, undertake an impartial investigation regarding the case, offer full reparations to Jessica Lenahan and her next-of-kin, reform existing legislation – and adopt measures aimed at ensuring enforcement – and promote the eradication of discriminatory socio-cultural patterns that impede women and children's full protection from domestic violence.[90]

Shifting to the European system, monetary compensation (just satisfaction under Article 41 ECHR) is granted to victims of domestic violence, or their relatives in cases of femicide, when the state is found responsible for not taking measures to prevent and to investigate violations of the applicants' rights recognised by the ECHR. The victim's health conditions can play a role in determining the amount of the reparations. Hence, for example, in *Opuz v. Turkey* the Court noted that 'the applicant ha[d] undoubtedly suffered anguish and distress,' and granted her, on an equitable basis, €30,000 as reparation.[91] Similarly, in determining reparations in *Valiulienė*, the Court considered the applicant's 'suffering and frustration,' hence the mental effects of DV, which could not be compensated for 'by a mere finding of a violation.'[92] In *Talpis v. Italy* the Court decided that Elisaveta Talpis was entitled to €30,000 as moral damages. Referring to *Opuz,* in *Bălşan* the ECtHR noted the 'anguish and distress' suffered by the applicant 'on account of the authorities' failure to take sufficient measures to prevent the acts of domestic violence perpetrated by her husband,' and awarded her €9,800.[93] In the latter case, however, the Court could have appreciated, in deciding how much to award as non-pecuniary damages, the effect on Bălşan's child of having witnessed DV. Turning to general measures, the ECtHR found that the adoption by the government of a strategy to prevent domestic violence had not ensured that the judicial system would be responsive, which granted impunity to the aggressors.[94] The mental health of Selma Civek's children was also taken into account by the Court when determining that the applicants in *Civek* were entitled to compensation amounting to €50,000 because of the 'anguish' suffered as a consequence of their mother's death.[95]

Rape

Context and legal background

Rape is a form of sexual violence. Sexual violence, in the recent definition provided by the African Commission on Human and People's Rights (African Commission), means 'any non-consensual sexual act, a threat or attempt to perform such an act, or compelling someone else to perform such an act on a third person,' and it includes sexual harassment, rape, sexual assault, forced abortion, forced sterilisation and human trafficking.[96] The 2011 Council of Europe Istanbul Convention defines rape as a form of sexual violence consisting in 'non-consensual vaginal, anal or oral penetration of a sexual nature of the body of another person with any bodily part or object,' where consent 'must be given voluntarily as the result of the person's free will assessed in the context of the surrounding circumstances' (Article 36).

Sexual violence is gender-based, because, although men and boys are victims of it, women are particularly and disproportionately subjected to this form of violence, and are subjected to rape in armed conflict more often than men.[97] Rape can amount to a war crime, a crime against humanity or even genocide. In the *Elements of Crimes* under the Rome Statute of the International Criminal Court, rape is included among the categories crimes against humanity and war crimes (Articles 7(1)g–1, 8(2)b(xxii)–1).

The absence of consent represents the key element of the crime, keeping in mind that force and coercion, which characterise armed conflict, negate consent. The CEDAW Committee contended that lack of consent rather than the use of force must be at the centre of the offence, and that sexual crimes must be considered as violations of a person's right to bodily security, not as offences against decency.[98] In *M.C. v. Bulgaria*, the ECtHR compared the legislation of European countries regarding rape, and affirmed that 'the definition of rape contains references to the use of violence or threats of violence by the perpetrator,' and that 'it is significant … that in case-law and legal theory lack of consent, not force, is seen as the constituent element of the offence of rape.'[99] Considering national legislation, as well as international criminal law jurisprudence, the European Court concluded that 'any rigid approach to the prosecution of sexual offences, such as requiring proof of physical resistance in all circumstances, risks leaving certain types of rape unpunished and thus jeopardising the effective protection of the individual's sexual autonomy.'[100] It stressed that rape is a violation of personal autonomy and self-determination. In so doing, it considered this particular aspect of harm, 'avoiding a paternalistic approach.'[101] In *Zontul v. Greece* the Court expanded the definition of harm in sexual intercourse, by including anal penetration.[102]

Lack of consent, which seems to be undisputable, has nonetheless been highly controversial. Definitions of rape at national level differ a great deal. As Vanessa Munro argued, 'even in jurisdictions where the doctrinal trigger for criminalization in the law of rape is non-consensual intercourse conducted with requisite blameworthy intent or inadvertence, the force requirement has remained rather tenacious in practice,' and 'the consent threshold is operationalized against a context of profound suspicion of female sexuality and acute concern over false allegations, often (mis)represented as easy for malicious women to make.'[103] According to the then SR on VAW, Radhika Coomaraswamy, even though consent has been defined as the 'legal dividing line between rape and sexual intercourse … the argumentation over consent, however, often degenerates into a contest of wills and credibility,' and 'many courts are reluctant to find the defendant guilty of rape in the absence of physical injuries.'[104]

There is an inherent stereotype in the crime of rape. Women's sexuality has been usually perceived as men's property. As Susan Brownmiller contended in her pioneer work *Against Our Will*, published in 1975, 'women were wholly owned subsidiaries and not independent beings … Woman, of course, was viewed as the property.' Rape was therefore deemed as a crime by a man against another man, a crime that was not committed against the woman, but rather against her father, husband or brother, in other words against the person who was entitled of a sort of 'right to property' in women.[105] In Italy, for example, only as late as 1996 did rape come to be considered a crime against a person and not a crime against public morality and decency. As Cook and Cusack argued in their landmark work

Gender Stereotyping, 'when women are stereotyped as men's sexual property, the stereotype operates to privilege male sexuality and to enable sexual exploitation of women through sexual assault and violence.'[106]

In international law, whether rape is committed in times of peace or in times of war, it is a clear example of VAW, a violation of women's human rights,[107] and, for my book's purposes, of VAWH, because it affects women's rights to health and to reproductive health.

In this section I will limit my analysis to rape committed in peace-time because 'rape as a war crime is not merely rape that occurs during the course of war … rape is war.'[108] The jurisprudence of international criminal tribunals will therefore not be the object of specific analysis here.[109] During war, the rape of women is an instrument of war. The context is so specific that it may influence the definition of rape, prove the existence of rape and be essential in elevating a rape to an international crime.[110]

Rape, as I will find in the cases that I am going to analyse in the following sub-sections, amounts to VAWH, because it affects a woman's sexuality and her capacity to decide how her own body should be treated. It can have an impact on mental and physical health, it does cause minor, moderate or severe physical injuries, and it may be the cause of sexually transmitted infections, or of unplanned pregnancies.[111]

Judgments and decisions

The selected decisions will explore the impact of rape on women's health and reproductive health, and will be categorised as follows: marital rape, rape committed by organs of the state (such as individuals representing the state) and rape committed by private persons, with a focus on gang rape.

'Marital rape' requires a few introductory notes. It should be named spousal rape or intimate partner rape, because it does not matter whether the relationship consists in a marriage, occurs *de facto* or is regulated by a contract. *Rape in Marriage* is the title of the landmark work by Diane Russell, published in 1982.[112] At that time, only six states in the USA criminalised rape within marriage. Marital rape came to be considered as a form of VAW in the UN Declaration on Elimination of Violence against Women of 1993. More than twenty-five years have passed from this affirmation at the international level, and marital rape is still lawful in some countries in the world. In 'The Global Rape Epidemic' of 2017, the association Equality Now reported that rape of a woman or a girl by her husband is expressly legal in at least ten jurisdictions (out of eighty-two considered), namely Ghana, India, Indonesia, Jordan, Lesotho, Nigeria, Oman, Singapore, Sri Lanka and Tanzania.[113] In four of these, marital rape is expressly legal even when the wife is a child, and the 'marriage' is in violation of laws setting a minimum age for marriage.

In many countries, marital rape is not explicitly a crime under the law.[114] Where it is, this is a recent development.[115] In Italy, not until 1976 did a court condemn a husband for sexual violence against his wife, and only five years later did the legislator repeal Italian provisions on honour crimes.[116] In the UK, to propose another example, rape within marriage was criminalised as late as the early 1990s, after a report of the Law Commission published on 13 January 1992 stated that Lord Hale's dictum – a man 'cannot be guilty of a rape committed by himself upon his lawful wife,' since 'by their mutual matrimonial consent and contract the wife hath given up herself in this kind unto her husband, which she cannot retract'[117] – is now 'unsupportable.'[118] The report followed the House of Lords judgment in *R. v. R.* arguing that 'the husband's immunity … no longer exists.'[119] In the USA, a marital rape exemption has persisted for a long time, transforming marriage into a 'safe haven for rapists.'[120] Despite being now illegal in all American states, marital exemptions are still contemplated. Nonetheless, courts went beyond the provisions of some states' laws and clearly acknowledged the illegality of the exemptions. While DV is acknowledged to be a violation of human rights, 'the specifically sexual component of violence against women in intimate relationships, including rape in marriage, is drastically under-recognised.'[121] Regional jurisprudence and international quasi-jurisprudence is scarce on the issue, as well.[122] I will follow in the following sub-sections the three axes of analysis, distinguishing the 'types' of rape as illustrated above.

Who is the applicant?

Let us start with marital rape, on which, as mentioned above, there have been few cases at the international and regional levels. The ECtHR ruled on two distinct but similar cases, decided on 22 November 1995, that there had been no violation of Article 7 ECHR (no punishment without law) with regard to the applicants, charged and convicted at national level with rape and sexual assault against their wives.[123] The applicants were alleged to have committed rape, but relied on Lord Hale's dictum that such a crime could not exist. The national court concluded that, through interpretation, judges had elaborated an increasing number of exceptions to the rule. Despite being interesting in the affirmation of the crime of marital rape, the two cases are not relevant for my analysis, since they make no reference to the impact of violence on women's health.

To investigate marital rape in the light of the right to health, it is necessary to have a look at domestic jurisprudence as well. Two judgments are relevant here, the first handed down by the Court of Nepal in 2002.[124] The applicants – the Forum for Women, Law and Development based at Thapathali, (police) ward no. 11 of Kathmandu municipal corporation, and Advocate Meera Dhungana – filed a writ petition challenging the legitimacy of No. 1 of the chapter on rape in the criminal code of the country, which does not include in the definition of rape sexual intercourse between a couple without the woman's consent. The second case occurred in India. Even though marital rape is not an offence in this country,[125] the High Court in Gujarat at Ahmedabad reflected on marital rape within a spousal dispute, during which the wife refused the sexual perversions of her husband and sexual intercourse was forced.[126] In its decision of 2018, the court applied several provisions of the Indian criminal code.

Moving to cases of rape committed by state organs, it should be said at the start that an action by a state organ entails state responsibility in international law.[127] At first sight, it seems less pertinent to add a comment on violence committed by organs of the state when discussing the horizontal dimension of VAWH. Under my paradigm, however, the vertical dimension does not relate to the nature of the perpetrator – private individual or state organ – but, rather, to the fact that in the horizontal dimension violence involves a violation of the applicant's right to health whereas in the vertical dimension a state's policies, or practices in the health sector, cause VAW. Accordingly, the behaviour of state organs is relevant to both dimensions. In the European and the Inter-American systems of protection of human rights, rape committed by state organs (individuals representing the state) has been considered as amounting to torture, inhuman or degrading treatment. That was the conclusion, for example, of the IACommHR in the case *Raquel Martín de Mejía v. Peru*,[128] decided in 1996. The complaint was filed by Raquel Martín de Mejía, by associations for protecting human rights and on behalf of Martín de Mejía's husband, who had been tortured and killed by a group of military personnel who accused them of being members of the Movimiento revolucionario Tupac Amaru (Tupamaros). For the purpose of my research, I will focus on Martín de Mejía's complaint of rape committed by state organs only. The couple lived in Oxapampa. One night, a number of military personnel with their faces covered entered the couple's house, accusing them of being subversives. They repeatedly raped Martín de Mejía, and kidnapped her husband. She reported the abduction of her husband the following day, but was not heard. Her husband's body was found a few days later. Martín de Mejía tried to obtain an effective remedy for the violations suffered, without success. She was continuously threatened with further reprisals against herself and her family, to induce her to withdraw the case, so escaped, first to the USA then to Sweden, where she asked for protection. Martín de Mejía claimed to have suffered a violation of her rights to humane treatment (Article 5) and to privacy (Article 11) in connection with Article 1(1) of the American Convention.

The case of the *'Las Dos Erres' Massacre*,[129] decided by the Inter-American Court of Human Rights (IACHR) in 2009, also involved violation of women's rights to health and reproductive health. It concerned the massacre and mass rape of 216 people, committed in 1982 by a group of special forces soldiers. In 1982, a military junta was installed in Guatemala, and military operations were undertaken with the knowledge of the highest authorities of the state. In the case, the applicants were the Office of Human Rights of the Archdiocese of Guatemala and the Center for Justice and International Law. They initially accepted a friendly settlement, then decided to continue the proceedings in front of the Commission, which presented its report in 2008, where it recommended the state investigate the facts rigorously and impartially. When Guatemala failed to implement its recommendations, the Commission submitted the case to the Court. Even though the state acknowledged its responsibility, the Court found it necessary to make further specifications in the determination of the facts of the case. The judicial body considered as victims the 2 survivors of the massacre, and 153 next-of-kin of the deceased.

The following year, the IACHR decided *Inés Fernández Ortega v. Mexico.*[130] Inés, a young member of the indigenous group Tlapanec, was raped by military officers in the state of Guerrero. After the violence, she was taken to hospital and, along with her counsel and an interpreter, reported the incident to the authorities. At the hospital, a practitioner performed a physical and gynaecological examination from which she determined that 'there was no evidence of violence.'[131] The state's Attorney-General referred the case to the Military Prosecution Service. Fernández Ortega asked for the case not to be tried under military jurisdiction; this was denied. She filed an *amparo*, but her case was considered inadmissible. She filed a petition with the IACHR with the support of human rights associations. The Commission, which issued a report in 2008 containing recommendations to the state, referred the case to the Court and asked the latter to declare the state responsible for violating Articles 5 (right to humane treatment), 8 (right to a fair trial) and 25 (right to judicial protection) of the American Convention.

In December 2018 the IACHR decided a case in which female protestors were raped in Texcoco and San Salvador Atenco. The case, *Women Victims of Sexual Torture in Atenco v. Mexico*, was filed by eleven women, who had been verbally, physically and sexually abused by the police in May 2006 while protesting against a ban on selling flowers at the Texcoco market. Their petition was filed with the Inter-American Commission by the Miguel Agustín Pro Juárez Human Rights Center and the Center for Justice and International Law, alleging several violations of the rights protected by the American Convention.[132] After a report on admissibility in 2011, the Commission referred the case to the Inter-American Court on 17 September 2016.[133]

Turning to the ECtHR system, the relevant case is *Şükran Aydin v. Turkey*, decided in 1997.[134] The applicant, Şükran Aydin, was a Turkish citizen of Kurdish origin, 17 years old at the time of the facts. In 1993, she was questioned, along with her family and other families in the village where she lived, by the authorities, which wanted to know whether members of the Kurdistan Workers' Party (PKK) had visited the family home. She was then taken to the police headquarters, where she was separated from her father, beaten, raped and humiliated. Once released, she reported the violence to the authorities, and the public prosecutor started an investigation, which proved ineffective. Aydin eventually decided to file a complaint with the European Commission of Human Rights, which issued a report concluding that Turkey had violated Articles 3 and 6 ECHR. The case was then brought to the ECtHR.

After discussing rape committed by state organs as revealed in the jurisprudence of regional human rights courts and UN treaty bodies, let us now turn to cases of rape committed by individuals who do not represent the state and do not belong to the victim's household. In *M.C. v. Bulgaria*, mentioned earlier, the ECHR decided the case of a woman, 14 years old at the time of the act of violence, who after a night spent in a bar was raped twice by a group of young men that she knew. It considered the events under both Articles 3 and 8 ECHR. M.C. and her mother had reported the case to the police. The prosecutor had refused to investigate the rape, and later dismissed a request to institute criminal proceedings against the alleged perpetrators. M.C. filed a complaint with the ECtHR, which considered rape as a violation of the prohibition of torture, inhuman or degrading treatment under the European Convention.

The IACHR did not consider rape as torture in the well-known case *Cotton Field*, but it applied other articles of the American Convention when ruling, upon referral of the case by the Commission,[135] on the disappearance and death of three women – Laura Berenice Ramos Monárrez, Claudia Ivette González and Esmeralda Herrera Monreal – at Ciudad Juárez, Mexico. The death of at least 370 women had been reported over a period of ten years.[136] The city, at the border between Mexico and the United States, has been called the 'city of migrants' and, from the 1960s onwards, saw the establishment of *maquiladora* (or *maquila*) factories in which the majority of the murdered women had worked. The Asociación Nacional de Abogados Democráticos A.C., the Latin American and Caribbean Committee for the Defense of Women's Rights, the Red Ciudadana de No Violencia y por la Dignidad Humana and the Centro para el Desarrollo Integral of the Mujer A.C. represented the alleged victims, who were relatives of the women who had disappeared and been brutally killed at Ciudad Juárez. The Inter-American Commission asked the Court to declare the state responsible for violating Articles 4 (right to life), 5 (right to humane treatment), 8 (right to a fair trial), 19 (rights of the child) and 25 (right to judicial protection) of the American Convention, and also of Article 7 of the Belém do Pará Convention (state's obligations in cases of violence against women). In *Cotton Field*, rape had not been committed by state organs so, according to a rigorous and traditional interpretation of the crime, it could not amount to torture.

A *revirement* in the jurisprudence eventually occurred with the decision in *Linda Loaiza López Soto and her relatives v. The Bolivarian Republic of Venezuela*, referred to the IACHR by the Commission on 2 November 2016.[137] The Commission issued its report on 29 July 2016. Linda Loaiza López was abducted by Luis Carrera Almoina in Caracas in 2001, at the age of 18, and deprived of her liberty for several months until she was able to escape and call for help. During the kidnapping, she suffered physical, sexual and psychological violence, causing her permanent injuries. In the complaint, the applicants – López Soto and her relatives – claimed that the state had not investigated the case effectively, despite López Soto's sister repeatedly reporting her disappearance. The Court decided the case on 26 September 2018, and for the first time it considered rape committed by private actors to be 'sexual torture.'[138]

Shifting to the African continent, there was an indirect reference to the victim's right to health in the decision in *Equality Now v. Ethiopia*, handed down by the African Commission in 2015.[139] The applicant is a non-governmental organisation (NGO), which brought to court the case of an Ethiopian girl – aged 13 at the time of the violence – who was abducted and raped by a man who wanted to marry her. She was forced to sign a marriage contract. In 2003, the High Court found that she had consented to the marriage and accordingly to sexual intercourse, and the following year the Oromia Supreme Court concluded that there was no ground to judge the case, dismissing the appeal. The Commission lent its good offices to resolve the dispute in an amicable way upon request by the parties. However, the amicable settlement process was interrupted on 5 October 2012, and from that point only the merits stage continued.

Has the right to health been applied directly? In which ways was women's health relevant in the judgment?

The ECtHR case is almost irrelevant for examining marital rape, because no reference to the woman's right to health was included in the legal reasoning.[140]

Much more of interest for the purpose of my analysis is the judgment rendered by the Court of Nepal in 2002. The court referred in its legal reasoning to international legal instruments protecting women's rights and criminalising rape. It argued that rape is 'an inhuman act,' which violates women's human rights and has a 'serious impact on individual liberty and [the] right to self-determination of victim wom[e]n.'[141] The right to health is indirectly mentioned in several paragraphs of the decision. The court acknowledged, for example, that marital rape not only has an 'adverse impact on [the] physical, mental, family and spiritual life of victim women, it also adversely affects [the] self-respect and existence of women.' It then contended that 'murder destroys [the] physical being of a person, but the offence of rape … destroys the physical, mental and spiritual position of victim women. Thus, it is a heinous crime.'[142] It also argued that 'where a wife is treated as an object or property or a means of entertainment and exploitation, her personal health and her needs are ignored in an irrational and inhuman manner and in that situation, an unnatural and brutal act of rape of [the] wife is committed.'[143] Marital rape is defined as a 'brutal act', and as a 'social evil.' The court pointed out that 'it cannot be said that [the] Hindu religion and traditions exempts the heinous act of rape [of a] wife. Sexual intercourse in conjugal life is a normal course of behaviour, which must be based on consent. No religion may ever take it as lawful because the aim of a good religion is not to hate or cause loss to anyone.'[144] The Court concluded that it was 'appropriate, reasonable and contextual' to define marital rape as a criminal offence.[145] Nonetheless, it quashed the petition because the definition of rape was not *per se* inconsistent with the Constitution. It rather recommended that the Ministry of Law, Justice and Parliamentary Affairs introduce a bill bringing the necessary amendments to identified gaps in the legislation, namely the prohibition of marital rape.[146]

The High Court in Gujarat at Ahmedabad followed a similar reasoning, by arguing that 'the total statutory abolition of the marital rape exemption [still in force in India, as anticipated] is the first necessary step in teaching societies that dehumanized treatment of women will not be tolerated and that the marital rape is not a husband's privilege, but rather a violent act and an injustice that must be criminalized.'[147] The judge also stressed that, by contracting marriage, women are not deprived of their rights, in particular 'their right to have control over and decide freely and responsibly on matters related to their sexuality, including sexual and reproductive health, free of coercion, discrimination and violence.'[148] He concluded that a husband could not be prosecuted for the offence of rape under the existing legislation, but could be prosecuted for unnatural sex under another section of the criminal code.[149] In both domestic cases, judges pushed the legislator to amend the existing laws in order to include a prohibition of marital rape.

As for cases of rape committed by state organs, the IACommHR acknowledged, in *Martín de Mejía*, that 'sexual abuse committed by members of security forces … constitutes a violation of the victims' human rights, especially the right to physical and mental integrity.'[150] When analysing the elements of the crime of torture as applied to the case, the Commission stressed the effects of rape on women's health. In the words of the Commission, rape causes 'physical and mental suffering in the victim,' the victims are 'commonly hurt,' or become pregnant as a consequence of the rape. Furthermore, it pointed out, 'the fact of being made the subject of abuse of this nature also causes a psychological trauma that results, on the one hand, from having been humiliated and victimized, and on the other, from suffering the condemnation of the members of their community if they report what has been done to them.'[151] The Commission showed that all three elements of the crime of torture were present in the case at issue, and accordingly found Peru responsible for violating Article 5 of the American Convention, along with Article 11 (right to privacy), and Article 1(1) concerning states' obligation to respect the rights and freedoms of the people subject to their jurisdiction.[152]

In a later case, *Inés Fernández Ortega v. Mexico,* the IACHR specifically referred to the Belém do Pará Convention to point out that VAW constitutes not only a violation of human rights, but also 'an offence against human dignity,' and 'a manifestation of the historically unequal power relations between women and men.'[153] In light of my analysis of the right to health, it is worth noting that the Court confirmed precedent arguments made by the Commission in its report on the merits in 2008, which found that rape amounts to torture. In order to prove the commission of an act of torture, the Court stressed 'the severe suffering of the victim' as 'inherent in rape, even when there is no evidence of physical injuries or disease.'[154] It is interesting to observe that Inés Fernández Ortega underwent a gynaecological examination performed by a medical practitioner, who certified that there was no evidence of violence. This certificate did not prevent the Court from analysing the case, which was indeed reinforced by the testimony of Fernández Ortega, who never claimed that she had physically resisted the attack.[155] The element of force is not essential – confirmed the Court – and 'evidence of the existence of physical resistance to such acts cannot be required.'[156] Even though Mexico acknowledged its international responsibility in relation to what happened to Fernández Ortega, the Court decided to determine certain facts and it assessed that the criminal investigation had failed to comply with unacknowledged aspects of the guarantees arising from Articles 8(1) and 25(1) of the American Convention, in relation to Articles 1(1) and 2 thereof, and also from Article 7 of the Belém do Pará Convention (state's obligations in cases of violence against women) and Articles 1, 6 and 8 of the Inter-American Convention to Prevent and Punish Torture.[157] There was a clear element of gender discrimination in the case, and the Court interestingly stressed how the general obligations stemming from the American Convention were 'complemented and enhanced' by the Belém do Parà Convention.[158] Intersectional discrimination against women was also a key element of the analysis.[159]

The female applicants in *'Las Dos Erres' Massacre* were pregnant women who had been subjected to induced abortions, rape and 'acts of extreme cruelty,' which provoked 'grave damages to their mental integrity.'[160] Their psychological health was immediately affected. The Court reiterated the findings in the *Plan de Sánchez v. Guatemala* case of 19 November 2004,[161] according to which 'the rape of women was a state practice, executed in the context of massacres, directed to destroying the dignity of women at a cultural, social, family, and individual level.'[162] The Court concluded that the state had violated several rights under the American Convention by not effectively investigating the massacre, and also Article 7 of the Belèm do Pará Convention (state's obligations in cases of violence against women). The health of the victims/survivors was a relevant factor to confirm the violation of the American Convention, and the right to be free from violence under Article 6 of the Belém do Pará Convention.

In the *Atenco* case, the applicants claimed that several human rights had been violated, including Articles 5 (human treatment) and 25 (judicial protection) of the American Convention, along with Articles 6 (right to be free from violence) and 7 (state's obligations in cases of violence against women) of the Belém do Pará Convention, and with the provisions of the Inter-American Convention that aim to prevent and punish torture. What is relevant for the purpose of this paragraph is the existence of several acts of physical and psychological violence and rape to which the applicants were subjected. The Commission, in its report, considered these acts to have been torture and determined that the women had been victims of physical, psychological and sexual torture during their apprehension, transfer to and arrival at the detention centre. Furthermore, the state was responsible for not having investigated the acts with due diligence and in reasonable time. The Commission also ruled that violations of the physical and moral integrity of the victims' families had occurred. The IACHR confirmed the findings in its judgment of 2018, describing the violence suffered by the applicants as torture.[163] It did not consider the right to health, but stated that the following all applied: the right to physical, mental, and moral integrity enshrined in Article 5(1) of the American Convention, the prohibition of torture under the Inter-American Convention against torture and the right to be free from violence under Article 6 of the Belém do Pará Convention. The impact of violence on the woman's health and sexual health clearly emerges from several parts of the judgment. In particular, the Court stressed how sexual violence affects 'essential aspects of a person's private life,' constitutes an interference in sexual life and 'annuls [a person's] right to freely take decisions' to have sexual intercourse, 'completely losing control over personal and intimate decisions.'[164] In particular, it found that, even though men were also subjected to an excessive use of force, women were subjected to a 'differentiated form of violence,' having a clear sexual character and focused on intimate parts of their bodies.[165] The Court also acknowledged that 'medical violence' had occurred, because the health personnel provided a 'degrading and stereotyped' treatment to the women, which became part of the sexual violence to which they were exposed.[166] The authorities' exercise of the duty to investigate demonstrated the persistence of stereotypes. According to the Court, the investigation and the medical examination both lacked a gender perspective; the women suffered verbal and physical aggression, and were addressed in sexist terms, which was done to exercise social control and perpetuate long-standing stereotypes of the roles of women in Mexican society.[167]

Turning to the ECtHR system, issues related to the woman's health in the *Aydin v. Turkey* case were relevant to prove the violation of Article 3 ECHR. The applicant was in severe pain, and 'experienced the acute physical pain of forced penetration, which … left her feeling debased and violated both physically and emotionally.'[168] She was detained, and she was kept 'in a constant state of physical pain and mental anguish.'[169] The Court concluded that 'the accumulation of acts of physical and mental violence inflicted on the applicant and the especially cruel act of rape to which she was subjected amounted to torture in breach of Article 3 of the Convention.'[170] With regard to Article 13 ECHR, the Court contended that an effective remedy would have entailed the payment of the compensation and a thorough and effective investigation capable of identifying those responsible of the crime. In the case under analysis, authorities only conducted an incomplete inquiry, and ordered examinations which were not objective, but circumscribed by instructions given by the prosecutor. The Court hence confirmed that Turkey also violated Article 13 ECHR.

As for rape committed by non-state actors, the relevant case in Europe is *M.C. v. Bulgaria*. The Court did not dwell on the impact of rape on M.C.'s health, but rather focused on the elements of the crime of rape, in particular the lack of consent. It concluded that the authorities had failed to sufficiently investigate the circumstances of the rape, owing to excessive emphasis on 'direct' proof of rape. The Bulgarian authorities were criticised because they did not consider the particular vulnerability of the applicant, minor at that time, and the special 'psychological factors' involved.[171] The reference to the psychological consequences of the violence is the only element linked to the right to health that can be found in the judgment. Judge Tulkens, concurring, emphasised the violation of both the right to personal integrity – physical and psychological – under Article 3, and the right to autonomy which falls under Article 8 ECHR.

In the Inter-American system of protection of human rights, the *Cotton Field* case, decided on 26 November 2009, plays a key role in recognising the gender dimension of the violence, and the systemic discrimination against women. The killings that occurred in Ciudad Juárez had a common trait: their being gender-based. The state was found in violation of several articles of the American Convention and of Article 7 (state's obligations in cases of violence against women) of the Belém do Pará Convention, because the authorities had not effectively investigated the crimes committed in Ciudad Juárez. The psychological consequences of the deaths and disappearances for the victims' relatives were also taken into account in the legal reasoning. Nonetheless, even though the Court found a violation of Article 5 of the American Convention (right to humane treatment), it did not describe the acts as 'torture'. The position it adopted was criticised by Judge Cecilia Medina Quiroga.[172]

The turning point in the jurisprudence of the IACHR, as mentioned earlier, was *Linda Loaiza López Soto*. In that case, the applicants claimed that the state had not investigated a case of abduction and abuse effectively, despite the fact that Linda López Soto's disappearance was reported to the authorities by her sister. They claimed that this was a case of torture, an example of 'institutional violence and re-victimization suffered by the women who are victims of sexual violence and seek justice in Venezuela.'[173] López Soto, who had been abducted, was found to have suffered severe injuries, both physical and psychological, later confirmed by the forensic medical examinations. She had also endured several violations of her right to reproductive health, demonstrated by signs of genital trauma. The reports on her mental health confirmed the statements she made. The right to health could not be directly considered by the Commission, but factors concerning López Soto's health and reproductive health were pivotal in its concluding that she had suffered violations of her rights to personal integrity, private life, autonomy and dignity, personal liberty, to equality and non-discrimination and to live a life free from violence.[174] The Commission emphasised the gender-based nature of the violations of López Soto's rights and that the acts could be described as torture. To support this argument, it referred to the UN Manual on effective investigation and documentation of torture and other cruel, inhuman or degrading treatment or punishment of 2004.[175] Had the jurisprudence not been enough, the Commission relied on 'soft law' to show that 'sexual torture' starts with forced nudity, and that verbal threats, insults and sexual jokes are part of sexual torture, because they increase the humiliation.[176] The Commission found that the Venezuelan state had been 'acquiescent and tolerant of the torture to which Linda Loaiza López was victim.'[177] It applied the 'powerlessness' requirement well developed by the then Special Rapporteur Manfred Nowak,[178] and referred to the jurisprudence of the ECtHR in a paragraph which is worth reporting *in extenso*:

> The Commission agrees with these developments under other protection systems, which, upon analyzing elements that would constitute conduct prohibited under Article 5(2) of the American Convention, have found that acts of physical,

> psychological, and sexual violence committed by non-State actors can be classified as such prohibited conduct, with emphasis on the characteristics of this type of violence and the serious effects it has on its victims. As far as the elements of State participation, the cited standards are consistent in considering failure in the duty to prevent and protect can be understood as a form of State tolerance and acquiescence with the corresponding legal implications of the ban on torture in a case like this one.[179]

The Commission concluded that Venezuela had violated all the rights López Soto mentioned in the complaint.[180] The pioneer position of the Commission, in describing sexual violence as torture, was then confirmed by the IACHR. López Soto's health is a recurrent element in the decision. The Court acknowledged that the proceedings had regarded as proved the 'outrageous acts of physical, verbal, psychological and sexual violence' suffered by Linda Loiza López Soto, which had impacted on her rights to personal integrity, dignity, autonomy and private life, as well as to her right to live free from violence.[181] The state, which admitted that it had failed in the investigation, rejected the allegation that it could have been aware of the risks the victim was facing. Nonetheless, the Court interestingly argued that an alleged episode of VAW requires 'a reinforced due diligence.'[182] This means that the response of the authorities to a risk of violence must be prompt and immediate, especially when there is a risk to the woman's life and bodily integrity. In particular, a report that a woman has disappeared or been abducted is, in itself, sufficient for the state's due diligence obligation to be triggered. As interestingly argued, 'the Court thus departed from prior decisions [*Cotton Field*] where it had additionally required proof of the State's awareness of a context of violence against women.'[183] To demonstrate that in this specific case sexual violence had amounted to torture, the Court further highlighted the impact on López Soto's health: her kidnapper had exercised a control over every aspect of her life, including her feeding and her physiological needs, 'leading to a status of absolute defencelessness.'[184] Her abduction had also amounted to sexual slavery, an aspect which cannot be explored further here.[185] The Court showed in this judgment that its legal reasoning has evolved to include a reflection on the specific character of states' obligations to prevent violence and on the nature of this violence. The state was found responsible for violating several rights of López Soto, including the rights to personal integrity, personal liberty, dignity, autonomy, private life, the prohibitions of torture and of slavery, and the right to be free from violence under the Belém do Pará Convention.

The final case proposed in these pages was decided by the African Commission in *Equality Now v. Ethiopia*. The applicant complained of violation of the woman's rights to equal protection under the law (Article 3); protection from cruel, inhuman or degrading treatment (Articles 5 and 4); protection from discrimination (Article 2); and to bodily integrity and security of the person (Articles 6 and 4 African Charter). At the time of the events, prosecution for rape was excluded when the perpetrator married his victim. The law was repealed in 2005; nonetheless, the practice of abducting, raping and forcing a woman to marry the perpetrator remained common at the time of the complaint. The language used by the Commission is particularly strong, and condemns 'one of the most repugnant traditional practices,' that recalls 'a proverbial ancient past' when a man could 'hunt' the woman he wanted.[186] The respondent state did not deny what happened to the woman, and also acknowledged that the police officers and prosecutor had not investigated the events diligently. The Commission invoked Article 1 of the African Charter, which obliges state parties to give effect to the rights enshrined in the Charter, and to respect, protect, promote and fulfil those rights. In a remarkable passage of the decision, the Commission pointed out that 'by rape, the victim is treated as a mere object of sexual gratification against his or her will and conscience,' and that 'the victim is treated without regard for the personal autonomy and control over what happens to his or her body.'[187] Turning to the consequences for the victim's health, the Commission highlighted that '[i]nevitably, rape may, and often does, inflict physical pain and invokes in the victim a sense of helplessness, worthlessness, and gross debasement, which cause unimaginable mental anguish beyond the physical suffering. Clearly, rape degrades and humiliates the victim.'[188] In considering violations of rights protected by the Charter, the Commission contended that the state 'was aware' or 'must be deemed to have been aware' of the practice of marriage by abduction and rape, and of the fact that girls were under 'the continuing threat of being abducted, raped and forcibly married.'[189] This argument recalls the immediacy of the risk elaborated by the European and the Inter-American jurisprudence, and will be relevant for the identification of states' obligations. The Commission failed however to acknowledge that this was a case of discrimination against women. It argued that not all forms of VAW 'necessarily [amount] to or ought to be termed "discrimination" to be condemned as violations of women's rights.'[190] However, VAW is a form of discrimination against women; it affects women because they are women, or affects women disproportionately. The fact that the Commission could not use a comparator – how men are treated in the same situation – should not have prevented it from finding a violation of the principle of non-discrimination. It is indeed because of the role of women in that society that ancient practices such as marriage by rape continue and affect women only. Even so, the decision is remarkable for addressing issues of VAW under a human rights law perspective and focusing on the impact of violence on the woman's health.

Reparations

The Inter-American system of protection of human rights has showed an interesting evolution in the determination of reparations as a consequence of the assessment of state responsibility for acts of sexual violence against women committed by state organs or private parties. It is beyond question that the victims and/or their relatives should be awarded adequate compensation once a violation of their human rights has been assessed by an adjudicatory body. It is also agreed that the defendant state must conduct an impartial and effective investigation.[191] What has emerged from the most recent reports issued by the Inter-American

Commission and from the judgments rendered by the IACHR, however, is the gradual inclusion of health concerns in determining reparations. For example, in *Cotton Field* Mexico was required by the Court not only to provide compensation to the victims' relatives and to continue investigation of their deaths, but also to provide appropriate medical support free of charge to all the next-of-kin.[192] In *Fernández Ortega*, the Court granted the victims different amounts of money as compensation, considering several elements, among them 'the sufferings caused to the victims and the way they have been treated,'[193] and found that reparations should also consist in 'appropriate care for the physical and psychological effects suffered by the victims, which attend to their gender and ethnicity.'[194] In *Mariana Selvas Gómez (Atenco)*, the IACommHR recommended that the victims receive full compensation, including moral damages, for violations of their human rights. Furthermore, it decided that the state should provide free medical and psychological treatment to the victims and continue the investigation with due diligence and in reasonable time. The IACHR followed the Commission's approach, and argued that, given the severe consequence to the victims' personal integrity, reparations must pay adequate attention to their physical and mental suffering. It specifically ordered the state to provide free medical treatment to the victims, including immediate psychological and psychiatric treatment, whether requested by the victims within six months from the judgment or not.[195] The Court also decided that the state had an obligation to continue investigation – despite the important steps forward that had been taken – and to reinforce the mechanism for prosecuting cases of sexual torture of women. The victims were awarded US$70,000 each for non-material damage.[196]

Under the European system for protecting human rights, it is worth highlighting how, in *Aydin*, the right to health was relevant in determining the amount of compensation. Given 'the enduring psychological harm' Aydin suffered as a consequence of rape, the Court awarded her £25,000 sterling as non-pecuniary damages.[197] The African Commission requested Ethiopia to adopt general measures, including the publication of convictions to put prospective offenders on notice, and the elaboration of statistics on cases of marriage by abduction and rape.[198] In setting monetary compensation, the Commission considered the physical, psychological and emotional trauma in deciding to award US$150,000.[199]

Female genital mutilation/cutting

Context and legal background

Female circumcision, female genital surgery, female genital mutilation and female genital cutting all describe procedures which affect female genital organs for non-medical reasons. Female circumcision seems the most misleading word, since the procedure does not resemble male circumcision.[200] Female genital mutilation is the expression used by several NGOs and international organisations, including the WHO, to describe 'all procedures that involve partial or total removal of the external female genitalia, or other injury to the female genital organs for non-medical reasons.'[201] In the analysis that follows, I will use the expression chosen by UNICEF: female genital mutilation/cutting (FGM/C). There are four major types of FGM/C, described by the WHO as follows:[202]

> Type I – Partial or total removal of the clitoris and/or the prepuce (clitoridectomy).
> Type II – Partial or total removal of the clitoris and the labia minora, with or without excision of the labia majora (excision).
> Type III – Narrowing of the vaginal orifice with creation of a covering seal by cutting and appositioning the labia minora and/or the labia majora, with or without excision of the clitoris (infibulation). When it is important to distinguish between variations in infibulations, … subdivisions are proposed: …
> Type IV – All other harmful procedures to the female genitalia for non-medical purposes, for example: pricking, piercing, incising, scraping and cauterization.

The practice is ancient. It was reported by Herodotus as early as the fifth century BCE and practised by the Phoenicians, Hittites and Ethiopians.[203] It was also known in Roman times.[204] According to a recent study by UNICEF, FGM/C is highly concentrated in countries 'from the Atlantic coast to the Horn of Africa, in areas of the Middle East such as Iraq and Yemen and in some countries in Asia like Indonesia.'[205] The practice has also been reported in some countries in South America (Colombia), and in Asia, Malaysia, Oman, Saudi Arabia and the United Arab Emirates. It is performed in immigrant communities in Europe, Australia and North America. It was reported that in the UK, between October and December 2016, 2,332 attendances at NHS trusts and GP practices were reported where FGM was identified or a procedure for FGM was undertaken.[206] In the world, 200 million women and girls in 30 countries have undergone the procedure, of which 44 million are girls below 14. The origins of the practice, which is not generally supported by governmental or religious authorities,[207] are not easy to track. Social pressure, control of women's sexuality (virginity, chastity), a ritual of 'admission' to a community, intertwined with socially constructed roles for women and men, count among the reasons explaining FGM/C. Refusing the practice might lead to a woman being excluded from her community of origin, or her community in a destination country. It may even be considered a stain on the honour of the family and a matter of deep shame.

From a medical point of view, all forms of FGM/C can cause severe physical and psychological harm.[208] Immediate medical complications include bleeding, and health hazards relating to performance outside healthcare facilities and poor sterilisation of the cutting instruments. Infections as a consequence of the procedure might lead to the woman's or girl's death,[209] and have an impact on her physical and psychological health. In the long term, type III in particular can cause urinary tract and chronic pelvic infections, cysts and complications during, before and after childbirth.

From a legal point of view, the practice has been generally condemned at the international level. Article 5 CEDAW requires states to take all appropriate measures 'to modify the social and cultural patterns of conduct of men and women, with a view to achieving the elimination of prejudices and customary and all other practices which are based on the idea of the inferiority or the superiority of either of the sexes or on stereotyped roles for men and women,' and the Convention on the Rights of the Child of 1989 clearly protects children from harmful practices prejudicial to their health (Article 24(3)). The CEDAW Committee drew up a GR on female circumcision in 1990, requiring states to 'take appropriate and effective measures with a view to eradicating the practice of female circumcision.'[210] A few years later, more than 170 countries committed to work to end FGM/C in the ICPD Programme of action (Cairo 1994), and in the Bejing platform (1995). Other bodies have condemned the practice: for example, in 2008 the then UN Special Rapporteur on torture and other cruel, inhuman or degrading treatment or punishment, Manfred Nowak, affirmed that 'even if a law authorizes the practice, any act of FGM would amount to torture and the existence of the law by itself would constitute consent or acquiescence by the State.'[211] In its GC No. 21, the ESCR Committee, despite acknowledging the existence of an individual and a collective right to take part in cultural life,[212] posited that 'female genital mutilation and allegations of the practice of witchcraft, are barriers to the full exercise by the affected persons of the right enshrined in Art. 15, para. 1 (a) [ICESCR].'[213]

At a regional level, prohibition of FGM/C is included in the 2003 Protocol to the African Charter on Human and Peoples' Rights on the Rights of Women in Africa (Article 5), and in the Council of Europe Istanbul Convention of 2011 (Articles 38 and 42). The latter also includes grounds for jurisdiction that allow the prosecution of female genital mutilation committed abroad by or against nationals or residents of the ratifying states (Article 44(1) and (2)).[214] The Istanbul Convention requires states to criminalise the following behaviours: excising, infibulating or performing any other mutilation to the whole or any part of a woman's labia majora, labia minora or clitoris; coercing or procuring a woman to undergo any of these procedures; inciting, coercing or procuring a girl to undergo any of these procedures.

At a European level, the EU and the Council of Europe institutions have repeatedly condemned FGM/C, at least the first three types, without exception. National laws in all regions of the world have gradually outlawed the practice, or at least some types of FGM/C.[215] Sudan, for example, made infibulation illegal in 1946.

Before examining some key judgments and decisions that are relevant to the horizontal dimension of my analysis, it is worth considering the cultural perspective to understand whether the practice can be accepted and, if so, under which circumstances. Might we identify different levels of harm in order to allow certain types of FGM/C and not others? What about medicalising it: a procedure performed in a secure environment, using sterile instruments? Is that legitimate or not? Is the prohibition a form of Western cultural imperialism or a commitment to protect women's human rights? The International Federation of Gynecology and Obstetrics (FIGO) has repeatedly condemned all forms of FGM/C, and asked healthcare professionals not to perform it, even though performing the practice in a sterile environment might reduce the most severe consequences. As it has recently stated, 'medicalisation of FGM/C – encouraged by some healthcare professionals – is not an acceptable practice because it violates medical ethics and further legitimises and perpetuates the practice.'[216] The reason lies in the fact that the procedure has no medical purpose, and violates a woman's rights to health and to reproductive health. As I have argued elsewhere,[217] FGM/C constitute VAW, in all their forms, because they are performed without the consent of the woman or girl – except re-infibulation, which I will discuss in chapter 2[218] – and they cause irreparable physical and psychological damage. This does not mean that the 'Western' point of view should prevail in defining which individual human rights deserve protection. These harmful practices are also criminalised in Africa and Asia, but they persist in some communities. FGM/C are also practised in immigrant communities in European countries. They cause physical and psychological harm to girls and women and have no explanation other than tradition or 'religion'.[219]

Judgments and decisions

Courts, especially national courts, have played a key role in the prohibition of FGM/C and in shaping the general perception of this practice as a violation of women's rights. As far as I am aware, no court has ever found the practice justified on cultural grounds. Lower sanctions might have been applied, depending on the gravity of the injury, but the violation of a woman's or girl's rights has never been condoned by courts. I will investigate the cases summarised in the next sub-section along my three axes of analysis, taking into consideration that there have been different decision typologies: decisions on the legitimacy of the practice; decisions related to the prosecution of individuals who performed FGM/C; decisions on requests for refugee status coming from women who risk being subjected to the procedure in their country of origin. For the following analysis, I found more interesting cases relating to FGM/C at the national level than at the regional level.

Who is the applicant?

Let us start from decisions on the legitimacy of the practice. Two judgments rendered by national courts in Africa and South America are worth discussing here. The first is *Law and Advocacy for Women in Uganda v. Attorney General*,[220] filed in 2007 and decided by the Ugandan Constitutional Court in 2010. The applicant was an NGO that required the court to declare FGM a violation of several articles of the Ugandan Constitution. The petition was supported by five affidavits, including one presented by a professional practitioner. The applicant presented evidence of the consequence of FGM on the lives of women and girls.

Moving to South America, which has rarely been mentioned as an area where the practice is performed, in 2008 the Juzgado Promiscuo Municipal [Municipal Court] in Colombia received a complaint that 16-day-old infants had been abused and, as a consequence of genital mutilation in the Emberá-Chamí community (Río San Juan Embera-Chamí native reservation), developed fever and vomiting owing to an acute infection.[221] The Court received reports from the municipal police and from the Ombudsman of Pueblo Rico of alleged abuses against indigenous girls. Through a writ issued soon after, the Court chose to start proceedings on behalf of the three new-born girls. It heard evidence from doctors, a nutritionist and anthropologists, before deciding the merits of the case.

Shifting to cases concerning the prosecution of individuals for performing the practice, it should be said at outset that, even though generally prohibited by law, FGM/C is frequently practised within immigrant communities in European countries. Few cases have been brought to the attention of national courts, though.[222] The UK first prohibited FGM/C in 1985 with the Prohibition of Female Circumcision Act; replaced this with the Female Genital Mutilation Act of 2003, which came into force in 2004; and amended the 2003 Act by sections 70 to 75 of the Serious Crime Act 2015. These sections extended the scope of extraterritorial offences, in light of the Istanbul Convention (which the UK has signed but not yet ratified), granted victims lifelong anonymity and introduced the offence of failing to protect a girl from the risk of FGM.[223] France, without specifically criminalising the conduct,[224] registered dozens of cases against West African immigrants during the 1980s and 1990s, starting from 1983, when the Cour de Cassation ruled FGM a mutilation that falls within the scope of the rule prohibiting personal injury.[225] In Italy, after the entry into force of the 2006 law criminalizing FGM,[226] the first case brought to court concerned G.O., a Nigerian midwife living in Verona, who practised FGM on a 2-month-old child. G.O. and the mother of the victim (X) were charged with the offence under Article 583*bis* of the Italian criminal code. G.O. was also charged with the offence of attempting to commit the crime, as she was arrested while entering a house where another infant lived. The proceedings were initiated by the Italian authorities.[227]

In a landmark case decided by the Supreme Court of New South Wales, Australia, three people were convicted and sentenced to 15 months' imprisonment – and referred to be assessed for suitability for home detention – for committing acts contrary to section 45 of the Crimes Act 1900 (NSW), adopted in 1994, which prohibits FGM. The defendants, who all belonged to the Dawoodi Bohra community, a sect of Shia Islam, were A2 (the mother of C1 and C2), KM (a retired midwife) and Mr Vaziri, the highest authority among the Dawoodi Bohra in Sydney. They were accused of performing FGM/C on two young girls, C1 and C2. The case was reported to the Department of Family. None of the children needed to be removed from the care of their parents. The applicant in the criminal proceedings was the Crown.[228]

The majority of cases that I could find at both national and regional levels involved requests for refugee status submitted by women who feared being subjected to the practice once back to their country of origin. In a report published in 2014 covering the EU, it was estimated that around 16,000 women and girls who arrived in the EU in 2013 could potentially have already endured FGM at the time of their arrival.[229] The UNHCR estimated that, although little or no data on the point had been collected by national asylum authorities, more than 2,000 asylum claims on grounds of FGM/C may have been received in 2011 in the EU.[230]

Starting at the regional level, the ECtHR has dealt with FMG/C in cases related to women seeking asylum in order to escape the practice in their country of origin, and concluded that the cases were not admissible.[231]

National courts have demonstrated themselves more open to the requests of women escaping countries where they might be subjected to FGM/C. Countries that have ratified the Council of Europe Istanbul Convention are obliged to afford refugee status to women escaping violence, under its Article 60. I will put forward two European examples, in Italy and the UK (only the former is a state party to the Istanbul Convention), and a US case. In *Fornah*, decided in the United Kingdom in 2005, the applicant was a young woman aged 15 who had escaped from Sierra Leone. She asked for refugee status because she feared undergoing FGM if returned to her country of origin. The Secretary of State for the Home Department granted her leave to remain until she turned 18, and could have extended the period for a further three years on humanitarian grounds. Zainab Fornah asked to be recognised as a refugee. The Court of Appeal held that FGM of 'young, single and uncircumcised Sierra Leonean women' does not constitute persecution 'for reasons of' their membership of a 'particular social group' for several reasons, among which were the fact that 'however harshly we may stigmatize the practice as persecution for the purpose of Article 3, it is not, in the circumstances in which it is practised in Sierra Leone, discriminatory in such a way as to set those who undergo it apart from society.'[232] Fornah's appeal against this decision was allowed by the then House of Lords in 2006. In its decision, the then House of Lords referred to another judgment, decided in 2005 in the United States, *Mohamed v. R. Gonzales*.[233] Mohamed had applied for asylum in the USA when she was 17 years old, and declared her fear of persecution if returned to Somalia, where she had already been subjected to FGM. Past persecution was put forward as ground for refugee status. When her request was refused, she appealed, but the Board of Immigration Appeals (BIA) denied it. Her motion to reconsider was dismissed by the same board; the US Court of Appeals, Ninth Circuit, with which the complaint was eventually filed, considered this decision 'rife with errors and inconsistencies.'[234]

As for Italy, the Corte d'Appello in Catania (Court of Appeal) handed down a landmark judgment in 2012, granting refugee status to a woman who had escaped from Nigeria where people of her community had tried to force her to undergo FGM.[235]

Has the right to health been applied directly? In which ways was women's health relevant in the judgment?

Despite the evident impact of FGM/C on the health of women and girls, the rights to health and to reproductive health have been seldom invoked in the decisions under analysis.

As illustrative example, in *Law and Advocacy for Women in Uganda* the Ugandan Constitutional Court referred, on one hand, to Article 37 of the Constitution, which recognises the right to culture, and on the other hand, to Article 44 of the same legal instrument, which provides that no derogation is admitted to freedom from torture, cruel, inhuman or degrading treatment or punishment. The Court concluded that 'the practice of female genital mutilation is a custom which is wholly inconsistent with the above mentioned provisions and it is now the duty of this court to declare the custom void.'[236] The judge also acknowledged that, while the case had still been pending, the government had started a discussion on a new law outlawing the practice. The right to health was not directly applied, even though the Constitution contains a provision which grants all Ugandans 'access to health services.'[237]

Turning to South America, in the *Emberá-Chamí Community FGM* case, the Colombian Court referred to Article 246 of the Colombian Constitution which recognises the authority of indigenous peoples to exercise jurisdictional functions 'within their territorial scope, in accordance with their rules and procedures, provided that they are not contrary to the constitution and the laws of the republic.' Previous jurisprudence had established that limitations to the exercise of this jurisdiction were confined to a hard core of rights – the right to life, the prohibition of slavery, the prohibition of torture, respect for due process – determined according to the beliefs of the respective indigenous tribe, and, in criminal matters, the lawfulness of crimes and punishments.[238] The Court did not consider the practice as DV, despite being committed within the family, but as a custom within the Emberá-Chamí indigenous community. From a procedural point of view, the decision of the court is fundamental, because the indigenous authorities, which normally have jurisdiction over DV cases, were not found competent to decide FGM/C cases. The Court posited that FGM/C 'is a conduct that violates human rights and that must be subject to a different treatment [than DV],'[239] and concluded that 'since FGM threatens the lives and personal integrity of indigenous girls, it violates fundamental constitutional rights that are senior to the constitutional values of ethnic diversity. Thus, we cannot uphold the autonomy of the indigenous community in said matter.'[240] The Court also recognised that the agreement concluded between the government and the indigenous community, which included a commitment to oppose harmful practices, did not work and could not protect children. Not considering FGM as DV, the Court found that the law on DV could not be applied and that violence suffered by the children was not a matter to be resolved through family protection laws. It also did not decide family protection measures, but declared that FGM performed in the Emberá-Chamí community was 'a barbaric and inhumane practice that violates the rights of the women and girls of that community, and is arbitrary and unjustifiable,' and that 'it disregards the National Constitution and International Human Rights Treaties signed by Colombia.'[241] Furthermore, the Court found that the rights which were violated, namely the right to life and to bodily integrity, 'have greater weight and, as a consequence, override the constitutional rights derived from the respect for cultural diversity and autonomy of indigenous peoples.'[242]

Turning now to cases relating to the prosecution of alleged perpetrators of the practice,[243] in the Australian cases that I mentioned in 'Who is the applicant?' above the Supreme Court found that mutilation had occurred, and that the degree of injury or harm would have been relevant for determining the penalty after conviction.[244] The jury found the alleged perpetrators guilty on 15 November 2015. The children were heard as witnesses. The Supreme Court determined the penalty – 15 months' imprisonment – in 2016, marking the first case of prosecution and conviction for FGM/C in Australia.[245] A2 (the children's mother) made a formal apology and other elements could have been taken into account in mitigating the sentence imposed on the defendants, but the Court posited that, in the case of FGM/C, general deterrence was necessary to 'point to an ongoing pattern of attitudinal change in the Dawoodi Bohra Community, against a background of centuries old adherence to the practice of *khatna.*'[246] It also explained that the sentence could not be taken as a model for further cases occurring after 20 May 2014, when the maximum penalty was raised from 7 to 21 years' imprisonment. There was no reference to the girls' right to health. One commentator, considering that the physical harm was not severe, asked 'where is the harm [in this case]?'[247] I will discuss the level of harm, which is both physical and psychological, in chapter 2, 'Consent and autonomy in the horizontal dimension: FGM/C'.

Shifting to cases in which fear of FGM/C could be considered a ground for recognising refugee status, the ECtHR has been reluctant to extend international protection to women escaping violence in their country of origin, arguing, for example, that the applicant could have moved to another part of the country instead of leaving it or that the woman's family could have protected her, being opposed to the practice.[248] In these cases, the right to health was not an issue, although the Court found that FGM can amount to torture, inhuman or degrading treatment or punishment, because of the severe impact these practices have on physical integrity.

Turning to national judgments on refugee status, in *Fornah*, decided by the then UK House of Lords, Lord Bingham posited that 'women in Sierra Leone are a group of persons sharing a common characteristic which, without a fundamental change in social mores, is unchangeable, namely a position of social inferiority as compared with men ... it is a characteristic which would exist even if FGM were not practised, although FGM is an extreme and very cruel expression of male dominance' and went on to acknowledge that 'there is a perception of these women by society as a distinct group. And it is not a group defined by persecution: it would be a recognizable group even if FGM were entirely voluntary, not performed by force or as a result of social pressure.'[249] The right to health was not mentioned in the case, and the reasoning of the House was rather guided by a sort of 'assessment' of the patriarchal culture of the country of origin. As stressed by Ruth Mestre and Sara Johnsdotter, 'it is important that courts in Europe have access to knowledge about culture-specific contexts when they handle suspected cases of FGM in criminal courts,' which does not mean arguing in favour of cultural relativism, but rather that courts need to demonstrate 'multicultural sensitivity.'[250]

The US Court of Appeals, Ninth Circuit, in *Mohamed v. Gonzales*, affirmed that there is no doubt that FGM amounts to persecution under US asylum law,[251] and that Mohamed had been persecuted 'on account of her membership to a social group,' which the Court identified either as Somalian women, or more narrowly, as young girls in the Benadiri clan.[252] According to the Court, 'it was the only plausible construction.'[253] It compared FGM to forced sterilisation, described in a previous case as a 'continuing harm that renders a petitioner eligible for asylum, without more.' That is the closest reference to the rights to health and reproductive health which can be found in this judgment. Mohamed's motion to have her petition reopened and reconsidered was eventually granted.[254]

The Italian Corte d'Appello in Catania, in *A.F.*, affirmed that A.F.'s situation deserved analysis under refugee law, as she had expressed a reasonable fear of being subjected to gender-based violence 'being [a] woman.' Furthermore, she faced the risk of being subjected in her country of origin to an inhuman and degrading treatment, 'like infibulation is.' The Court based its reasoning on A.F.'s deposition, which was supported by 'reliable sources' such as a report prepared by Amnesty International and UN documents. The decision of the lower tribunal was overruled and A.F. was granted refugee status.[255]

Reparations

Compensation to the victims of FGM/C was not an issue in the decisions on the legitimacy of the practice, nor in the prosecution of the alleged perpetrators. In prosecutions, parallel proceedings could have been started in order to obtain redress from the perpetrator. In the case filed by *Law and Advocacy for Women in Uganda* and in the case of the Emberá-Chamí community, given the nature of the proceedings, compensation was not an issue. However, the Colombian state authorities were required to urgently ban the practice of FGM/C in the Emberá-Chamí community, and private entities and NGOs were asked to take action to support the immediate and urgent elimination of FGM.

In all cases on refugee status,[256] reparations consisted either in a re-examination of the applicant's case or in the direct acceptance of her request.

The vertical, 'state policies' dimension

Abortion

Context and legal background

The purpose of this section of the chapter is to reflect on cases concerning abortion in order to identify the elements of violence against women's health that pertain to the second, 'vertical' dimension of my analysis. The issue is extremely sensitive, because it entails considerations that go beyond law and touch upon ethics and morality.[257] I have selected cases decided by courts at both the national and regional levels, and by UN treaty bodies. I will study the cases under analysis through an innovative lens, which builds on my paradigm, and allows me to eventually unravel the challenging 'conflict' between the interests of the pregnant woman and those of the foetus. The reasoning that I will elaborate does not exclude the potential for the foetus to become a person,[258] but rather emphasises the fact that, in the name of the foetus, decisions that are pivotal for the woman's health have been left in the hands of 'others', thereby adumbrating a stigmatised vision of 'woman' that cannot but want to become mother and needs protection in order to make what the society considers the 'correct' choice.[259] Even though it is not the purpose of this book to take a position on the concept of personhood,[260] a few preliminary remarks seem unavoidable. It is worth pointing out that it is extremely difficult to determine the moment at which an embryo or foetus is 'morally entitled to, at least, consideration.'[261] Prenatal personhood has been sustained or denied by scholars, activists, religious authorities and courts,[262] but, as one author contends, 'prenatal personhood is often not something that is taken seriously by its proponents; rather it is a vehicle for justifying restrictions on women's sexual and reproductive rights and, more specifically, for trumping the right to choose.'[263] Who is the focus of the 'narrative'? The woman, or the foetus, or both? Sifris has made the argument that states restricting access to abortion 'generally fail to provide practical support to help prevent unwanted pregnancies from occurring in the first place and to assist such women when they become mothers,' with the consequence that 'legislation restricting access to abortion rests on discriminatory assumptions about women and does not only rest on concern for the rights of the foetus.'[264]

At the international level, it is hard to argue that abortion is a stand-alone right.[265] The Protocol to the African Charter on Human and Peoples' Rights on the Rights of Women in Africa (Maputo Protocol) is the only regional binding legal instrument which openly acknowledges 'the reproductive rights of women,' and authorises medical abortion 'in cases of sexual assault, rape, incest, and where continued pregnancy endangers the mental and physical health of the mother or the life of the mother or the foetus.'[266] This provision directly 'situat[es] abortion as a human right that is recognised in the substantive provisions of a regional treaty.'[267] Where other explicit provisions are not present in regional and international legal instruments, women's right to have access to abortion services is protected by international human rights law, under which denial of abortion amounts to a violation of women's rights.[268]

The criminalisation of abortion, in particular a criminalisation without exceptions, is an example of VAW, and, I am arguing, also of VAWH, that originates from a state health policy. The close relation between the criminalisation of abortion and the rights to health and reproductive health was emphasised by Rebecca Cook:

> When a state criminalizes induced abortion …, it is constructing its social meaning as inherently wrong and harmful to society. Through criminal prohibition, a state is signaling conditions in which abortion is criminally wrong, reflecting the historical origin of crime in sin that can and should be punished. In contrast, the legal framing of abortion as a health issue constructs meanings of preservation and promotion of health. A state is signaling that abortion is a public health concern, and should be addressed as a harm reduction initiative.[269]

The working group on the issue of discrimination against women in law and in practice has correctly categorised the control exercised by the state over decisions taken by women as a form of 'instrumentalisation of women's body': 'patriarchal negation of women's autonomy in decision-making leads to violation of women's rights to health, privacy, reproductive and sexual self-determination, physical integrity and even to life.'[270] Instrumentalisation includes the discriminatory use of criminal law, such as provisions on termination of pregnancy, the enforcement of which 'generates stigma and discrimination.'[271]

Abortion laws differ from country to country,[272] and they are highly influenced by religious communities, in particular the Catholic Church,[273] and traditions. According to a study published in 2013 by the UN Department of Economic and Social Affairs, 97 per cent of governments permit abortion to save a woman's life; two-thirds of countries permit abortion when the physical or mental health of the mother is endangered, but only half of the countries surveyed do so when the pregnancy results from rape or incest or in cases of foetal impairment.[274] Only about one-third of countries permit abortion for economic or social reasons or on request. On one hand, we can find countries such as Sweden that grant free, safe and legal abortion for all women to the extent of preventing physicians from invoking conscientious objection; on the other hand, there are countries such as Ireland, which criminalised abortion in 1861 and amended its Constitution in 1983 to include a provision giving the unborn equal right to life with the mother.[275] This provision was challenged by a referendum in 2018, which led to the adoption of the Health (Regulation of Termination of Pregnancy) Act in December of that year, allowing abortion care on request up to the twelfth week of pregnancy, so long as a three-day waiting period has elapsed.[276] A total ban on abortion is written in the laws of the Dominican Republic, El Salvador,[277] the Holy See, Malta and Nicaragua.[278] After twenty-eight years of criminalisation Chile has recently enacted a new law which ensures women have access to abortion in specific situations.[279] In Muslim-majority countries, it has been reported that the approach to abortion varies from state to state, although it is widely permitted when there are risks to the pregnant woman's life or health, and in cases of rape (incest being far less often discussed).[280] In the Middle East and North Africa, the laws may require authorisation by more than one practitioner or require the husband's approval.[281] In Africa 'virtually all member states of the African Union have regulated abortion through a crime and punishment model that has been indifferent to women's reproductive health,' and African abortion laws mirror those in the countries that colonised them, without respect for women's rights.[282]

The situation has gradually changed since the adoption of the Maputo Protocol. Ethiopia and South Africa have the most liberal laws, Nigeria and Malawi the most restrictive ones.[283] Several African countries now recognise rape, incest or foetal malformations as grounds for abortion, as well as risks to the pregnant woman's health.[284] States belonging to a federal system, such as the United States or Australia, may significantly differ in the approach to abortion within the country, at the expense of women's rights.[285] In Asia abortion is permitted in countries such as China and Japan, but prohibited, for example, in South Korea.[286]

Judgments and decisions

The cases I have selected, which do not include cases of forced abortion,[287] will demonstrate how states can cause, or create the conditions of, violence against women. I will separately investigate cases of abortion hampered by the law, and cases of abortion hampered by practical difficulties in the implementation of the law (including conscientious objection). The former is a situation of *de jure* prohibition of abortion, while the latter is a form of *de facto* prohibition of abortion. The jurisprudence of both national and regional human rights courts, as well as the quasi-jurisprudence of UN treaty bodies, will be under scrutiny, and will be analysed along the three main axes that guided the *anamnesis* in the horizontal dimension.[288]

Abortion hampered by the law

Under this category, I will consider cases in which abortion is completely banned under the law in force, or in which abortion is only partly banned but the reason for abortion invoked by the applicant(s) was not among the options recognised by the law.

I will reflect on how landmark judgments handed down by domestic courts and views by the HRC have been capable of unsettling the almost total ban on abortion existing in some countries, stressing the importance of the protection of women's rights. A legal change is also encouraged by the IACommHR, which has urged states to adopt 'comprehensive, immediate measures to respect and protect women's sexual and reproductive rights,' arguing that 'denying access by women and girls to legal and safe abortion services or post-abortion care can cause prolonged and excessive physical and psychological suffering to many women, especially in cases involving risks to their health, unviability of the foetus.'[289]

Who is the applicant?

Let us start from Latin American countries. A pivotal domestic case that put into question the *de jure* prohibition of abortion was decided by the Constitutional Court of Colombia, which 'liberalised' the Colombian abortion law in 2006.[290] The law prohibited abortion without exceptions. The importance of the judgment lies in the fact that 'it was one of the of the first judicial decisions in the world to uphold abortion rights on equality grounds and the first decision by a constitutional court to review the constitutionality of abortion in line with a human rights framework.'[291] The judges argued that the Constitution requires the provision of abortion services in cases of rape and incest.[292] The applicants, Colombian nationals Mónica del Pilar Roa López, Pablo Jaramillo Valencia, Marcela Abadía Cubillos, Juana Dávila Sáenz and Laura Porras Santillana, requested in separate complaints a declaration that some articles of Law No. 599 (2000) criminalising abortion – in particular Article 122 – were unconstitutional.

In Brazil, the penal code adopted by decree during the Vargas dictatorship in 1940 makes abortion a serious criminal offence.[293] Abortion is a crime in all circumstances except rape and when the life of the woman is at risk. Women who undergo abortions can be punished with one to three years' imprisonment; physicians who provide abortions are sentenced up to twenty years' imprisonment.[294] Since 2012, abortion has become legal when the foetus is diagnosed with anencephaly.[295] This hypothesis was contemplated by the Federal Supreme Court in a pioneer decision presented on 12 April 2012.[296] The case had been brought before the courts in 2004 as a claim of non-compliance with a fundamental precept by the Confederação Nacional dos Trabalhadores na Saúde, which represented dozens of cases of women delivering an anencephalic child,[297] in particular Gabriela de Oliveira Cordeiro, a poor woman aged 19 living in the suburbs of Rio de Janeiro.[298] Luis Roberto Barroso, at the time a lawyer and constitutional law professor, then judge of the Supreme Court, wrote the complaint on behalf of the Confederação. The complaint did not address the constitutionality of the provisions in the penal code criminalising abortion, but rather asked the courts to interpret these provisions in order to include among the justifications for abortion anencephaly in the child.[299] The development of Brazilian jurisprudence gained momentum with writ of *habeas corpus* no. 124.306, decided by the first panel of the Federal Supreme Court on 29 November 2016.[300] The case concerned healthcare providers at a clandestine abortion clinic in Rio de Janeiro who were arrested for providing illegal abortion services. The decision challenged the pre-trial detention of doctors and nurses of the clinic.

Another Southern American court gave a broad interpretation to the few exceptions allowed under a law prohibiting abortion in order to legitimise the termination of pregnancy in cases of anencephaly, but in itself the judgment was, as I will contend, a form of violence against women's health. The Supreme Court of Argentina mitigated the Argentinean abortion prohibition in the 2000 judgment *T., S. v. Gobierno de la Ciudad de Buenos Aires*.[301] The applicant was a woman who was denied the induction of labour or a caesarean after her foetus was diagnosed with anencephaly; she then started an *amparo* action against the Hospital Materno Infantil Ramón Sardá complaining that her rights to health and to physical integrity had been violated.

El Salvador bans abortion under all circumstances, even where health issues endanger the pregnant woman's life.[302] Women are arrested, investigated and eventually imprisoned if they experience complications during their pregnancies that require medical intervention.[303] This is a clear example of VAWH, since it not only bars women from access to abortion even in cases where their life is at risk, but also stigmatises them and puts them at risk when imprisoned in detention centres. The Supreme Court has not helped encourage a change in the law.[304] In 2013, Beatriz, a pregnant woman carrying an anencephalic foetus and suffering from lupus and kidney disease, was denied access to abortion by the Salvadoran Constitutional Chamber because the threat to her life was not 'actual and imminent.' The Chamber argued that 'the rights of the mother cannot be privileged over those of the foetus.'[305] The case was brought before the IACHR as a matter of urgency.[306] More recently, in March 2017, the IACommHR ruled admissible the case of *Manuela y Familia v. El Salvador,* supported by the US-based Center for Reproductive Rights. Manuela was a poor illiterate woman living in a rural area. She had been diagnosed with cancer in 2006. In 2008, seven months pregnant, she experienced a miscarriage and was taken to hospital, where the doctor reported the case to the authorities. She was arrested, investigated and sentenced to 30 years' imprisonment. Conditions in the prison, including vaginal inspections, caused her huge suffering and her health deteriorated. She was eventually moved to a hospital, where she started chemotherapy. She died in 2010. The case was brought before the IACommHR, which considered that the requirement for exhaustion of domestic remedies had been met.[307]

In Europe, my focus will be on Ireland, where abortion law has been the object of investigation by both the ECtHR and the HRC.[308] *A., B., C. v. Ireland* was decided by the ECtHR in 2010.[309] Here, I will limit my analysis to the first two applicants. A. and B. claimed that the prohibition of abortion for all reasons other than risk to the woman's life was a violation of Articles 3, 8, 13 and 14 ECHR. Applicant A. had four young children, was unmarried, unemployed and lived in poor conditions. She had borrowed money to travel abroad to seek abortion. Once back in Ireland, she started bleeding and was taken to hospital; after being discharged, she did not seek further medical advice. B. also faced difficulties meeting travel costs. She was told that her pregnancy could be ectopic but, before undergoing the procedure, she discovered that this was not the case. She travelled to London, alone, for an abortion and sought medical assistance back in Ireland, asking for a clinic affiliated to the English one. The HRC examined two cases, *Mellet v. Ireland* and *Whelan v. Ireland,*[310] in which the situation of the two women was similar to *A., B., C.* – having to travel abroad because their case was not contemplated by domestic law – but differed since the foetuses were affected by a congenital malformation. Foetal impairment was not at that time a ground for termination of pregnancy in Ireland, so both women were recommended either to travel abroad or to 'wait for nature to take its course.'[311] Both women decided to fly to Liverpool. The physicians at the Irish hospital dealing with Amanda Mellet attempted to dissuade her from getting an abortion and provided little information on options for undergoing the procedure in the UK. Mellet had her abortion in the 24th week of pregnancy, Whelan in the 21st. Neither received any financial assistance and both had to fly back to Ireland soon after the procedure. The former received no support at the Irish hospital, but was offered access to post-abortion counselling at a family planning organisation. Whelan received medical care once back in Ireland, though she was never offered any counselling. They both complained that their rights protected by the ICCPR had been infringed.

Moving east, in the judgment of 11 April 2019,[312] the South Korean Constitutional Court decided that two provisions of the Criminal Act (as amended in 1995) which criminalise abortion, were not in conformity with the Constitution. The applicant was an obstetrician-gynaecologist who was charged with the offence of procuring abortions for sixty-nine women between 2013 and 2015 in violation of the law. While the decision was pending before the lower court, the applicant filed a motion to refer the case to the Constitutional Court for constitutional review.

Has the right to health been applied directly? In which ways was women's health relevant in the judgment?

In the judgments under analysis, the adjudicatory bodies often took the right to health and the right to reproductive health, when enshrined in the constitutions of the country, into account in their legal reasoning, and also referred to the women's right to autonomy.

In case C-355/2006 decided by the Constitutional Court of Colombia, the applicants invoked several articles of the Constitution, including Article 49 on the right to health, which was directly applied to the case. In particular, the Court contended that women's right to health includes reproductive health, and that the constitutional protection granted to this right includes protection against intrusion or interference by the government or any third party.[313] Moreover, 'this latter dimension of protection from violation, or obligation on the state to not interfere, is closely related to the duty of every individual to be responsible for his or her own health. From this perspective, certain measures adopted by the legislature that disproportionately restrict the right to health are unconstitutional.'[314] The Court seems to refer to the principle of proportionality and the principle of the 'undue burden' as elaborated by US courts,[315] when it concluded that the criminalisation of abortion in cases of rape and incest 'amounts to a disproportionate and unreasonable infringement on the liberty and dignity of women.'[316] When the pregnant woman's health or life is at risk, the judges described the criminalisation of abortion as 'excessive':

> If the criminal penalty for abortion rests on valuing the life of the developing foetus over other constitutional interests involved, then criminalization of abortion in these circumstances would mean that there is no equivalent recognition of the right to life and health of the mother.[317]

Considerations of the woman's right to health were also incorporated into the final stages of the Brazilian complaint before the Federal Supreme Court, stressing that the ban on abortion where foetal anencephaly is diagnosed puts women's physical integrity at risk. Human dignity constituted the backbone of advocate

Barroso's argument, and emerged in the final 2012 decision of the Court, adopted by a vote of eight to two.[318] In particular, one of the judges stressed that 'the termination of pregnancy of [an] anencephalic foetus is a measure protective of the physical and emotional health of women, avoiding psychological disorders she would suffer were she forced to carry on a pregnancy that she knew would not result in life.'[319] The Court did not discuss the right to life of the foetus, and did not comment on other foetal malformations. It clearly concluded that the judgment was limited to pregnancies involving an anencephalic foetus.[320] This situation was more 'accepted' than other forms of disability because the lack of brain activity was perceived as impairing the exercise of the right to life after delivery.[321] As correctly outlined, 'because it lacks cerebral functioning, granting the anencephalic foetus constitutional protection is inappropriate because it has neither life nor the potential for life.'[322] The debate in Brazil has recently been resumed after the spread of the Zika virus and its correlation with the increased number of new-born babies presenting microcephaly. In August 2016 a group of attorneys filed a petition with the Brazilian Supreme Court to allow women who have contracted the Zika virus and are in a state of 'great mental suffering' access to abortion.[323] The case has not been decided yet.[324]

In a 2016 decision of the Supreme Federal Court, concerning the detention of healthcare providers at a clandestine abortion clinic in Rio de Janeiro, two of the judges argued that there were no legitimate conditions for detention, while the other three, Justices Luis Roberto Barroso, Rosa Weber and Edson Fachin, put directly into question the criminalisation of abortion during the first trimester of pregnancy. Even though the judgment only applies to the case at issue, it has paved the way for further reflections in legal scholarship. The rights to health and to reproductive health emerged in the reasoning of the three judges constituting the majority. They considered that prohibition of abortion during the first trimester violates the sexual and reproductive rights of women, 'who cannot be forced by the State to maintain an unwanted pregnancy,'[325] the autonomy of the woman, the physical and psychological integrity of the pregnant woman and gender equality. The Court acknowledged that the foetus's right to life is a matter for debate, but at the same time it found that the dependence of the foetus on the woman's body is *de facto* indisputable.[326] A paragraph of the judgment is of utmost interest, because it stressed that 'a central aspect of [the woman's] autonomy is the power to control her own body and to take decisions', including 'on termination of pregnancy,' and then raised a question: how could a state, through its organs, 'impose on a woman', at the beginning of her pregnancy, the duty to bring it to an end 'as if it were a womb in the service of society, and not an autonomous person,' capable of being, thinking and living?[327] Criminalisation leads to the consideration of women as instruments for the perpetuation of society. As to proportionality, the Court considered that criminalisation did not reduce the number of abortions, it simply made them more dangerous; that other measures were more effective than criminalisation, such as education and distribution of contraceptives, and that criminalisation was disproportionate in the narrow sense, because it produced social harms. The Court put into question the very existence of the crime, which was relevant for how the pre-trial detention was taken into account. An element for criticism is the reference the Court made to the practice of 'developed and democratic' countries with regard to the termination of pregnancy. The 'shadow of "Northern legal hegemony"' – as one author put it[328] – risks reducing the importance of the judgment in recognising of women's sexual and reproductive rights. Few months after the judgment, in March 2017, the Socialism and Freedom party presented a petition – an Arguição de Preceito Fundamental (Interrogation of Fundamental Principles) – to the Brazilian Supreme Court to request the decriminalisation of abortion up to the 12th week of pregnancy.[329]

In Argentina, the *T., S.* case is highly problematic. Even though the Supreme Court of Argentina mitigated the Argentinean prohibition of abortion by its decision, it did not take into consideration women's rights. The legal reasoning was indeed based on the impossibility that the child could survive as a consequence of anencephaly. From this, the Court determined that the premature delivery of an anencephalic foetus – *not* its abortion – could not be considered a crime provided that this occurred after the twenty-eighth week of pregnancy, since the foetus's death would be a consequence of its condition *and not* of the procedure. This decision, based on a fictitious 'viability', is capable of causing even further violence against women, in the form of distress and agony while waiting for the point that such 'premature delivery' can take place.[330]

In the *Matter of B.*, one day before the decision of the Constitutional Chamber, the IACHR granted provisional measures requiring El Salvador to take all necessary measures to protect Beatriz's life and personal integrity. El Salvador agreed that Beatriz could undergo a caesarean section, technically not an abortion. The new-born died a few days later. In *Manuela y Familia,* the complaint filed with the IACommHR referred to the violation of several articles of the American Convention, including the right to life, the prohibition of torture, the right to personal integrity and the prohibition of discrimination, but also of Article 7 of the Belém do Pará Convention (state's obligations in cases of violence against women). On the basis of the latter article, in particular paragraphs (a) and (e), it seems that the Commission, whose findings are non-binding, could argue that El Salvador had caused VAW by enacting and applying a total ban on abortion. The abortion law of El Salvador is currently under review and its Congress has been asked to examine a proposal, highly urged by UN experts, to allow the termination of pregnancy in the case of risk to the life of the woman, when it is the result of rape and in all circumstances in which the foetus would not survive.[331]

Turning to Ireland, *A., B., C.* was examined by the Grand Chamber of the ECtHR, which dismissed the complaints under Article 2 (proposed by C.) and under Article 3 ECHR; the Chamber did not consider it necessary to separately examine the applications under Articles 13 and 14. Concerning A. and B., the Court reiterated its main findings in *Vo v. France,* confirming that it was not possible to answer the question whether the unborn was a person under Article 2 ECHR, 'so that it would be equally legitimate for a State to choose to consider the unborn to be such a person and to aim to protect that life.'[332] The core issue was the following: since an interference with the right enshrined in Article 8 ECHR had occurred, to what extent did this interference pursue a legitimate aim and was it necessary in a democratic society? In other words, how wide is a state's margin of appreciation to determine on which grounds abortion is legitimate? The Court found that Ireland had pursued a legitimate aim of 'protection of morals of which the protection in Ireland of the right to life of the unborn was one aspect,'[333] and that a broad margin of appreciation must in principle be accorded to the state.[334] Despite a quite wide consensus among the contracting states of the Council of Europe towards allowing abortion on less restrictive grounds than those accorded under Irish law, 'the Court [did not] consider that this consensus decisively narrow[ed] the broad margin of appreciation of the State.'[335] In particular, considering that women could lawfully travel abroad to have access to abortion, and had access to appropriate information and medical care, Ireland was not infringing Article 8 ECHR. Needless to repeat, the right to health was not directly considered since such a provision is not present in ECHR; however, the applicants' health was at the core of the complaints. The Court referred to the psychological effects of not having access to abortion, without elaborating further on the effect on the health of A., B. and C. As for the attitude of the Court towards abortion, some authors have argued that recognition by the judges of a European consensus on abortion might lead in the future to a 'more interventionist' approach in abortion cases, given the development of the Court's jurisprudence concerning transsexual cases.[336] Very different was the outcome of the two complaints filed with the HRC, which focused on the prohibition of torture and cruel, inhuman or degrading treatment (Article 7 ICCPR), the right to privacy (Article 17 ICCPR), the right to freedom of expression (Article 19 ICCPR), the right to equality before the law (Article 26), the prohibition of discrimination (Article 2(1)) and the equal rights of men and women (Article 3). The Committee examined the allegations under Articles 7, 17 and 26. The right to health was not directly invoked but the physical and mental health of Mellet and Whelan constituted the backbone of the Committee's reasoning, which considered the 'intense stigma and loss of dignity' to which they had been subjected, along with 'a high level of mental anguish' attributable to a 'combination of acts and omissions of the State party.'[337] Lack of key, medically indicated information, which 'exacerbat[ed] her distress,' was also a factor cited by the Committee to show violation of the prohibition of cruel, inhuman or degrading treatment.[338] It is with regard to the right to privacy that the most striking differences between the reasoning of the ECtHR and that of the HRC can be found. In both cases, the HRC considered that the state's interference with the woman's decision was unreasonable and arbitrary in violation of Article 17 of the Covenant. In particular, the Committee argued that the balance that the state party had chosen 'to strike between protection of the foetus and the rights of the woman … cannot be justified.'[339] The mental condition of both Mellet and Whelan – the prohibition of abortion was a cause of 'intense suffering' – were again at the core of the main argument. In *Whelan*, the Committee stressed that the interference had been 'intrusive.'[340] On the principle of non-discrimination, the Committee departed from the main arguments presented in the complaint by stressing that there had been discrimination within the same gender and not *between* genders. In other words, the experts found that the treatment of patients after miscarriage or delivery of a stillborn child diverged from that of women who choose to terminate a non-viable pregnancy.[341] However, the Committee's members highlighted that discrimination on the basis of sex had *also* occurred. Sarah Cleveland, in her opinion concurring with the views in *Mellet*, posited that 'the near-comprehensive criminalisation of abortion services denies access to reproductive medical services that only women need, and imposes no equivalent burden on men's access to reproductive health care.'[342] She concurred also with the findings in *Whelan,* and agreed with Yadh Ben Achour, who affirmed that Whelan had been subject to a gender-based stereotype according to which 'a woman's pregnancy should be continued no matter what the circumstances.'[343]

In the final case I am analysing here, decided by the South Korean Constitutional Court, four judges argued that the provisions on the criminalisation of abortion, which 'force a pregnant woman to continue her pregnancy by imposing criminal punishment on the woman who violates the ban,' did not conform with the Constitution, and ordered the legislative to amend them by 30 December 2020. Most of the judges referred to the principle of human dignity enshrined in the Constitution, endorsed the medical view that a foetus is viable at around twenty-two weeks' gestation, and reflected on the consequences of the ban:

> It forces her to seek out expensive procedures to procure an abortion, making it difficult for her to seek relief in the event of medical malpractice during an abortion, and rendering her vulnerable to retaliatory harassment that could be committed by her ex-boyfriend or civil lawsuits involving domestic matters that could be filed by her ex-partner.

The few exceptions provided by the Mother and Child Health Act in force could not cover economic and social reasons for seeking an abortion. Even considering the state's aim to protect the foetus, the majority of the judges concluded that the principle of the balance of interests had not been respected, because the law was 'heavily in favour of the public interest in protecting foetal life,' which had 'absolute and unilateral superiority' over women's autonomy.[344] This pivotal judgment will pave the way for intervention by the legislative.

Reparations

Given the nature of the judgments examined in this section, some of them handed down by the highest courts of the country, the issue of reparations becomes more complex, or not even an issue. For instance, in case 355/06 the Constitutional Court of Colombia confirmed the constitutionality of Article 122 of the penal code, provided that abortion is decriminalised in three circumstances:

a) when the continuation of the pregnancy presents risks to the life or the health of the woman, as certified by a medical doctor;
b) when there are serious malformations of the foetus that make the foetus not viable, as certified by a medical doctor; and
c) when the pregnancy is the result of any of the following criminal acts, duly reported to the authorities: incest, rape, sexual abuse, or artificial insemination or implantation of a fertilized ovule without the consent of the woman.[345]

Similarly, in the case filed by the Confederação Nacional dos Trabalhadores na Saúde, the Brazilian Federal Supreme Court did not decide on any form of compensation to women who were forced to carry a foetus until the scheduled delivery knowing that it could not live, but, within its competences, it broadened the interpretation given to the limited exceptions to the prohibition of abortion provided by the law.

The Constitutional Court of South Korea did not repeal the challenged provisions, but it ordered their application to be temporary, setting a time limit for the legislative to amend them.

Cases in which a complaint is filed with a judicial (quasi-judicial) body competent to receive individual complaints for alleged violations of human rights are different. In the twin cases *Mellet* and *Whelan v. Ireland,* the HRC concluded that the respondent state was under an obligation to provide women with an effective remedy, including 'adequate compensation' and 'any needed psychological treatment.' The state was also encouraged to amend the law on termination of pregnancy, 'including if necessary its Constitution,' to ensure compliance with the Covenant, 'including effective, timely and accessible procedures for pregnancy termination … and take measures to ensure that health care providers are in a position to supply full information on safe abortion services without fearing being subjected to criminal sanctions.'[346] In the *Matter of B.*, the IACHR ordered the state to adopt the measures needed to allow doctors to perform 'opportune and desirable' procedures to avoid permanent harm to women's rights to life, personal integrity and health. No reparation was decided by the ECtHR in *A., B., C.* case for A. or B., whose complaint was not successful. The case of C. is discussed in the next section of this chapter.

Abortion hampered by obstacles to implementation of the law

Even when abortion is liberalised, usually within the first months of pregnancy, and when a pregnant woman faces one of the conditions for legitimate abortion admitted by law, she can encounter practical difficulties in gaining access to abortion services. In this sub-section, different conditions will be considered: economic difficulties; conscientious objection; denial of access to services, including lack of complete information or provision of misleading information; pressure from third parties, etc. Conscientious objection means that a person refuses to perform an action or to provide a service on the grounds that doing so is against their conscience.[347] Granting the right to such objection is meant to protect 'the right of individuals to differ in thought, belief and opinion for religious, political, philosophical, humanitarian or other reasons.'[348] Used to refuse to perform compulsory military service, conscientious objection might be invoked by physicians who do not want to perform abortions; however, it has correctly been argued that 'the legitimate exercise of conscientious objection is much more delicate when it is used against a person in a vulnerable position.'[349] National jurisprudence has determined that conscientious objection cannot be used as justification by judicial officers,[350] by administrative assistants,[351] or by midwives whose only task is to coordinate the work of a labour ward.[352] In cases concerning abortion hampered by obstacles to the implementation of the law, behaviour or personal beliefs of health personnel emerge as a pivotal factor barring a woman from access to abortion.

As confirmed by the CEDAW Committee in its GR No. 35 of 2017, acts committed by private actors 'empowered by the law of that State to exercise elements of the governmental authority, including private bodies providing public services, such as health care or education, or operating places of detention' shall be considered as 'acts attributable to the State itself.'[353] When I examine 'pressure' from third parties, which might include pro-life activists and religious communities, the vertical dimension of my analysis seems, at first sight, to turn into the horizontal one. Although such pressure cannot be defined as interpersonal violence, it can be seen as a form of interference within the community that the state must prevent; interference that in some cases turns into violence. Despite interference from third parties, what matters from a legal point of view is the behaviour of health personnel, whose actions determine the access or the lack of access to abortion services.

Who is the applicant?

A pivotal case in which economic difficulties constituted an obstacle to access to abortion is *Lakshmi Dhikta v. Nepal*, handed down by the Supreme Court of Nepal in 2009. Nepal had a very restrictive law on abortion, which was amended in 2002 to allow abortion on broad grounds. Despite the evolution of the law, however, poor women continued to face enormous difficulties in gaining access to the service. In the judgment, the Court recognised abortion as a 'constitutionally protected fundamental right.'[354] The applicants represented a poor woman living with her husband and five children in far-western rural Nepal.[355] Another child would have meant an enormous additional financial burden. She went to hospital with her husband to request an abortion, under the amended legislation, which makes abortion legal within the first three months of pregnancy. However, the fee for an abortion amounted to 1,130 rupees, which the family could not afford at that time.

Turning to the second example of obstacles to the access to abortion service, conscientious objection, a paramount case comes from Italy, where abortion is available but women still encounter many difficulties in gaining access to it. Under Law no. 194 (1978),[356] abortion is lawful in Italy during the first three months of pregnancy, when 'the continuation of the pregnancy, childbirth, or motherhood would seriously endanger [women's] physical or mental health,' and also where justified by '[the pregnant women's] state of health, their economic, social, or family circumstances, the circumstances in which conception occurred, or the probability that the child would be born with abnormalities or malformations.'[357] After the first ninety days, voluntary termination of pregnancy 'may be performed … a) where the pregnancy or childbirth entails a serious threat to the woman's life; b) where the pathological processes constituting a serious threat to the woman's physical or mental health, such as those associated with serious abnormalities or malformations of the foetus, have been diagnosed.' Conscientious objection is recognised by law, although it does not exempt health personnel from providing care prior to and following any termination of pregnancy. Nonetheless, access to abortion in Italy is reduced in practice by the high number of conscientious objectors. A complaint about this situation was brought by the Confederazione Generale Italiana del Lavoro (CGIL) before the European Committee of Social Rights in 2013.[358] The competence of the Committee is based on the European Social Charter, as amended in 1996, a Council of Europe treaty that guarantees social and economic rights. The monitoring system consists in collective complaints filed by social partners and other NGOs. The outcome is not binding, but still relevant because it derives its strength from a binding legal instrument. In the case under analysis, the applicant, an Italian labour union, argued that Article 9 of Law no. 194 of 1978, which regulates the conscientious objection of medical practitioners and other medical personnel in relation to abortion services, is not 'properly applied in practice.'[359]

As my third example, I have chosen the denial of abortion services as example of VAW, which might severely impair pregnant women's rights. I will move from the international to the regional and eventually the domestic level. In this area, two cases decided by UN treaty bodies with regard to Peru are worth mentioning. In Peru, abortion is admitted to save the mother's life or to avoid serious and permanent harm to her health. In *Karen Noelia Llantoy Huamán v. Peru*, decided in 2005 by the HRC,[360] Karen Huamán became pregnant aged 17 and discovered that she was carrying an anencephalic foetus. A gynaecologist at the hospital in Lima informed her of the foetal abnormality and the risks to her life should she continue the pregnancy. The director of the hospital refused to authorise an abortion, since abortion in cases of malformation of the foetus is illegal under Peruvian law and only when the pregnant woman's health is severely impaired is there a legitimate ground for abortion. Huamán eventually gave birth to an anencephalic baby girl, who died four days later. She was obliged to breastfeed her baby during the few days of her life. After her daughter's death, Huamán fell into deep depression. Since no administrative remedy would have allowed her to terminate the pregnancy on therapeutic grounds, nor any effective and quick judicial remedy, the UN treaty body considered the complaint admissible.

Six years later, Peruvian abortion law was brought to the attention of the CEDAW Committee, in *L.C.*[361] The applicant, who like Huamán was a minor, got pregnant after suffering sexual abuse. She fell into depression and attempted suicide. L.C. survived but risked permanent disability. Surgery was delayed because of her pregnancy, and when she asked for therapeutic abortion the medical board of the hospital denied the request because it considered that the life of their patient was not at risk. She submitted an appeal. In the meanwhile, she miscarried and, only after that, was she operated on. After the operation L.C. needed intensive physical therapy and rehabilitation, which her family could not afford. The CEDAW Committee found the case admissible, because neither the *amparo* nor a civil action for compensation had been deemed appropriate to offer effective relief to L.C.[362]

Three cases filed with the ECtHR against Poland, concerning women encountering different difficulties during their pregnancies, pertain to my analysis. In Poland, the 1993 Family Planning Act provides that abortion can be carried out only by a physician where there are risks to the mother's life or health; where prenatal tests show that the foetus will be severely damaged or suffer from an incurable, life-threatening ailment; or where there are strong grounds for believing that the pregnancy is the result of a criminal act.[363] In the first two cases, abortion can be performed until the foetus becomes viable, whereas in the third case it is available until the end of the twelfth week of pregnancy. In *Alicja Tysiac v. Poland,*[364] decided by the ECtHR in 2007, the applicant was a pregnant woman who suffered from severe myopia, which, in the opinion of three ophthalmologists, would have worsened if the pregnancy carried to term. A general practitioner issued a certificate in which he declared that the pregnancy constituted a threat to Alicja Tysiac's health. Nonetheless, the head of the gynaecology and obstetrics department at a clinic in Warsaw declined her request to terminate the pregnancy. Without the possibility of access to a timely procedure to review the doctor's decision, Tysiac carried her pregnancy to term, and her eyesight seriously deteriorated to the extent that she was qualified as significantly disabled according to the Polish social system. She then tried to get compensation, filing complaints with domestic courts, but all her claims were rejected. She eventually brought the case before the ECtHR.

In *R.R. v. Poland*,[365] decided by the fourth section of the ECtHR in 2011, the applicant was a Polish woman who, although she had already been informed that the foetus might be affected by Turner syndrome, could not gain access to the medical test needed to ascertain its actual impairment. After medical practitioners delayed all tests, she was not eligible for an abortion within the time limits proscribed by Polish law. R.R. sought compensation at national level. The Supreme Court, to which the case was referred, quashed the judgment of a lower court which had awarded her an inadequate sum in compensation. The Kraków Court, to which the case was remitted, awarded a higher amount. R.R. complained before the ECtHR that she could not get access to the genetic tests that were needed to assess the foetus's possible malformation, and that her rights to be free from torture, from inhuman or degrading treatment, and to private and family life had been violated.

In a case concerning a minor who became pregnant in consequence of a rape, the fourth Chamber of the ECtHR had the opportunity to reflect on the application of legal provisions allowing abortion. In *P. and S. v. Poland*, decided in 2012, the applicants were a girl (P.) who had been raped by a boy her own age and reported the fact to the authorities, and her mother (S.), who helped P. to gain access to abortion. P. encountered numerous difficulties in doing so, including failures of confidentiality and contradictory information given by personnel at the hospital, and delays in the examination of her case. One doctor advised S. 'to get her daughter married.' Another doctor asked her to sign a statement that she understood that the procedure could lead to P.'s death. Both P. and her mother faced criminal proceedings, to the extent that S.'s parental rights were put into question by Catholic and pro-life associations which released confidential information on P. (a minor), whom they approached to try to convince her not to undergo abortion. P. was also arrested in the execution of a court ruling, which decided to place her in a juvenile centre. P. did manage to gain access to abortion in the end, but 'the events surrounding the determination of the … applicant's access to legal abortion were marred by procrastination and confusion,' since the applicants (P. and her mother) were given 'misleading and contradictory information.'[366] Furthermore, even though the Ministry of Health authorised the procedure, it was carried out many kilometres away from the applicants' home city, and conducted – despite being legal – in a 'clandestine' manner. P. and S. filed complaints with the prosecution authorities, but one court found that cases of teenage pregnancy give rise to controversy and are legitimate subjects for discussion by social and church organisations. The government suggested that the applicants could have started civil litigation, but the ECtHR found that such litigation would not have offered good prospects and therefore deemed the case to be admissible.[367]

The *A., B., C. v. Ireland* case is relevant in this analysis, because applicant C., who had been treated for a rare form of cancer, underwent a series of tests for cancer, contraindicated during pregnancy, without being aware of that fact. She could have been given access to abortion, according to the law. However, she failed to obtain complete information on the effects of the tests on her foetus and on the effect of her health conditions on the pregnancy itself, so decided to fly to England to gain access to abortion services. Once back home, she complained about not having received adequate post-abortion care.

Moving to the Inter-American system of protection of human rights, the case of *Paulina del Carmen Ramírez Jacinto v. México* was filed with the IACommHR and concluded with a friendly settlement agreement.[368] Paulina Jacinto, 14 years old at the time, fell pregnant in consequence of rape. Under Mexican law, she could have been given access to abortion, but she faced manipulation and misinformation by personnel at the hospital, and pressure from representatives of the Catholic Church to withdraw her request for the procedure. In the end, Jacinto's mother decided to refuse the procedure.

Moving to North America, one US case is worth mentioning: *Whole Woman's Health et al. v. Hellerstedt*,[369] decided in 2016. The USA falls into the category I am analysing in this sub-section, because several states have adopted restrictive laws on abortion, therefore hampering *de facto* access to the procedure. These statutory provisions have been adopted despite the affirmation in *Roe v. Wade* of a woman's *right* to an *abortion* prior to the viability of the foetus as protected by the Constitutional right to privacy.[370] The *Whole Woman's Health* judgment struck down House Bill 2, enacted in 2013 in Texas with the declared purpose of protecting women's health. My purpose here is not to analyse the dispute in detail, but to highlight the main aspects of the Supreme Court's judgment that are pivotal for this book. The applicants were not women, but abortion providers in Texas, supported by associations for the protection of women's rights, and they challenged the Texas law which fixed two requirements for abortion services to meet: admitting privileges (a physician performing abortion must show admitting privileges at a hospital within 100 miles of the abortion site), and a requirement that abortion providers meet the minimum standards for surgical centres. As a consequence of the law, abortion centres closed. The case reached the US Supreme Court after a complex legal dispute.[371]

Laws can also oblige practitioners to provide misleading or inaccurate information to women seeking abortion, or to perform ultrasounds before granting abortion. In the United States, for example, several states' counselling laws require health personnel to make statements to patients about specific 'risks,' including infertility, linked to abortion procedures. Ian Vandewalker has called them 'biased counselling laws,' because 'they are not intended to ensure that patients give their informed consent to abortion, but rather are intended to make women less likely to terminate their pregnancy.'[372] This approach was adopted by Indiana, through the adoption of the House Enrolled Act 1210 in 2011, which obliged practitioners of Planned Parenthood Indiana to inform women seeking an abortion that 'objective scientific information' shows that 'a foetus can feel pain at or before twenty weeks of post-fertilization age.'[373] Planned Parenthood Indiana brought the case before US courts, and sought to obtain a preliminary injunction.[374] In a more recent case, Planned Parenthood Indiana challenged a provision of the Indiana code, amended in 2016, which required the performance of an ultrasound at least eighteen hours before access to abortion.[375] The law mainly affected women with a low income or precarious jobs, or victims of domestic violence, who were obliged, first, to travel to the (few) premises offering ultrasound scans, and then, after the mandatory eighteen hours, had to make another journey to the clinic, and meet further costs, to get access to abortion.

Has the right to health been applied directly? In which ways was women's health relevant in the judgment?

In the ground-breaking decision in *Lakshmi Dhikta,* the Supreme Court of Nepal analysed issues of equality, sexuality and motherhood. The Court also tackled the challenging issue of personhood, by saying that 'what we do know is that a foetus does not have a separate existence and it can only exist within a mother's womb. That's why even if we do recognize a foetal interest, we cannot say that it shall prevail over a mother's interest.'[376] The Court referred to many rights, including the right to reproductive health, which is enshrined in Article 20(2) of the Constitution, and contended that 'women are … considered to have the right to make decisions relating to reproduction free from interference. This means that a woman is the master of her own body.' In an interesting passage, the Court stated that 'when forced, the … pregnancy can become [a] cause of violence against women.'[377] Cook, Dickens and Fathalla, in their pioneer work, clearly made the point that 'there is little to choose between *coerced contraception, sterilization*, or *abortion*, because society does not want the child, and *coerced motherhood*, because society wants the child. Both interventions deny women the dignity of making a choice in their reproductive lives.'[378]

In the conscientious objection case *CGIL v. Italy*, the European Committee of Social Rights directly applied the right to health, as enshrined in the Revised European Social Charter.[379]

Cases of denial of access to abortion examined by UN bodies are much more interesting in terms of application of the rights to health and to reproductive health. In *K.N.L.H. v. Peru*, the HRC found that Peru had violated Articles 2 (obligations of state parties), 7 (prohibition of torture), 17 (prohibition of unlawful interference with privacy) and 24 (right of the child to measures of protection) of the ICCPR. In particular, it stressed the vulnerability of K.N.L.H., who had been a minor at the time of the pregnancy, and the effect of the denial of access to abortion services on her mental conditions. The right to health was not directly considered because it is not provided in the ICCPR, but K.N.L.H.'s health was relevant when the Committee described the suffering she faced.[380] These views were entirely based on her declarations, given the lack of information provided by the state party. Consideration of the right to health eventually came with the case *L.C. v Peru*, in which the CEDAW Committee directly applied Article 12 CEDAW (which ensures women access to healthcare services on a non-discriminatory basis) and emphasised the failure of the state to protect women's reproductive rights, which is even more severe given the vulnerable condition of L.C., being a minor and a victim of sexual abuse.[381] Two elements are particularly interesting in these views, beyond the direct application of the right to have access to health care services in a non-discriminatory way.[382] The first is the Committee's affirmation that 'legislation to recognise abortion on the grounds of sexual abuse and rape are facts that contributed to L.C.'s situation.'[383] Bearing in mind my paradigm, this means that the legislation caused or created the conditions in which violence against the applicant occurred. The second element concerns the violation of Article 5 CEDAW, laying down the actions states must take to eliminate prejudices against and stereotypes of the roles of women in society. The Committee argued that 'the decision to postpone the surgery due to the pregnancy was influenced by the stereotype that protection of the foetus should prevail over the health of the mother.'[384]

At regional level, the ECtHR focused on Article 8 ECHR in *Tysiac*, and concluded that Poland had violated Tysiac's right to respect for private and family life, because it did not provide 'any effective mechanisms capable of determining whether the conditions for obtaining a lawful abortion had been met in her case.'[385] The Court referred to her health in terms of the 'severe distress and anguish' that Tysiac suffered, and stressed the absence of compensation granted by the Polish authorities to cover 'the irreparable damage to her health.'[386] In *R.R. v. Poland*, the Court applied Article 8 ECHR, ruling that Poland had violated R.R.'s right to respect for private and family life by not providing 'any effective mechanisms that would have enabled the applicant to seek access to a diagnostic service, decisive for the possibility of exercising her right to take an informed decision as to whether to seek abortion or not.'[387] The Court, 'in an unprecedented move,'[388] also found Poland in violation of Article 3 ECHR, since R.R. had 'suffered acute anguish' and 'humiliation,' as a consequence of the fact that her concerns 'were not properly acknowledged and addressed by the health professionals dealing with her case.'[389] Furthermore, delays in the provision of services had prevented her from making an informed decision within the time limit provided by the law. Article 3 ECHR was also applied in *P. and S. v. Poland*, along with the rights enshrined in Articles 8 and 5. The Court in Strasbourg concluded that Poland had been responsible for violating the applicants' rights. In particular reference to Article 8, P. and her mother had received 'misleading and contradictory information,' and been deprived of 'appropriate and objective medical counselling.'[390] Furthermore, civil courts could not provide them an effective remedy, because no case law featured compensation for the damage caused to a woman by 'the anguish, anxiety and suffering entailed by her efforts to obtain access to abortion.'[391] This is the closest affirmation of P.'s health conditions. In *A., B., C. v. Ireland*, specifically C.'s case, the ECtHR acknowledged the existence of guidelines for practitioners, which should have helped identify the legitimate grounds for abortion, but considered that they did not provide clear criteria for doctors in assessing the risks related to the pregnancy. This uncertainty had a chilling effect on practitioners' acceptance of permission to perform abortion, owing to the risk of 'a serious criminal conviction and imprisonment in the event that a decision taken in medical consultation, that the woman was entitled to an abortion in Ireland given the risk to her life, was later found not to accord with Article 40.3.3 of the Constitution.'[392] Furthermore, C.'s interests could not have been said to be protected by the availability of judicial proceedings, since, according to the Court, 'constitutional courts [a remedy also invoked by the government] are [not] the appropriate forum for the primary determination as to whether a woman qualifies for an abortion which is lawfully available in a State.'[393] As a consequence, Ireland had no effective and accessible procedures in place, demonstrating a 'striking discordance' between the provisions of the law and its practical implementation.[394] Ireland was therefore found in violation of Article 8 ECHR.

The case of *Paulina Ramírez Jacinto* was settled and the agreement between Ms Ramírez Jacinto and the Mexican States was endorsed by the IACommHR. The Commission stressed that women 'cannot fully enjoy their human rights without having a timely access to comprehensive health care services, and to information and education in this sphere,' and that 'the health of sexual violence victims should be treated as a priority in legislative initiatives and in the health policies and programs of Member States.'[395] Nonetheless, the agreement only contained the government's assent 'to strengthen their commitment toward ending violations of the right of women to the legal termination of a pregnancy,'[396] and failed to refer to practices within the healthcare system that had contributed to reproductive rights violations.[397]

With regard to the law in Texas that had raised significant obstacles to the provision of abortion services, the US Supreme Court, in a five to three decision, shed light on the controversial issue of abortion in the USA. Judge Breyer delivered the opinion of the Court, joined by four judges. The judgment referred to criteria including viability elaborated by previous Supreme Court jurisprudence, in particular *Roe v. Wade* and *Planned Parenthood of Southeast Pennsylvania v. Casey*.[398] The latter introduced the concept of 'undue burden', which means that a law is unconstitutional when 'its purpose or effect is to place a substantial obstacle in the path of a woman seeking an abortion before the foetus attains viability.'[399] In *Whole Woman's Health*, the majority of the judges concluded that the health provisions in force in Texas had no health benefit for women seeking abortion, and posed an 'undue burden on their constitutional right to do so.'[400] The right to health was not addressed, and references to women's health were scant and only focused on the absence of health benefits deriving from the law, not on the consequences of such provisions for women's health. The relevance of women's health was however stressed by an *amicus curiae* brief in support of the petitioners, presented by social science researchers. They emphasised that the delays and the increased costs stemming from the application of the Texas law 'hurt women – physically, psychologically, and economically.'[401] Furthermore, there was an intrinsic element of discrimination, also reported in the final judgment, which unravelled the fact that other outpatient procedures were not subject to the same restrictive rules. What is striking is the fact that women's rights, in particular reproductive rights, are nowhere mentioned in the text of the judgment. It is possible to argue that the recognition of women's rights is implicit in determining the 'undue burden' posed by the statutory provisions. I can also support the fact that the Court tried to clarify the practical meaning of the test, but, still, it would have been a good opportunity for the Supreme Court to affirm women's rights, in particular the right to health and the right to reproductive health. It is even more striking to see that the dissenting opinions focused more on the state's interest than on women's rights. Judge Thomas argued that the 'made-up test' decided by the majority to achieve a specific outcome 'seriously burdens States, which must guess at how much more compelling their interests must be to pass muster and what "common sense inferences" of an undue burden this Court will identify next.'[402] He also disagreed with the premise that women have a right to obtain abortion protected by the Constitution.[403]

In terms of transmission of 'misleading information' to women seeking abortion, in *Planned Parenthood Indiana*, suspending the case for other legal reasons, the US Court of Appeals for the Seventh Circuit argued that 'requiring Planned Parenthood Indiana Practitioners to state that "objective scientific information shows that a foetus can feel pain at or before twenty week of postfertilization age"' may be 'false, misleading, and irrelevant.'[404] The decision was guided by the acknowledgement that Planned Parenthood only performed abortions during the first trimester, and it specifically referred neither to the bias underlying the law, which confirmed the state's patriarchal attitude towards women, nor to the potential effects on women's health. In the most recent complaint filed by Planned Parenthood of Indiana and Kentucky, on the requirement for an ultrasound scan at least eighteen hours before an abortion, the US Court of Appeals for the Seventh Circuit did not refer to women's right to health, nor to the intersectional discrimination underlying the law – poor women, with a precarious job, and women subjected to DV were much more affected by the requirement imposed by law. However, by upholding the findings of the District Court it addressed these points indirectly.[405]

Reparations

Reparations have taken very different forms according to the procedure. In *Lakshmi Dhikta*, for example, the Supreme Court in Nepal ordered the state to adopt a series of measures, including a comprehensive abortion law, a government fund to cover the costs of abortion procedures for poor women, the promotion of access to safe services for all women and campaigns to educate the public about abortion rights.[406] The *CGIL v. Italy* decision by the European Committee of Social Rights did not envisage any form of compensation, since the applicant was not a direct victim but, as provided by this system of complaints, an association acting on behalf of (currently or potentially) pregnant women in Italy not able to access abortion owing to the significant number of conscientious objectors.

Turning to the denial of access to abortion services, the decisions by UN treaty bodies are of utmost interest, despite their non-binding character. In *K.N.L.H.*, decided by the HRC, the respondent state was required to provide K.N.L.H. with an effective remedy, 'including compensation,' and, as general measures, to 'take steps to ensure that similar violations do not occur in the future.'[407] In *L.C.*, the CEDAW Committee required the state to provide reparation, such as adequate compensation, covering rehabilitation as well as material and moral damages, and to adopt a series of general measures, including reviewing its laws to establish a mechanism for 'effective access to therapeutic abortion,'[408] which I will discuss further in chapter 3, 'Methodology for treatment, Positive obligations of result, To provide access to health services'.

Moving to the European system, in one of the three judgments against Poland, Tysiac was awarded €25,000 in non-pecuniary damages and €14,000 to cover fees and expenses by the ECtHR. Interestingly, non-pecuniary damages took into account the 'considerable anguish and suffering, including fear about her physical capacity to take care of another child and to ensure its welfare and happiness.'[409] As for *A., B., C. v. Ireland*, C. was not granted just recompense for her journey abroad to gain access to abortion, because she had not invoked the abortion regulatory provisions in force in Ireland. She could indeed have legitimately asked for an abortion, given her state of health, but not being provided the necessary information, she decided to travel abroad. Nonetheless, she was awarded €15,000 in non-pecuniary damages for the anxiety caused by the obstacles to abortion.

In the agreement that concluded *Ramírez Jacinto*, a more detailed set of remedies was envisaged, including monetary compensation (legal expenses, money to pay for education and school supplies for the child, etc.), non-repetition remedies such as legislative proposals, public acknowledgement of the violation and a national survey to ascertain progress in implementating a national programme for preventing and raising attention about domestic and sexual abuse, and violence against women.[410]

In the USA, reparations were not an issue in the Supreme Court decision in *Whole Women's Health*. The Supreme Court reversed the lower court's judgment, which had upheld Texas law. In *Planned Parenthood Indiana* of 2011, the Court of Appeals granted the applicants' motion for a preliminary injunction against the plaintiffs' restrictions on first-trimester abortions.[411] In the 2018 judgment, the Court upheld the lower court's ruling that requiring an ultrasound to take place at least eighteen hours before an abortion constitutes an 'undue burden' on women.[412]

Involuntary sterilisation

Context and legal background

Involuntary sterilisation consists in the surgical removal or impairment of a person's reproductive organs being performed without full and informed consent. It can be imposed on all genders, but women – and transgender and intersex persons – have been disproportionately subjected to the procedure.[413] As reported in a 2014 interagency statement drafted by several bodies including UN Women and the WHO, coercive and involuntary sterilisation was one instrument used by states to control populations and public health between 1870 and 1945, a period during which several eugenic laws were enacted (in Germany, Japan and the United States, for example).[414] Eugenics purported to 'improv[e] the human gene pool by eliminating genes deemed undesirable.'[415] In 1922, nineteen US states had in force eugenic sterilisation laws which targeted 'confirmed criminals,' the 'feeble-minded,' and also 'idiots,' 'imbeciles,' 'hereditary insanity or incurable chronic mania or dementia,' 'epileptics' and those addicted to drugs or alcohol.[416] In 1948 Japan adopted a Eugenic Protection Law, which forced sterilisation and abortion on people with intellectual and mental illness and severe disabilities, and included among the grounds for abortion the woman's or her spouse's hereditary mental or physical illness.[417] The purpose was to 'prevent the proliferation of genetically inferior offspring and to promote the growth of a "healthy" population.'[418]

Despite the Japanese example, eugenic laws were gradually abandoned after the Second World War,[419] although sterilisation has been used to control populations, in particular minority populations, in almost all continents during recent decades. In China, the fear that overpopulation would lessen national economic development and social advancement led to the adoption of the 'One Child Policy' in 1979 to limit the population to a manageable level.[420] Implementation of the policy included abortion, sterilisation, economic incentives and huge fines on those breaking the law.

Why women? Involuntary sterilisation reflects the unequal power relations existing between women and men in a given society. Sifris argues that 'women's bodies continue to be objectified and viewed as the property of society as a whole.'[421] Women are subjected to sterilisation more often than men because of the 'false stereotype of women as incapable of making rational decisions.'[422] Johanna Bond makes the point that, in particular in patriarchal societies (and indirectly even in those where *de facto* discrimination is still recurrent), women's reproduction is 'the prerogative of men.'[423]

Why women living in particular conditions? Sterilisation has generally affected marginalised women, such as HIV-positive women, poor and uneducated women, women belonging to minorities, women in jail and disabled women.[424] States have relied on sterilisation as an instrument of health policy, with the purpose of fighting HIV, disregarding the fact that the use of anti-retroviral drugs reduces the transmission of HIV from mother to child to below 5 per cent.[425] Minorities and indigenous women have been targeted for involuntary sterilisation, as well. The IACommHR expressed its concern about involuntary sterilisation of indigenous women in Canada in a statement in January 2019.[426] States have used sterilisation against minorities to safeguard the majority population – striking in that respect is the declaration of the Slovak Minister of Health in 1995: '[t]he government will do everything to ensure that more white children than Romani children are born.'[427] Also women in jail: the California State Auditor reported in 2013 that, from 2005 to 2012, 144 female inmates were sterilised by bilateral tubal ligation, and that 'the *state entities* responsible for providing medical care to these inmates … sometimes failed to ensure that inmates' consent for sterilization was lawfully obtained.'[428] According to Alexandra Minna Stern, guiding a team on this issue at the University of Michigan:

> [T]he majority of these female inmates were first-time offenders, African-American or Latina. Echoing the rationale of the eugenicists who championed sterilization in the 1930s, the physician responsible for many of these operations blithely explained they would save the state a great deal of money 'compared to what you save in welfare paying for these unwanted children – as they procreated more.'[429]

A bill banning sterilisation in California state prisons was eventually approved in 2014,[430] but the case reopened the debate on the violation of women's rights in detention centres.

Disabled women constitute another vulnerable group. In 1927, the US Supreme Court upheld Virginia's eugenic sterilisation law in *Buck v. Bell*, concerning the sterilisation of three women considered 'feeble-minded.'[431] Judge Holmes argued that a law enforcing sterilisation on individuals suffering from mental disability or epilepsy did not violate the equal protection and due process clauses. His infamous sentence reads: 'it is better for all the world, if instead of waiting to execute degenerate offspring for crime, or to let them starve for their imbecility, society can prevent those who are manifestly unfit from continuing their kind[;] three generations of imbeciles are enough'. For many years it was written in stone, and it is now taken as an example of the paternalistic attitude of judges and legislators in matters pertaining to women's autonomy.[432]

Given the above, involuntary sterilisation is not only a form of discrimination against women, but also a clear example of intersectional discrimination, based on different *multiply interrelated* grounds, including gender, ethnicity, health, and personal economic or social condition. Women are sterilised not only because they are women, but because they are women *and* HIV-positive, or women *and* black, etc. The term 'intersectionality' was coined in 1989 by Kimberlé Crenshaw 'to capture the applicability of black feminism to anti-discrimination law,'[433] and it has been widely explored in feminist scholarship.[434] Nonetheless, when examined by courts, the aspect of intersectionality is rarely taken into account. Catharine MacKinnon has argued that:

> [t]he conventional framework fails to recognise the dynamics of status and the power hierarchies that create them, reifying sex and race not only along a single axis but also as compartments that ignore the social forces of power that rank and define them relationally within and without. In this respect, conventional discrimination analysis mirrors the power relations that form hierarchies that define inequalities rather than challenging and equalising them.[435]

The question is, on one hand, whether or not the person subjected to sterilisation was correctly informed before the performance of the procedure, and on the other, whether the behaviour of the health personnel involved was guided by discrimination, and if so on which grounds. The element of intersectionality, as I will demonstrate, matters to states' obligations.[436]

Needless to say, involuntary sterilisation is a violation of human rights, including the right to privacy, and of women's rights to health and to reproductive health.[437] It may amount to torture, inhuman, cruel or degrading treatment, or punishment.[438] When it is part of a widespread or systematic attack against a civilian population, enforced sterilisation constitutes a 'crime against humanity' according to Article 7(1)(g) of the Rome Statute. It is also a form of violence against women considered in the vertical dimension of my paradigm. As the then SR on VAW argued in one of her reports, 'direct State action violative of women's reproductive rights can be found, for example, in government regulation of population size, which can violate the liberty and security of the person if the regulation results in compelled sterilization and coerced abortion.'[439]

Judgments and decisions

In the analysis that follows, I will investigate decisions, judgments and views regarding sterilisation of HIV-positive women, and women belonging to minorities or to other vulnerable groups. In addition to the three axes that have guided my analysis so far, I will also reflect on whether the court or human rights body being examined has taken into consideration the element of intersectionality in the merits of its decision. I have decided not to investigate cases of forced sterilisation during armed conflict; as explained earlier, war is *sui generis*, and would require consideration of the context of coercion in which the act occurred.

Women with disabilities have also been subjected to involuntary sterilisation for a long time. In this section, however, I will not delve into specific cases of sterilisation of disabled women for two main reasons. First, once eugenic laws are repealed, the sterilisation of women and girls with disabilities is decided by courts, often on request of people that are responsible for their care and on medical opinion. Courts have elaborated over time a jurisprudence that is guided by the pursuance of the 'best interest' of the person with disabilities.[440] The challenging issue is whether and to what extent it is possible to avoid having to obtain the consent of the person with disabilities.[441] This is a topic that goes beyond the scope of my research, even though my paradigm could open future reflection on the issue. Secondly, sterilisation is often imposed on minors, a fact that entails further ethical and legal consideration of parental authority.[442] It should be remembered that the UN Convention on the Rights of Persons with Disabilities, adopted in 2006 and entering into force in 2008, states that '[p]ersons with disabilities, including children, retain their fertility on an equal basis with others' (Article 23). UN bodies have widely acknowledged the need to obtain the consent of a person with disabilities before performing sterilisation.[443]

Who is the applicant?

One landmark judgment concerning HIV-positive women comes from Namibia, where coerced sterilisation has not diminished despite the adoption by the government of a national plan to fight against HIV/AIDS. In *L.M. and others v. Government*, decided on 30 July 2012,[444] the High Court of Namibia granted compensation to three women who were sterilised in a procedure to which they had not consented. The Supreme Court of Namibia upheld the judgment on 3 November 2014, dismissing the government's appeal. The applicants were surgically sterilised at two state hospitals between 2005 and 2007. The procedure was performed at the same time as caesarean sections. The three women sought compensation for violation of their rights to personality or alternatively to human dignity, the right to liberty and the right to found a family guaranteed by the Namibian Constitution. The applicants proposed a second claim, arguing that they had been sterilised *because* they were HIV-positive. Only one of the plaintiffs could understand and read English. Nurses had talked to the patients in their own language (Oshiwambo), but had not provided all the information needed for fully informed consent.

Other cases can be mentioned in this connection, still pending before national courts (one before the IACommHR). In South Africa, it was reported that 7 per cent of the respondents included in a study conducted by the Human Sciences Research Council (10,473 people, HIV-positive) declared that they had been coerced into being sterilised.[445] In 2015 three women's rights advocacy groups filed a complaint with the national Commission for Gender Equality denouncing the forced and coerced sterilisation of women living with HIV in South Africa. The complaint was supported by forty-eight documented cases of involuntary sterilisation occurring in Gauteng and KwaZulu-Natal between 1986 and 2014. In some cases, consent had been obtained while the women were in labour. The applicants asked the Commission to launch an investigation. The Commission, which accepted the complaint, was asked to investigate episodes of coerced sterilisation in public hospitals and to propose remedial actions, including law reforms and compensation.[446]

Another case is pending before the High Court of Kenya, filed by six applicants (four victims and two advocacy groups).[447] Alicia Ely Yamin, Policy Director of the Francois-Xavier Bagnoud Center for Health and Human Rights, stressed in the complaint both the violation of women's health and reproductive rights and the aspect of intersectional discrimination.[448]

The final pending case on HIV-positive women that I would like to mention here is *F.S. v. Chile*, which was filed with the IACommHR. The applicant is a HIV-positive woman living in a rural town in Chile. When she discovered her HIV status, she started an anti-retroviral therapy and arranged for a caesarean delivery. During the delivery, she was sterilised without her consent. Vivo en Positivo,[449] a HIV people's rights association, brought F.S.'s case to the Chilean court system in 2002 as a domestic complaint, without success. The association, along with the US Center for Reproductive Rights, then filed a complaint within the Inter-American system of protection for human rights. The IACommHR has found the case admissible.[450]

As anticipated, women belonging to minorities have been widely affected by involuntary sterilisation. Several cases have been decided by UN bodies and regional human rights courts alike. In 2006, the CEDAW Committee handed down its views in *Andrea Szijjarto v. Hungary*,[451] which was the first case in which a UN body found a state party to the CEDAW responsible for failure to obtain fully informed consent in a reproductive health procedure.[452] The applicant, a Hungarian Roma woman, was sterilised in 2001 at a Hungarian hospital during surgery to remove her dead foetus. She had countersigned a hand-written note added to the bottom of a form, where the Latin word for sterilisation was used. Within seventeen minutes of Andrea Szijjarto's arrival at the hospital, the caesarean section had been performed, the dead foetus removed and her fallopian tubes tied. The sterilisation had a profound impact on her life, and she was later treated for depression. Szijjarto sought redress before the CEDAW Committee.

Moving to the regional system, in *V.C. v. Slovakia*, decided by the ECtHR in 2011,[453] the applicant, of Roma origin, was sterilised in a public hospital during the delivery of her second child via caesarean section. She signed a consent form after she was told that either she or the baby would have died if any future pregnancy continued to delivery. The record of V.C.'s pregnancy and delivery reported her Roma origin. She had sought redress both in civil proceedings and through a constitutional complaint, but was not successful. A similar case is *N.B. v. Slovakia*, where N.B. underwent sterilisation without giving informed consent during the delivery of her second child via caesarean section.[454] She sued the hospital for damages, started a criminal complaint against the doctors and initiated a constitutional complaint, and only obtained around €1,500 in compensation. In another case brought before the Court by three women of Roma origin, *I.G., M.K. and R.H. v. Slovakia*,[455] the first applicant had been a minor at the time of her sterilisation. I.G. and M.K. were sterilised without giving consent, while R.H. signed a document without understanding its content. They had tried all the forms of complaint available in Slovakia.

Turning to the Inter-American system, it is worth mentioning the case of María Mamérita Mestanza Chávez, a 33-year-old Peruvian indigenous woman, mother of seven children, who died from an aggravated infection caused by the absence of medical attention after being sterilised.[456] María Mestanza Chávez, who lived with her partner in the Encañada district, was approached by district health professionals applying a Voluntary Surgical Contraception Program, who visited her and tried to convince her, upon threat of being sent to jail, to undergo sterilisation. She and her partner initially refused. She eventually decided to undergo the procedure, without however receiving either appropriate information or medical attention. She died a few days after the operation. Her husband filed a complaint for negligent homicide, but his request was never heard by the authorities. Several NGOs brought an action against Peru on behalf of the Chávezes before the IACommHR. It was closed in 2001 by amicable settlement.

A first, and almost unique,[457] instance of sterilisation of a migrant woman was decided in 2016 by the IACHR. In *I.V. v. Bolivia*,[458] the applicant was the Ombudsperson (Defensor del Pueblo de la República de Bolivia) of Bolivia, and brought the action on behalf of a Peruvian woman, mother of three children, who was subjected to a tubal ligation procedure during a caesarean section in a Bolivian public hospital in 2000. At the age of 17, I.V. was accused of 'apology [for] terrorism' and arrested in Peru. While in detention, she was subjected to several forms of physical and psychological violence. After many years, she managed to flee to Bolivia, where she was granted asylum. In 2000, I.V., pregnant, went to the Women's Hospital in La Paz, where she underwent a caesarean section during which her fallopian tubes were tied. I.V. and her partner were informed of the procedure only after it had been performed. Even if she had been consulted during the operation (which would have involved oral consent at best), I.V. argued that her consent would have been vitiated by anaesthesia and surgical stress. The Public Prosecution Office filed criminal charges against the doctor who performed the sterilisation for causing severe bodily harm, but after four years two judicial resolutions terminated the proceedings. The case was first decided on the merits by the IACommHR, which found several violations of the rights enshrined in the American Convention and of Article 7 of the Belém do Pará Convention (state's obligations in cases of violence against women). The Commission then referred the case to the IACHR.

Has the right to health been applied directly? In which ways was women's health relevant in the judgment?

Involuntary sterilisation clearly affects women's rights to health and to reproductive health. In *L.M. and others v. Government*, decided by the High Court of Namibia, reporting Judge Elton focused on the concept of autonomy and informed consent. He argued that informed consent is not just written consent, and that 'the patient should be informed of advantages and disadvantages of alternative contraception methods.'[459] The applicants also argued that they had been sterilised because they were HIV-positive. This argument was dismissed by the Court, which was convinced that there was no evidence to support any claim of discrimination based on HIV status. The rights to health and to reproductive health were not directly considered in the decision. Some concerns can be raised about the judgment's dismissal of the second argument proposed by the applicants.[460] Discrimination on the basis of the applicants' health status should have been at the core of the Court's reasoning, along with the impairment of the physical and psychological health of the three women. Intersectionality should have played a major role. There were three elements worthy of attention in the case: gender, health and ethnicity.[461] Intersectionality would have emphasised the 'motivating reason for forced and coerced sterilisations,' which is 'to deny specific populations the ability to procreate due to a perception that they are less than ideal members of society.'[462]

Concerning Roma women, *Andrea Szijjarto* claimed before the CEDAW Committee that Hungary had violated Articles 10(h) (right to get information and advice on family planning), 12 (elimination of discrimination in access to healthcare services), and 16(1)e (right to decide freely and responsibly on the number and spacing of children) CEDAW. From a procedural point of view, it is interesting to note that the Committee found the complaint admissible even though the sterilisation had occurred before the CEDAW Protocol for Hungary came into force. It acknowledged that the procedure was permanent in its effects, and that the facts of the case could be considered as continuous in nature. Therefore, admissibility *ratione temporis* was justified.[463] In the merits, the Committee concluded that Hungary had violated all of the articles of the Convention invoked by Szijjarto. It argued that the right protected by Article 10(h) CEDAW includes the right to receive specific information on sterilisation and alternative procedure for family planning. Andrea Szijjarto had arrived at the hospital in poor health, so 'any counselling must have been given under stressful and inappropriate conditions.'[464] Her right to access appropriate health services (Article 12 CEDAW) had also been violated. In particular, the Committee noted that 'it is not plausible that during that [short] period of time hospital personnel provided the author with thorough enough counselling and information about sterilization, as well as alternatives, risks and benefits,' to ensure that Szijjarto could make 'a well-considered and voluntary decision to be sterilized.'[465] Intersectionality was not mentioned, although it was clear that this had been a case of discrimination based on both gender and ethnicity. The case anticipated some of the decisions of the ECtHR.[466]

Turning to that court's jurisprudence, in *V.C. v. Slovakia* it acknowledged that sterilisation constitutes 'a major interference with a person's reproductive health status,' which 'concerns one of the essential bodily functions of human beings,' and 'bears on manifold aspects of the individual's personal integrity including his or her physical and mental well-being.'[467] The fact that sterilisation had not been a case of life-saving surgery was relevant; nor, in the case at issue, was it of immediate necessity from a medical point of view.[468] Taking into account the effects of the sterilisation procedure – which provoked feelings of 'fear, anguish and inferiority' and affected V.C's relationship with her husband – the Court concluded that Slovakia had violated Article 3 ECHR. It posited that there was 'no indication that the medical staff acted with the intention of ill-treating the applicant,' but acknowledged that 'they nevertheless displayed gross disregard for her right to autonomy and choice as a patient.'[469] VAW had occurred despite no intent to harm the patient being proven, and the state was found responsible for this violence. The Court also found a violation of V.C.'s right to private and family life (Article 8 ECHR), because Slovakia had not complied with its positive obligation to secure her sufficient protection, 'giving special consideration to the reproductive health of the applicant as a Roma woman.'[470] Although this affirmation evoked the principle of non-discrimination, the Court did not find it necessary to separately consider a violation of Article 14 ECHR (non-discrimination).[471] In *N.B.*, the Court referred to the impairment of N.B.'s reproductive health in determining that Article 8 ECHR had been violated.[472] Nonetheless, it did not separately analyse the case under Article 14 ECHR, having already determined one violation of the rights enshrined in the Convention. In *I.G., M.K. and R.H.*, the first and the second applicants – R.H. died during the proceedings and her children were not granted standing to continue it – the Court found a procedural and substantive violation by Slovakia of Articles 3 and 8 ECHR. It referred to the judgments mentioned above to elaborate its conclusions. It is striking that the Court failed again to consider the violation of the principle of non-discrimination (Article 14 ECHR), which is far from being a secondary aspect. As correctly argued by Judge Ljiljana Mijović in her dissenting opinion to the *V.C.* judgment, the application of Article 14 was 'the very essence of the case.' In particular, the fact that V.C.'s record mentioned her ethnic origin was a clear sign of discrimination affecting a specific minority. Mijović recommended the application of Article 14 ECHR by arguing that 'the sterilisations performed on Roma women were not of an accidental nature, but relics of a long-standing attitude towards the Roma minority in Slovakia.'[473]

In the agreement which settled *María Mamérita Mestanza Chávez*, Peru acknowledged the violation of Chávez's rights, namely the rights to life, to human treatment and to equal protection as enshrined in the American Convention, and the violation of Article 7 of the Belém do Pará Convention.

In the landmark case *I.V. v. Bolivia*, the IACommHR, with which the case was initially filed, found that Bolivia had not only violated several rights of I.V. enshrined in the American Convention, including the right to personal integrity, but also Article 7 of the Belém do Pará Convention, and argued that 'non-consensual surgical procedure [is] not only a form of discrimination, but also a form of violence.'[474] It stressed the 'multiple forms of discrimination suffered by the victim.'[475] The Commission referred the case to the IACHR, which handed down its judgment on 30 November 2016. It is not my purpose here to analyse in depth the decision of the Court, but to highlight the main aspects which are relevant for the *anamnesis*. Although the American Convention does not encompass either the right to health or the right to reproductive health, the Court referred to I.V.'s right to reproductive health several times, by emphasising how the procedure had constituted a violation of 'sexual and reproductive rights', which affected her reproductive capacity, 'causando infertilidad e imponiendo un cambio físico grave y duradero sin su consentimiento,' as well as deep suffering, both physical and mental. The Court found a violation of I.V.'s right to bodily integrity.[476] The attitude of the health personnel, who had assumed that sterilisation was the best option for I.V., was described as 'unjustified paternalistic medical intervention' without a 'free, full and informed consent,' which severely 'restricted [the patient's] autonomy concerning her body and her reproductive health.'[477] The Court also delved into the issue of multiple discrimination, distinguishing it from intersectional discrimination, the latter defined as the intersection of several elements which characterise a particular discrimination.[478] As such, it is not the mere sum of grounds of discrimination, but a form of specific discrimination where more elements operate simultaneously.[479] In this case, the Court did not find that the decision to sterilise I.V. had specifically been guided by her national origin, her refugee status or her socio-economic situation.[480] Nonetheless, it considered that these grounds of discrimination, as interrelated, could determine the magnitude of the harm I.V. suffered. The Court also found that the social and economic conditions and I.V.'s migrant status had impaired her ability to gain access to justice.[481]

Reparations

Monetary compensation is the most common way that violations suffered by the victims of involuntary sterilisation have been redressed. In *L.M. and others*, for example, the High Court of Namibia, to which the Supreme Court referred the case after dismissing an appeal filed by the government, determined the quantum of damages payable to the women.

General measures addressed to the government are also fundamental, though. Thus the views issued by the CEDAW Committee in *Szijjarto v. Hungary* are relevant for my analysis. The state was asked to provide appropriate compensation to Szijjarto, 'commensurate with the gravity of the violations of her rights,' and to adopt general measures: to ensure that the personnel in private and public health centres were informed of the content of the CEDAW Convention and of the relevant CEDAW General Recommendations; to review domestic legislation on the principle of informed consent in cases of sterilisation; and to monitor public and private centres to ensure that all patients express fully informed consent before any sterilisation procedure.[482]

In the ECtHR judgments on involuntary sterilisation, which highlighted the shortcomings of the national legislation at the time of the facts,[483] the applicants were awarded sums of money in non-pecuniary damages and expenses; no particular consideration was given to the impact of the violence on women's health in determining the sums.[484]

The agreement which settled *María Mamérita Mestanza Chávez* tackled the issue of reparations via a commitment by the state to redress the violation of Chávez's rights. Her health and the lack of informed consent were taken into account in the determination of reparations. In particular, the settlement required Peru to pay monetary compensation to Chávez's relatives, along with US$7,000 to cover psychological support. Mr Chávez was also granted health insurance for the rest of his life, and US$20,000 to buy land or a house; their children were given free education in public schools.[485] The state was required to adopt a series of general measures to investigate cases of violation of women's rights, to ensure that centres where sterilisation is conducted respect the requirements established by the state family-planning programme, to ensure that health professionals attend courses in reproductive rights, violence against women, human rights and gender equality and to implement mechanism to file and tackle cases reported to the authorities quickly.[486]

In *I.V. v. Bolivia,* the IACHR ordered the state to provide I.V. with free, immediate and effective medical treatment and compensation for monetary and non-monetary damages, and to include the family in the therapy.[487] The Court stressed that reparations should pay adequate attention to I.V.'s physical and psychological suffering, taking into account the gendered nature of the discrimination.[488] The different grounds of discrimination at the basis of involuntary sterilisation were relevant in determining the amount of compensation as a consequence of the violation of I.V.'s right to personal integrity.[489] The state was also required to make the judgment public and acknowledge responsibility, to ensure that consent to sterilisation is always obtained in advance, free, informed and full, to provide clear and accessible information on women's rights to reproductive health and to adopt permanent programmes for medical students and professionals on informed consent.[490] Despite the achievement of this judgment, an author has argued that the Court should have addressed society at large, with awareness-raising education and campaigns, and that I.V.'s children should have been awarded compensation, beyond being involved in the rehabilitation.[491]

Maternal health

Context and legal background

Several legal instruments contain human rights provisions that seek to advance safe motherhood.[492] The ICESCR, for example, provides, at Article 10(2), that '[s]pecial protection should be accorded to mothers during a reasonable period before and after childbirth.' Article 12(2) CEDAW requires states parties to ensure that women have access to 'appropriate services in connection with pregnancy, confinement and the post-natal period.' In 1985, the WHO and the Pan-American Health Organization organised a conference on appropriate technology for birth, which led to the adoption of a long list of recommendations, some of them aimed at preventing mistreatment during birth. These included free access to a chosen member of the woman's family during birth, and women's right to decide about clothing, food, disposal of the placenta and other culturally significant practices.[493] The international conference on safe motherhood held in Nairobi in 1987 considered maternal health a means to improve women's status in the economic, social and political spheres, and identified strategies for safe motherhood.[494] Ensuring universal access to sexual and reproductive health and reproductive rights is included as Sustainable Development Goal No. 5 (5.6) in the Agenda 2030 of the United Nations.[495] Notwithstanding these achievements, human rights in safe motherhood have traditionally been given small importance.[496]

Safe motherhood means both access to emergency obstetric care to prevent complications and maternal death, and freedom from mistreatment during labour and delivery. Maternal mortality, mistreatment and abuse during labour (known as 'obstetric violence' or OV) are 'the greatest social injustice of our times,' which highlight 'the failure and refusal of political, religious, health and legal institutions to address the most fundamental way in which women differ from men.'[497] Nonetheless, if on one hand public health policies and programmes have been adopted over the years to reduce maternal health,[498] on the other hand obstetric violence has received less attention.

Maternal mortality is defined by the WHO as 'the death of a woman while pregnant or within 42 days of termination of pregnancy, irrespective of the duration and site of the pregnancy, from any cause related to or aggravated by the pregnancy or its management but not from accidental or incidental causes.'[499] According to the data provided by the organisation, every day approximately 830 women die from preventable causes related to pregnancy and childbirth. Maternal mortality dropped by about 44 per cent between 1990 and 2015, and the goal is to reduce the global maternal mortality rate to less than 70 per 100,000 live births before 2030.[500] Maternal mortality is higher in less developed countries and it is linked to the status of the woman in the society: women belonging to minorities, poor women and women living in rural areas have proved to be disproportionately affected. Maternal mortality and morbidity have been addressed in numerous concluding observations adopted by UN treaty bodies.[501]

OV occurs in all countries in the world even though it is not yet fully recognised.[502] In 2014, the WHO eventually issued a statement in which it acknowledges that 'many women across the globe experience disrespectful, abusive or neglectful treatment during childbirth in facilities.'[503] It stressed that 'abuse, neglect or disrespect during childbirth can amount to a violation of a woman's fundamental human rights.'[504] In 2015, UN and regional human rights experts, the Rapporteur on the rights of women of the IACommHR and the Special Rapporteurs on the rights of women and human rights defenders of the African Commission on Human and Peoples' Rights issued a joint statement explicitly calling on states to address 'acts of obstetric and *institutional* violence.'[505] Mistreatment and abuse during childbirth include physical, verbal and sexual abuse, discrimination and neglect, denial of privacy or of confidentiality and poor-quality care. More than fifty years ago, the *Ladies' Home Journal* in the USA published a shocking article under the title 'Cruelty in maternity wards,' which reported the stories of nurses and women about inhuman treatment in labour and delivery.[506] In 1958, a Society for the Prevention of Cruelty to Pregnant Women was established in the United Kingdom. The situation has not improved in recent years.[507] In a report of 2011 by the Perseu Abramo Institute in Brazil, 25 per cent of the 2,365 women interviewed reported some form of violence during childbirth, including verbal abuses and vaginal examination.[508] In September 2017, the Osservatorio sulla violenza ostetrica Italia (Ovo), published a report on obstetric violence, based on interviews of 5 million Italian women aged 18 to 54 with at least one child aged 14 or less.[509] The inquiry, which was followed by the protest of thousands of women through the campaign '#Basta tacere' on Twitter, showed that four in ten women considered their child's birth as harmful to their dignity and psycho-physical integrity. Approximately 1 million women in Italy – 21 per cent – claimed to have been victim of a form of physical or psychological OV during their first child's birth.

Experts from different countries have documented cases of beatings, hitting, slapping, kicking, pinching, the use of mouth gags and bed restraints, of harsh or rude language, of judgmental or accusatory remarks.[510] Coercive or unconsented medical procedures, such as forced caesarean surgery (sometimes through a court order), episiotomy, the Kristeller manoeuvre and induced labour – when they are not clinically justified – and also detention of women and their new-borns in facilities after birth for inability to pay constitute other examples of obstetric violence. OV also consists in the refusal to provide relief for pain during labour, with possible negative consequences for the woman's rights to health and reproductive health. Obstetric practices 'inadvertently perpetuate VAW by using coercion.'[511] In the most severe cases, OV leads to the woman's death. As one author outlined, 'this is a problem that resides at the intersection of astonishing progress in medical technology on the one hand, and regressive attitudes about the rights and responsibilities of pregnant women on the other.'[512]

OV found legal recognition in Venezuela's 2007 Organic Law on women's right to a life free from violence, which first defined obstetric violence as

> the appropriation of a woman's body and reproductive processes by health personnel, in the form of dehumanizing treatment, abusive medicalization and pathologisation of natural processes, involving a woman's loss of autonomy and of the capacity to freely make her own decisions about her body and her sexuality, which has negative consequences for a woman's quality of life.[513]

Article 51 of the same law includes some examples of OV, such as incapacity to respond to obstetric emergencies, forcing women to deliver lying on their backs with their feet in stirrups, preventing the mother and child from staying together after birth, altering the natural process of delivery by using induced labour without 'voluntario, expreso e informado' consent, performing a coerced caesarean section when the conditions for a natural childbirth were present, without fully informed consent. The law requires the perpetrator ('al responsible o la responsible', irrespective of gender) to pay a fine and a copy of the judgment to be sent to the professional association which can decide whether to proceed against its member.

In 2009, the Argentinean congress admitted that 'the provision of maternal care in health facilities had become a source of VAW,' and it adopted in 2009 the Integral Law for the Sanction, Prevention, and Eradication of Violence against Women.[514]

In a report presented in 2012 as a follow-up mechanism to the Belém do Pará Convention, the Committee of Experts recommended that states include provisions that 'not only make obstetric violence a punishable offense, but that also elaborate on the elements of what constitutes a natural process before, during and after birth, without excessive reliance on medication.'[515]

In Italy, a draft law aimed at the protection of women in labour and the new-born, and at the promotion of natural childbirth was presented on 11 March 2016.[516] Although not all the provisions were in line with the law's declared purpose to protect women's dignity, the draft law marked a huge step forward in defining obstetric violence as 'the actions or omissions' of health personnel which 'deprive the woman of her autonomy and dignity during childbirth' (Article 14 of the draft).

These laws attempt to respond to a paternalistic view of medicine, which has led both to the phenomenon of 'over-medicalisation' – the use of medical procedures where not strictly necessary and without fully informed consent[517] – and of 'under-medicalisation', for example the denial of pain relief during birth. As clearly put by Erdmann, 'a health system wears the inequalities of the society in which it functions.'[518]

Judgments and decisions on 'obstetric violence'

In this paragraph, I will analyse cases of OV. The difficulties that emerged in the selection of cases for analysis derive from several factors. Firstly, compared to abortion, obstetric violence has been dealt with by judges more in terms of negligence of health personnel than of violation of women's human rights. In the

United States, a scholar has reported that 'justice is elusive for many American women who experience obstetric violence,' even though the common law of tort 'in most jurisdictions provides that anyone subjected to unconsented touching may sue for battery.'[519] Cases of obstetric violence are usually dealt by the civil justice system in the United States, with the consequence that 'it treats the matter as either a medical error or an interpersonal conflict similar to a fistfight on a street corner.'[520] In particular, OV has come to court usually when it caused more or less permanent physical damage, which might lead to malpractice lawsuits. Secondly, OV is not perceived as violence by women themselves. From a feminist point of view, it is possible to argue that a male-centred society underestimates the harm caused to women while bearing children. If women are conceived as reproductive objects, and the birth of children as a 'normal' part of every woman's life, it is easier to understand why OV has only recently attracted interest. Women's suffering has always had a purpose: to serve society by giving birth to a child.[521]

A specific case of OV which affects women in prison is perinatal shackling, which I consider a form of VAW in its vertical dimension. It is also a form of intersectional discrimination, combining multiple and intersecting grounds of discrimination: gender, social and health condition, and ethnicity. Perinatal shackling in prison is an example of VAWH directly committed by states' officials, and it has been a standard practice in the United States, even after the adoption of laws prohibiting it. The first SR on VAW, Radhika Coomaraswamy, acknowledged in her report of 1999 on the United States that 'women in labour are also shackled during transport to hospital and soon after the baby is born,' and that she 'heard of one case where shackles were kept on even during delivery.'[522] She concluded that 'the use of these instruments violates international standards and may be said to constitute cruel and unusual practices.'[523] In 2006, the UN Committee against Torture expressed its concerns about 'incidents of shackling of women detainees during birth,' and recommended the United States 'adopt all appropriate measures to ensure that women in detention are treated in conformity with international standards.'[524] More than ten years after Coomaraswamy's report, the SR Rashida Manjoo stressed that despite the efforts and the existence of a Federal Bureau of Prisons' policy on shackling, pregnant women have been reported to be routinely shackled on their way to and from hospital, and sometimes even during labour, delivery and after delivery.[525] Even when laws prohibiting the use of shackles on women in labour have been adopted, they are seldom applied.[526] A report published in May 2016 by the Prison Birth Project and Prisoners' Legal Services of Massachusetts found that Massachusetts prisons and jails had violated their newly adopted anti-shackling law by continuing to 'subject pregnant women to illegal, unsafe, and degrading treatment.'[527]

Who is the applicant?

As anticipated, judgments relating to mistreatment during childbirth have often been dealt with by courts in terms of compliance with legal standards of clinical practice by health professionals. The civil justice system is mainly used to address

OV. Hence, for example, in *G., M.C.Y. v. Hospital Luis Lagomaggiore*, the Third Chamber of Mendoza, Argentina, analysed the case of a young woman who was subjected to a caesarean section and an episiotomy in terms of tort liability.[528] The former was not clinically necessary, and the episiotomy was 'incorrectly performed' and caused severe health consequences to G., including uterine infections and damage to her sphincter muscles. In particular, the episiotomy was not performed by experienced healthcare staff. G. did not consent to either procedure.

Cases in Italy of malpractice during childbirth, which can amount to manslaughter (*omidicio colposo*), are generally linked to harms suffered by – or the death of – the new-born,[529] or to maternal mortality or morbidity. In a case decided by the Italian Cassazione sez. civile (Supreme Court) in 2010, a woman was subject to episiotomy during childbirth which caused her severe and permanent health consequences (incontinence), and affected her intimate relationship with her husband.[530] The woman and her husband both sued the hospital and asked for compensation, for the injury and for the damage to their matrimonial life. They obtained compensation in both instances, but considered the amount too little given the permanent incontinence affecting the woman after the delivery. Accordingly, they appealed to the Cassazione.

A recent case of OV was decided by the High Court of Kenya at Bungoma in March 2018, which applied a human rights-based approach to the case.[531] J.O.O., a low-income woman, suffered abuse and mistreatment while in labour at the Bungoma County Referral Hospital, which should have provided maternal health services at no charge. She received no assistance while in labour, and was forced to walk alone to the delivery room. J.O.O. eventually gave birth on the floor as the delivery room was occupied by other patients, and was shouted at by two nurses. She sought redress from the hospital and both national and local governments before the Kenyan Court, invoking her human rights.

The ECtHR has not specifically dealt with cases of obstetric violence, but in *Dubská and Krejzova v. Czech Republic* it tackled the complaint of a woman who, choosing home birth as a consequence of OV, suffered during her first delivery.[532] The case was first decided by a Chamber of the Court and then referred to the Grand Chamber. The case is relevant here to reflect on the possibility that forced or coerced hospitalisation for delivery is a form of violence against women in its vertical dimension. Home birth is not prohibited in the Czech Republic, and there is no record of midwives being prosecuted for attending home births *per se.* Midwives, however, have been prosecuted for alleged malpractice during home births. Šárka Dubská endured OV during her first delivery so she decided to give birth to her second child at home. She could not find a midwife willing to assist her and finally she gave birth alone. The second applicant, Alexandra Krejzová, gave birth to her first two children with the assistance of a midwife. During her third pregnancy she was not able to find anyone available to assist her, and when she was informed that home birth was not covered by public insurance, she chose a maternity hospital, which did not respect all her wishes. One of the applicants had sought redress in front of the constitutional court, which dismissed the appeal.

A famous case on perinatal shackling was filed in 1993 in the USA as a class action. The plaintiffs were female prisoners incarcerated in three facilities in the District of Columbia. They complained of sexual harassment and inadequate obstetric and gynaecological care offered to female prisoners. In the judgment of the District Court, it was reported that 'when Defendants transport pregnant women prisoners on medical visits they customarily place women in leg shackles, handcuffs and a belly chain with a box that connects the handcuffs and belly chain,' and that 'a physician's assistant stated that even when a woman is in labour "their ankles and their hands are cuffed".'[533] Twenty-five years later, in the case *Shawanna Nelson v. Correctional Medical Services*, the US Court of Appeals for the Eighth Circuit marked a pivotal step in the protection of female inmates' rights.[534] Shawanna Nelson was assigned to the McPherson Correctional Unit in Newport, Arkansas, after being convicted for credit fraud. When she went into labour, she was first denied a transfer to the hospital, then finally escorted there by a female correctional officer. Her legs were placed in shackles. Despite the request of the nurse and the physician, the applicant remained shackled for most of the procedure, until shortly before her baby was born. She experienced a hip dislocation and an umbilical hernia. After childbirth she was immediately reshackled to her hospital bed by an officer who had replaced the first one. She was unshackled only on the second night of her stay at the hospital.[535]

Has the right to health been applied directly? In which ways was women's health relevant in the judgment?

In *G., M.C.Y. v. Hospital Luis Lagomaggiore*, decided by the Third Chamber of Mendoza, Argentina, the right to health was considered in terms of the practitioner's duty to ensure women's health during childbirth. The judges concluded that the obstetrician had been negligent. The core of the judgment was the behaviour of the practitioner, rather than G.'s individual rights.

Turning to the Italian case of malpractice during childbirth, with health consequences for the woman, the Cassazione, to which the couple appealed, acknowledged that separate cases had to be considered for the couple, because the impact of the medical procedure was different for the woman and her husband. In particular, the Court referred to the dignity of the *affectio coniugalis* and to 'the constitutional value of the marriage,' meaning that 'it is not only a matter of health, but of the essence of matrimonial life.' It is striking to note that the reproductive and sexual health of the woman only mattered inasmuch they affected the matrimonial life of the couple. The right to reproductive and sexual health is a component of the right to health, as affirmed in international human rights law, and a more gender-sensitive approach would have highlighted how episiotomy not only caused incontinence – with severe consequences in daily life – but also affected the reproductive and sexual health of the *woman*, not of the woman *in her relationship* with her husband.

The High Court of Kenya referred to the constitutional right to health and to the legal instruments the country had ratified. It concluded that J.O.O. had been in a vulnerable state, and that the behaviour of the nurses was inexcusable, leading to a violation of J.O.O.'s rights 'as a woman.'[536] The judgment went further, since the complaint had been filed against the national and local governments as well. In the assessment of the Court, the authorities 'have not devoted adequate resources to health care services, have not put in place effective measures to implement, monitor and provide minimum acceptable standards of health care, thus violating our [very own] Constitution and international instruments that we have acceded to as a country.'[537] The Kenyan Court declared that J.O.O.'s rights to dignity and to be free from cruel, inhuman or degrading treatment had been breached, and that the violation was caused by the national and county governments failing to ensure adequate health care services. By finding the authorities responsible for violating J.O.O.'s rights, the Court acknowledged that the state, through inadequate implementation of the law and the lack of guidelines on free maternal care, had contributed to the violence she had suffered.

In *Dubská and Krejzova* the ECtHR approached the case from the angle of positive obligations to ensure respect for the applicants' private life, and analysed whether the interference in private life had been 'in accordance with the law,' 'necessary in a democratic society' for the pursuit of 'legitimate aims.'[538] It said that the interference was provided by the law, which allowed home births only when the activity of the midwife met specific requirements. The law was foreseeable and clear.[539] The Court accepted that the Czech state's policy was aimed at protecting the health and safety of mothers and children during delivery.[540] On the legitimacy of the interference, it recognised a wide margin of appreciation given to states in deciding whether to allow or prohibit home birth. Following a line of argument similar to one used in abortion cases, the Court pointed out that there was no consensus among the member states of the Council of Europe with regard to home birth. National authorities can make the first assessment of where a fair balance must be struck. The courts must then supervise whether 'the interference constitutes a proportionate balancing of the competing interests involved.'[541] A majority of twelve judges agreed that the interference had not constituted a violation of Article 8 ECHR, and encouraged the Czech authorities to keep the relevant legal provisions under constant review in order to 'reflect medical and scientific developments whilst fully respecting women's rights in the field of reproductive health, notably by ensuring adequate conditions for both patients and medical staff in maternity hospitals across the country.'[542]

As for perinatal shackling, the District Court of the District of Columbia, deciding on the shackling of female prisoners in the District, held that '[w]hile a woman is in labor … shackling is inhumane,' and the practice violated her Constitutional rights, in particular the Eight Amendment, which reads that 'excessive bail shall not be required, nor excessive fines imposed, nor cruel and unusual punishment inflicted.'[543] In *Shawanna Nelson,* the US Court of Appeals stated that the law 'clearly established' that shackling a female prisoner during labour and delivery, without evident security justification, constituted 'cruel and unusual punishment' and violated the Eight Amendment. The appellate court argued that the corrections officer should have been aware that her actions were not Constitutional, and concluded by a majority of six to five that she was not entitled to qualified immunity.[544] The details of the judgment will not be reported here,[545] but it is worth highlighting that there was no reference to the impact of perinatal shackling on Shawanna Nelson's rights to health and to reproductive health. The only reference to health matters consists in the description of shackling practices as 'degrading, barbaric, humiliating, and life threatening to both mother and child.'[546] What about the state? A complaint could have been filed with the IACommHR raising the issue of violation of Articles VII (special protection to women during pregnancy and nursing period), and XXV (right to humane treatment during custody) of the American Declaration. The case of perinatal shackling is a clear example of gender-based violence against women, which is characterised by being based on two specific conditions relating to the woman: pregnancy and detention. Another condition determining the treatment of women in detention is ethnicity. As argued by Priscilla Ocen, perinatal shackling appears 'as a manifestation of the punishment of "unfit" or "undesirable" women for exercising the choice to become mothers. Within the prevailing punishment regime, undesirability is synonymous with race, as the impulse to punish such women is rooted in the stereotypical constructions of Black women.'[547] Perinatal shackling is a way to 'export' rules in prison, which are male-centric, to the hospital.[548] In *Nelson*, the officer was a woman, but the 'prison' is a male actor, in which the subordination of women to men is perpetuated to the extent of being normalised and felt as compulsory by female officers as well as male. Perinatal shackling is a violation of human rights, including the right to health, and it also disregards the UN Standard Minimum Rules which require that prisons make special accommodation for the care and treatment of pregnant women.[549]

Reparations

Reparations in cases of OV mainly consist in monetary compensation, usually as a consequence of the permanent impairment of the woman's life. In *G., M.C.Y. v. Hospital Luis Lagomaggiore,* for example, compensation was granted to the applicants. However, as Vacaflor has argued, the judges did not consider the absence of consent to the procedures, which in itself would have amounted to a form of violence even if no physical harm had resulted. What is more, 'the judicial reasoning in this case focused on awarding relief for the physiological malpractice during childbirth, but failed to recognize the damages to women's emotional, and psychosocial needs, or consider their choices and preferences.'[550]

In the Italian case, the amount of the compensation was determined by the court of appeal to which the Cassazione referred the case. However, as I contended above, the issue here is that the Court diminished the impact of this form of violence on the woman's health, by referring only to the 'essence of matrimonial life' threatened by the procedure.

The Kenyan Court awarded Kshs. 2,500,000 (around €21,000) to J.O.O. as compensation for the violation of her rights and ordered that a formal apology by the hospital and the nurses be made to her.

In the US class action on perinatal shackling, the Court ordered the defendants to 'develop and implement a protocol concerning restraints used on pregnant and postpartum women,' providing that 'a pregnant prisoner shall be transported in the least restrictive way possible consistent with legitimate security reasons.'[551] In *Nelson*, the Court sent the case back for jury trial, which determined compensatory damages in the amount of $1.[552]

Judgments and decisions on maternal mortality

In GR No. 24, the CEDAW Committee contended that under Article 12(2) CEDAW states have the legal obligation to 'ensure women's right to safe motherhood and emergency obstetric services and they should allocate to these services the maximum extent of available resources.'[553] The Human Rights Council, in its Resolution No. 11/8 adopted in 2009, identified human rights directly implicated by maternal mortality and morbidity, including the rights to life, to be free to seek, receive and impart information, and to enjoy 'the highest attainable standard of physical and mental health, including sexual and reproductive health.'[554] Some cases decided by the CEDAW Committee, domestic and regional human rights courts are worth exploring here.

Who is the applicant?

The pivotal case with regard to maternal mortality is *Alyne da Silva Pimentel Teixeira (deceased) v. Brazil*, decided by the CEDAW Committee in 2007.[555] In the words of Rebecca Cook, *Teixeira* marks 'the first decision of an international treaty body [to hold] a government accountable for a preventable maternal death.'[556] The applicant was Alyne Teixeira's mother, Maria de Lourdes da Silva Pimentel, who filed a complaint in her own name and on behalf of the family of her deceased daughter with the Committee, claiming violation of Articles 1, 2 and 12 CEDAW. Teixeira, a poor woman of Afro-Brazilian descent aged 28, who already had a child, visited a private clinic in the state of Rio de Janeiro presenting symptoms of a high-risk pregnancy. The physician sent her home. She returned to the hospital, where the doctor was unable to detect foetal heartbeat. She gave birth to a stillborn foetus, and the placenta was only removed fourteen hours later. Given her medical conditions, Teixeira was transferred to a public healthcare institution, but had to wait another eight hours. When she arrived at the hospital, she was hypothermic, and her blood pressure dropped to zero. She died after 21 hours of agony without medical attention. The autopsy found the official cause of death to be digestive haemorrhage. The pathologist said that it was attributable to the delivery of the stillborn foetus. However, when Maria Pimentel returned to the hospital, doctors argued that her daughter's death was due to the fact that she had carried a dead foetus in her womb for several days. Two lawsuits were filed on behalf of Teixeira, one at domestic, the other at international level. In

November 2007, the Center for Reproductive Rights and Advocacia Cidadã pelos Direitos Humanos filed a complaint with the CEDAW Committee.

In the European system, Strasbourg judges dealt with a case of maternal health in *Byrzykowski v. Poland,* decided in 2006.[557] The applicant was Byrzykowski's husband. She died after going into coma as a consequence of epidural anaesthesia, necessary to perform a caesarean section. Investigations were still ongoing at the time of the complaint before the ECtHR; after more than seven years, no final decision had been taken in any of the domestic proceedings. In a more recent case, *Z. v. Poland,* decided in 2012,[558] Z.'s daughter was diagnosed with ulcerative colitis while pregnant. She was admitted to a number of hospitals without success. Her condition rapidly deteriorated, and the doctors, after finding that the foetus had died in her womb, removed it. Z.'s daughter died later of septic shock. Z. started different proceedings in front of Polish judicial authorities, before filing a complaint with the ECtHR. The following year, the Court decided a complaint, *Şentürk v. Turkey,* submitted by the husband and the son of a woman who had died in a private ambulance, without the support of medical staff.[559] She had suffered huge pain and gone to several hospitals which discharged her, one after another. She was examined by a midwife and not a doctor in the first three hospitals. On arrival at the fourth hospital, she was finally examined by a gynaecologist, who performed an ultrasound scan that showed that her foetus was dead and needed to be removed. Since she could not afford the fee for the operation, she was transferred to another hospital, but died during the journey. An investigation led to an open verdict, concluding that the doctors had committed no fault. The Supreme Administrative Court upheld the appeal, and the applicants filed a complaint with the European Court.

Turning to the Inter-American system, in 2010, the IACHR dealt with the issue of maternal mortality in its judgment *Xákmok Kásek Indigenous Community v. Paraguay,* which concerned the right of an indigenous community to ancestral property.[560] The case was submitted to the Court by the Inter-American Commission, which issued a report on 17 July 2008 including specific recommendations for the state. The application was filed by members of the organisation Tierraviva a los Pueblos Indígenas del Chaco on behalf of and in representation of the members of the Community. Among the deaths that had occurred in the community, one is relevant for my analysis. Remigia Ruíz died in 2005 because, while pregnant, she did not receive adequate medical care. She represented an example of death during labour without access to health services, lack of documentation on cause of death and exclusion for extreme poverty.[561]

At national level, I have found remarkable the judgments issued by Indian courts. In *Laxmi Mandal v. Deen Dayal Harinagar Hospital*, the High Court of Delhi decided a case filed on behalf of Shanti Devi, a poor woman who was refused adequate maternal care despite being entitled to free services according to the existing state-sponsored schemes.[562] Shanti Devi, who suffered from anaemia, became pregnant for the sixth time, and died in January 2010 after giving birth at home to a daughter who was two months premature; the daughter survived. In another case, the High Court started proceedings on its own, following a newspaper report of a destitute woman who had died on a busy street after giving birth to a baby girl, to address discrimination and denial of medical care to homeless women, and lactating women.[563]

Has the right to health been applied directly? In which ways was women's health relevant in the judgment?

In *Alyne da Silva Pimentel Teixeira (deceased) v. Brazil*, the Committee rejected the argument presented by the state that Teixeira's death was non-maternal and that the probable cause of her death was digestive haemorrhage. The Committee was convinced that Teixeira's death had been linked to obstetric complications related to pregnancy, and that there was a link between gender and the possible medical errors committed.[564] It found Brazil responsible for failure to control private institutions providing medical services, and that this was in violation of Article 2(e) CEDAW providing for the elimination of discrimination by any organisation or enterprise.[565] According to the Committee, appropriate maternal health services in the state party had failed to meet 'the specific, distinctive health needs and interests of women,' which constituted a violation of Article 12 (2) CEDAW, but also discrimination against women under Articles 12(1) and 2 CEDAW. It is interesting to note the emphasis put on the intersecting forms of discrimination that Teixeira suffered, 'not only on the basis of sex, but also on the basis of her status as woman of African descent and her socio-economic background.'[566] The convergence or association of the different elements – posited the Committee – 'may have contributed to the failure to provide necessary and emergency care to her daughter, resulting in her death.'[567] Rebecca Cook says that this was the first time that a UN treaty body considered discrimination in a country's healthcare system from the perspective of a poor woman belonging to a minority, and the first time that maternal death was declared to be preventable, 'and when governments fail to take the appropriate preventive measures, that failure violates women's human rights.'[568] The Committee concluded that the state had violated the principle of non-discrimination by failing to accommodate sex-specific health care.[569]

Compared to the views in the *Pimentel Teixeira* case, the judgments handed down by the ECtHR are quite limited, because they do not reflect on the issue of maternal mortality as a matter of concern in European countries. Even though it is clear that the right to health could not be applied to these cases – since no such provision is in the ECHR – a reference to the fundamental rights of a woman, as linked to or as a part of the right to life, and to international legal instruments on the topic would have been positive. In *Byrzykowski v. Poland*, the Court found that the state had violated the right to life enshrined in Article 2 ECHR by not effectively investigating the case of a woman who died after going into coma as a consequence of epidural anesthesia, necessary to perform a caesarean section. The Court reiterated its previous jurisprudence, saying that:

> positive obligations require States to make regulations compelling hospitals, whether public or private, to adopt appropriate measures for the protection of their patients' lives. They also require an effective independent judicial system to be set up so that the cause of death of patients in the care of the medical profession, whether in the public or the private sector, can be determined and those responsible made accountable.[570]

In all cases in which the harm has not been caused intentionally – the Court pointed out – the positive obligation does not require the provision of a criminal law remedy. It is enough that the system provides a remedy in civil courts, 'either alone or in conjunction with a remedy in the criminal courts,' which enables 'any liability of the doctors concerned to be established and any appropriate civil redress, such as an order for damages and for the publication of the decision, to be obtained.'[571] Despite the medical question being complex, the Court pointed out that the overall length of the investigation had been unjustified.[572]

Similarly, in *Z. v. Poland*, it was a matter of procedural obligations under Article 2 ECHR. The ECtHR concluded that the authorities had dealt with the case with the level of due diligence required by Article 2 ECHR, and that there had been no violation of Z.'s daughter's rights.[573] It did not focus on conscientious objection, which Z. argued was the reason why health personnel had refused her daughter a full endoscopy, because it was not established that this was the factor that determined the medical decision. Z. contended that her daughter had been subjected to inhuman and degrading treatment 'as a result of the doctors' deliberate failure to provide the necessary medical treatment.'[574] The Court argued that, while there was no doubt that 'the applicant's daughter's illness caused her inordinate pain,' she had received 'treatment in various specialised hospitals and [been] subject to various medical tests,' and 'it is not [the Court's] function to question the doctors' clinical judgment as regards the seriousness of Y's condition or the appropriateness of the treatment they proposed.'[575] The case presented some disputed facts, which could have mattered in terms of relevance to women's reproductive health. Z., for example, submitted that during her stay her daughter had been humiliated by a doctor, but the hospital denied the accusation.[576]

The following year, in *Şentürk v. Turkey*, the ECtHR argued that positive obligations under Article 2 ECHR imply 'that a regulatory structure be set up, requiring that hospitals, be they private or public, take appropriate steps to ensure that patients' lives are protected.' States are also required to put in place an efficient and independent judicial system to assess the cause of death of an individual.[577] The Court noted that 'the deceased woman, victim of a flagrant malfunctioning of the hospital departments, was deprived of the possibility of access to appropriate emergency care.'[578] Judges were convinced that it was not a mere error or medical negligence, but rather that the doctors working there, 'in full awareness of the facts and in breach of their professional obligations, did not take all the emergency measures necessary to attempt to keep their patient alive.'[579]

As for the Inter-American system, in *Xákmok Kásek Indigenous Community* the Court found that the state had violated Remigia Ruíz's right to life, that she had died because of lack of adequate medical assistance during childbirth, and requested that it adopted several measures to prevent maternal mortality.[580] No account was specifically taken of the violation of Ruíz's right to reproductive health, and the legal reasoning did not take into account the existence of intersectional discrimination: it should be said, however, that the case was particularly complex owing to the large number of applicants and of alleged violations of human rights.

At national level, in *Laxmi Mandal*, the High Court of Delhi stressed the inefficiency of the support schemes: 'instead of making it easier for poor persons to avail of the benefits, the efforts at present seem to be to insist upon documentation to prove their status as "poor" and "disadvantaged".'[581] Reference to the right to reproductive health and the right to life is clear in the judgment. The Court stressed that the complaint focused on the right to health, a 'survival right' that formed part of the right to life, which included 'the right to access and receive a minimum standard of treatment and care in public health facilities, and in particular the reproductive rights of the mother.'[582] The Court also mentioned the relevant international human rights law instruments on women's rights to health and to reproductive health,[583] and acknowledged the right to maternal health care as a constitutionally protected right.

Reparations

In terms of reparations, *Pimentel Teixeira* is the most interesting case. The Committee presented several recommendations to the state, including ensuring 'women's right to safe motherhood and affordable access for all women to adequate emergency obstetric care;' providing 'adequate professional training for health workers, especially on women's reproductive health rights;' and ensuring that private health care facilities comply with relevant national and international standards on reproductive health care. These recommendations will be thoroughly analysed in chapter 3.[584] The state was asked to provide adequate financial compensation to the relatives of Teixeira, 'commensurate with the gravity of the violations against her.'[585] After ten years, in 2013, the Rio de Janeiro Trial Court awarded moral damages and a pension to Teixeira's daughter, retroactively from her mother's death until she turned 18.

The ECtHR has granted monetary compensation to victims, or victims' relatives. In *Byrzykowski*, judges only granted the applicant, Byrzykowski's husband, non-pecuniary damages (€20,000), dismissing his request for pecuniary damages to covering the lost earnings of his late wife and the cost of the medical care which was necessary for his son.[586]

The judgment of the IACHR in the case concerning the Xákmok Kásek Community was considered *per se* a form of reparation. The state was requested to pay compensation amounting to US$260,000 to the leaders of the Community, who would then distribute the amount among its members.[587] The Court ordered Paraguay to establish a permanent health clinic, equipped with the supplies and medicines necessary to provide adequate health care.[588]

The High Court of Delhi, which acknowledged the right to maternal health care as constitutionally protected, granted financial compensation to Mandal's relatives, and in particular to her daughter, and addressed the main shortcomings of the scheme that had been meant to help poor people gain access to medical services. In a later judgment, started by the High Court itself after the death of a destitute woman on a street, the Court held that the government of Delhi had an obligation 'to demarcate or hire or create at least two shelter centres meant for destitute pregnant women and lactating women so that proper care can be taken to see that no destitute woman is compelled to give birth to a child on the footpath.'[589]

Access to emergency contraception

Context and legal background

In this section, I will specifically deal with emergency contraception (EC), which has raised several ethical issues in scholarship. EC has been defined by the WHO as 'methods of contraception that can be used to prevent pregnancy after sexual intercourse.'[590] In GC No. 22, the ESCR Committee posited that it is an essential medicine, and should be available.[591] Individuals have the right to receive information on all aspects of sexual and reproductive health, including on contraceptives.[592]

Depending on the perspective adopted, whether based on ethics, culture or religion, EC has been considered either an abortifacient or a contraceptive measure. It has been reported for example that between 2000 and 2010 high courts in Latin American countries decided several cases on the legitimacy of the selling of EC.[593] If, on one hand, some courts have acknowledged the perceived abortive effects of EC or based their argument on the 'reasonable doubt' attributable to the scientific status of research on the effects of EC,[594] other courts have contended that EC has only contraceptive, and not abortive, effects.[595] Four authors have pointed out that 'the event in human reproduction from which personhood or individuality can be considered to have begun will probably never be conclusively determined, since decisive events are selected to serve different and sometimes conflicting purposes;'[596] nonetheless, the definition provided by the WHO does not leave much doubt that EC is contraception. The updated WHO factsheet states that EC pills prevent or delay ovulation and 'do not induce an abortion,' they cannot interrupt an established pregnancy or harm a developing embryo.[597] The IACommHR held hearings during its 149th session from 24 October to 8 November 2013, during which it 'received troubling information on barriers that exist in terms of women's access to emergency contraception.'[598] In particular, the Commission received information confirming 'the major challenges women face for complete access to emergency contraception, as well as a troubling tendency to restrict or ban its availability.'[599] Limited access to emergency contraception has been proved to be related to high rates of clandestine abortions, especially for teen pregnancy – which is often the result of sexual violence – and cases of suicide among adolescent girls. In a joint statement issued in 2015, UN experts argued that 'the criminalization of or other failure to provide services that only women require, such as abortion and emergency contraception, constitute discrimination based on sex, and is impermissible.'[600]

Judgments and decisions

Judgments and decisions relating to access to EC are not as numerous as the ones analysed in this chapter relating to other forms of violence. The reason is that it is difficult to demonstrate, in a specific case, the causal link between the lack of access to contraceptives, in particular EC, and, for example, the death of a woman after an unsafe abortion.

Who is the applicant?

I will propose in this sub-section, exceptionally, given the scant jurisprudence on the matter, the CEDAW inquiry on the Philippines related to Executive order No. 3 of 2000 issued in Manila.[601] The case was brought to the attention of the CEDAW Committee by a group of NGOs. Despite a clear prohibition on the use of modern contraception not being included in the order, in practice implementation of the order severely limited women's access to sexual and reproductive health services, resulting in unavailability of modern contraceptives in Manila. The Executive order recalled the 'sanctity of life' and the protection of the lives of the mother and the unborn child, and it affirmed that the city of Manila would have promoted 'responsible parenthood.'

In the Inter-American system for protecting human rights, the US-based Center for Reproductive Health, along with Promsex, DEMUS and Paz y Esperanza, has filed a complaint against Peru with the IACommHR on behalf of an adolescent rape survivor who was denied access to essential medical treatment following the assault on her.[602] The case concerns Peru's ban on the distribution of EC in public hospitals.[603] The survivor, Maria, was kidnapped, drugged and gang-raped. She eventually gained access to EC in a private pharmacy, but received no information on how to take the medicine. The Inter-American Commission will have the opportunity to assess the compatibility of these state measures with the protection of fundamental human rights, including, hopefully, the rights to health and to reproductive health.

At national level, the Colombian Constitutional Court decided in 2012 the case of 1,280 women who filed a joint *tutela*, objecting to false information on EC provided by the Attorney-General of Colombia.[604] He had publicly stated that the medicine for EC is an abortifacient, and that the right to life is granted by the Constitution.

A related issue is conscientious objection in the provision of contraception, in particular EC. The Attorney-General of Colombia, in the case just mentioned, was accused of encouraging this. In a case concerning the selling of contraceptives (not EC), the ECtHR dismissed a complaint presented by two pharmacists who claimed that their right to freedom of thought, conscience and religion had been infringed after they were convicted in France for refusing to dispense contraceptives to three women who held medical prescriptions. The Court of Cassation confirmed the decisions of the lower courts arguing that 'personal convictions ... [could] not constitute for pharmacists, who have the exclusive right to sell medicines, a legitimate reason' under the Consumer Code to refuse the purchase.[605]

Has the right to health been applied directly? In which ways was women's health relevant in the judgment?

As assessed by the CEDAW Committee in the case of Manila, an order which in practice limited access to contraceptives led to the 'withdrawal of all supplies of modern contraceptives from all health facilities funded by the local government, in the refusal to provide women with family planning information and counselling ... and in misinformation about modern methods of contraception, including those methods listed on the World Health Organization Model List of Essential Medicines.'[606] The Committee demonstrated the existence of a ban on modern methods of contraception 'in all public health facilities run by the local government, namely hospitals, health centres and "lying-in clinics".'[607] It further noted that the prohibition of EC was 'indicative of the ideological environment prevailing at the time and its retrogressive impact on the provision of reproductive health services and commodities.'[608] The Committee concluded in its inquiry that the Philippines had violated Article 12 CEDAW, since 'given that only women can become pregnant, lack of access to contraceptives is ... bound to affect their health disproportionately.'[609] In other words, the policy had caused a violation of women's right of access to health care. The UN treaty body also 'took note' of the 'potentially life-threatening consequences of unplanned and/or unwanted pregnancies as a direct consequence of the denial of access to the full range of contraceptive methods, as well as of the strict criminalisation of abortion without any exemptions provided for in the State party's legislation,' and acknowledged that 'complications resulting from unsafe and illegal abortion are a prominent cause of maternal death in Manila.'[610]

The Colombian Constitutional Court, considering the affirmation of the Attorney-General that EC is an abortifacient, based its legal reasoning on the Constitution, and on Article 12 CEDAW, to affirm the right to information on reproductive health. In particular, it acknowledged that 'reproductive rights are implicit in the fundamental rights to human dignity and life, to equality, to the free development of personality, to information, to health and to education, among others.'[611] In the Court's view, women's rights to health and to reproductive health also encompass a right to adequate and unbiased information.

Reparations

The Inquiry on the Philippines did not lead to reparations, given the nature of the proceedings, but rather to a series of recommendations by the CEDAW Committee, which called upon the government to ensure, to adults as well as to adolescents, 'universal and affordable access to the full range of sexual and reproductive health services, commodities and related information ... including oral contraception and emergency contraception.'[612] It further asked the state, which was found responsible for the action of the Manila government, to 'reintroduce emergency contraception ... to prevent early and unplanned pregnancies and in cases of sexual violence,' and 'to promote and raise awareness about the benefits of emergency contraceptives in such situations, in particular among adolescent girls.'[613]

As reparation to the 1,280 women who had filed the *tutela*, the Colombian Constitutional Court ordered the Attorney-General, within forty-eight hours from the notification of the judgment, to make a public statement to explain that EC is not an abortifacient, and that in no case can women be charged with the crime of abortion when buying it.[614]

Conclusions: paving the way for the diagnosis

The conclusion of the *anamnesis* constitutes the diagnosis, which will be the object of chapter 2. These cases, which, admittedly, constitute a small portion of the cases that have been decided in the world,[615] have been important to guide my analysis of the two dimensions of violence as conceived in this book. The two dimensions are different in nature, but at the same time they share some key aspects: the effects on women's rights to health and to reproductive health, the fact that violence is grounded in the stereotyped role of women in society and the responsibility of states for directly or indirectly causing violence, or for 'tolerating' and not preventing interpersonal violence.

As for the actor starting the proceedings, I noticed that, varying with the type of complaint, the applicants were women subjected to violence, victims' relatives, associations representing women's interests, an Ombudsperson, the alleged perpetrators of an offence, or professionals providing health services for women. As anticipated in the introduction, I am not considering the women involved as 'patients' in a very simplistic way, but rather as victims/survivors and as agents of change who, by filing complaints with national or international fora, contribute to the evolution and the protection of women's rights. Agents of change can include a victim's relatives, or the associations that file complaints on behalf of women, giving them voice and an instrument for seeking redress.

As highlighted throughout this chapter, the right to health and the right to reproductive health have not always entered the legal reasoning of the courts and the UN treaty bodies. This is not because the importance of these rights is minor, but rather attributable to the intrinsic limits on the competence of the judiciary and quasi-judicial bodies. The health of women who endure and/or survive violence has been taken into consideration in many proceedings without implying the direct application of the rights to health and reproductive health, which, as I will demonstrate, means that the content of these rights has been indirectly promoted by applying other rights enshrined in the relevant legal instrument.

In few cases have the reparations awarded by judicial and quasi-judicial bodies been innovative. The innovation brought by some judgments and decisions was, nonetheless, ground-breaking. Beyond monetary compensation, as I will argue further, reparations must include measures that disrupt the underlying causes of violence in the two dimensions that are theorised in this book. In some judgments, reparations were not even an issue, because of the nature of the proceedings that, for example, challenged the constitutional legitimacy of a provision of the law.

I will now turn to the identification of the 'illness' in its diagnosis, conceptualising the new idea of VAWH, and I will discuss states' obligations in chapter 3.

Notes

1 Leavy, *The Psychoanalytic Dialogue,* p. 8.
2 J. Felson Duchan, 'The social construction of relationships in healing interactions from ancient times to the present', in R.J. Fourie (ed.), *Therapeutic Processes for Communication Disorders* (Hove and New York: Taylor and Francis, 2011) 153, p. 157.
3 See this distinction in Sir Nigel Rodley, 'International human rights law', in M.D. Evans (ed.), *International Law* (Oxford: Oxford University Press, 2018) 774, pp. 784, 785. However, the author conceived the vertical dimension as one in which the state is directly responsible and the horizontal as describing when it is indirectly responsible for acts committed by private persons or entities. My understanding is slightly different and is crucial to the analysis of the relationship as conceptualised in my book.
4 Available at www.who.int/violenceprevention/approach/definition/en/.
5 C. Chinkin, 'Gender and economic, social, and cultural rights', in E. Riedel, G. Giacca and C. Golay (eds), *Economic, Social, and Cultural Rights in International Law* (Oxford: Oxford University Press, 2014) 134, p. 144.
6 UN Commission on Human Rights, preliminary report submitted by the SR on VAW, Ms Radhika Coomaraswamy, E/CN.4/1995/42, 22 November 1994, para. 117*ff.* See also M. Schuler, *Freedom from Violence: Women's Strategies from around the World* (New York: UNIFEM, 1992), p. 14.
7 Sterilisation can be forced (physically compelled), coerced (under circumstances that compel women) or compulsory (provided by law). See R. Sifris, *Reproductive Freedom, Torture and International Human Rights* (London: Routledge, 2014), p. 5.
8 On the ethical aspects, see R.C. Cook, B.M. Dickens, C. Ngwena and M.I. Plata, 'The legal status of emergency contraception', *International Journal of Gynecology & Obstetrics* 75 (2001) 185.
9 See, among others, WHO, *Safe Abortion: Technical and Policy Guidance for Health Systems* (Geneva: World Health Organization, 2012); R. Cook, J.N. Erdman and B.M. Dickens (eds), *Abortion Law in Transnational Perspective: Cases and Controversies* (Philadelphia: University of Pennsylvania Press, 2014); R.J. Cook and D.M. Dickens, 'Human rights and abortion laws', *International Journal of Gynecology & Obstetrics* 65 (1999) 81; R.J. Cook, 'Abortion laws', in L. Breslow, *Encyclopedia of Public Health* (New York and Detroit: Macmillan Reference USA, 2002) 5; C. Zampas

and J.M. Gher, 'Abortion as human right – international and regional standards', *Oxford Human Rights Law Review* 8 (2008) 249; R. Sifris, 'Restrictive regulation of abortion and the right to health', *Medical Law Review* 18 (2010) 185; C.G. Ngwena, 'Inscribing abortion as a human right: significance of the Protocol on the Rights of Women in Africa', *Human Rights Quarterly* 32 (2010) 783; R.C Cook and B.M. Dickens, 'Upholding pregnant women's right to life', *International Journal of Gynecology & Obstetrics* 117 (2012) 90; R.C. Cook and M.F. Fathalla, 'Women, abortion and the new technical and policy guidance from WHO', *Bulletin of the World Health Organization* 90 (2012) 712.

10 P. Abrams, 'Bad mothers: stigma, abortion, and surrogacy', *Journal of Law, Medicine & Ethics* 43 (2015) 179, p. 185.

11 R.J. Cook and C.G. Ngwena, 'Women's access to health care: the legal framework', *International Journal of Gynecology and Obstetrics* 94 (2006) 216.

12 Statement of the WHO, 2014, available at http://apps.who.int/iris/bitstream/10665/134588/1/WHO_RHR_14.23_eng.pdf.

13 See further, chapter 2, 'Consent and autonomy in the vertical dimension'.

14 M.M. Dempsey, *Prosecuting Domestic Violence: A Philosophical Analysis* (Oxford: Oxford University Press, 2009), p. 116.

15 Dempsey, *Prosecuting Domestic Violence*, p. 115.

16 Meyersfeld, *Domestic Violence*, p. 106.

17 Meyersfeld, *Domestic Violence*, p. 111.

18 A/RES/48/104, Article 1.

19 UN GA Resolution No. 58/147, UN Doc. A/RES/58 (19 February 2004), para. 1.

20 Resolution No. 58/147, para. 1.

21 Resolution No. 58/147, para. 1.

22 Resolution No. 58/147, para. 4.

23 UN GA Resolution No. 71/170, UN Doc. A/RES/71/170 (7 February 2017), preamble.

24 J. Herring, 'The Istanbul Convention: is domestic violence abuse against women?', in G. Douglas, M. Murch and V. Stephens (eds), *International and National Perspectives on Child and Family Law* (Cambridge: Intersentia, 2018) 205, p. 209.

25 Cusack, 'Eliminating judicial stereotyping', p. 3.

26 Cusack, 'Eliminating judicial stereotyping', p. 23.

27 Article 572, Italian criminal code.

28 C. Pecorella and P. Farina, 'La risposta penale alla violenza domestica: un'indagine sulla prassi del tribunale di Milano in materia di maltrattamenti contro familiari e conviventi (Art. 572 cp)', *Diritto penale contemporaneo* 1 (2018) 11, p. 24.

29 See, for example, *Angela González Carreño v. Spain* (n. 40 below and related text), and *Bălşan v. Romania* (n. 37 below and related text).

30 J. Caputi and D. Russell, 'Femicide: speaking the unspeakable', Sep/Oct 1990, in *MS Magazine* (published as 'Femicide, sexist terrorism against women', in D. Russell and J. Radford, *Femicide: The Politics of Woman Killing* (New York: Twayne Publishers, 1992). Femicide is considered to be 'on the extreme end of a continuum of anti-female terror that includes a wide variety of verbal and physical abuse … Whenever these forms of terrorism result in death, they become femicides.'

31 Views of 6 August 2007, *Fatma Yildirim v. Austria*, Communication No. 6/2005 and *Şahide Goekce*, Communication No. 5/2005 (both CEDAW).

32 Report of 16 April 2001, no. 54/01, case 12.051, *Maria da Penha Maia Fernandes v. Brazil* (IACommHR).

33 Judgment of 23 February 2016, Appl. No. 55354/11, *Civek v. Turkey* (ECtHR).

34 Views of 26 January 2005, *A.T. v. Hungary*, Communication No. 2/2003 (CEDAW).

35 Views of 15 October 2008, *V.K. v. Bulgaria*, Communication No. 20/2008 (CEDAW Committee).

36 Judgment of 26 March 2013, Appl. No. 33234/07, *Valiulienė v. Lithuania* (ECtHR).

37 Judgment of 23 May 2017, Appl. No. 49645/09, *Bălşan v. Romania* (ECtHR).

38 Report of 21 July 2011, case 12.626, *Lenahan (Gonzáles) et al. v. US* (IACommHR). *Cf.* R. McQuigg, 'Domestic violence and the Inter-American Commission on Human Rights: *Jessica Lenahan (Gonzáles) v. United States*', *Human Rights Law Review* 12 (2012) 1, and J. Koshan, 'State responsibility for protection against domestic violence: the Inter-American Commission on Human Rights decision in *Lenahan (Gonzáles)* and its application in Canada', *Windsor Yearbook of Access to Justice* 30 (2012) 39.

39 The entire story of the case is reported in E. Kate, 'A "supremer" court? How an unfavorable ruling in the Inter-American Commission on Human Rights should impact United States domestic violence jurisprudence', *Wisconsin International Law Journal* 28:3 (2010–11) 430, pp. 435–7, and C. Bettinger-Lopez, '*Jessica Lenahan (Gonzáles) v. United States of America*: implementation, litigation, and mobilization strategies', *Journal of Gender, Social Policy & the Law* 21 (2013) 207.

40 Views of 16 July 2014, Communication No. 47/2012, *Angela González Carreño v. Spain* (CEDAW).

41 Judgment of 2 March 2017, Appl. No. 41237/14, *Elisaveta Talpis v. Italy* (ECtHR). See the details of the case and the legal analysis in S. De Vido, 'States' positive obligations to eradicate domestic violence: the politics of relevance in the interpretation of the European Convention on Human Rights', *ESIL Reflection* 6:6 (2017).

42 *Yildirim*, para 12.1.4. It is the 'immediacy test', discussed in chapter 3, 'Methodology for the treatment'.

43 *Yildirim*, para. 12.1.5, and 12.3.

44 *Da Penha*, para. 47.

45 *Da Penha*, para. 58.

46 Judgment of 28 October 1998, Appl. No. 23452/94, *Osman v. United Kingdom.*

47 *Osman*, para. 116.

48 *Civek*, para. 48.

49 *Civek*, para. 50.

50 *Civek*, para. 50.

51 *Civek*, para. 57.

52 *Civek*, para. 20.

53 *Civek*, para. 50.

54 *A.T.*, para. 9.3.

55 *A.T.*, para. 9.4.

56 *V.K.*, para. 9.8.

57 *V.K.*, para. 9.12. On the fact that authorities often consider DV a private matter, see ECtHR, judgment of 12 June 2008, Appl. No. 71127/01, *Bevacqua and S. v. Bulgaria.*

58 *V.K.*, para. 9.14.

59 *Valiulienė*, para. 68.
60 See, in that sense, De Vido, *Donne, Violenza*, p. 67*ff*.
61 On the lack of coherence of the ECtHR jurisprudence concerning DV, see R. McQuigg, 'The European Court of Human Rights and domestic violence: *Valiulienė v. Lithuania', International Journal of Human Rights* 18 (2014) 756.
62 *V.K.*, concurring opinion of Judge De Albuquerque.
63 *Bălşan*, para. 60.
64 *Bălşan*, para. 57.
65 *Bălşan*, para. 66.
66 *Bălşan*, para. 85.
67 *Lenahan (Gonzáles) et al.*, para. 66.
68 *Lenahan (Gonzáles) et al.*, para. 129.
69 *Lenahan (Gonzáles) et al.*, para. 141.
70 *Lenahan (Gonzáles) et al.*, para. 161.
71 See the analysis in De Vido, 'States' due diligence obligations', and below, chapter 3, ' … in particular the positive obligation of due diligence'.
72 *Lenahan (Gonzáles) et al.*, para. 199.
73 *González Carreño*, para. 9.4. See also the *amicus curiae* brief prepared by S. Cusack, 2 February 2014, available at www.womenslinkworldwide.org/files/gjo_amicus_brief_Simone_Cusack_angelagonzalez_en.pdf, para. 17: 'it is essential that gender stereotyping does not lead authorities to prioritise the visitation and custody rights of male perpetrators over the rights of women and their children to life and physical and mental integrity.'
74 *González Carreño*, para. 9.5.
75 *González Carreño*, para. 9.8.
76 *González Carreño*, para. 9.8.
77 Judgment of 9 June 2009, *Opuz v. Turkey*, Appl. No. 33401/02, para. 127.
78 *Talpis*, para. 30.
79 See, in more detail, De Vido, 'States' positive obligations'.
80 See, among others, M. Evans and S. Konstadinides (eds), *Remedies in International Law: The Institutional Dilemma* (Oxford: Hart, 1998); C. Gray, *Judicial Remedies in International Law* (Oxford: Clarendon, 1987); D. Shelton, *Remedies in International Human Rights Law* (Oxford: Oxford University Press, 2nd edn, 2005); G. Bartolini, *Riparazione per violazione dei diritti umani e ordinamento internazionale* (Naples: Jovene, 2009).
81 GR No. 33, 'Women's access to justice', CEDAW/C/GC/33 (CEDAW Committee), 23 July 2015.
82 *Yildirim*, para. 12.3.
83 *Yildirim*, para. 12.3.
84 *A.T.*, p. 13, I.
85 *A.T.*, p. 13, II. The reasoning is similar in *V.K.*, para. 9.16, although in the latter there was no reference to the measures being proportional to the physical and mental harm suffered by V.K.
86 *González Carreño*, para. 11.
87 STS (Contencioso-Administrativo) de 17 de julio 2018, Rec. de Casación núm. 1002/2017, p. 28. See, in that respect, www.ohchr.org/SP/NewsEvents/Pages/DisplayNews.aspx?NewsID=23849&LangID=S.

88 *Da Penha*, para. 61. See also IACommHR, 'Legal standards related to gender equality and women's rights in the InterAmerican human rights system: development and application updates from 2011 to 2014', 2015, para. 24.
89 Law no. 1134/2006, also known as the Maria da Penha Law, entered into force on 22 September 2006.
90 *Lenahan (Gonzáles) et al.*, para. 201.
91 *Opuz*, para. 210.
92 *Valiulienė*, para. 91.
93 *Bălşan*, para. 93.
94 *Bălşan*, para. 88.
95 *Civek*, para. 74.
96 African Commission's guidelines on combating sexual violence and its consequences, May 2017, p. 14. Available at www.achpr.org/files/instruments/combating-sexual-violence/achpr_eng_guidelines_on_combating_sexual_violence_and_its_consequences.pdf.
97 M. Sjöholm, *Gender-Sensitive Norm Interpretation by Regional Human Rights Law Systems* (Leiden, Boston, MA: Brill, 2018), p. 229.
98 Report of CEDAW to the General Assembly (A/57/38), 2004, paras 333–4, referring to Hungary; Report of CEDAW to the General Assembly (A/67/38), 2012, p. 31.
99 Judgment of 4 December 2003, Application no. 39272/98, *M.C. v. Bulgaria*, para. 159.
100 *M.C.*, para. 166.
101 Sjöholm, *Gender-Sensitive Norm Interpretation*, p. 287.
102 Judgment of 17 January 2012, Appl. No. 12294/07, *Zontul v. Greece* (ECtHR).
103 V. Munro, 'Sexual autonomy', in M.D. Dubber and T. Hörnle, *The Oxford Handbook of Criminal Law* (Oxford: Oxford University Press, 2014) 747, p. 753.
104 SR on VAW, Report of 12 February 1997, E-CN.4–1997–47, para. 36.
105 Brownmiller, *Against our Will*, p. 18.
106 R.J. Cook and S. Cusack, *Gender Stereotyping* (Philadelphia: University of Pennsylvania Press, 2011), p. 27, and M. Eriksson, *Defining Rape: Emerging Obligations for States under International Law?* (Leiden, Boston, MA: Martinus Nijoff, 2011), p. 37.
107 See also C. McGlynn, 'Rape as "torture"? Catharine Mackinnon and questions of feminist strategy', *Feminist Legal Studies* 16 (2008) 71, pp. 80–1.
108 Eriksson, *Defining Rape*, p. 124.
109 See, among a huge *corpus* on the issue, T. Meron, 'Rape as a crime under international humanitarian law', *American Journal of International Law* 87 (1993) 424; C. Chinkin, 'Rape and sexual abuse of women in international law', *European Journal of International Law* 5 (1994) 326; A. Healey, 'Prosecuting rape under the statute of the War Crimes Tribunal for the Former Yugoslavia', *Brooklyn Journal of International Law* 21 (1995) 327; F. Londras, 'Prosecuting sexual violence in the ad hoc international criminal tribunals for Rwanda and the former Yugoslavia', in M. Albertson Fineman (ed.), *Transcending the Boundaries of Law* (Abingdon: Routledge, 2011) 290, p. 295; and K.D. Askin, 'Crimes against women under international criminal law', in B.S Brown (ed.), *Research Handbook on International Criminal Law* (Cheltenham: Elgar, 2011) 85. See also S. De Vido, 'Collective memory of rape', *Sociologia del diritto* 3 (2016) 101, and references therein.

110 Eriksson, *Defining Rape*, p. 124.
111 T. Bryant-Devis, S. Tillman and P.A. Counts, 'Sexual assault: a matter of reproductive justice', in J.C. Chrisler (ed.), *Reproductive Justice: A Global Concern* (Santa Barbara, CA, Denver, CO, Oxford: Praeger, 2018) 77, pp. 81–3.
112 D. Russell, *Rape in Marriage* (New York: Macmillan, 1982), p. 261.
113 Equality Now, 'The Global Rape Epidemic', 2017, p. 26. Available at https://www.equalitynow.org/the_global_rape_epidemic_campaign.
114 See http://wbl.worldbank.org/data/exploretopics/protecting-women-from-violence.
115 S. Fredman, *Discrimination Law* (Oxford: Oxford University Press, 2011), p. 39.
116 Cassazione penale, judgment of 16 February 1976, no. 12855. Law 5 August 1981, n. 442, GU no. 218 of 10 August 1981.
117 Lord Hale, *Historia placitorum coronæ* (*The history of the Pleas of the Crown*), in the Savoy London, printed by E.R. Nutt, R. Gosling, 1736, pp. 628–9.
118 Law Commission No. 205, HC 167.
119 [1991] 2 WLR 1065, 1074 B–C.
120 R. Augustine, 'Marriage: the safe haven for rapists', *Journal of Family Law* 29 (1990–91) 559. See also S.A. Adamo, 'The injustice of the marital rape exemption: a survey of common law countries', *American University International Law Review* 4 (1989) 555; J.E. Hasday, 'Contest and consent: a legal history of marital rape', *California Law Review* 88 (2000) 1373. On the evolution of US legislation, see the in-depth analysis by M. Anderson, 'Marital immunity, intimate relationships, and improper inferences: a new law on sexual offenses by intimates', *Hastings Law Journal* 54 (2003) 1463.
121 M. Randall and V. Venkatesh, 'The right to no: the crime of marital rape, women's human rights, and international law', *Brooklyn Journal of International Law* 41 (2015) 153, p. 155.
122 The CEDAW Committee has repeatedly encouraged countries to criminalise marital rape. See, for example, 'Concluding observations on India', CEDAW/C/IND/CO/3 (2 February 2007), and on Indonesia, CEDAW/C/IDN/CO/6–7 (7 August 2012).
123 Judgments of 22 November 1995, *C.R. v. United Kingdom*, Appl. No. 20190/92, and *S.W. v. United Kingdom*, Appl. no. 20166/92 (ECtHR). See Eriksson, *Defining Rape*, p. 163.
124 Supreme Court Special Bench, Order Writ No. 55 of the year 2058 BS (2001–2), *on behalf of the Forum for Women, Law and Development, Thapathali, ward No. 11 of Kathmandu Municipal Corporation and on her own, Advocate Meera Dhungana, 33 v. His Majesty's Government, Ministry of Law, Justice and Parliamentary Affairs*, The House of Representatives, The National Assembly, available in English here www.globalhealthrights.org/wp-content/uploads/2013/10/The-Forum-for-Women-Law-and-Development-Nepal-2002.pdf.
125 K. Yllö, 'Prologue', in Yllö and Torres, *Marital Rape*, 1, p. 2. In India, exception 1 to Section 375 of the Indian Penal Code states: 'Sexual intercourse or sexual acts by a man with his own wife, the wife not being under fifteen years of age, is not rape.' The exception to marital rape was considered as inapplicable to minor wives by the Supreme Court in *Independent Thought v. Union of India*, Writ Petition (Civil) No. 382 of 2013, 11 October 2017 (Judge Gupta) – summary and comment at https://reproductiverights.org/sites/default/files/documents/Independent-Thought-Factsheet-0118.pdf.

126 In the High Court of Gujarat at Ahmedabad, R/Criminal Misc., Application No. 26957 of 2017, 2 April 2018, Mr Justice J.B. Pardiwala, para. 130.7 – summary and comment can be found at this website on Indian law, https://indiankanoon.org/doc/185050052/

127 Draft Articles on State Responsibility for internationally wrongful acts, Article 4.

128 Report of 1 March 1996, case no. 10.970, final no. 5/96, *Raquel Martín de Mejía v. Peru.*

129 Judgment of 24 November 2009 (IACHR). See also the judgment of the IACHR in the case *Gladys Carol Espinoza Gonzáles v. Peru*, 20 November 2014 (details on vawh.wordpress.com).

130 Judgment of 30 August 2010, *Fernández Ortega et al. v. Mexico* (IACHR).

131 *Fernández Ortega*, para. 115.

132 Case 12.846, *Mariana Selvas Gomez et al. v. Mexico (Atenco)* (IACommHR).

133 Judgment of 28 November 2018, *Mujeres Víctimas de Tortura Sexual en Atenco v. Mexico* (IACHR). A first comment appears in D. Kravetz, 'Holding states to account for gender-based violence: the Inter-American Court Of Human Rights' decisions in *López Soto v. Venezuela* and *Women Victims of Sexual Torture in Atenco v. Mexico*', EJIL Talks! 21 January 2019, available at www.ejiltalk.org/holding-states-to-account-for-gender-based-violence-the-inter-american-court-of-human-rights-decisions-in-lopez-soto-vs-venezuela-and-women-victims-of-sexual-torture-in-atenco-vs-mexico/.

134 Judgment of 25 September 1997, Appl. No. 57/1996/676/866, *Şükran Aydin v. Turkey.*

135 Report of 9 March 2007, No. 28/07, *González et al. ('Cotton Field') v. Mexico* (IACommHR).

136 K. Tiroch, 'Violence against women by private actors: the Interamerican Court's judgment in the case of *Gonzales et al. (Cotton Field) v. Mexico*', *Max Planck Yearbook of United Nations Law* 14 (2001) 371.

137 Report of 29 July 2016, No. 33/16, case no. 12.797, *Linda Loaiza López Soto and relatives v. Venezuela.*

138 Judgment of 26 September 2018, *Linda Loaiza López Soto y otros v. Venezuela* (IACtHR).

139 Communication 341/2007, *Equality Now and Ethiopian Women Lawyers Association (EWLA) v. Federal Republic of Ethiopia* (African Commission on Human and Peoples' Rights during the 19th Extra-Ordinary Session, from 16 to 25 February 2016). Available at www.escr-net.org/caselaw/2016/equality-now-and-ethiopian-women-lawyers-association-ewla-v-federal-republic-ethiopia.

140 In national law, violation of a woman's right to health did play a role in some ancient judgments in Australia, which challenged Lord Hale's affirmation. An analysis is provided on vawh.wordpress.com.

141 *Forum for Women, Law and Development*, p. 7.

142 *Forum for Women, Law and Development*, p. 7.

143 *Forum for Women, Law and Development*, p. 11.

144 *Forum for Women, Law and Development*, p. 11.

145 *Forum for Women, Law and Development*, p. 12.

146 *Forum for Women, Law and Development*, p. 12.

147 Appl. No. 26957, para. 130.7.

148 Appl. No. 26957, para. 114.
149 Appl. No. 26957, para. 130.2.
150 *Martín de Mejía*, p. 18.
151 *Martín de Mejía*, p. 19.
152 In the case *Ana, Beatriz and Celia González Pérez v. Mexico*, case no. 11.565, Report No. 53/01, IACommHR (2001), para. 52, the right to health was not expressly mentioned in the Commission report; however, the abuses which targeted 'the physical, mental and moral integrity of the three sisters' collectively demonstrated that this was a case of torture.
153 *Fernández Ortega*, para. 118.
154 *Fernández Ortega*, para. 124.
155 *Fernández Ortega*, para. 115.
156 *Fernández Ortega*, para. 115.
157 *Fernández Ortega*, para. 190.
158 *Fernández Ortega*, para. 190.
159 *Fernández Ortega*, para. 200.
160 Judgment of 24 November 2009, *Las Dos Erres Massacre v. Guatemala* (IACHR), para. 139.
161 Judgment of 19 November 2004, *Plan de Sánchez Massacre v. Guatemala*, Reparations and Costs (IACHR).
162 *Plan de Sánchez*, para. 49.19.
163 *Mujeres Víctimas (Atenco)*, para. 198.
164 *Mujeres Víctimas (Atenco)*, para. 179.
165 *Mujeres Víctimas (Atenco)*, para. 179.
166 *Mujeres Víctimas (Atenco)*, para. 208.
167 *Mujeres Víctimas (Atenco)*, paras 211*ff.*, and 270*ff.*
168 *Aydin*, para. 84.
169 *Aydin*, para. 84.
170 *Aydin*, para. 86.
171 *M.C.*, para. 182.
172 Judge Quiroga's opinion in *M.C.*, in particular para. 2 of it.
173 *Loaiza López* (IACommHR), para. 13.
174 *Loaiza López* (IACommHR), para. 199.
175 Submitted to the United Nations High Commissioner for Human Rights 9 August 1999: available at www.ohchr.org/Documents/Publications/training8Rev1en.pdf.
176 *Loaiza López* (IACommHR), para. 203.
177 *Loaiza López* (IACommHR), para. 224.
178 *Loaiza López* (IACommHR), para. 213.
179 *Loaiza López* (IACommHR), para. 219.
180 Another case pending before the IACommHR is *Brisa Liliana De Angulo Losada v. Bolivia* (Report no. 25/17, Petition 86–12, admissibility), which was considered admissible on 18 March 2017 (see details and update on vawh.wordpress.com).
181 *Loaiza López* (IACHR), para. 124.
182 *Loaiza López* (IACHR), para. 136. See further in chapter 3, 'Positive obligations of due diligence in specific cases: to investigate without delay'.
183 Kravetz, 'Holding states'.
184 *Loaiza López* (IACHR), para. 180.

185 *Loaiza López* (IACHR), para. 121.
186 *Equality Now*, para. 107.
187 *Equality Now*, para. 120.
188 *Equality Now*, para. 120.
189 *Equality Now*, para. 126.
190 *Equality Now*, para. 149.
191 See, for example, in the cases *Martín de Mejía*; *González Pérez*; *Fernández Ortega*; *Las Dos Erres*.
192 *Cotton Field*, para. 549. In 2013, the Court left open the mechanism by which the state might comply with its obligation to provide free medical, psychological and psychiatric support to the relatives of the victims (Resolución de la Corte Interamericana De Derechos Humanos de 21 de mayo de 2013, *Caso González y otras ('Campo Algodonero') v. México*, Supervisión de Cumplimiento de Sentencia). See also chapter 3, 'Positive obligations of result: to provide effective remedies'.
193 *Fernández Ortega*, para. 293.
194 *Fernández Ortega*, para. 251. Medical treatment was granted by the state (Resolución de la Corte).
195 *Mujeres Víctimas (Atenco)*, para. 341.
196 *Mujeres Víctimas (Atenco)*, para. 376. Similar reasoning is found in *Loaiza López* (IACHR), para. 293 (medical treatment). Interestingly, the Court ordered the state to pay for López Soto's and her sister's education, given the fact that the violence they had experienced permanently affected her future. It also ordered the state to set up, reasonably promptly, the tribunals on violence against women as envisaged in the Ley de Reforma de la Ley Orgánica sobre el Derecho de las Mujeres a una Vida Libre de Violencia, *Gaceta Oficial* No. 40.548, 25 November 2014, Articles 119–20.
197 *Aydin*, para. 131.
198 *Equality Now*, para. 153.
199 *Equality Now*, para. 158.
200 Cook *et al.*, *Reproductive Health*, p. 265. See also P. Levitt and S.E. Merry, 'Making women's human rights in the vernacular: navigating the culture/rights divide', in D. Hodgson (ed.), *Gender and Culture at the Limits of Rights* (Philadelphia: University of Pennsylvania Press, 2011) 81, p. 86, and G.C. Denniston, F.M. Hodges and M. Fayre Milos (eds), *Genital Cutting: Protecting Children from Medical, Cultural, and Religious Infringements* (Dordrecht, Heidelberg, New York, London: Springer, 2013), discussing the harm caused to boys by male circumcision.
201 Available at https://www.who.int/en/news-room/fact-sheets/detail/female-genital-mutilation.
202 Available at www.who.int/reproductivehealth/topics/fgm/overview/en.
203 N. Toubia, 'Female genital mutilation and the responsibility of reproductive health professionals', *International Journal of Gynecology & Obstetrics* 46 (1994) 127.
204 Infibulation derives from *fibula*. V. Marotta, 'Politica imperiale e culture periferiche nel mondo romano: il problema della circoncisione', *Index* XII (1982/84) 405.
205 Available at www.unicef.org/media/files/FGMC_2016_brochure_final_UNICEF_SPREAD.pdf.
206 Available at http://digital.nhs.uk/catalogue/PUB23494.
207 On the legislation in Africa, see, extensively, D. Scolart, 'Quando il diritto affronta le tradizioni culturali: le mutilazioni genitali femminili e la violenza contro le donne',

in S. Angioi, M. Lanna, C. Mariconda, G. Palermo and D. Scolart (eds), *Donne violate. Un'analisi interdisciplinare della violenza contro le donne* (Naples: Cuam University Press, 2014) 241.

208 See also the recent report of the Council of Europe Steering Committee for Human Rights, 'Female genital mutilation and forced marriage' (Strasbourg, August 2018).

209 R. Cook, B.M. Dickens and M.F. Fathalla, 'Female genital cutting (mutilation/circumcision): ethical and legal dimensions', *International Journal of Gynecology and Obstetrics* 79 (2002) 281, p. 283, Toubia, 'Female genital mutilation', p. 128.

210 GR No. 14, ninth session, 'Female circumcision' (1990).

211 Report of the SR Manfred Nowak, 15 January 2008, A/HRC/7/3, para. 53. See also GR No. 14 of the CEDAW Committee, 1 February 1990, in which the UN body stated that the practice is harmful to the health of women and children.

212 L. Pineschi, 'Cultural diversity as a human right? General Comment No. 21 of the Committee on Economic, Social and Cultural Rights', in S. Borelli and F. Lenzerini (eds), *Cultural Heritage, Cultural Rights, Cultural Diversity* (Leiden: Martinus Nijhoff Publishers, 2012) 29, p. 36.

213 GC No. 21, para. 64.

214 S. De Vido, 'Culturally motivated crimes against women in a multicultural Europe. The case of criminalization of FGM in the 2011 CoE Istanbul Convention', in L. Zagato and M. Vecco (eds), *Citizens of Europe* (Venice: Ca' Foscari Digital Publishing, 2015), available at https://edizionicafoscari.unive.it/it/edizioni/libri/978–88–6969–054–9/culturally-motivated-crimes-against-women-in-a-mul/), p. 93.

215 African Parliamentary Conference, 'Violence against women, abandoning female genital mutilation: the role of national parliaments'. Dakar, Senegal, 4 and 5 December 2005.

216 'FIGO reaffirms support for 2017's International Day of Zero Tolerance to Female Genital Mutilation (6 February 2017)', available at www.figo.org/sites/default/files/uploads/News/FIGO%20reaffirms%20support%20for%20FGM%20Day%20 2017_6.pdf.

217 De Vido, 'Culturally motivated crimes'. See also S. Engle Merry, *Human Rights and Gender Violence: Translating International Law into Local Justice* (Chicago and London: University of Chicago Press, 2006), p. 9.

218 As for consent to re-infibulation, the situation is far more complex than it seems. Even though the practice might have an impact on the woman's health, re-infibulation can be based on her (genuine and free) consent – but not if she is a minor. See further in chapter 2, 'Consent and autonomy in the horizontal dimension: FGM/C'.

219 Report of the SR Coomaraswamy 2013, p. 132. On the effects of the practice, many reports have been adopted. See, for example, E. Vloeberghs, *Veiled Pain: A study in the Netherlands on the psychological, social and relational consequences of female genital mutilation* (Utrecht: Pharos, 2011).

220 *Law and Advocacy for Women in Uganda v. Attorney-General* [2010] UGCC 4; Constitutional Petition No. 8 of 2007, 28 July 2010.

221 *Emberá-Chamí Community FGM Case*, Juzgado Promiscuo Municipal [Municipal Jurisdiction Court], 24 July 2008, Radicación No. 66572–40–89–001–2008–00005–00 (Colom.). Translation available at www.globalhealthrights.org/wp-content/uploads/2013/08/Translation-Caso_Risaralda_Mutilacipn_Genital_Femenina_Colombia.pdf.

222 See, for an analysis, a report prepared for the European Commission: S. Johnsdotter and R.M. Mestre i Mestre, 'FGM in Europe: an analysis of court cases' (Brussels, 2015), and, by the same authors, 'Female genital mutilation in Europe: public discourse *versus* empirical evidence', *International Journal of Law, Crime and Justice* 51 (2017) 14, p. 17. See further on vawh.wordpress.com.

223 Available at www.cps.gov.uk/legal-guidance/female-genital-mutilation-legal-guidance.

224 FGM/C can be treated as a crime under Articles 222(1), 222(3) and 222(5) code pénal (Criminal code) (acts of torture and barbarity), and Articles 222(9) and 222(10) (bodily harm causing permanent infirmity or mutilation). Committing the offence against a minor is considered an aggravating circumstance that increases the penalty.

225 Cour de Cassation, chambre criminelle, No. de pourvoi: 83-92616, 20 August 1983.

226 In Italy, Law no. 7 of 9 January 2006 introduced the offence in Art. 583*bis* of the criminal code. For a detailed analysis, see De Vido, 'Culturally motivated crimes'.

227 Tribunale di Verona, 14 April 2010, No. 279, and Court of Appeal in Venice, 23 November 2012 (dep. 21 February 2013), No. 1485.

228 *R v. A2*; *R v. K.M.*; *R v. Vaziri (No. 2)* [2015] NSWSC 1221 (27 August 2015).

229 UN High Commissioner for Refugees (UNHCR), 'Female genital mutilation and asylum in the European Union. A statistical update', March 2014, p. 3.

230 UNHCR, *Too Much Pain*, February 2013, available at www.unhcr.org/protection/women/531880249/pain-female-genital-mutilation-asylum-european-union-statistical-overview.html.

231 See, extensively, S. De Vido, 'Escaping violence: the Istanbul Convention and violence against women as a form of persecution', in G.C. Bruno, F. Palombino and A. Di Stefano (eds), *Migration Issues before International Courts and Tribunals* (Rome: National Research Council of Italy, forthcoming, open access). The cases under analysis are: Decision on admissibility of 8 March 2007, Application no. 23994/05, *Collins and Akaziebie v. Sweden*; Decision on admissibility of 17 May 2011, Application no. 43408/08, *Enitan Pamela Izevbekhai and others v. Ireland*, and Decision on admissibility of 20 September 2011, Application no. 8969/10, *Mary Magdalene Omeredo v. Austria*. The Court of Justice of the European Union has never dealt directly with cases of FGM. See, however, vawh.wordpress.com for an analysis of Joined Cases C-71/11 and C-99/11, *Federal Republic of Germany v. Y* (C-71/11), *Z* (C-99/11). The ECtHR found two other cases admissible, but did not conclude that there had been a violation of the applicants' rights: Judgment of 7 June 2016, Application no. 7211/06, *R.B.A.B. and others v. The Netherlands*, and judgment of 19 January 2016, Application no. 27081/13, *Sow v. Belgium* (ECtHR). See also a similar case, decided as inadmissible by the CEDAW Committee, *M.N.N. v. Denmark*, Communication No. 33/2011, 15 July 2013.

232 Court of Appeal, *Zainab Esther Fornah v. Secretary of State for the Home Department* [2005] EWCA Civ 680, 9 June 2005, para. 44.

233 *Mohamed v. R. Gonzales* [2005] USCA9 150; 400 F.3d 785 (10 March 2005).

234 *Mohamed v. Gonzales*, para. 7.

235 Corte d'appello di Catania, Sez. della Famiglia della Persona e dei Minori, *A.F. v. Ministro dell'Interno*, dep. 17 December 2012.

236 *Law and Advocacy for Women in Uganda*, p. 20.

237 Provision XIV, Constitution of the Republic of Uganda, 1995, available at https://ulii.org/node/23824.
238 *Emberá-Chamí Community*, Judgment T-349 of 1996, quoted at para. 3.5.
239 *Emberá-Chamí Community*, p. 18.
240 *Emberá-Chamí Community*, p. 21.
241 *Emberá-Chamí Community*, p. 26.
242 *Emberá-Chamí Community*, p. 26.
243 For an account of the Italian cases, see extensively De Vido, 'Culturally motivated crimes'.
244 *R v. A2*; *R v. K.M.*; *R v. Vaziri (No. 2)* [2015] NSWSC 1221 (27 August 2015), para. 255.
245 *R v. A2; R v. K.M.; R v Vaziri (No. 23)* [2016] NSWSC 282 (18 March 2016). Comment by M. McLean, at www.hrlc.org.au/human-rights-case-summaries/three-convicted-and-sentenced-in-australias-first-female-genital-mutilation-trial.
246 *R v A2; R v KM; R v Vaziri (No. 23)*, para. 136.
247 J. Brough Rogers, 'The first case addressing female genital mutilation in Australia. Where is the harm?', *Alternative Law Journal* 4 (2017) 235.
248 See, extensively, S. De Vido, 'Escaping violence'.
249 House of Lords, *K. (F.C.), Fornah (F.C.) v. Secretary of State for the Home Department*, [2006] UKHL 46, 18 October 2006, para. 31.
250 Mestre and Johnsdotter, 'Female genital mutilation', p. 19.
251 *Mohamed v. Gonzales*, para. 25. See the report by Y. Kim, 'Female genital mutilation as persecution: when can it constitute a basis for asylum and withholding of removal?', CRS Report for Congress, 2008, p. 12, available at www.ilw.com/immigrationdaily/news/2009,1230-crs.pdf.
252 *Mohamed v. Gonzales*, para. 31.
253 *Mohamed v. Gonzales*, para. 31.
254 *Mohamed v. Gonzales*, para. 49.
255 See, in more detail, De Vido, 'Culturally-motivated crimes'.
256 Other similar cases are reported here: http://refugeelegalaidinformation.org/fgmc-case-law-and-other-legal-documents.
257 See a complete account of all the positions from a philosophical and legal point of view in K. Greasley, *Arguments about Abortion: Personhood, Morality, and Law* (Oxford: Oxford University Press, 2017); in a comparative perspective, Fredman, *Comparative Human Rights*, p. 187*ff*.
258 The 'gradualist' perspective tries to respond to the question whether or not the foetus has a moral status by acknowledging that 'at some point late in pregnancy, the foetus [deserves] the very strong moral protection due to newborns.' M.O. Little, 'Abortion and margins of personhood', *Rutgers Law Journal* 39 (2007–8) 331. See also Nelson, *Law, Policy*, p. 115.
259 Cook and Cusack, *Gender Stereotyping*, pp. 85–7, and R. Siegel, 'Reasoning from the body: a historical perspective on abortion regulations and questions of equal protection', *Stanford Law Review* 44 (1992) 262, p. 277.
260 See, *inter alia* in the philosophical scholarship, J.J. Thompson, 'A defense of abortion', *Philosophy and Public Affairs* 1 (1971) 47, and R.P. George and C. Tollefsen, *Embryo: A Defense of Human Life* (Princeton, NJ: Witherspoon Institute, 2nd edn, 2011). In detail, Greasley, *Arguments*.

261 G.T. Laurie, S.H.E. Harmon and G. Porter (eds), *Law and Medical Ethics* (Oxford: Oxford University Press, 10th edn, 2016), p. 322. There is a trend to accord protection to a foetus that is 'viable,' which means when it is capable of being born alive. The concept of viability originated in the USA (Laurie *et al.*, *Law and Medical Ethics*, p. 356).

262 The ECtHR has never taken a strong position in that respect. On the EU legal system, see N. Koffeman, *Morally Sensitive Issues and Cross-Border Movement in the EU* (Mortsel: Intersentia, 2015), p. 21.

263 A. Madrazo, 'Narratives of prenatal personhood in abortion law', in Cook *et al.*, *Abortion Law in Transnational Perspective*, 327, p. 344.

264 Sifris, *Reproductive Freedom*, p. 126.

265 R. Sifris and S. Belton, 'Australia: abortion and human rights', *Health and Human Rights Journal* 19 (2017) 209, p. 210.

266 Article 14(2)(c).

267 Ngwena, 'Inscribing abortion as a human right', p. 810.

268 See, for example, GC No. 22 ESCR Committee (2016), paras 10 and 34.

269 Cook, 'Stigmatized meanings of criminal abortion law', in Cook *et al.*, *Abortion Law in Transnational Perspective*, 347, p. 347.

270 A/HRC/32/44, para. 63.

271 A/HRC/32/44, para. 76.

272 See http://worldabortionlaws.com/ and the update database elaborated by WHO and UN, available at https://esa.un.org/gapp/.

273 J. Lemaitre, 'Catholic constitutionalism on sex, women, and the beginning of life', in Cook *et al.*, *Abortion Law in Transnational Perspective*, 239.

274 UN Department of Economic and Social Affairs, 'Abortion policies and reproductive health around the world' (New York: UN, 2014), p. 3.

275 For the evolution of Irish law see I. Bacik, 'Abortion and the law in Ireland', in A. Quilty, C. Conlon and S. Kennedy (eds), *The Abortion Papers Ireland: Volume 2* (Cork: Cork University Press, 2015) 104, and Fredman, *Comparative Human Rights*, p. 197.

276 No. 31 of 2018, available at https://data.oireachtas.ie/ie/oireachtas/act/2018/31/eng/enacted/a3118.pdf.

277 Center for Reproductive Rights, 'Marginalized, persecuted and imprisoned' (New York: 2014), p. 18, available at www.reproductiverights.org/sites/crr.civicactions.net/files/documents/El-Salvador-CriminalizationOfAbortion-Report.pdf.

278 UN Department of Economic and Social Affairs, 'Abortion policies', p. 3.

279 The Chilean law, passed by Congress in August 2017, decriminalises abortion if the life of the pregnant woman is at risk, if the pregnancy is the result of rape or if the foetus is not expected to survive due to severe impairment.

280 See G.K. Shapiro, 'Abortion law in Muslim-majority countries: an overview of the Islamic discourse with policy implications', *Health Policy and Planning* 29 (2014) 488.

281 R. Dabash and F. Roudi-Fahimi, 'Abortion in the Middle East and North Africa', Population Reference Bureau (2008), available at www.prb.org/pdf08/MENAabortion.pdf.

282 C.G. Ngwena, 'Conscientious objection to abortion and accommodating women's reproductive health rights: reflections on a decision of the Constitutional court of

Colombia from an African regional human rights perspective', *Journal of African Law* 58 (2014) 183, p. 187.

283 E. Brookman-Amissah and T. Kachika, 'Reducing abortion-related maternal mortality in Africa: progress in implementing objective 5 of the Maputo plan of action on sexual and reproductive health', in C. Ngwena and E. Durojaye (eds), *Strengthening the Protection of Sexual and Reproductive Health and Rights in the African Region through Human Rights* (Pretoria: Pretoria University Law Press, 2014) 31, p. 33.

284 Ngwena, 'Conscientious objection', p. 189.

285 For the USA, see 'Abortion hampered by obstacles to implementation of the law: Has the right to health been applied directly?' For Australia: Sifris and Belton, 'Australia', p. 211.

286 According to the Criminal Act (amended by Act No. 5057 of 29 December 1995), women who have abortions in South Korea can face up to a year in prison and can be fined up to 2 million won (US$1,780), while doctors or healthcare workers who help terminate a pregnancy can be jailed for up to two years. W. Kyu Sung, 'Abortion in South Korea: the law and the reality', *International Journal of Law, Policy and the Family* 26 (2012) 278. However, see note 312 and the text relating to it for the recent judgment of April 2019.

287 Forced abortion has been reported in Colombia, where the FARC obliged female combatants to undergo abortion in order to be able to continue fighting.

288 For a list of judgments see the bibliography prepared by the International Reproductive and Sexual Health Law Program Faculty of Law, University of Toronto, published here: https://reprohealthlaw.wordpress.com.

289 'IACHR urges all states to adopt comprehensive, immediate measures to respect and protect women's sexual and reproductive rights.' Press Release No. 165/17, 23 October 2017.

290 C-355/2006, 10 May 2006, expedientes D- 6122, 6123 y 6124 Demandas de inconstitucionalidad contra los Arts. 122, 123 (parcial), 124, modificados por el Art. 14 de la Ley 890 de 2004, y 32, numeral 7, de la ley 599 de 2000 Código Penal. See also Ngwena, 'Conscientious objection', p. 186.

291 A. Ruibal, 'Movement and counter-movement: a history of abortion law reform and the backlash in Colombia 2006–2014', *Reproductive Health Matters* 22 (2014) 42.

292 R. Cook, C-355/2006 foreword to a commentary on the case by Women's Link Worldwide, 2007, available at www.law.utoronto.ca/utfl_file/count/documents/reprohealth/colombia-2006-excerpts-english-trans.pdf, p. 10.

293 K.S. Rosenn, 'Recent important decisions by the Brazilian Supreme Court', *University of Miami Inter-American Law Review* 45 (2014) 297, p. 314.

294 B. Galli, 'Negative impacts of abortion criminalization in Brazil: systematic denial of women's reproductive autonomy and human rights', *University of Miami Law Review* 65 (2011) 969, p. 972.

295 D. Diniz, 'The architecture of a Constitutional case in three acts – anencephaly at the Brazilian Supreme Court', *Revista de Direito da Universidade de Brasília* 1 (2014) 155, p. 158.

296 Supremo Tribunal Federal, ADPF 54, 12 April 2012. Available at http://redir.stf.jus.br/paginadorpub/paginador.jsp?docTP=TP&docID=3707334.

297 L.R. Barroso, 'Bringing abortion into the Brazilian public debate: legal strategies for anencephalic pregnancy', in Cook *et al.*, *Abortion Law in Transnational Perspective*, 258, p. 259.

298 Diniz, 'The architecture', p. 163*ff.*

299 Rosenn, 'Recent important decisions', p. 316.

300 Supremo Tribunal Federal, *Habeas Corpus* 124.306, Rio de Janeiro, 29 November 2016. A first comparative comment in I-CONnect Symposium 'Five perspectives on the Brazilian abortion ruling', *International Journal of Constitutional Law* blog, 7 March 2017, at www.iconnectblog.com/2017/03/symposium-on-brazilian-abor tion-ruling-five-perspectives.

301 Judgment of 26 December 2000, *T., S. v. Gobierno de la Ciudad de Buenos Aires* (Tribunal Superior de la Ciudad Autónoma de Buenos Aires).

302 A. Januwalla, 'Human rights law and abortion in El Salvador', *Health and Human Rights Journal* blog (2016), available at www.hhrjournal.org/2016/08/human-rights-law-and-abortion-in-el-salvador/.

303 Some of their stories are included in the report of the Center for Reproductive Rights, 'Marginalized, persecuted and imprisoned'.

304 In March 2019, the Supreme Court of El Salvador commuted the 30-year sentences of three women who had been imprisoned for abortion convictions. They had already spent ten years in detention on aggravated homicide charges for allegedly having abortions.

305 Available at www.ijrcenter.org/2013/06/05/inter-american-court-issues-provision-al-measures-el-salvador-allows-caesarean-for-seriously-ill-pregnant-woman-de-nied-abortion/.

306 *Matter of B.* Provisional measures, order of 29 May 2013 (IACHR).

307 *Manuela y Familia v. El Salvador*, Report No. 29/17, case no. 424/12, 18 March 2017, OEA/Ser.L/V/II.161 (IACommHR). The case was referred by the Commission to the IACHR on 10 October 2019.

308 See further on vawh.wordpress.com.

309 *A.B.C. v. Ireland*, Appl. No. 25579/05, Judgment of 16 December 2010 (ECtHR).

310 *Amanda Jane Mellet v. Ireland*, CCPR/C/116/D/2324/2013 (HRC), 31 March 2016; *Siobhán Whelan v. Ireland*, CCPR/C/119/D/2425/2014 (HRC), 17 March 2017.

311 *Whelan*, para. 2.1.

312 헌재 2019. 4. 11. 2017헌바127, 영문판례집(2019), 1 [헌법불합치], [2017 Hun-Ba 127, 11 April 2019], English translation at http://search.ccourt.go.kr/ths/ep/selectThsEp0101List.do.

313 C-355/2006, p. 42.

314 C-355/2006, p. 42.

315 For a critique of the 'undue burden', see C.E. Borgmann, 'In abortion litigation, it's the facts that matter', *Harvard Law Review Forum* 127 (2014) 149.

316 C-355/2006, p. 53.

317 C-355/2006, p. 54.

318 Barroso, 'Bringing abortion', p. 275. The two dissenting judges contended that the foetuses were human lives.

319 Translation of this passage in Barroso, 'Bringing abortion', p. 275.

320 Barroso, 'Bringing abortion', p. 266.

321 On the challenges posed by this argument, see I.W. Sarlet, 'The Brazilian Supreme Court and the right to life – commentaries to the Court's decision on ADPF 54, regarding pregnancy interruption in cases of fetal anencephaly', *Revista de Direito da Universidade de Brasília* 1 (2014) 178, p. 190.
322 Rosenn, 'Recent important decisions', p. 318.
323 C. Collucci, 'Brazilian attorneys demand abortion rights for women infected with Zika', *British Medical Journal* (2016) 354, available at www.bmj.com/content/354/bmj.i4657.
324 A. Greenberg, 'Will the Zika virus enable a transplant of *Roe v. Wade* to Brazil?', *University of Miami Inter-American Law Review* 49 (2018) 51. The Court was supposed to hear the case on 22 May 2019, but it removed the case from the schedule and no new date has been fixed.
325 Supremo Tribunal Federal, 124.306, para. 29.
326 Supremo Tribunal Federal, 124.306, para. 22.
327 Supremo Tribunal Federal, 124.306, para. 25, author's translation.
328 C.-J. Chen, 'A progressive voice from the South', I-CONnect Symposium, available at www.iconnectblog.com/2017/03/symposium-on-brazilian-abortion-ruling-five-perspectives/.
329 P. Guimarães and S. Corrêa, 'Brazil: abortion rights at the Supreme Court', 11 April 2017, available at http://sxpolitics.org/abortion-rights-at-the-brazilian-supreme-court/16796.
330 Barroso, 'Bringing abortion', pp. 270–71.
331 'El Salvador: UN experts urge Congress to allow termination of pregnancy in specific circumstances', 8 May 2017, available at www.ohchr.org/EN/NewsEvents/Pages/DisplayNews.aspx?NewsID=21595&LangID=E.
332 *A.B.C.*, para. 222, citing Judgment of 8 July 2004, Appl. No. 53924/00, *Vo v. France* (ECtHR).
333 *A.B.C.*, para. 227.
334 *A.B.C.*, para. 231.
335 *A.B.C.*, para. 236.
336 B. Rainey, E. Wicks and C. Ovey, *Jacobs, White and Ovey, The European Convention on Human Rights* (Oxford: Oxford University Press, 6th edn, 2014), p. 399.
337 *Whelan*, paras. 7.3, 7.7. See, in that sense, Sifris, *Reproductive Freedom*, p. 126.
338 *Mellet*, para.7.3.
339 *Whelan*, para. 7.8.
340 *Whelan*, para. 7.9.
341 *Whelan*, para. 7.11. See, in that respect, the critical analysis by K. Sękowska-Kozłowska, 'A tough job: recognizing access to abortion as a matter of equality. A commentary on the views of the UN Human Rights Committee in the cases of *Mellet v. Ireland* and *Whelan v. Ireland', Reproductive Health Matters* 26:54 (2018) 25.
342 *Mellet*, para. 13.
343 *Whelan*, para. 19.
344 2017 *Hun-Ba* 127. Three judges contended that the Court should have argued in favour of simple unconstitutionality, while two dissenting judges argued that they could see no difference between a foetus and a person born alive.
345 C-355/2006, p. 61.
346 *Mellet,* para. 9.

347 M.R. Wicclair, *Conscientious Objection in Health Care. An Ethical Analysis* (Cambridge: Cambridge University Press, 2011).
348 Ngwena, 'Conscientious objection', p. 199.
349 E. Bribosia and I. Rorive, 'Seeking to square the circle. A sustainable conscientious objection in reproductive health care', in S. Mancini and M. Rosenfeld (eds), *The Conscience Wars* (Cambridge: Cambridge University Press, 2018) 392.
350 T-388/09, 28 May 2009, Colombian Constitutional Court, *En el proceso de revisión del fallo proferido por el Juzgado Segundo Penal del Circuito de la ciudad de Santa Marta*, reported at www.globalhealthrights.org/wp-content/uploads/2013/08/BB-OBO-AA-SaludCoop-E.P.S.-T-388-09.pdf. Ngwena, 'Conscientious objection', p. 186.
351 See *Janaway v. Salford Area Health Authority* [1988] 3 All ER 1079 (UKHL).
352 *Doogan v. Greater Glasgow and Clyde Health Board* [2015] UKSC 68.
353 GR No. 35, para. 24.
354 See the analysis also in M. Upreti, 'Towards transformative equality in Nepal: the *Lakshmi Dhikta* decision', in Cook *et al.*, *Abortion Law in Transnational Perspective*, 279. Summary and excerpts of the judgment are available at www.reproductiverights.org/sites/crr.civicactions.net/files/flash/LBS_LAKSHMI%20DHIKTA_FINAL%20NOV2010.pdf.
355 The case was a public interest lawsuit brought by the Forum for Women, Law and Development (FWLD), Pro-Public and a group of human rights lawyers. The US Center for Reproductive Rights submitted a memo.
356 Law No. 194 of 22 May 1978 on the social protection of motherhood and the voluntary termination of pregnancy, GU 22 May 1978, no. 140.
357 Law No. 194 (1978), Article 5.
358 Decision of 12 October 2015, published on 11 April 2016, complaint No. 91/2013, *CGIL v. Italy* (European Committee of Social Rights).
359 *CGIL v. Italy*, para. 2. See also Decision of 10 September 2013, published on 10 March 2014, Complaint No. 87/2012, *International Planned Parenthood Federation – European Network (IPPF EN) v. Italy*.
360 Views of 24 October 2005, Communication No. 1153/2003, *Karen Noelia Llantoy Huamán (K.N.L.H.) v. Peru* (HRC).
361 View of 17 October 2011, Communication No. 22/2009, *L.C. v. Peru* (CEDAW Committee).
362 *L.C.*, para. 8.4.
363 Family Planning (Protection of the Human Foetus and Conditions Permitting Pregnancy Termination) Act, 1993.
364 Judgment of 20 March 2007, Application No. 5410/03, *Tysiac v. Poland* (ECtHR).
365 Judgment of 26 May 2011, Application No. 27617/04, *R.R. v. Poland* (ECtHR).
366 Judgment of 30 October 2012, Application No. 57375/08, *P. and S. v. Poland* (ECtHR).
367 *P. and S.*, para. 117.
368 *Paulina del Carmen Ramírez Jacinto v. Mexico*, Friendly Settlement Agreement, Report No. 21/07 (2007) (IACommHR).
369 *Whole Woman's Health et al. v. Hellerstedt, Commissioner, Texas Department of State Health Services, et al.*, *Certiorari* to the United States Court of Appeals for the Fifth Circuit No. 15–274. Argued 2 March 2016–Decided 27 June 2016.

370 410 US 113 (1973).
371 See a comment in *Harvard Law Review* 130 (2016) 316.
372 I. Vandewalker, 'Abortion and informed consent: how biased counseling laws mandate violations of medical ethics', *Michigan Journal of Gender and Law* 19 (2012) 1, p. 3.
373 2011 Indiana Legislative Services Agency P.L. 193–2011, Sec. 6.
374 *Planned Parenthood of Indiana v. Commissioner of Indiana State Department of Health*, No. 11/2464 (United States Court of Appeals for the Seventh Circuit), 24 June 2011.
375 *Planned Parenthood of Indiana and Kentucky, Inc. v. Commissioner of Indiana State Department of Health*, No. 17/1883 (United States Court of Appeals for the Seventh Circuit), argued 6 November 2017, decided 25 July 2018.
376 *Lakshmi Dhikta v. Government of Nepal,* Writ No. 0757, 2067 (2009), Supreme Court of Nepal. Translation provided on Reproductive Rights website: see note 354 above.
377 *Dhikta*, p. 8.
378 Cook *et al.*, *Reproductive Health and Human Rights*, p. 316.
379 See the complete analysis in S. De Vido 'Conscientious objection and access to abortion in the case *CGIL v. Italy* decided by the European Committee of Social Rights', *Hitotsubashi Journal of Law and Politics* 47 (2019) 45, available at http://hermes-ir.lib.hit-u.ac.jp/rs/bitstream/10086/30079/1/HJlaw0470000450.pdf.
380 *K.N.L.H.*, paras 6.2, 6.3.
381 *L.C.*, paras 8.15 and 8.18.
382 E. Kismödi *et al.*, 'Human rights accountability for maternal death and failure to provide safe, legal abortion: the significance of two ground-breaking CEDAW decisions', *Reproductive Health Matters* 20 (2012) 31.
383 *L.C.*, para. 8.18.
384 *L.C.*, para. 8.15.
385 *Tysiac*, para. 124.
386 *Tysiac*, para. 125.
387 *R.R.*, para. 208.
388 F. Fabbrini, *Fundamental Rights in Europe* (Oxford: Oxford University Press, 2014), p. 235. See, in that respect, the partly dissenting opinion of Judge Bratza.
389 *R.R. v. Poland*, para. 159.
390 *P. and S.*, para. 108.
391 *P. and S.*, para. 110.
392 *A.B.C.*, para. 254.
393 *A.B.C.*, para. 258.
394 *A.B.C.*, para. 264.
395 *Ramírez Jacinto*, para. 19.
396 *Ramírez Jacinto*, part IV, twelve.3.
397 C. O'Connell, 'Litigating reproductive health right in the Inter-American system: what does a winning case look like?', *Health and Human Rights* 16 (2014) 116, p. 121.
398 *Planned Parenthood of Southeast Pennsylvania v. Casey*, 505 US 833 (1992).
399 *Planned Parenthood of Southeast Pennsylvania*, p. 878.
400 *Whole Woman's Health*, p. 36.

401 *Amici curiae* brief in support of the petitioners, *Whole Woman's Health*, p. 25.
402 Thomas's dissenting opinion, *Whole Woman's Health*, pp. 10–11.
403 *Roe v. Wade* is being challenged by new anti-abortion laws such as the law signed by the Georgia Governor Brian Kemp on 7 May 2019 (see http://www.legis.ga.gov//Legislation//en-US//display//20192020//HB//481). See further on vawh.wordpress.com.
404 *Planned Parenthood Indiana*, p. 42.
405 *Planned Parenthood Indiana and Kentucky*, p. 42.
406 An unresolved question is whether access to abortion also implies access to health insurance, both private and public. The debate arose in the USA after *Roe v. Wade*, during the 1970s. See R. Copelon and S.A. Law, 'Nearly allied to her right "to be" – medical funding for abortion: the story of *Harris v. McRae*', in E. Schneider and S.M. Wildman (eds), *Women and the Law Stories* (New York: Foundation Press, 2011) 207. See also chapter 3, 'Methodology for treatment, Positive obligations of result, To provide access to health services'.
407 *K.N.L.H.*, para. 8. The government announced the payment of compensation more than ten years after the views: www.un.org/apps/news/story.asp?NewsID=53033#.WZMik1EjEdX.
408 *L.C.*, para. 9.
409 *Tysiac*, para. 152. With regard to *P. and S. v. Poland*, the Committee of Ministers urged the Polish authorities to take rapidly the measures necessary for executing the judgment, and 'expressed serious concern that, more than six years after the judgment became final, no measures have been taken to ensure access to lawful abortion throughout Poland.' 1340th meeting (12–14 March 2019).
410 O'Connell, 'Litigating reproductive health right', p. 123.
411 *Planned Parenthood Indiana*, p. 43.
412 Indiana filed a writ of *certiorari* on 4 February 2019, asking the Supreme Court to uphold its law requiring an ultrasound be performed on women seeking an abortion at least 18 hours before the procedure. See www.theindianalawyer.com\\articles\\50212-indianas-abortion-ultrasound-petition-listed-at-us-supreme-court.
413 OHCHR, UN Women, UNAIDS, UNDP, UNFPA, UNICEF and WHO, 'Eliminating forced, coercive and otherwise involuntary sterilization. An interagency statement' (Geneva: WHO, 2014), p. 3.
414 OHCHR *et al.*, 'Eliminating … sterilization', p. 2.
415 L.C. Ikemoto, 'Infertile by force and federal complicity: the story of *Relf v. Weinberger*', in Schneider and Wildman, *Women and the Law Stories*, 179, p. 183.
416 Ikemoto, 'Infertile by force', p. 183.
417 R. Odawara, 'Rights of women vs. rights of the disabled people: eugenics in Japan after 1968', paper presented at the International Conference organised by the European Association for Japanese Studies in 2017 in Lisbon.
418 H. Maruyama, 'Abortion in Japan: A feminist critique', *Wisconsin Women's Law Journal* 10 (1995) 131, p. 133.
419 In Japan, a law which allows the payment of reparations to victims of involuntary sterilisation has been recently adopted. Law No. 14 Heisei 31 (2019), in force as of 24 April 2019, available at http://elaws.e-gov.go.jp/search/elawsSearch/elaws_search/lsg0500/detail?lawId=431AC0000000014. For the first time, the Sendai District Court acknowledged on 28 May 2019 that the Eugenic law had

violated Constitutional rights, but it did not grant any compensation to the victims, because the twenty-year statute of limitations had expired. The story is available on www.japantimes.co.jp/news/2019/05/28/national/crime-legal/sendai-court-rules-de-funct-eugenics-law-unconstitutional-denies-damages-due-statute-limitations/.

420 S. Chang, 'Time to phase out the one child policy', *Prospect: Journal of International Affairs at UCSD* (2013), available at https://prospectjournal.org/2013/10/04/time-to-phase-out-the-one-child-policy-2/; N.M. Skalla, 'China's one-child policy: illegal children and the Family Planning Law', *Brooklyn Journal of International Law* 30 (2004) 329. China has abandoned the one-child policy in favour of a two-child policy.

421 R. Sifris, 'Involuntary sterilization of HIV-positive women: An example of intersectional discrimination', *Human Rights Quarterly* 37 (2015) 464, p. 473; Sifris, *Reproductive Freedom*, p. 135.

422 Cook and Cusack, *Gender Stereotyping*, p. 85.

423 J.E. Bond, 'Intersecting identities and human rights: The example of Romani women's reproductive rights', *Georgetown Journal of Gender and the Law* 5 (2004) 897, p. 906.

424 R. Sifris, 'The involuntary sterilisation of marginalised women: power, discrimination, and intersectionality', *Griffith Law Review* 25 (2016) 45; C. Soohoo and F. Diaz-Tello, 'Torture and ill-treatment: Forced sterilization and criminalization of self-induced abortion', in C. Soohoo and F. Diaz-Tello, *Gender Perspectives on Torture* (Washington, DC: Center for Human Rights and Humanitarian Law, 2015) 279, p. 283.

425 Available at https://www.who.int/hiv/topics/mtct/about/en/. OHCHR, 'Busting the myth that sterilization can end AIDS', 2012, www.ohchr.org/EN/NewsEvents/Pages/ForcedSterilization.aspx.

426 Available at www.oas.org/en/iachr/media_center/PReleases/2019/010.asp.

427 Reported in L. Hoyle, '*V.C. v. Slovakia*: a reproductive rights victory misses the mark', *Boston College International and Comparative Law Review* 36 (2014) 17, p. 19. See also S. Curran, 'Intersectionality and human rights law: an examination of the coercive sterilisations of Romani women', *Equal Rights Review* 16 (2016) 132.

428 California State auditor, 'Sterilization of female inmates: some inmates were sterilized unlawfully, and safeguards designed to limit occurrences of the procedure failed', Report 2013–120, available at www.auditor.ca.gov/pdfs/reports/2013–120.pdf. Emphasis added.

429 A. Minna Stern, *Eugenic Nation* (Oakland: University of California Press, 2015), and her article 'That time the United States sterilized 60,000 of its citizens', 2016, published at www.huffingtonpost.com/entry/sterilization-united-states_us_568f35f2e-4b0c8beacf68713.

430 Senate Bill No. 1135 (2014) prohibits sterilisation for the purpose of birth control of an individual under the control of the Department of Corrections and Rehabilitation or a county correctional facility. Available at https://leginfo.legislature.ca.gov/faces/billTextClient.xhtml?bill_id=201320140SB1135.

431 *Buck v. Bell*, 274 US 200 (1927).

432 One of the girls condemned in *Buck v. Bell* later became an honour student: Ikemoto, 'Infertile by force', p. 184. See also R. Cepkot, 'Involuntary sterilization of mentally disabled women', *Berkeley Women's Law Journal* 8 (1993) 122.

433 See her interview here: www.newstatesman.com/lifestyle/2014/04/kimberl-crenshaw-intersectionality-i-wanted-come-everyday-metaphor-anyone-could and K. Creshaw, 'Mapping the margins: intersectionality, identity politics, and violence against women of color', *Stanford Law Review* 43 (1991) 1241, p. 1242.

434 See, to name just a few, *European Journal of Women's Studies* 13:3 (2006); on the dialectical notion of unity-in-difference for intersectional studies, L. Gunnarsson, 'Why we keep separating the "inseparable": dialecticizing intersectionality', *European Journal of Women's Studies* 24 (2017) 114; P. Hill Collins and S. Bilg, *Intersectionality* (Cambridge: Polity, 2016); L. Sosa, *Intersectionality in the Human Rights Legal Framework on Violence against Women* (Cambridge: Cambridge University Press, 2017).

435 C.A. MacKinnon, 'Intersectionality as method: a note', *Signs: Journal of women in culture and society* 38 (2013) 1019, p. 1023.

436 See, in that respect, P. Patel, 'Forced sterilization of women as discrimination', *Public Health Reviews* 38 (2017) 15, p. 17.

437 GR No. 35, para. 18.

438 GC No. 28 (2000) on Article 3 ECHR, 'The equality of rights between men and women' (HRC). See the in-depth analysis by Sifris, *Reproductive Freedom*, and the report by the then SR against torture, Manfred Nowak, A/HRC/7/3, paras 38–9.

439 E/CN.4/1999/68/Add.4, para. 44.

440 See, for example, UK jurisprudence based on the *Bolam* test: Laurie *et al.*, *Mason and McCall Smith's Law and Medical Ethics* (Oxford: Oxford University Press, 11th edn, 2019) p. 297*ff.*

441 J. Tobin and E. Luke, 'The involuntary, non-therapeutic sterilisation of women and girls with intellectual disability – can it ever be justified?' *Victoria University Law and Justice Journal* 4 (2013) 17, p. 45: 'the sterilisation of a woman or girl with a profound intellectual disability in the absence of her free and informed consent is not necessarily a violation of these standards if this treatment can be justified as being reasonable and necessary to protect her right to health.'

442 See, for example, L. Steele, 'Disability, abnormality and criminal law: sterilisation as lawful and good violence', *Griffith Law Review* 23 (2014) 467.

443 GC No. 5 (1994) on persons with disabilities, 11th session (ESCR Committee), para. 31.

444 *L.M. and Others v Government of the Republic of Namibia* (I 1603/2008, I 3518/2008, I 3007/2008) [2012] NAHC 211 (30 July 2012). Available at http://namibialii.org/na/cases/NAHC/2012/211.pdf.

445 Available at www.stigmaindex.org/south-africa.

446 Available at http://wlce.co.za/wp-content/uploads/2017/02/WLC-_Media-Release_Coerced-Sterilisation_141116.pdf.

447 Petition 605 of 2015.

448 Petition 605 of 2015, p. 4.

449 P. Nair, 'Litigating against the forced sterilization of HIV-positive women: Recent developments in Chile and Namibia', *Harvard Human Rights Journal* 23 (2010) 223, pp. 227–8.

450 Report No. 52/14, petition 112–09, report on admissibility, 21 July 2014. For 2017 hearing of the case, see https://reproductiverights.org/press-room/inter-american-commission-holds-hearing-on-forced-sterilization-of-chilean-woman-living-w.

451 Views of 14 August 2006, Communication No. 4/2004, *Andrea Szijjarto v. Hungary* (CEDAW).
452 S. Cusack and L. Pusey, 'CEDAW and the rights to non-discrimination and equality', *Melbourne Journal of International Law* 14 (2013) 54.
453 Judgment of 8 November 2011, Appl. No. 18968/07, *V.C. v. Slovakia* (ECtHR).
454 Judgment of 12 June 2012, Appl. no. 29518/10, *N.B. v. Slovakia* (ECtHR).
455 Judgment of 13 November 2012, Appl. no. 15966/04, *I.G., M.K. and R.H. v. Slovakia* (ECtHR).
456 Report No. 71/03, case. no. 12.191, amicable settlement, *María Mamérita Mestanza Chávez v. Peru*, 10 October 2003 (IACommHR).
457 Many cases have never reached a court. See some examples on vawh.wordpress.com.
458 Judgment of 30 November 2016, *I.V. v. Bolivia*, Excepciones Preliminares, Fondo, Reparaciones y Costas (IACHR).
459 *L.M.*, paras 66 and 70.
460 C. Badul and A. Strode, '*LM and Others v. Government of the Republic of Namibia*: the first sub-Saharan African case dealing with coerced sterilisations of HIV-positive women – *quo vadis*?', *African Human Rights Journal* 13 (2013) 214, p. 226.
461 Sifris, 'Involuntary sterilisation', p. 481.
462 Patel, 'Forced sterilization', p. 23.
463 *Szijjarto*, para. 10.4.
464 *Szijjarto*, para. 11.2.
465 *Szijjarto*, para. 11.3.
466 An application against Hungary was found inadmissible by the ECtHR because the applicant could have obtained compensation at national level. Appl. no. 54041/14, *G.H.* v. *Hungary*, 9 June 2015.
467 *V.C.*, para. 106.
468 *V.C.*, para. 116.
469 *V.C.*, para. 119.
470 *V.C.*, para. 154.
471 On this weak aspect of the judgment, see R. Rubio-Marín and M. Möschel, 'Racial and gender-based violence as discrimination under the European Court of Human Rights' in M. Balboni (ed.), *The European Convention on Human Rights and the Principle of Non-Discrimination* (Naples: Scientifica, 2017) 171, p. 193.
472 *N.B.*, para. 98.
473 *V.C.*, dissenting opinion of Judge Mijovic, para. 4.
474 Report No. 72/14, case no. 12.655 (IACommHR), paras 104, 179.
475 *I.V.* (IACommHR), para. 161.
476 *I.V.* (IACHR), paras 266–7.
477 *I.V.* (IACHR), para. 246.
478 *I.V.* (IACHR), para. 247.
479 See the analysis by N. Bamforth, M. Malik and C. O'Cinneide, *Discrimination Law: Theory and Context* (London: Sweet & Maxwell, 2008), p. 534.
480 *I.V.* (IACHR), para. 248.
481 *I.V.* (IACHR), para. 318.
482 *Szijjarto*, para. 11.5. In 2011, the Hungarian Helsinki Committee reported that the country had failed to comply with the CEDAW Committee recommendations.
483 *V.C.*, para. 153.

484 *V.C.*, para. 182*ff.*; *N.B.*, para. 169*ff.*; *I.G. and others*, para. 169*ff.*
485 *Mestanza Chávez*, part IV of the agreement.
486 *Mestanza Chávez*, part IV of the agreement. In 2011, Peru's Office of the Public Prosecutor notified the Inter-American Commission that it would have reopened the investigation into her case. In January 2014, the Peruvian state closed the investigation, alleging lack of evidence to support the claims of forced sterilisation, but the investigation reopened in 2015 (see www.reproductiverights.org/press-room/peru-reopens-criminal-investigation-into-mass-forced-sterilizations).
487 *I.V.* (IACHR), para. 332.
488 *I.V.* (IACHR), para. 332.
489 'No obstante, la Corte considera que estos aspectos incidieron sobre la magnitud de los daños que sufrió I.V. en la esfera de su integridad personal' (*I.V.* (IACHR), para. 248).
490 *I.V.* (IACHR), paras 340 and 342. After two years, the state was found to have complied with almost all the measures requested by the Court. In 2018, the Court left open the monitoring procedure with regard, among other things, to the provision of medical support to I.V. (Resolución de la Corte Interamericana de derechos humanos de 21 de noviembre de 2018, *I.V. v. Bolivia*, supervision de cumplimiento de sentencia).
491 D. Alaattinoğlu, 'Gender-sensitive reparations in the *I.V. v. Bolivia* case: a missed opportunity?' available at https://ilg2.org/2017/03/24/gender-sensitive-reparations-in-the-i-v-v-bolivia-case-a-missed-opportunity/.
492 See the analysis by R.J. Cook and B.M. Dickens, *Advancing Safe Motherhood through Human Rights* (Geneva: WHO, 2001), p. 21*ff.*
493 Available at http://iris.paho.org/xmlui/bitstream/handle/123456789/6579/25821.pdf?sequence=1.
494 S.A. Cohen, 'The safe motherhood conference', *International Family Planning Perspectives* 13 (1987) 68.
495 For a feminist critique of Agenda 2030, see, for example, the special issue 'The gender discourse of Sustainable Development Goals and other instruments for gender equality: Advancing feminist agenda in Africa?', *Agenda* 32 (2018) 1.
496 J. Erdmann, 'Bioethics, human rights, and childbirth', *Health and Human Rights Journal* 17 (2015) 29, p. 43.
497 R. Cook, 'Advancing safe motherhood through human rights', *SOGC Journal* (1999) 363, p. 364. The author referred to maternal mortality only, but her remarks can be extended to obstetric violence (OV).
498 See also GR No. 24 (CEDAW), para. 27.
499 Available at www.who.int/healthinfo/statistics/indmaternalmortality/en/.
500 Available at www.who.int/mediacentre/factsheets/fs348/en/.
501 See, for example, CEDAW Committee Algeria (A/60/38), para. 131; Czech Republic (A/57/38), para. 85; India (CEDAW/C/IND/CO/3), para. 40; Saint Kitts and Nevis (A/57/38), para. 88; Sri Lanka (A/57/38), para. 217; Turkey (CEDAW/C/TUR/CC/4–5), para. 38; Lao People's Democratic Republic (CEDAW/C/LAO/CO/8–9), para. 39; Congo (CEDAW/C/COG/CO/7), para. 45; Mexico with regard to indigenous women (CEDAW/C/MEX/CO/9), para. 41e; Malaysia (CEDAW/C/MYS/CO/3–5), para. 39.
502 F. Diaz-Tello, 'Invisible wounds: obstetric violence in the United States', *Reproductive Health Matters* 24 (2016) 56, p. 57.

503 WHO statement 2014, http://apps.who.int/iris/bitstream/10665/134588/1/WHO_RHR_14.23_eng.pdf?ua=1&ua=1.

504 WHO statement 2014.

505 Available at www.achpr.org/news/2015/09/d192/.

506 G.D. Schultz, 'Cruelty in maternity wards', *Ladies' Home Journal* (1958), pp. 44–5,152–5.

507 See the study by H. Goed, 'Cruelty in maternity wards: fifty years later', *Journal of Perinatal Education* 19 (2010) 33.

508 S.G. Diniz, A.F. Pires Lucas D'Oliveira and S. Lansky, 'Equity and women's health services for contraception, abortion and childbirth in Brazil', *Reproductive Health Matters* 20 (2012) 94, p. 97.

509 The report is available, in Italian, at https://ovoitalia.wordpress.com/.

510 M.A. Bohren, J.P. Vogel, E.C. Hunter, *et al.*, 'The mistreatment of women during childbirth in health facilities globally: a mixed-methods systematic review', *PLoS Medicine* 12 (2015), available at https://journals.plos.org/plosmedicine/article/file?id=10.1371/journal.pmed.1001847&type=printable. R. Khosla *et al.*, 'International human rights and the mistreatment of women during childbirth', *Health and Human Rights Journal* 18 (2016) 131, p. 132. For Venezuela, see P. Terán *et al.*, 'Violencia obstétrica: percepción de las usuarias', *Revista de Obstetricia y Ginecología de Venezuela* 73 (2013) 171; for Nigeria, I.I. Okafor, E.O. Ugwu and S.N. Obi, 'Disrespect and abuse during facility-based childbirth in a low-income country', *International Journal of Gynaecology and Obstetrics* 128(2015) 110.

511 S. Charles, 'Obstetricians and violence against women', *American Journal of Bioethics* 11 (2011) 51.

512 E. Nelson, 'Reconceiving pregnancy: expressive choice and legal reasoning', *McGill Law Journal / Revue De Droit De McGill* 49 (2004) 593, p. 596.

513 Available at https://www.acnur.org/fileadmin/Documentos/BDL/2008/6604.pdf. R. Pérez d'Gregorio, 'Obstetric violence: a new legal term introduced in Venezuela', *International Journal of Gynaecology and Obstetrics* 3 (2010) 201.

514 Law 26485, article 6(e), Argentina. C. Herrera Vacaflor, 'Obstetric violence in Argentina: a study on the legal effects of medical guidelines and statutory obligations for improving the quality of maternal health', 2015, p. 2, available at https://tspace.library.utoronto.ca/handle/1807/70430, and C. Herrera Vacaflor, 'Obstetric violence: a new framework for identifying challenges to maternal healthcare in Argentina', *Reproductive Health Matters* 24 (2016) 65.

515 Second Hemispheric Report on the Implementation of the Belém do Pará Convention, available at www.oas.org/en/mesecvi/docs/MESECVI-SegundoInforme Hemisferico-EN.pdf, p. 39.

516 No. 3670, 'Norme per la tutela dei diritti della partoriente e del neonato e per la promozione del parto fisiologico', available at www.camera.it/_dati/leg17/lavori/stampati/pdf/17PDL0039650.pdf.

517 See, among others, A.F. D'Oliveira, S.G. Diniz and L.B. Schraiber, 'Violence against women in healthcare institutions: an emerging problem', *Lancet* 359:9318 (2002) 1681; A.F. D'Oliveira, S.G. Diniz and L.B. Schraiber, 'Institutional violence, medical authority, and power relations in maternity hospitals from the perspective of health workers', *Cadernos de Saúde Pública* 29 (2013) 2287; J. Faneite, A. Feo and

J. Toro Merlo, 'Grado de conocimiento de violencia obstétrica por el personal de salud', *Revista de Obstetricia y Ginecología de Venezuela* 72 (2012) 4.

518 Erdmann, 'Bioethics', p. 48.

519 Diaz-Tello, 'Invisible wounds', p. 59.

520 Diaz-Tello, 'Invisible wounds', p. 60.

521 A. Rich, *Of Woman Born – Motherhood as Experience and Institution* (New York: Bantam Books, 1976), pp. 152–62.

522 E/CN.4/1999/68/Add.2, 4 January 1999, para. 53.

523 E/CN.4/1999/68/Add.2, para. 54.

524 Conclusions and Recommendations of the Committee against torture, United States of America, 36th Session, para. 33, CAT/C/USA/CO/2, May 2006.

525 A/HRC/17/26/Add.5, 6 June 2011, para. 42.

526 See C.L. Griggs, 'Birthing barbarism: the unconstitutionality of shackling pregnant prisoners', *American University Journal of Gender Social Policy and Law* 20 (2011) 247.

527 Available at http://theprisonbirthproject.org/wp-content/uploads/2016/05/Breaking-Promises_May2016.pdf.

528 Cámara 3ra de Apelaciones en lo Civil, Comercial, Minas, de Paz y Tributaria de Mendoza [Third Appellate Chamber on Civil, Commercial, Mining, Peace and Tax Law of the Province of Mendoza], 5 September 2014, *G., M.C.Y v. Hospital Luis Lagomaggiore s/d y p*, 2014, RCyS2015-III, 137, at 4–5 (Argentina). The case is reported and discussed in Vacaflor, 'Obstetric violence', p. 43.

529 See, for example, Cassazione penale, sez IV, 24 January 2013, dep. 11.03.2013, n. 11493, commentary by F.G. Seregni, 'Osservazioni a Corte di Cassazione penale, del 24 gennaio 2013, n. 11493', *Rivista italiana di medicina legale* 2 (2013), p. 967.

530 Cassazione civile, sez. III, 17 May 2010, dep. 17.05.2010, n. 11958.

531 *J.O.O. (also known as J.M.) v. The Attorney-General & 4 others* [2017] eKRL, Petition No.5 of 2014 (Kenya at High Court in Bungoma), commentary by Naitore Nyamu, available at https://reprohealthlaw.wordpress.com/tag/south-africa/.

532 *Dubská and Krejzová v. Czech Republic*, Appl. No. 28859/11 and 28473/12, judgment of 15 November 2016. Referral to the Grand Chamber.

533 *Women Prisoners of D.C. Department of Corrections v. District of Columbia*, 877 F. Supp. 634, 668–69 (D.D.C. 1994), pp. 646–7. Then *vacated in part* and *modified in part on other grounds*, 899 F. Supp. 659 (D.D.C. 1995), *remanded*, 93 F.3d 910 (D.C. Cir. 1996). See B. Dignam and E.Y. Adashi, 'Health rights in the balance: the case against perinatal shackling of women behind bars', *Health and Human Rights* 16 (2014) 14.

534 *Nelson v. Correctional Medical Services*, 583 F.3d 522 (8th Cir. 2009), *en banc*. For a detailed history of the case see E. Alexander, 'Unshackling Shawanna: the battle over chaining women prisoners during labor and delivery', *University of Arkansas at Little Rock Law Review* 32 (2010) 435; and Griggs, 'Birthing barbarism'.

535 Alexander, 'Unshackling Shawanna', p. 442.

536 *J.O.O.*, paras 62 and 64.

537 *J.O.O.*, para. 70.

538 *Dubská and Krejzová*, paras 165–6.

539 *Dubská and Krejzová*, para. 171.

540 *Dubská and Krejzová*, para. 171.
541 *Dubská and Krejzová*, para. 184.
542 *Dubská and Krejzová*, para. 189. See, however, finding a violation of Article 8 ECHR, judgment of 14 December 2010, Appl. No. 67545/09, *Ternovszky v. Hungary* (ECtHR). See also the critical comment by F. Van Leeuwen, 'Milestone or stillbirth? An analysis of the first judgment of the European Court of Human Rights on home birth', in M. Van de Brink, S. Burri and J. Goldschmid (eds), *Equality and Human Rights: Nothing but Trouble?* (Utrecht: SIM; 2015) 197, p. 203.
543 *Women Prisoners of DC*. See Dignam and Adashi, 'Health rights'.
544 Qualified immunity is described in 42 USC § 1983; see W. Baude, 'Is qualified immunity unlawful?' Public Law and Legal Theory Working Papers 620 (2017), available at http://chicagounbound.uchicago.edu/public_law_and_legal_theory/620.
545 See Alexander, 'Unshackling Shawanna'.
546 Griggs, 'Birthing barbarism', p. 253.
547 P.A. Ocen, 'Punishing pregnancy: race, incarceration, and the shackling of pregnant prisoners', *California Law Review* 100 (2012) 1239, p. 1244.
548 D. L. Sichel, 'Giving birth in shackles: a constitutional and human rights violation', *American University Journal of Gender, Social Policy and the Law* 16 (2007) 223, p. 235; D. Sussman, 'Bound by injustice: challenging the use of shackles on incarcerated pregnant women', *Cardozo Journal of Law and Gender* 15 (2009) 477, pp. 496 and 502.
549 'Standard minimum rules for the treatment of prisoners', UN Doc. A/CONF/1Annex 1, ESC res. 663C, UN ESCOR, 24th Sess., Supp. No. 1, UN Doc. E/3048, Rule 33(c) (31 July 1957). Article 23(1).
550 Vacaflor, 'Obstetric violence', p. 46.
551 Order for declaratory and injunctive relief, para. 35.
552 Ocen, 'Punishing pregnancy', p. 1283.
553 GR No. 24, paras 26–7.
554 HRC, 11th session, Resolution 11/8. 'Preventable maternal mortality and morbidity and human rights', para. 2.
555 Views of 25 July 2011, Communication No. 17/2008, CEDAW/C/49/D/17/2008.
556 R. Cook, 'Human rights and maternal health: exploring the effectiveness of the *Alyne* decision', *Journal of Law, Medicine & Ethics* 41 (2013) 103.
557 Judgment of 27 June 2006, Application no. 11562/05 (ECtHR), *Byrzykowski v. Poland*.
558 Judgment of 13 November 2012, Application no. 46132/08 (ECtHR), *Z v. Poland*.
559 Judgment of 9 April 2013, Application no. 13423/09 (ECtHR), *Şentürk v. Turkey*.
560 Judgment of 24 August 2010, *Xákmok Kásek Indigenous Community v. Paraguay*, merits, reparations and costs (IACHR).
561 *Xákmok Kásek Community*, para. 232.
562 *Laxmi Mandal v. Deen Dayal Harinagar Hospital* (2010) 172 D.L.T. 9 (High Court in Delhi, India).
563 Judgment 12 January 2011, *Court of its own motion v. Union of India*, W.P. (C) 5913/2010 (High Court in Delhi). See also *Sandesh Bansal v. Union of India and others*, W.P. no. 9061/2008, judgment of 6 February 2012. Follow-up complaint W.P. no. 11860/2013 (High Court in Delhi).

564 *da Silva Pimentel Teixeira*, para. 7.3. See the analysis in L. Cabal and S. Phillips, 'Reproductive rights litigation: from recognition to transformation', in M. Langford, C. Rodríguez-Garavito and J. Rossi (eds), *Social Rights Judgments and the Politics of Compliance: Making It Stick* (Cambridge: Cambridge University Press, 2017), pp. 418–19.
565 *Pimentel Teixeira*, para. 7.5.
566 *Pimentel Teixeira*, para. 7.7.
567 *Pimentel Teixeira*, para. 7.7.
568 Cook, 'Human rights', pp. 108–9.
569 On state compliance, see also K.L. Caldwell, *Health Equity in Brazil: Intersections of Gender, Race, and Policy* (Champaign: University of Illinois Press, 2017), chap. 5.
570 *Byrzykowski*, para. 104.
571 *Byrzykowski*, para. 105.
572 *Byrzykowski*, para. 115.
573 *Z.*, para. 105.
574 *Z.*, para. 136.
575 *Z.*, para. 137.
576 *Z.*, para. 23.
577 *Sentürk*, para. 81.
578 *Sentürk*, para. 97.
579 *Sentürk*, para. 104.
580 See below, chapter 3, 'Methodology for treatment, Positive obligations of result, To provide access to health services'.
581 *Mandal*, para. 48.
582 *Mandal*, para. 2.
583 *Mandal*, paras 21–6.
584 *Pimentel Teixeira*, para. 8.2.
585 *Pimentel Teixeira*, para. 8.1.
586 *Byrzykowski*, paras 123–7.
587 *Xákmok Kásek Community*, para. 232.
588 *Xákmok Kásek Community*, p. 78, operative para. 21.
589 *Court of its own motion v. Union of India*. See also chapter 3, 'Methodology for treatment, Positive obligations of result, To provide access to health services' for states' obligations.
590 Available at www.who.int/news-room/fact-sheets/detail/emergency-contraception.
591 GC No. 22, para. 13. See also the updated list of essential medicines of the WHO, at http://apps.who.int/iris/bitstream/handle/10665/273826/EML-20-eng.pdf?ua=1.
592 GC No. 22, para. 18.
593 J.F Gonzalez-Bertomeu and R. Gargarella (eds), *The Latin American Casebook: Courts, Constitutions, and Rights* (London: Routledge, 2016), p. 56. See also R. Villanueva Flores, *La anticoncepción oral de emergencia. El debate legal en América Latina* (San José, Costa Rica: Instituto interamericano de Derechos Humanos, 2008).
594 See, for example, *Portal de Belén Asociación Civil sin Fines de Lucro v. Ministerio de Salud de la Nación/ANMAT*, judgment of 5 March 2002 (Supreme Court of Argentina, 2002), reported in M. Hevia, 'The legal status of emergency contraception in Latin America', *International Journal of Gynecology & Obstetrics* 116 (2012) 87, p. 88.

595 In this sense, see Colombia, State Council, Chamber of Administrative dispute, Ref.: Expediente núm. 200200251 01, Actor: Carlos Humberto Gómez Arambula, 5 June 2008.
596 R.J. Cook, B.M. Dickens, C. Ngwena and M.I. Plata, 'Ethical and legal issues in reproductive health. The legal status of emergency contraception', *International Journal of Gynecology & Obstetrics* 75 (2001) 185.
597 Factsheet updated June 2017, available at www.who.int/mediacentre/factsheets/fs244/en/.
598 Available at www.oas.org/en/iachr/media_center/PReleases/2013/083A.asp.
599 Available at www.oas.org/en/iachr/media_center/PReleases/2013/083A.asp.
600 Joint Statement by UN human rights experts, 24 September 2015, available at www.ohchr.org/EN/NewsEvents/Pages/DisplayNews.aspx?NewsID=16490&LangID=E.
601 CEDAW Committee, 'Summary of the inquiry concerning the Philippines under article 8 of the Optional Protocol to the Convention on the Elimination of All Forms of Discrimination against Women', 22 April 2015. CEDAW/C/OP.8/PHL/1. See also Cusack and Cook, *Gender Stereotyping*, p. 60.
602 Available at www.reproductiverights.org/press-room/new-human-rights-case-filed-on-behalf-of-peruvian-rape-survivor-denied-emergency-contraception.
603 C. Puig Borràs and B. I. Alvarez Alvarez, 'The history of universal access to emergency contraception in Peru: a case of politics deepening inequalities', *Health Reproductive Matters* 26 (2018) 47. See also Committee against Torture, 'Concluding observations on Peru', 21 January 2013, para. 15, CAT/C/PER/CO/5–6; Report of the working group on the issue of discrimination against women in law and in practice Addendum Mission to Peru, A/HRC/29/40/Add.2, 26 June 2015, para. 65; Committee on the rights of the child, 'Concluding observations on Peru', CRC/C/PER/CO/4–5, 2 March 2016, para. 55.
604 Case T-627/12. Colombian Constitutional Court. Reported at www.globalhealthrights.org/wp-content/uploads/2014/07/Colombian-T-627–121.pdf. *Tutela* means proceedings started by an individual to obtain immediate protection of human rights. The case must be determined within ten days (Article 86 of the Colombian Constitution).
605 Judgment of 2 October 2001, Appl. No. 49853/99, *Pichon and Sajous v. France* (ECtHR).
606 CEDAW Committee, Philippines, para. 8.
607 CEDAW Committee, Philippines, para. 12.
608 CEDAW Committee, Philippines, para. 9.
609 CEDAW Committee, Philippines, para. 32.
610 CEDAW Committee, Philippines, para. 32.
611 Case T-627/12. Colombian Constitutional Court, p. 152.
612 CEDAW Committee, Philippines, para. 52(a).
613 CEDAW Committee, Philippines, para. 52(c).
614 See M. Roa and B. Klugman, 'Considering strategic litigation as an advocacy tool: a case study of the defence of reproductive rights in Colombia', *Reproductive Health Matters* 22 (2014) 31, p. 38.
615 New cases to support or to challenge my paradigm will be included in the blog vawh.wordpress.com.

2

The diagnosis: a conceptualisation of VAWH

Unravelling the notion of violence against women's health

The *anamnesis* leads us now to the diagnosis. In this chapter I will unravel the innovative notion of VAWH as conceived in this book, which will pave the way for the analysis of states' obligations in chapter 3 (the 'treatment'). Going back to the philosophical metaphor that I used as *fil rouge* of this book, Greek physicians undertook detailed histories and examinations of patients, noting all elements that were useful for the diagnosis, including the course of the disease over time.[1] In my book, these elements have been the judgments of human rights courts and national courts, and the views of UN treaty bodies, related to specific aspects of the relationship between VAW on one hand, and the rights to health and to reproductive health on the other. It should be said that my analysis might seem limited – I looked into around seventy decisions. A database is not the purpose of this book, which aims to reflect on a precise relationship and analyse it using a medical metaphor to achieve a reconceptualisation of states' obligations in the field. It is true, indeed, that Hippocratic medicine was also founded on the available – hence, surely not 100 per cent complete – evidence-based knowledge.[2] As interestingly argued by one author, who relied on the rhetorical theory, 'all theoretical discussions of international law are incomplete in one way or the other,' and the reason is that theorists 'choose,' they emphasise different aspects of the discipline.[3]

To paraphrase the most common definition of VAW – violence against women is a violation of women's human rights – violence against *women's health* constitutes a violation of *women's right to health* and *right to reproductive health*. From the analysis in chapter 1, the notion of VAWH can encapsulate both a vertical and a horizontal dimension of violence, namely the interpersonal dimension between individuals and an institutional one, which is characterised by laws and policies in the field of health. VAW always violates a woman's rights to health and to reproductive health. At the same time, state policies and laws in the field of health, such as the criminalisation of abortion (as showed in chapter 1), might themselves cause, or contribute to cause, violence. From the *anamnesis*, however, I draw the lesson that it is essential to consider as state policies and laws in the field of health the practice of private parties, such as health personnel and hospitals, exercising public functions. Sonya Charles first linked DV and forced medical treatment – respectively belonging to the horizontal and vertical dimensions of my analysis – and examined them both as forms of VAW.[4] Her argument anticipated mine. Nonetheless, from a legal point of view, although both are examples of VAW, in the case of DV the state is responsible for not preventing and/or suppressing VAW committed by private parties, whereas the state is responsible in cases of forced medical treatment because of its laws, or as a consequence of the action of its organs (for example the courts that authorise coercive practices), or because of the action of the health personnel, who are performing a public function in the field of health. In terms of state obligations, this difference matters.

One might wonder why the definition of VAW is not sufficient to encompass both the dimensions as I conceive them in this book. If we look at General Recommendation No. 35, adopted in 2017, it is clear that the CEDAW Committee conceived all forms of violence as potentially falling within the definition of VAW, including the criminalisation of abortion, for example. The Committee also argued that an international custom on the prohibition of VAW had consolidated. Nonetheless, I contended in the introduction that this latter affirmation – pivotal and progressive it might be – only partly corresponds to state practice.[5] VAW is usually conceived as interpersonal violence, in which the actors might also be organs of the state, and less as a system of health policies and laws which cause VAW.[6] However, if we look at VAW from the perspective of the right to health, then it is possible to argue that the macro-concept of VAWH can encapsulate both dimensions of violence. Like that of VAW, the concept of VAWH is not a term in criminal law, but rather an 'umbrella' definition that grasps the two dimensions of violence, each characterised by specific, gender-based crimes or practices. I will argue in these pages that, compared to the idea of VAW, this new concept can be enriched by another element, the limitation of women's autonomy, which will be construed in these pages along human rights-based lines.

In the introduction, I 'de-constructed' the idea of VAW, analysing it from five different perspectives; in this chapter I will 'construct' the concept of VAWH, in an attempt to provide the clearest conceptualisation of my argument. Being a framework definition, VAWH does not include the element of intent. Nonetheless, I will argue in favour of the identification of a pattern of conduct in relation to VAWH, which will be relevant for re-conceptualising states' obligations. I will conclude the chapter by reflecting on the public/private divide and how it might be challenged by the concept of VAWH.

What is violence against women's health?

The definition of VAW included in the Council of Europe Istanbul Convention, which reflects legal developments on this issue at the international level, constitutes an excellent starting point for the analysis. VAW means 'all acts of gender-based violence that result in, or are likely to result in, physical, sexual, psychological or economic harm or suffering to women, including threats of such acts, coercion or arbitrary deprivation of liberty, whether occurring in public or in private life' (Article 3(a), Istanbul Convention). The concept of VAWH can also encompass all acts that cause or are likely to cause harm to women. This book theorises that these acts can be either 'horizontal' or 'vertical' forms of violence. Like VAW, VAWH makes no reference to the gender or the nature of the perpetrator. It emerged from chapter 1 that the perpetrator is not necessarily a male actor. For example, it is common practice that FGM/C are performed by women belonging to the community of the girl who undergoes it. Obstetricians might be women. In my book, the state can also be a perpetrator, not just through its agents, but also through laws and policies in the field of health that cause, or create the conditions for, VAWH.

In this paragraph, I will specifically reflect on the term 'harm,' although my purpose is not to investigate all the theories that legal scholars have elaborated over the centuries on this legal concept. Harm is usually related to criminal law, but in this book I see VAWH as an 'umbrella' concept, rather than a distinct crime, which is more comprehensive and better describes the two dimensions of violence as I theorised them in chapter 1. In this section I will not consider harm in relation to specific crimes which fall under the concept of VAWH, either.

Let us start from an apparently easy question: what is harm? In 1859 John Stuart Mill elaborated the following principle:

> The sole end for which mankind are warranted, individually or collectively, in interfering with the liberty of action of any of their number, is self-protection. That the only purpose for which power can be rightfully exercised over any member of a civilised community, against his will, is to prevent harm to others. His own good, either physical or moral, is not sufficient warrant.[7]

In a very simple, and admittedly not exhaustive, description, harm consists in a violation of legally protected interests. In his famous work of 1984, the legal philosopher Joel Feinberg conceived harm as a 'wrongful setback to interests,'[8] which is an interesting definition even though a 'set-back to interests is not considered as harmful if it has been voluntarily consented to.'[9]

What protected interest is violated in cases of VAWH? When considering rape, it was argued that the harm 'lies in the violation of sexual autonomy and bodily integrity,' with the consequence that the protected interest can be precisely identified in sexual autonomy.[10] To turn to VAWH, I consider that the protected interests capable of embracing the two dimensions of violence are a woman's rights to health and to reproductive health, which include, but are not limited to, sexual and reproductive autonomy. Hence, harm consists (or, better, harms consist) in violation of those rights to health and to reproductive health. As has been argued, 'different harms may ensue from the same violations and one of the determining factors may be the gender of the victim.'[11]

The second, related, question concerns whether or not it is possible to 'measure' harm in international human rights law. In the *Valiulienė v. Lithuania* case decided at European level, for example, Loreta Valiulienė suffered DV at the hands of her former partner. Her physical injuries were minor, but she was repeatedly, and violently, verbally abused. Was the violation of her human right – in this case, freedom from torture, inhuman or degrading treatment – less severe because she was not permanently, physically injured? Psychological harm might be disregarded, and often has been, and considered 'less important' than physical harm. Quite to the contrary, psychological harm has long-lasting consequences. The ECtHR argued, in *Valiulienė*, that it could not 'turn a blind eye to the psychological aspect of the alleged ill-treatment … psychological impact is an important aspect of domestic violence,'[12] and it found that Lithuania had violated Article 3 ECHR. It can be argued that, according to this jurisprudence, there is no pre-determined 'threshold' below which an act of gender-based violence is considered as not violence. Confirming this point, in several cases of DV the ECtHR has applied Article 3 prohibiting torture, inhuman or degrading treatment, without proceeding to analyse the level of severity. In her dissenting opinion on *Valiulienė*, Judge Jŏcienė contended that the applicant's right to respect for private and family life had been violated, and *not* her right to be free from torture, inhuman or degrading treatment or punishment, because Article 3 ECHR requires a certain level of intensity to be triggered.[13] The position of the judge deserves some attention, and it is not devoid of legal arguments, but on one hand it raises doubts about how far severity should be considered in cases of DV, which risks minimising psychological harm, and on the other hand reference to the victim/survivor's right to privacy might be counter-productive, since it might bring the analysis back to the public/private divide that has been fought over by feminists for decades.

In her work on reproductive freedom and torture, Ronli Sifris considered that 'there is clearly no bright line dividing pain that is sufficiently intense to be categorised as severe, and pain that falls below this threshold.'[14] She then turned to restrictions on abortion, and argued that 'legally coercing a woman to carry an unwanted pregnancy to term is not only an abuse of her basic human rights, but may also be extremely damaging from a mental health perspective.'[15] The use of the adverb 'legally' is interesting for my purposes, because it identifies the perpetrator as the state, through its laws and policies. Restrictions on abortion might also have physical effects, especially when a woman decides to undergo 'unsafe abortions,' an expression which includes procedures carried out below the minimum medical standards and performed by individuals without the necessary skills.[16]

VAWH not only causes harm, manifesting as bodily injury, fear, anguish and psychological pressure, but also leads to the adoption of behaviours that limit women's autonomy, causing further harm. Consider, for example, that many women who have been raped adjust their behaviour because they fear being raped again – they might never leave their house alone, or at night – and suffer a new form of harm.[17] It is a double harm: the harm of rape, and the harm caused by the psychological consequences of rape. The same can be said for DV, when a woman, fearing abuse, decides to stay at home or to avoid contact with friends or relatives. Fear of being subjected to traditional practices such as FGM/C may prevent a woman from going back to her country of origin. The kind of harm that is discussed in these pages is fundamental where OV has occurred. As I saw in chapter 1, cases of obstetric violence tend to be brought to court only when they lead to permanent physical injuries to a woman and, as a consequence, to a complaint of malpractice or of negligent behaviour by a practitioner. Nonetheless, this is only a limited view of the problem, because in the majority of cases, I venture to say, OV causes psychological and possibly long-lasting harm(s).

Finally, harm must be considered in the social context of the unequal power relations of women and men. Harm is 'gendered'. Harm may be caused to women because they are women, or may affect women disproportionately, so is inflicted on women *as a group*. Needless to say, this does not mean that harm must be conceived as collective and not as individual. Such a position would echo some national laws that considered rape as a crime against 'morality,' against the male actor exercising his control over the woman.[18] Instead, it means that an act of violence that a woman endures is not just an individual act, but also the product of an 'institution,' which 'reinforces the group-based subordination of women to men.'[19] Ruth Rubio-Marín has contended in that respect that 'looking at the harms produced by violations allows for an understanding of rights violations ... as a distortion of relationships and network systems that are sustained by these rights in a way that is especially relevant for women.'[20]

VAWH as a form of discrimination against women: patterns of discrimination

VAWH is a form of discrimination against women *because* they are women and/or that affects women disproportionately, and it is structural, meaning that this form of violence is rooted in society, and based, as explained by the Council of Europe Istanbul Convention, on the 'crucial social mechanisms by which women are forced into a subordinate position compared with men.'[21] It is structural subordination, which is clarified by the control of sexuality exercised over girls through FGM/C, but also in the subjugation of women in rape and domestic violence. In the vertical dimension, the element of structural subordination is shown in the attitude towards women in the medical sector, where doctors decide on behalf of women, or after obtaining a 'coerced', not entirely informed or free, consent – and laws and policies allow them to do so. Even though juridical equality has been gradually accepted by states, and forms of subjugation of women have been legally removed, 'lifting legal impediments [i]s not sufficient to dislodge the deeply ingrained patterns of prejudice and disadvantage suffered by women.'[22] Substantive equality is far from being achieved.

From a legal point of view, the structural aspect of VAWH can be seen in 'patterns of discrimination', which will be useful when we come to reconceptualise states' obligations in chapter 3. A 'pattern of discrimination' means not just social and cultural patterns that are rooted in society, but also the persistence of and the 'tolerance' states demonstrate towards VAW, and in particular to VAWH, as it is conceived here. The 'societal' pattern of discrimination and the 'state' pattern of discrimination are, needless to say, interconnected and mutually reinforcing. This distinction is pivotal in terms of states' obligations: the state has legal obligations to prevent VAWH by changing cultural patterns that consider the woman as subordinated to the man,[23] but it also, as I will discuss in chapter 3, has obligations to disrupt the 'pattern of discrimination' represented by laws and policies in the health field that, directly or indirectly, perpetuate the stereotyped gender roles of women and men in society, and thereby cause violence. The ESCR Committee, in its GC No. 20, clearly defined systemic discrimination in this key passage:

> The Committee has regularly found that discrimination against some groups is pervasive and persistent and deeply entrenched in social behaviour and organization, often involving unchallenged or indirect discrimination. Such systemic discrimination can be understood as legal rules, policies, practices or predominant cultural attitudes in either the public or private sector which create relative disadvantages for some groups, and privileges for other groups.[24]

Let us focus first on the horizontal dimension. Both the Inter-American and the European mechanisms for protecting human rights have referred to 'patterns' of discrimination in judgments concerning DV. For instance, in *Maria da Penha v. Brazil*, the IACommHR held that:

> tolerance by the State organs is not limited to this case; rather, it is a pattern. The condoning of this situation by the entire system only serves to perpetuate the psychological, social, and historical roots and factors that sustain and encourage violence against women ... the violence ... is part of a general pattern of negligence and lack of effective action by the State in prosecuting and convicting aggressors ... general and discriminatory judicial ineffectiveness also creates a climate that is conducive to domestic violence.[25]

In *Lenahan (Gonzáles) v. United States*, the IACommHR found '[t]he systemic failure of the United States to offer a coordinated and effective response to protect Jessica Lenahan and her daughters from domestic violence [which] constituted an act of discrimination ... and a violation of their right to equality before the law.'[26] A 'more general context of gender violence and impunity' was emphasised in the report of the IACommHR in *López Soto v. Venezuela*,[27] and reinforced by the IACHR, which stressed how the 'judicial inefficiency' provoked an 'environment of impunity,' which in turn facilitated the repetition of acts of violence.[28] The IACommHR described sexual violence as a 'multi-dimensional problem,' the product of a 'social environment in which violence is tolerated.'[29]

Turning to the European human rights law system, in *Opuz v. Turkey* the ECtHR found Turkey responsible for violating Article 14 ECHR (prohibition of discrimination) because, although it had adopted a law to counter DV, discrimination resulted 'from the general attitude of the local authorities, such as the manner in which the women were treated at police stations when they reported domestic violence and judicial passivity in providing effective protection to victims.'[30] Despite the number of DV cases reported in the area where Nahide Opuz lived, the police did not investigate her complaints of DV and the courts easily dismissed them, reproducing the public/private divide which international human rights law had begun to disrupt starting from the 1990s. The ECtHR also emphasised how the 'general discriminatory judicial passivity … created a climate that was conducive to domestic violence.'[31] This outcome is confirmed in another judgment, *Talpis v. Italy*, where the Court found that Italian authorities had 'condoned' the violent acts against Elisaveta Talpis – whose son was killed by her husband – and that she had been a victim of discrimination. The Court also referred to the 'socio-cultural attitude of tolerance of DV.'[32] Quite interestingly, and surprisingly to a certain extent, the Court departed from a previous judgment also involving Italy, filed by Giulia Rumor,[33] explicitly saying that the circumstances were different, because in *Rumor* the legislative framework existing in Italy was effective in punishing the perpetrator, whereas in *Talpis* the criminal law system 'had not had an adequate deterrent effect.'[34] The reasoning of the Court regarding the application of Article 14 ECHR in *Talpis v. Italy* is thus not straightforward. I can argue that the reason lies in the fact that the Court mixed the patterns of discrimination discussed in this paragraph. As pointed out by Judge Eicke in his dissenting opinion, there was no 'appearance of discriminatory treatment of women who are victims of domestic violence on the part of the authorities such as the police, law-enforcement or health-care personnel, social services, prosecutors or judges of the courts of law.'[35] That is precisely the description of a pattern of discrimination in laws and policies of the state: accordingly, either the findings in *Rumor* were wrong, or in Italy this specific pattern of discrimination, which permeates state policies, cannot be demonstrated. The Court was right to state that social and cultural patterns of discrimination are still persistent in Italian society, though. A quick look at Italian newspapers will show, for example, that DV is routinely treated as an 'episode of insanity' by the partner, or a murdered woman's behaviour is scrutinised to find out whether she had cheated on her husband, as this would 'explain' or even 'justify' the act of violence.

In the case under analysis here, though, I can go a bit further, because one element of the facts of the *Talpis* case was not sufficiently discussed by the Court and could have led to identification of a pattern of discrimination by the state. Had it confirmed the existence of such a pattern, not in society but in the behaviour of the state and its organs, the Court could have concluded, in a more effective way, that Italy had violated the prohibition of discrimination as enshrined in Article 14 ECHR. Let us go back to the facts. Talpis had found refuge from her violent husband with a local association. However, after some months, the social services of the municipality of Udine notified the association that no funds were available to guarantee her another refuge or to pay for the refuge found by the association. Talpis then returned home. The government argued that the social services in Udine, which had developed a programme for victims of violence, were not in charge of the situation and therefore could not pay for a refuge managed by a private association; Mrs Talpis should have contacted the social services to ask for help. The Court could have chosen to apply Article 14 ECHR, and then held that, despite remarkable steps forward in protecting women from domestic violence, the Italian legislative framework *as applied by* the Udine authorities *systematically* discriminated against women.[36] The Italian authorities did discriminate by blaming Elisaveta Talpis for not having asked the competent authorities for help in due time, and by not supporting associations which assist women victims of abuse. This can be defined as a pattern of discrimination preventing abused women from having free and immediate access to social services.

In support of the main argument of these pages, I should also mention the views of the CEDAW Committee in *Angela González Carreño*, which clearly contended that:

> [w]hen there is evidence of systematic patterns of violence against women, or when the incidence of violence against women is inordinately high, as reflected in a high rate of domestic violence, it is clear that the State knows or should know of the risks faced by women who have complained of violence from their partners or former partners.[37]

Furthermore, in a case of rape and abduction, the African Commission stressed how the state does not respect its obligations 'when it tolerates a situation where private persons or groups act freely and with impunity in violation of the rights' under the African Charter.[38]

If we turn to the vertical dimension, the pattern of discrimination can be seen either in laws and policies in the field of health care that directly or indirectly cause VAWH – for example the criminalisation of abortion or provisions on forced sterilisation – or in the state's 'tolerance' of discriminatory behaviours by medical personnel, both in the public and the private sector, which cause VAWH. Hence, for example, in *CGIL v. Italy*, the European Committee of Social Rights argued in 2013, that, despite the law granting women access to abortion, and the monitoring activity started by the government, 'the shortcomings which exist in the provision of abortion services in Italy … remain unremedied.'[39] Another example of a pattern of discrimination taken from the case law analysed in chapter 1 concerns the provision of misleading information to women, either because directly required by the state, the male actor I have referred to several times, which can replace the woman in pivotal decisions concerning her body; or because medical personnel are guided by the stereotype that the woman will always decide to protect her foetus, no matter what medical treatment is necessary to do so. Health personnel, whether in public or in private healthcare, perform a public function in the field of health. With regard to abortion, from a social perspective, as Ronli Sifris has interestingly argued, 'coercing a woman to continue with a pregnancy has the effect of coercing her to become mother.'[40] The direct consequence of doing this is to reinforce a socially imposed construction of a woman's role in society, and to reduce the possibility, given the way many workplaces organise themselves, for her to live a professional life: 'legal restrictions on access to abortion discriminate against women in [a] myriad of ways. They are formulated and implemented in a social context in which gender inequality reigns.'[41]

The pattern of discrimination in the vertical dimension can be also seen in all cases of involuntary sterilisation. As I discussed in chapter 1, sterilisation without the consent of the woman, or without fully informed consent, can be imposed by the adoption of eugenic laws by the state. In this regard, the CEDAW Committee, in its concluding observations on Japan, noted that 'the State party, through the Prefectural Eugenic Protection Committee, *sought to prevent* births of children with diseases or disabilities and, as a result, subjected persons with disabilities to forced sterilization.'[42] It was a pattern of discrimination, in this case on the ground of disability, by means of a law in the field of health. Several cases of involuntary sterilisation have been reported in many countries, and the ECtHR has handed down pivotal judgments in which it applied the right to respect for private and family life and the prohibition of torture, inhuman or degrading treatment or punishment. Nonetheless, when it comes to the prohibition of discrimination under Article 14 ECHR, as I have already mentioned, the Court has missed the opportunity to tackle these cases as discrimination, and intersectional discrimination more specifically.[43] In *I.G. and others v. Slovakia*, for example, the Court first found that the practice of sterilising women without their prior, informed consent 'affected vulnerable individuals from various ethnic groups,' but then noticed that 'it cannot be established … that the doctors involved acted in bad faith, that the first and second applicants' sterilisation was a part of an "organised policy," or that the hospital staff's conduct was intentionally racially motivated.'[44] Before a decree of the Ministry of Health in 2013, which set out procedures to guarantee that a woman could only be sterilised after free, prior and informed consent, the Public Health Act had allowed physicians 'to deliver the sterilization without the information procedure generally specified when it seems to be appropriate in given circumstances.'[45] The existence of a pattern of discrimination, at the time when sterilisation occurred, seemed to be confirmed by the most recent report of the UN Committee on the Elimination of Racial Discrimination (CERD) in Slovakia, which, with regard to the right to health, expressed its concern 'about reports of discriminatory treatment by medical personnel against Roma and segregation of Roma, particularly women and girls, in different hospital departments.'[46] The Committee acknowledged that, despite the measures adopted to prevent forced sterilisation, access to justice for those who suffered involuntary sterilisation still remained difficult.[47] Where women belong to minorities, the woman's body is 'used' to discriminate against an entire group, and women are considered as 'incapable of making rational decisions.'[48] Why not promote campaigns of contraception or sterilisation for men? Ronli Sifris has clearly answered this question:

> If a woman's body belongs to the men in her life and the male paradigm of the State, then it is logical that involuntary sterilisation procedures should be carried out on women more than men, even though the medical procedure for men is much simpler than that for women.[49]

The relevance of intersectionality in describing patterns of discrimination

The term 'intersectionality' was first introduced by Kimberlé Crenshaw in the late 1980s, to stress the specific conditions of Black women in US society. It is not a concept that applies only to marginalised groups, it is rather 'an aspect of social organisation that shapes our lives,' with the consequence that 'groups may be advantaged or disadvantaged by structures of oppression.'[50] Intersectionality has not had much attention in legal scholarship, though. Defined as an 'analytical tool,'[51] it has rarely been invoked in court. In these pages, I use the definition of intersectionality proposed by Lorena Sosa, who, in her remarkable book, considers intersectionality 'a tool for interpreting human rights in general, and for violence against women in particular, consisting of an explicit interdisciplinary approach to the study of race, gender, class and other social categories of distinction.'[52] This idea, she argues, captures the 'socio-structural nature of inequality.'[53] From a legal point of view, intersectionality can be used as 'interpretative methodology' for exploring international legal norms on VAW,[54] and for 'empowering these norms.'[55]

Why is intersectionality appropriate for conceptualising the idea of VAWH?
Although the issue of intersectionality has mainly emerged in connection with involuntary sterilisation, intersectionality permeates all the types of violence that I proposed in chapter 1. Starting from the horizontal dimension, in cases of DV the 'tolerance' of the state for episodes of DV, manifested in lack of or delay in investigation, and absence of effective remedies, can become more intense in all cases in which the woman belongs to a minority. Hence, for example, in *Lenahan (Gonzáles)*, *amici curiae* presented several reports during the proceedings before the IACommHR, one of which precisely concerned the effects of DV on minority women and children and the law enforcement response.[56] Even though the Commission, deciding the case, did not consider intersectionality as an issue in its report, it stressed the existence of multiple grounds of discrimination, recognising that 'certain groups of women face discrimination on the basis of more than one factor during their lifetime, based on their young age, race and ethnic origin, among others, which increases their exposure to acts of violence.'[57] This has consequences in terms of measures that the state must adopt in order to change socio-cultural patterns of discrimination.

Intersectionality is relevant when a woman is raped, because she is a woman, and because she belongs to a specific minority. The decision of the IACHR in *Inés Fernández Ortega v. Mexico* is an example in that respect. The Court elaborated the state's obligation to guarantee access to justice by referring to the specific situation of indigenous women. As I will elaborate further, the pattern of intersectional discrimination in cases of FGM/C seems much more apparent in state reactions to such cases than in reactions to other violations of a woman's physical integrity.[58] Without denying that FGM/C is a form of VAWH, as I will contend, the response of the state to these violations of women's rights to health and reproductive health has proved to be discriminatory, especially against *adult* women belonging to minorities in which this practice is performed.

Turning to the vertical dimension, from the *anamnesis* elaborated in chapter 1 I can draw several cases of intersectional discrimination. It seems that another ground of discrimination is specifically relevant to access to abortion, for example: the social and economic conditions of the woman seeking such access. When access is withheld because abortion clinics do not exist in the area where the woman lives,[59] or because practitioners opt for conscientious objection,[60] or because the fees are too high,[61] or because the law does not allow women access to abortion and they are obliged to travel,[62] it is evident that these health laws and policies cause VAWH, and their impact is much more severe for those who do not have the economic means to gain access to safe abortions. Unsafe abortions are extremely dangerous for women's health.

Ethnicity as a ground for discrimination combined with gender is seen both in cases of involuntary sterilisation, and in cases of OV. Going back to its recent report on Slovakia, CERD affirmed that it had received information relating to 'verbal and physical violence faced by Roma women when accessing sexual and reproductive health services.'[63]

The *anamnesis* was particularly useful in highlighting how some courts, in particular the ECtHR, have been reluctant to apply the concept of intersectional discrimination, or, despite recognising the existence of different grounds of discrimination, have not drawn adequate conclusions about the state's obligations. In its GR No. 35, the CEDAW Committee acknowledged that 'because women experience varying and intersecting forms of discrimination,' VAW 'may affect some women to different degrees, or in different ways, so appropriate legal and policy responses are needed.'[64] This means, in other words, that intersectionality, far from being a mere feminist naïveté, is fundamental to accurately identifying states' obligations, such as the obligation to provide access to effective remedies. In my analysis of VAWH, the concept is especially pertinent because intersectionality particularly matters in the field of health policies and laws, with regard to women's rights to health and to reproductive health, and it matters in both dimensions of violence explored in this book.

As I will show further in chapter 3, the notion of intersectionality allows us to reflect on the 'costs' of services for women. Should emergency contraception be free? Should access to abortion be covered by health insurance? What about the differences in access to health and social services for poor women and women belonging to minorities? I am referring not only to the US system, characterised by a system of private insurances, but also, for example, to travel insurance. Without mentioning any particular company (since I am sure similar provisions appear in many contracts), a travel insurance purporting to cover costs related to injuries and illnesses while abroad clearly excludes 'voluntary termination of pregnancy,' 'assisted reproduction' and 'related complications.' Accordingly, a woman who seeks abortion outside her home country has to bear all the costs of the procedure plus the risks deriving from possible medical complications.

VAWH as a form of gender-based violence

Violence against women, as repeatedly confirmed in international and regional legal instruments alike, is based on gender. VAWH is also gender-based, because, to quote GR no. 35 adopted by CEDAW in 2017, it is founded on stereotypes rooted in our societies, it is a 'social – rather than individual – problem, requiring comprehensive responses, beyond specific events, individual perpetrators and victims/survivors.'[65] The Council of Europe Istanbul Convention also 'link[ed] gender-based violence to gender stereotypes,'[66] and the expression of gender-based violence is understood 'as aimed at protecting women from violence resulting from gender stereotypes.'[67]

A stereotype is 'a generalized view or preconception of attributes or characteristics possessed by, or the roles that are or should be performed by, members of a particular group (e.g., women, lesbians, adolescents).'[68] Stereotypes are ancient and persistent. They are ancient – it is possible to find traces of them in literature and in popular idioms. Bruna Bianchi argued that DV is 'widespread in all social classes and cultural contexts, invisible, silenced, condoned, often the object of complacent humour which crystallised in popular idioms, songs and nursery rhymes.'[69] As early as the beginning of the nineteenth century feminists started to fight against stereotypes that depict women as vulnerable, incapable of taking autonomous decisions and completely dependent on their husbands or male relatives. Stereotypes are persistent because, for all that feminists could achieve excellent results in promoting gender equality in the law, VAW and VAWH characterise all societies of today. As has interestingly been argued, 'when a State applies, enforces or perpetuates a gender stereotype in its laws and policies, it institutionalises the stereotype giving it the force and the authority of law and custom.'[70]

Stereotypes can be seen in all the cases I analysed in chapter 1. As with the cases of intersectional discrimination, human rights courts have not always been ready to construct their arguments on the existence of stereotypes. UN treaty bodies have demonstrated themselves more attentive in assessing the existence of stereotypes in cases of VAW. For example, in *A.T. v. Hungary* the CEDAW Committee referred, in a case of DV, to the 'persistence of entrenched traditional stereotypes regarding the role and responsibilities of women and men in the family.'[71] In the views on a rape case, *Vertido v. The Philippines*, the CEDAW Committee stressed that:

> the judiciary must take caution not to create inflexible standards of what women or girls should be or what they should have done when confronted with a situation of rape based merely on *preconceived notions* of what defines a rape victim or a victim of gender-based violence, in general.[72]

In this case, Karen Vertido was raped by a senior colleague after a dinner to which she and another male colleague had been invited. She could not obtain justice, since the national court acquitted the perpetrator on the basis that it was not clear 'why the woman had not escaped when she allegedly appeared to have had so many opportunities to do so.' The stereotype of the woman that must demonstrate resistance to rape or be assumed to have consented to it permeated the national court's judgment. Another gender bias was the court's affirmation that 'an accusation for a rape can be made with facility,' implying that women may lie when it comes to reporting unwanted sexual intercourse.[73] Viewed through the lens of VAWH, rape caused Vertido both physical and psychological harm, which was exacerbated by the re-victimisation she suffered during proceedings in front of the domestic court. The Committee found that the Philippines had violated Articles 2(f) and 5(a) of the CEDAW Convention because the state had failed to respect its due diligence obligations to banish gender stereotypes.[74] The affirmation is particularly strong and not devoid of legal consequences, in terms of actions that the state must adopt to eradicate prejudices.

At first sight we can argue that courts have responded to FGM/C through judgments that, although not always directly, have emphasised the stereotyped role of women in the societies where this practice is performed. Courts have granted refugee status to women escaping countries in which there was a risk of being subjected to FGM/C, a practice that has been defined as 'cultural,' 'barbaric,' 'torture.' These judgments must be welcomed, although I will try to go a bit further in the analysis. I am convinced that, even though it is practised by women, and has a ritual and ancestral meaning, FGM/C is a form of VAWH, which entails severe consequences for women's and girls' health and reproductive health. It is based on stereotypes that identify a specific role for women in society. Nonetheless, as I will discuss further, courts themselves, while condemning FGM/C, and while accepting requests for refugee status, perpetuate stereotypes. If we look at the language used by the courts, this argument is crystal-clear. The Constitutional Court of Uganda, in the pivotal case *Law and Advocacy for Women in Uganda v. Attorney-General*, condemned FGM/C by also referring to Article 33(1) and (3) of the Ugandan Constitution, which states that 'women shall be accorded full and equal dignity of the person with men,' and that 'the state shall protect women and their rights taking into account their unique status and natural maternal functions in society.'[75] This assumes that the state can better protect women, since they occupy a condition of vulnerability. I am not arguing that national courts should not have condemned the practice, quite the contrary; but when it comes to my paradigm and my notion of VAWH, I cannot disregard practices that, despite having similarly permanent and dangerous effects for a woman's health, are accepted by society without any – or with very little – concern. Fighting stereotypes using other stereotypes of women does not seem the most adequate approach to identifying and eradicating the rooted causes of VAWH.

The vertical dimension shows many examples of stereotypes. The recurrent stereotype of the mother who cannot decide what is best health practice for her child and herself is pervasive. One author calls it the 'ideology of motherhood,' which may lead to prohibitions on contraception and abortion, and is characterised (given the stereotyped role of women as caretakers) by a lot of emphasis on, for example, 'the importance of breastfeeding for children's nutrition, the bond between mother and child established through pregnancy and women's sensitive and caring nature.'[76] The CEDAW Committee examined a tragic case of lack of access to abortion, and acknowledged for the first time 'the impact of stereotyping on the rights of individual women.'[77] In *L.C. v. Peru*, the stereotype was to regard the woman as a vessel for reproduction, letting the interests of the foetus prevail over those of L.C. This stereotype caused a doctor to delay the decision to perform spinal surgery on a minor who had been raped and attempted suicide, severely injuring herself. L.C. was also refused therapeutic abortion. Similar stereotypes operate to restrict access to contraception: pharmacists and health personnel in public dispensing have claimed, for example, their right to conscientious objection in refusing to accept requests for contraceptives and refusing to fill a doctor's prescription of contraceptives.[78]

Conversely, involuntary sterilisation goes in the direction of denying women motherhood. The stereotype here sees the woman as not capable of deciding what is the best for her, because she is HIV-positive or because she is a convicted criminal (say), and others – practitioners or the state directly – as better qualified to decide on her behalf. Ethnic biases are particularly prevalent in cases of involuntary sterilisation, as I realised after investigating issues of intersectional discrimination where the state has decided that women belonging to a particular minority must be prevented from having children.

Finally, the stereotype is evident in OV. If a woman's role is to have children, and she is not considered 'complete' without them, one might assume that she will do whatever she is asked to achieve this outcome, without questioning too much the practitioner's opinion: when deciding on an unnecessary caesarean section, say,[79] or manoeuvres or other practices during the birth. The stereotype is also normalised by women, who do not report cases of OV, believing that they are 'normal' practices.

The *anamnesis* confirmed the main arguments in the feminist discourse regarding the female body and the approach of medicine over time. Laura Purdy has contended that the process of 'medicalisation' of women's health, meaning the 'tendency to define normal events in women's lives … and natural states … as pathological and requiring medical attention,' is surely an aspect of our times, but that it cannot be simply demonised. As she pointed out, 'a medical approach to bodily conditions (medicalisation) is not the problem, but rather the culture of medicine itself.'[80]

VAWH as a violation of the right to health and the right to reproductive health

VAWH consists in violations of the women's rights to health and to reproductive health. In the *anamnesis* in chapter 1 my analysis of case law showed that these rights are seldom invoked. The outcome is not surprising. The right to health is not included in the ICCPR, nor in the European and American regional conventions on human rights. The American Convention (Article 5(1)) and the Belém do

Pará Convention (Article 4(c)) provide rights to respect for physical and mental integrity, but do not include the right to the 'highest attainable standard of health' as elaborated in the ICESCR. Accordingly, failure to apply the rights to health and to reproductive health does not suggest that the right to health is regarded as less justiciable, but simply that this right was not envisaged in regional human rights legal instruments characterised by developed monitoring mechanisms of compliance. Courts have referred to the health conditions of the applicant in many judgments, as have UN treaty bodies in their views, and found violations of three major human rights: the right to privacy, which includes the respect for reproductive autonomy; the right to life, in the most serious cases that have led to the death of the woman or of one of her relatives; the right to freedom from torture, inhuman or degrading treatment or punishment.

In cases of DV, the ECtHR has often based its main argument on the physical and psychological conditions of the woman. In *Valiulienė*, as discussed in 'What is violence against women's health?', the Court emphasised the severe mental consequences of DV.[81] In *Opuz*, references to the health condition of Sahide Opuz were relevant to assessing that her right to be free from torture, inhuman or degrading treatment had been violated.[82] Even though the ECtHR cannot apply a right that the European Convention does not convey, it observed that, among the 'factors that can be taken into account in deciding to pursue a prosecution,' authorities must consider 'the continuing threat to the health and safety of the victim.'[83] The IACHR referred to the rights to privacy and to humane treatment in pivotal cases of rape committed by the military such as *Ana, Beatriz and Celia González Pérez v. Mexico* and *Ortega v. Mexico*. The right to privacy includes sexual and reproductive autonomy. In *López Soto* the IACommHR stressed in its report the violations of Linda López Soto's physical integrity, and characterised her kidnapping, and the sexual assault she suffered, as 'expression of acute cruelty … of an extreme intensity', violating her rights to humane treatment, personal liberty, privacy, autonomy and dignity.[84] The protection of personal integrity was also mentioned by the Municipal Court of Pueblo Rico in a case of FGM/C within the Emberá-Chamí indigenous community.

Turning to the vertical dimension, the rights to personal integrity and to freedom from violence were mentioned in the report of the IACommHR in the case *Manuela y Familia v. El Salvador*, regarding a woman who was imprisoned after having a miscarriage and died while in detention.

The lack of access to abortion has been examined under several provisions of both the ECHR and the ICCPR, and the aspects relating to health have been mentioned in order to support conclusions that a specific right had been violated. In *Mellet,* for example, the HRC highlighted the 'high level of mental anguish' Amanda Mellet suffered. In *Tysiac v. Poland*, the ECtHR referred to the 'terrible anguish' Alicja Tysiac, who was refused abortion, was subjected to, while in *R.R. v. Poland* it applied for the first time Article 3 ECHR in a case which resembled *Tysiac* in terms of the obstacles to gaining access to abortion services. With no right to health, but referring to the health consequences of violence, the Court has relied on other human rights to ascertain the effects of violence on women's health.

Some national courts have directly applied the rights to health and to reproductive health in cases brought to their attention. For example, in the C-355/2006 judgment, the Colombian Constitutional Court ruled that a law criminalising abortion in all circumstances was unconstitutional. In particular, it argued that women's right to health encompasses reproductive health, including freedom from state interference in women's decisions. The Supreme Court of Nepal applied the constitutionally granted right to health in *Lakshmi Dhikta*, which concerned economic difficulties in gaining access to abortion.

At national level, the rights to health and to reproductive health were also mentioned in the *G., M.C.Y. v. Hospital Luis Lagomaggiore* judgment on OV decided by the Court of Mendoza in Argentina, and by the High Court of Delhi in a case regarding maternal mortality.[85]

At regional level, it is worth mentioning the decision in *CGIL v. Italy*, where the European Committee of Social Rights applied the right to health in the analysis of the *de facto* difficulties in gaining access to abortion services attributable to the number of conscientious objectors operating in Italian hospitals. The mechanism of collective complaints provided by the European Committee, although unique, is not capable of filling the gap in the jurisprudence of the ECtHR where social and economic rights are not protected in its founding treaty, however.

At the international level, needless to say the CEDAW Committee has offered the best protection of the rights to health and to reproductive health, given that its governing convention includes the principle of non-discrimination in the field of health care (Article 12(1)), and obliges state parties to ensure to women appropriate services in connection with pregnancy, confinement and the post-natal period (Article 12(2)). Cases such as *L.C.* on access to abortion, *Andrea Szijjarto v. Hungary* concerning involuntary sterilisation and *Alyne da Silva Pimentel Teixeira v. Brazil* on maternal health are excellent examples of the affirmation of the right to health as justiciable. Let us focus on these cases to assess whether the outcome of these decisions was different to those in cases in which the right to health was indirectly applied. If the focus is (only, although importantly) on the right of the victim/survivor to receive justice, and on compensation for the harm suffered because of the violation of human rights, applying the rights to health and to reproductive health, whether directly or indirectly, does not seem to change much, at least at first sight. As one author has argued about a case of DV, 'the inclusion of the right to health may not have changed the outcome of the decision, but it would have provided the Court with a far more honest and accurate assessment of the harms that were suffered' by women.[86] I would say that the outcome would be similar, but not identical. Application of the rights to health and to reproductive health can better shape states' obligations, as I will discuss in chapter 3, in the form of positive obligations to provide health services to women.

The main objection to this argument is that, even if my assertion is so, and application of the rights to health and to reproductive health would change the outcome of a case, we cannot alter the nature of legal instruments that are the product of the will of the state. It is up to states to amend provisions included in international treaties. One might also object that the cases in which the rights to health and to reproductive health have been applied were brought before either the courts of states whose constitutions include the right to health, or the CEDAW Committee whose founding convention encompasses these rights and whose decisions are not binding. Still, even without specific provisions, the ECtHR and the IACHR, along with the HRC, have been able to address issues of health in their judgments/views. In other words, international and regional jurisprudence has not directly ensured respect for the right to health; rather, it has indirectly *promoted the right's content by applying other, more 'justiciable' rights*. The expression 'more justiciable rights' does not imply different levels of justiciability but that some rights have been more easily applied, owing to the way the complaint has been presented or a body's competence not extending into key areas. This is of interest for my purposes. Until the recent judgment in *López Soto*, the case law of human rights courts has had a 'knock-on effect', upholding individual rights in several articles of the conventions of which they are the guardians, and could pave the way for amendments to those conventions or the addition of new protocols to them.[87] This does not mean 'inventing' new rights or placing excessive burden on human rights courts, but rather implies conceiving a material right that already exists in other legal instruments, and has been the object of interpretation by courts. The future could bring some light and some 'justiciability' to the right to health before UN treaty bodies, thanks to the entry into force of the Protocol to the ICESCR, giving the corresponding committee competence to accept individual complaints against the states that have ratified it (at the moment, few).

Direct application of the rights to health and to reproductive health would have some fundamental consequences. First, even though we can agree with the courts that DV and rape amount to torture, inhuman or degrading treatment or punishment, it is also true that where regional courts get rid of the assessment of the level of intensity their reasoning is not always straightforward. Furthermore, the right to be free from torture, inhuman or degrading treatment or punishment, application of which is almost automatic in cases of DV and rape, is not necessarily applicable in all cases of VAWH. The IACHR has not applied the prohibition of torture in cases of DV or rape committed by private individuals, for example,[88] because of the specific characteristics of the crime of torture.[89] In cases of lack of access to abortion, the first judgment in which the ECtHR applied Article 3 ECHR was handed down in 2011, two years after the well-known *Opuz* judgment on DV.[90] Second, as I will show, the main consequence of considering the violation of the rights to health and to reproductive health concerns states' obligations. Third, application of the rights to health and to reproductive health – the latter as part of the former – will reinforce the justiciability of the right to health, which as a social and economic right has suffered the same status of 'Cinderella right' as the other rights included in the ICESCR. If direct application is not possible, considerations on the right to health and reproductive health should permeate more extensively the legal reasoning of courts and human rights bodies. Fourth, from a feminist legal perspective, this argument would help women, because application of the rights to health and to reproductive health would better emphasise the multiple angles of VAWH, which causes serious physical and psychological harm, and would embrace both the dimensions I discuss in this book. Julie and Sandra Levison have argued that 'although violence and abuse are an integral part of the lives of many people, and the single greatest cause of injury to women, the subject of violence has not been systematically addressed as a major issue in women's health.'[91] They refer to data and national surveys, but I realised in my research how the rights to health and to reproductive health have only been protected indirectly, and how they would play a fundamental role in enhancing the protection of women's rights at the international level. As was reported in a manual of the National Academy of Women's Health, women's health:[92]

> includes the values and knowledge of women and their own experience of health and illness; recognizes the diversity of women's health needs over the life cycle and how these needs reflect differences in race, class, ethnicity, culture, sexual preference and levels of education; includes the empowerment of women … to be informed participants in their own health care.

VAWH and intent

In the short analysis of the definition of VAW contained in the introduction,[93] I argued that intent is not a necessary element of the definition, and that VAW can be conceived as a framework encompassing acts of gender-based violence against women rather than a distinct crime or behaviour. I have already shown in this chapter that VAWH grasps both dimensions of violence, and describes well the relationship between VAW on one hand, and the rights to health and to reproductive health on the other. I will confirm the absence of the element of intent in the definition of VAWH conceived in this book, and further explore an element that I outlined in 'VAWH as a form of discrimination against women: patterns of discrimination', namely the 'pattern of discrimination' that can be found in both dimensions of violence.[94]

I am not discussing here the concept of intent in criminal law, which goes beyond the scope of this book, and would require a comparative analysis of different legal systems and of international criminal law.[95] Intention, in a very simple and clearly non-exhaustive summary, is related to the purpose of an action. It is the 'guilty mind' of the perpetrator.[96] It could be said that the purpose of VAWH is to discriminate against women because they are women. Nonetheless, discrimination is structural, and permeates societies to the extent that it might be difficult to prove that an individual and/or the state intended to discriminate against women while committing an act of violence. VAW, and VAWH as it is conceptualised here, *is* defined as a form of discrimination against women. In other words, acts of violence may not aim to discriminate against women, but *constitute themselves* forms of discrimination, are directed against women because they are women and/or affect women disproportionately.

The concept of intent is extremely complex in international law, especially when it concerns states. Could a state have a 'guilty mind'? As put by Ronli Sifris, who interestingly has analysed limitations to reproductive freedom from the point of view of the crime of torture, 'when a State legally restricts access to abortion, can it be viewed as intending to cause severe pain or suffering'?[97] Relying on an argument made by Rhonda Copelon,[98] she concluded that, since severe pain and suffering is 'a foreseeable consequence of both involuntary sterilisation and restrictions on abortion,' the requirement for intention is 'satisfied in both of these cases.'[99] This analysis is of utmost interest. Nonetheless, it has proved very difficult not only to consider intention on the part of the state, a collective entity,[100] but also to examine state responsibility for the sole exercise of the legislative power.[101] Furthermore, the responsibility of the individual must be distinguished from the responsibility of the state. As I have argued with regard to genocide, if we consider the state as a *de facto* entity, we might say that it has a 'guilty mind', although intention would manifest itself in a different way: not as 'mental, individual status,' but rather as 'state policy' and a 'pattern of conduct.'[102]

Let us consider a case taken from the vertical dimension. When a practitioner communicated misleading information to a woman seeking abortion, was there an intent to cause VAWH as a form of discrimination against women? From the point of view of the responsibility of the individual, the analysis should be conducted in terms of medical malpractice litigation, and it would lead to the assessment of the 'negligence' of the practitioner rather than of the intentions.[103] This level of analysis is not relevant here, however, because I am not discussing the intent of the perpetrators of the single actions that can be referred to VAWH, but the intent – or the lack of intent – in the concept of VAWH itself. Since VAWH is not conceived as a distinct crime but as a framework, the analysis of intent seems superficial. Nonetheless, the *anamnesis* suggests that a 'pattern of conduct' by the state, in my case 'a pattern of discrimination,' exists in all cases of VAWH intended in its vertical dimension, and whenever a repeated tolerance is demonstrated in the horizontal dimension. The 'pattern of conduct', in other words, associates both dimensions as conceived in this book. This argument will prove useful in elaborating states' obligations, in particular the policies and laws that must be adopted in the long term to eradicate violence, and will emphasise the importance of the principle of non-discrimination in human rights cases.

In *Opuz*, the ECtHR contended that there was no need to prove intent while assessing state responsibility for violating Opuz's human rights in a case of DV.[104] However, while deciding whether Turkey had violated Article 14 ECHR, the Court referred to the general attitude of the authorities, and concluded that it had.[105] I saw that the ECtHR has not demonstrated in all cases a structural tolerance by national authorities investigating cases of DV.[106] In a case on involuntary sterilisation, hence concerning the vertical dimension, *I.G. and others v. Slovakia*, the Court argued that there was no evidence that the practitioners had acted in bad faith or that sterilisation was part of an organised policy, and it did not proceed to investigate the case under Article 14 ECHR. In this case, however, a pattern of discrimination could have been demonstrated, given a long-standing attitude in the health sector to discriminate against Romani people.

Considering the vertical dimension, it should be said that, directly or indirectly, the pattern of discrimination can be showed in all cases in which health laws and policies cause VAWH: directly, when the law itself causes VAWH, for example by criminalising abortion; or indirectly, for example when, despite a law granting access to abortion, services and practitioners responsible for a public interest activity (in the field of health care) *do* cause VAWH. Back in the 1980s, one author contended that, in the United States, 'legislative proposals to allow involuntary sterilisation of certain groups on eugenic grounds have a long history,' and the public policy showed 'a systematic, state-sanctioned character of involuntary sterilisation,' which was later replaced by sterilisation programmes 'more subtle but nonetheless motivated by population control objectives.'[107] The only context in which it seems that the pattern of discrimination cannot be demonstrated is when the individual's action is not related to any form of policy of the state or the structure, e.g. hospital, for which he/she works.

In the horizontal dimension, a pattern of discrimination can be verified, as human rights courts have underlined, when the state shows 'tolerance' for acts of gender-based violence. Is 'negligence' showed by organs of the state sufficient to demonstrate state responsibility for VAWH? Where pain and severe suffering are the consequences of negligence, the requirements for considering an act as torture are not met (because to be torture, there must have been an intent, and a very strong one). In other words, negligence is not enough to demonstrate that torture has been committed.[108] Nonetheless, I would argue that negligence by state organs might be sufficient to prove state responsibility for VAWH because of the existence of a pattern of discrimination against women. By tolerating violence or by promoting policies that perpetuate the subordination of women in society, states repeatedly 'tolerate' a form of discrimination against women and, to paraphrase the ECtHR in a case of domestic violence, create 'a climate that [is] conducive' to VAWH.[109]

Consent and autonomy in the concept of VAWH

The conceptualisation of VAWH does not seem complete without exploring the issue of the woman's consent (or lack of consent), which is not, *prima facie*, part of the definition. The concept of VAW, as elaborated in international and regional legal instruments, does not refer to consent either. However, consent is relevant for both the horizontal and vertical dimensions: lack of consent is an element of the offence of rape, just as lack of 'informed' consent characterises, for example, forced sterilisations.

Consent is an expression of autonomy, and 'autonomy is self-determination.'[110] Francesca Rescigno has defined self-determination as 'a fundamental right,' which is not expressive of 'egoistic liberty,' but rather an 'aware [and informed] choice of the individual within a community and not against it.'[111]

In its GC No. 22, the ESCR Committee considered the right to sexual and reproductive health as 'indispensable to [women's] autonomy.'[112] As argued by Erin Nelson, autonomy is 'the ability to be self-determining and to act on one's own values in making decisions about reproduction.'[113] Autonomy is a pivotal concept in philosophy, bioethics and law; as outlined by Sheila McLean, it is 'the transcending principle of modern bioethics.'[114] Marilyn Friedman contends that autonomous choices are self-reflecting, in the sense that, on one hand, they are caused by a woman's 'reflection on wants and desires that characterise her,' and on the other hand they must reflect wants, desires, cares, values and commitments that someone reaffirms when attending to them.[115] Autonomy is, for the purpose of this analysis, the capacity of a woman to decide about her health, and her reproductive health more specifically.

There is a huge literature on autonomy, from different perspectives.[116] From a philosophical and ethical point of view autonomy would be of utmost interest to discuss, but I cannot even attempt to do it justice here. The purpose of this sub-section is not to dwell on all the existing theories on autonomy, but to assess how consent and autonomy matter for conceptualising the idea of VAWH, and how these are cross-cutting issues for both dimensions. A few preliminary notes seem useful, however.

Individualistic accounts of autonomy have prevailed since 'the change of emphasis' from paternalism, which was common in ancient medicine, to autonomy.[117] In the 1970s, feminists stressed how this notion of autonomy expressed a 'liberatory potential for women.'[118] Nonetheless, individualistic autonomy has been accused of disregarding social context, the network of duties and obligations, and relationships and interests, of the community.[119] This is why scholars, and feminist scholars in particular, turned in the 1980s, and more clearly in the 1990s, to a relational concept of autonomy, considering women as embedded in social relations. Hence, for example, Carol Gilligan, who theorised the 'different voice' of women characterised by responsibility for 'others,' saw care as complementary to individualistic autonomy.[120] Interpersonal relations were at the core of her reasoning. Susan Sherwin, who discussed this issue ten years after Gilligan, did not consider merely interpersonal relations, but rather, and to a great extent, 'the full range of influential human relations, personal and public.'[121] She elaborated a concept of relational autonomy, which was based on the understanding of 'how forces of oppression interfere with an individual ability to exercise autonomy.'[122] Her perspective belongs to radical feminism, which has repeatedly highlighted the limited control women have over healthcare institutions. Without denying the importance of the individual decision, relational theories show 'the damaging effects on autonomy of internalised oppression.'[123] In other words, what is internalised is structural *and* individual, pertains to society and is interiorised by the individual. In the words of Simone de Beauvoir, 'a free individual blames only himself for his failures, he assumes responsibility for them; but everything happens to a woman through the agency of others, and therefore these others are responsible for her woes … she insists on living in her situation precisely as she does – that is, in a state of impotent rage.'[124] In other words, anyone has a 'choice', but the constraints that shape women into women 'can make it virtually impossible for them to exercise this freedom in the world.'[125] Relations are therefore fundamental to understanding the patterns of oppression of women. Relational, in the understanding of Sherwin, means 'contextualised,' or 'socially situated.' In both individualistic and relational autonomy, Sherwin highlighted the importance of informed consent, which, in the case of her account of autonomy, must take into consideration the social location of the woman, and how this location can affect her autonomy.

Susan Dodds, more recently, followed the relational approach. Unlike Susan Sherwin, however, she reconceived the idea of consent, suggesting that 'an adequate understanding of respect for autonomy in health care must extend to an understanding of the development and exercise of the capacity for autonomous decision-making, rather than focusing solely on informed consent or even rational choice.'[126] Even though a person may have all the information she requires, this fact does not guarantee autonomy. The woman must have 'autonomy competencies' to determine 'how to choose authentically.'[127] Accordingly, what is needed is a process of counselling that helps a woman determine what she wants in the given context; this process should assist the person to 're-examin[e], when possible, one's preferences, goals, values.'[128] This theory, although interesting, especially when it reflects on the capacity to decide critically, is not devoid of criticism. Erin Nelson, for example, contends that the adjective 'relational' is unhelpful and might be risky, since 'it can be understood to mean that if you are not in the right kinds of relationships … you cannot be autonomous.'[129] It might lead to an effect that contradicts the initial purpose of countering oppression, by 'justifying paternalistic ideas and arguments about which decisions can legitimately count as autonomous.'[130] Furthermore, the activity of 'counselling' that Susan Dodds recommends can be in itself biased by stereotypes which might well have been internalised by the practitioners. I agree with Nelson when she endorses a 'social' conception of autonomy, which reconciles individualistic choice with feminist recognition of the reality of oppression, without entirely embracing the relational approach.[131]

Based on the right to autonomy is the doctrine of consent, which implies that 'decisions must be made following the provisions of information by a competent, non-coerced individual and [one] may even expect to see some evidence that the person has understood the information they have been given.'[132] The law on consent varies from country to country, but a general principle is encapsulated in the 1997 Convention for the Protection of Human Rights and Dignity of the Human Being with regard to the Application of Biology and Medicine (Oviedo Convention), under which an intervention in the health field 'may only be carried out after the person concerned has given free and informed consent to it' (Article 5). Furthermore, according to the Declaration adopted by the General Conference of UNESCO in 2005, 'any preventive, diagnostic and therapeutic medical intervention is only to be carried out with the prior, free and informed consent of the person concerned, based on adequate information' (Article 6). The meaning of 'adequate information' was clarified in the report on consent submitted by the International Bioethics Committee of UNESCO in 2008, which identified the following elements to be taken into account to show the consent of a patient to a medical intervention:

- the diagnosis and the prognosis;
- the nature and the process of the intervention;
- the expected benefits of the intervention;
- the possible undesirable side effects of the intervention; and
- possibilities, benefits and risks of alternative interventions.[133]

McLean has interestingly argued that, even though in theory consent *does* represent autonomy, when translated from ethical rhetoric to legal reality it seems to be a rather empty vehicle 'to protect doctors from liability.'[134] According to the theories on autonomy that I proposed, consent does not automatically guarantee autonomy, and I will unravel the problems inherent in both the individualistic and the relational approach by explaining how consent and autonomy matter in conceptualising the idea of VAWH. Before elaborating an autonomous notion of autonomy that, for the purpose of this research, will be 'contextualised' and 'human rights-based,' let us see how consent operates in the horizontal and in the vertical dimensions.

Consent and autonomy in the horizontal dimension

In the horizontal dimension that I have elaborated in this book, encompassing cases in which VAW within interpersonal relationships causes a violation of women's rights to health and to reproductive health, the lack of consent is the key aspect. When a woman endures FGM/C, rape or DV, she loses autonomy in the field of reproductive health, either because the practice permanently and severely affects her reproductive capacity or because, as with DV, her capacity to make decisions is impaired by the pressure coming from the violent partner.

Domestic violence

DV diminishes women's autonomy.[135] Nonetheless, the limitation of autonomy is not solely the result of the actions of the perpetrator. The authorities must intervene when a woman reports an episode of violence, but what happens if the abused woman wants to return to live with her abuser or when she withdraws her complaint to the police? Should the authorities disregard her consent, and act for her well-being?

The analysis in this area by Friedman is relevant for my purposes. She warned against posing the question why women stay, which patently blames the victim, and to turn it over: why do men abuse women?[136] On one hand, reasonable factors might lie behind her decision to stay, including the coercive environment in which she lives, the fear of losing custody of her children, incapacity to survive without the husband's financial resources. On the other hand, however, religious or moral norms might guide women to misunderstand what is happening to them.[137] According to Friedman, failing to prosecute the abuser would increase the risk of future abuses, and the negation of autonomy in the short run will be replaced by autonomy in the long run.[138] Nonetheless, to achieve this objective, authorities and police forces need to be adequately trained to avoid secondary victimisation, and act in a gender-sensitive way.[139] This disrupts the public/private divide: it means bringing DV into the public sphere, and criminalising behaviour that in the past only occurred within the husband–wife relationship. The disruption of this divide 'comes [at] a price,' namely loss of control over the legal consequences that follow DV, and short-term loss of autonomy.[140] From another perspective, however, even in the short run there is no lack of autonomy. Privacy, as Meyersfeld has interestingly pointed out, 'cannot be understood merely as the right to be left alone; rather, it is linked affirmatively to liberty, the right to autonomy and self-determination;' it means, in other words, that 'privacy is not in opposition to, but is an affirmation of, women's safety in the home.'[141] Technologies might be of help in that respect: for example, bracelets or wristbands can be designed to be life-saving devices, capable of detecting situations of danger for a woman who has already reported to the authorities episodes of violence, or has approached a women's rights association.

Rape

As I proceeded with the *anamnesis*, I saw how relevant the lack of consent is in cases of rape.[142] In *M.C. v. Bulgaria*, the ECtHR clearly argued that state practice demonstrates how lack of consent is the pivotal element of the crime in the majority of national criminal law systems, and how rape is a violation of sexual autonomy. In international criminal law, the *Elements of Crimes* of the International Criminal Court (ICC) provide that the crime against humanity of rape occurs when 'the invasion was committed by force, or by threat of force or coercion … or by taking advantage of a coercive environment, or the invasion was committed against a person incapable of giving genuine consent.'[143] Accordingly, proofs of non-consent are 'irrelevant in a context of inherent coercion.'[144] Theories of relational autonomy help us to understand the social context in which rape occurs, both in times of peace and in wartime. Requiring the 'utmost resistance' by the victim, as some judges have done,[145] means completely disregarding the role of women in society, trapped in a network of relations characterised by oppression. As for marital rape, it has only recently been considered from a legal point of view, and not by all countries, as a crime. Relational autonomy might explain why consent has been presumed, precisely because the relation between husband

and wife is supposed to imply consent. Nonetheless, minimal requirements for providing valid consent to sexual intercourse must be 'an assurance of a certain level of freedom, so that consent is not the result of either wrongful threat or oppression.'[146]

FGM/C

It is easy to say that girls a few months old who undergo FGM/C cannot express their consent to it. It is the family that decides for them. Nonetheless, there might be cases in which adult women ask to be re-infibulated after, for example, giving birth to a child. The key issue is then whether the consent of the woman is enough in these cases to authorise the practice. In other words, is the woman's consent expressive of her autonomy? If we consider the relations within which the woman is situated, it can be argued that the community and/or the family can significantly influence a particular decision, and even impose it. It would be possible to contend, following the interesting position elaborated by Sherwin, that oppression is internalised and that it is difficult to consider the genuine nature of the consent within the context of a network of existing (presumably oppressive) relations. However, the criticism to the relational approach proposed by Erin Nelson is especially relevant here. We risk endorsing a patriarchal and Western approach, which decides which relations are the best for the woman: the norms within the society of the host state prevail over those of the society of the country of origin. Although harm to young women's genitalia is never acceptable, regardless of how 'minor' the injury, because harm, as I explained, can also be psychological, and these practices affect a girl's rights to health and to reproductive health,[147] it is important to reflect on the possibility that the woman can give consent when she is adult. Some scholars might find this possibility unacceptable, but I think that it is not when we challenge the relational approach in order to avoid imposing a 'model' of autonomy which belongs to Western countries. For example, in the UK a case of re-infibulation requested by a woman after childbirth ended with the practitioner being acquitted, and this happened despite the strong legislation against FGM/C in force in the UK.[148] The judgments on FGM/C that I discussed in chapter 1 were actually based on 'relations,' because courts from different countries took into consideration the degree of oppression for women in their country of origin. In the majority of the interesting judgments I found, domestic courts accepted requests for refugee status filed by women who might have been subject to FGM/C if returned to their home country. From a legal point of view, and according to my analysis, the arguments were correct, because FGM/C does cause VAWH.[149] In all of these cases the woman refused consent to the practice, and escaped her country of origin. Nonetheless, there is a 'tendency to make "culture" more important than it is in explaining events in non-Western or minority cultures, whilst minimising its significance elsewhere.'[150] European and American societies call 'culture' something that 'we cannot otherwise understand.'[151]

Let us take for example another practice, genital cosmetic surgery (GCS). I can easily contend that it is culturally embedded in Western societies. Genital cosmetic surgery usually consists in labiaplasty, which means to reduce the size of the labia minora – the flaps of skin either side of the vaginal opening.[152] One might say that the woman consents to GCS, and that the practice does not affect new-born girls, so FGM and GCS are not comparable.[153] Nonetheless, in the United Kingdom, girls as young as 11 request the operation.[154] On its website the National Health Service says that the surgery *should not* be performed on girls younger than 18, but it is not prohibited on minors *per se*. This operation is also called 'designer vagina surgery,' which clearly stresses that, in the great majority of cases, it is unnecessary (there is no medical indication of its usefulness) and harmful (because it causes bodily injury). How genuine, meaning devoid of any form of actual or internalised oppression, is the consent of girls as young as 11 that do not like their genitalia and ask for them to be surgically altered? If we go back to relational autonomy, it is clear that the network of relations is fundamental to understanding the complexity of consent. The image of beauty in Western society is 'cultural' in the same sense as a practice that considers FGM/C the act of belonging to a community. Hence, the question is: why should FGM/C be prohibited and not GCS? There is no obvious answer to the question, which surely requires reflection at societal level. For the time being, it can be said that this practice is not often considered from the perspective of human rights law. It should be, just as FGM/C is considered as a violation of human rights. For the purpose of this chapter, I argue that both these practices constitute a form of VAWH. This is why consent matters in the elaboration of the notion of VAWH and in the definition of the offences that belong to this concept. GCS, which causes permanent injuries, can be equated with FGM/C, and should be prohibited when performed on minors who cannot express genuine and well-informed consent.[155] Furthermore, why should a woman, aged 18 or above, not be competent to ask for re-infibulation, but be competent to ask for GCS? A reconsideration of the elements of the crime of FGM/C, including the element of lack of consent, and consideration of when and how GCS violates human rights, would be helpful in addressing cases of VAWH. An adult woman can consent to both practices, and she can even accept that they are part of her group's tradition or a mere standard of beauty; what is relevant here is that she must be aware and fully informed of the consequences for her health so that she can express her genuine, non-coerced, consent.

Consent and autonomy in the vertical dimension

In the vertical dimension, informed consent is the key, as it was in my argument on FGM/C and GCS. As anticipated in explaining the general theories on autonomy, free and informed consent means that a person receives 'adequate information,' including the effects of medical intervention on her health.

Abortion

In terms of consent and autonomy, abortion is a highly controversial issue. What constitutes informed consent in the case of abortion? What information or counselling should a woman receive when deciding whether to undergo abortion? Are mandatory procedures such as transvaginal ultrasounds necessary to 'inform' her? More than in other cases, stereotypes and biases pervade consent in the field of access to abortion. As clearly contended by Cook:

> [t]here is a generalized view that all women should become mothers, irrespective of their distinctive reproductive health capacity and physical and emotional circumstances, or their individual priorities. It does not matter for purposes of defining the stereotype that an individual woman, say Mary, may not wish, for whatever reason, to become a mother. Precisely because Mary is categorized as a woman, it is believed that motherhood is her natural role and destiny.[156]

Stereotypes lead to biased information, which emphasises the foetus's interests at the expense of the woman's. The state, acting as a male actor, protecting the woman from 'wrongful' decisions, engages in 'reflecting what it sees as legitimate social policy,'[157] with the doctor becoming the 'mouthpiece' for state interests.[158]

> With the State and the doctor potentially bearing down on the patient with their own interests in the foetus, how is the distinctly private and individualistic nature of reproductive choice protected?[159]

Describing the situation in the United States, Pamela Laufer-Ukeles explains that doctors 'assume' what the woman wants to know, or should know, in order to take the 'right' decision, about the condition of the foetus and the possibility of foetal pain while performing abortion. Nonetheless, information can be 'unabashedly biased and reflect … ideological interests of the State as long as it is deemed not misleading or untruthful.'[160] In the USA, even though abortion was recognised as a right in *Roe v. Wade*, state laws seek to restrict women's ability to exercise this right through, for example, laws that require pre-procedure counselling with a list of information the physician must provide, laws providing waiting periods between the consultation and the procedure, and laws that oblige the woman to undergo an ultrasound.[161] The stereotype of the relationship between the woman (as potential mother) and the foetus is at the basis of this legislation, with the consequence that the gender dimension of discourses on abortion has been 'eclipsed, more specifically, by metaphysical or otherwise non-legal discourses that focus on the beginning of human life and the protection it deserves.'[162] Jennifer Hendricks considered the 'challenge' as being to 'assign appropriate value' to the relationship between the woman and the foetus 'without becoming deterministic about women's roles.'[163] Sheilah Martin contended that, when the law talks about 'foetal rights' or 'doctor knows best,' pregnant women are placed in 'a separate category, where their rights are frequently denied.'[164] Laufer-Ukeles suggested a relational perspective on informed consent, focusing on discussion, dialogue and 'the need to interact and understand the competing interests, influences and social pressures involved.'[165] She warns against denying the importance of the relationship, and focuses on the need to recognise the status of pregnancy 'for the purpose of supporting the pregnant person's autonomy and dignity, and to protect the unique relationship, not to undermine the woman's personhood for the sake of the foetus that grows inside her. The context and purpose of recognizing pregnancy matters.'[166] Accordingly, 'ignoring the inter-dependency and focusing on a woman's full individual autonomy does not enable consideration of the support women need during pregnancy both for their own sakes and for the sake of the foetus.'[167] Greasley interestingly pointed out that the foetus 'cannot partake in international relations of any kind … as can the neonate,' and that the foetus's engagement with the world is 'mediated through the body of the pregnant woman.'[168] Nonetheless, as argued by McLean, a more relational account of autonomy 'would see the pregnant women as intimately linked to her social network, perhaps especially to her embryo/foetus,' with the consequence that women 'should always and at all times act for the benefit of their foetuses.'[169] This route leads us to the elaboration of a notion of human-rights based autonomy: 'the relational account … may result in the deprivation of fundamental freedoms;' it means that women need equal rights, in particular 'the right not to have treatment (or punishment) imposed upon them in the purported interests of their embryos/foetuses.'[170]

In the judgments that I analysed in chapter 1, courts rarely took a position on the status of the embryo, hiding behind the wall of the state's margin of appreciation (ECtHR), or avoiding any reference to women's rights, by preferring to measure a state's provision for abortion against other standards (the undue burden in US jurisprudence, for example). In some cases, judgments have even caused VAWH, such as in *T., S. v. Gobierno de la Ciudad de Buenos Aires*, where abortion of an anencephalic foetus was admitted as 'premature delivery' with the obvious consequence of its death, and severe psychological harm for T. Accordingly, 'some women's lives [and health] have been effectively ruined by the law's failure to hold to the autonomy rights of individuals.'[171]

I anticipated in chapter 1 the sensitive ethical issue that lies beneath every legal discussion on abortion. The relationship between the pregnant woman and her foetus has been depicted as 'maternal/foetal conflict,' stressing the element of hostility. Put in this way, however, this 'conflict' might mean that the woman and her foetus are considered as two separate biological entities. It is not a matter of biology, though, but rather a decision that the legislator or courts can make, to 'highlight either foetal differentiation from, or connection to, the woman.'[172] The difficulties consist in the prevalence of 'non-legal arguments on abortion,' which 'place abortion discourses beyond the law's grasp, couching it in terms that appear to be non-negotiable for the law and that sit uncomfortably with modern legal arguments.'[173] If we follow the legal reasoning, it is possible to argue that the embryo has a 'status' – and we can even say a gradual status that grows week after week[174] – but it is not a holder of rights, at least according to the legal instruments in force and state practice. As outlined by Laufer-Ukeles, 'the full set of rights and interests of personhood begins at birth despite political, religious and humanitarian desires to protect foetal life.'[175] Having a status means that it is more than a simple group of cells, as described by the Committee of Inquiry into Human Fertilisation and Embryology (Warnock Committee) in 1984,[176] but that its interests cannot prevail over those ones of its mother. Birth is the turning point: 'a cataclysmic event [that] propels the foetus into the context in which it can … be brought into membership with other human beings.'[177] Moving to my concept of VAWH, I can argue a bit further that its interests cannot prevail when the lack of access to abortion causes VAWH. When state policies in the field of health directly or indirectly cause VAWH as conceptualised in these pages, the rights to health and to reproductive health of the woman must guide the reasoning. VAWH occurs, for example, when the woman cannot have access to abortion despite severe foetal impairments, or when her life and/or her physical and psychological health are at risk, or when she encounters insurmountable difficulties causing her anguish and psychological pressure. Using the paradigm elaborated in this book, it is not a conflict between the foetus and the mother that must be resolved. States *must prevent* VAWH and they have obligations in that respect, as I will discuss further in chapter 3; they also are obliged to provide adequate health services. This argument is further supported by the acknowledgement that 'the act of abortion cannot be separated from the social conditions in which impregnation occurs and pregnancy is experienced,' and that laws on abortion should first consider 'matters like sexual aggression, inadequate or unavailable contraception, special legal controls on the conduct of pregnant women, and the patchwork of provisions … on maternity leaves, pregnancy discrimination and childcare.'[178]

Involuntary sterilisation

The IACHR, in *I.V. v. Bolivia*, defined informed consent as 'the positive decision to undergo a medical act, derived from a previous, free and informed decision or process,' characterised by 'an interaction between the doctor and the patient, through which the patient actively participates in the decision making process, moving away from the paternalistic approach of medicine and focusing on individual autonomy.'[179] It combined the individualistic view on autonomy with the more relational aspect of the interaction between the doctor and the patient.

As explored in chapter 1, involuntary sterilisation occurs when misleading information is provided to a woman in order to coerce her to undergo the procedure. The consent of the woman in these cases does not grant autonomy, the coerced consent resulting in a form of VAHW. I analysed several cases in chapter 1, such as the CEDAW Committee views in *Szijjarto v. Hungary*, decided in 2006. Andrea Szijjarto, belonging to a minority, was induced while in hospital to have her Fallopian tubes tied, and to sign a document the content of which she could not understand. The Committee clarified that, in cases of this kind, hospital personnel must inform the woman and provide information and counselling about sterilisation, as well as about alternatives. As I explained, these cases are expressions of intersectional discrimination. The autonomy of a woman undergoing involuntary sterilisation is limited, not just because she is a woman, but also if she belongs to a specific minority, or is in one of several social or health conditions. Consent is not a genuine expression of autonomy in cases of involuntary sterilisation.

Obstetric violence and maternal health

As mentioned earlier, OV is a form of VAWH, and it is rarely recognised by laws and in courts, unless it leads to permanent and severe injuries or maternal death that call in question the responsibility of health personnel. Stereotypes interfere with the exercise of women's autonomy during pregnancy. Women's autonomy is impaired by decisions taken by others, or by health professionals, which affect reproductive freedom. The trend towards the 'medicalisation' of every process pertaining to women's reproductive rights is demonstrated by the state's male tendency to protect women even when this is not clinically necessary.[180] An example of non-consensual obstetric intervention, which amounts to VAWH, is forced caesarean section. Such interventions might be ordered by a court, with the aim of protecting the foetus, and against the woman's will.[181] Nonetheless, one could also reflect on the consent to vaginal delivery as the 'normal' and accepted form of delivery: should a woman be free to decide autonomously, informed of all possible consequences? Medicalisation does not only include forced interventions in the woman's body, but also tests and other technologies to which women consent. The 'normalisation of technology' in pregnancy is a concern for feminists, because it is not straightforward that the consent of the woman is 'sufficiently informed as to represent a genuine instance of informed choice.'[182] Normalising certain tests means that they are considered as a routine which is difficult to avoid, and even to question.

'Normalisation' also affects the place in which a woman gives birth to her child. The autonomy of the woman might indeed be limited when she cannot decide where to give birth, and is forced to choose a hospital over home birth. As Judge Tulkens pointed out in his opinion concurring with *Ternovszky*, decided by the ECtHR in 2010, in which a woman complained of not receiving adequate professional assistance during a home birth:

> Freedom may necessitate a positive regulatory environment which will produce the legal certainty providing the right to choose with effectiveness. Without such legal certainty there is fear and secrecy, and in the present context this may result in fatal consequences for mother and child.[183]

I argue that denying home birth might amount to a form of VAWH, especially when the woman prefers home birth in order to avoid a repetition of mistreatment or unconsented practices in hospitals that she experienced on a previous occasion. From a legal point of view, this is a violation of the woman's rights to health and to reproductive health, and her right to autonomously decide where to safely give birth to her child.

Access to contraception

Free and informed consent to contraception implies knowledge of the effects and side-effects of contraceptives pills. In particular, misleading information that EC is an abortifacient can impair a woman's decision, which should be autonomous and personal. Considerations related to this situation are similar to those I have already proposed for abortion and involuntary sterilisation.

A human-rights based autonomy: a new element for conceptualising VAWH?

I am borrowing the argument made by McLean to elaborate my own notion of autonomy, which helps the conceptualisation of VAWH. In her view, the language of human rights caused the relationship between doctor and patient to evolve during the twentieth century, and 'the rights that are central to every human rights declaration or treaty are essentially equivalent to respect for autonomy.'[184] As a consequence, the very idea of autonomy is inseparable from human dignity.[185] I would say that the very idea of autonomy is inseparable from the rights to health and to reproductive health. McLean also stressed how human rights are both individualistic and relational, therefore recognising that individual autonomy in the light of human rights law does not preclude consideration of the rights of groups and communities.[186] Autonomy permeates human rights law. The ECtHR refers to Article 8 ECHR (right to respect for private and family life) when dealing with cases of personal autonomy. For this reason, for example, in *Pretty v. United Kingdom*, the ECtHR brought the notion of personal autonomy within the scope of application of Article 8 ECHR, as an 'important principle underlying the interpretation of its guarantees.'[187] In *K.A. and A.D. v. Belgium*, the Court argued that the right to entertain sexual relationships comes from the right to dispose of one's body, which is *'partie intégrante'* of the notion of personal autonomy.[188]

A human rights-based autonomy contains both the dimensions we have discussed, namely the individual and the relational: the first, because it is the individual, as a human being, who has the right to make decisions about his/her own body, and the second, because the decision is taken in a context of relationships that inevitably affect it, even if we adhere to the purest model of individualism. A human rights-based autonomy is relevant when considering the legal instruments through which to realise the human rights to health and to reproductive health. For example, since no right to health is enshrined in the ECHR, the ECtHR referred to Article 8 as a legal pretext for discussing and protecting personal autonomy. Moreover, since free and informed consent is an expression of autonomy, then consent contributes to the realisation of this right.

In conceptualising the notion of VAWH, considering that the notion of autonomy is not part of the original definition of VAW, I argued that autonomy permeates both dimensions of the analysis. Common to both dimensions is the fact that a woman's autonomy diminishes when she is exposed to VAWH. It is also common that in both dimensions, the lack of consent – *rectius*, genuine consent – causes the violation of the woman's rights. In that respect, I could add a further element to my definition of VAWH, namely the limitation of women's autonomy. VAWH is therefore a violation of human rights and a limitation of women's autonomy.

A human rights-based autonomy encompasses the principle of non-discrimination, and hence contributes to a process of 'gendering' autonomy, with the consequent analysis of whether, and if so, to what extent, limitations of women's autonomy derive from the fact of their being women. The legal consequences of this argument can be appreciated in different contexts. As for FGM/C, for example, I suggested that other practices that impair women's and girls' rights to health and to reproductive health, such as GCS, should be conceived as violations of human rights, unless genuine, informed consent of a woman older than 18 can be proved. This conceptualisation of VAHW, as read in conjunction with the analysis of the principle of autonomy, could well allow a reconsideration of the crime of FGM/C itself.

The notion of autonomy and consent will also be pivotal in criminalising OV, which few countries consider as an offence in their national penal code, but also in paving the way for the adoption of guidelines and recommendations for practitioners, which would constitute codes for conducting the activity of public hospitals. Considering a human rights-based autonomy also means considering a woman as holding human rights when deciding in matters related to her rights to health and to reproductive health (*mutatis mutandis* the reasoning on a human-rights based concept of autonomy can be extended to all genders). A state's policies on abortion must not cause, or contribute to causing, VAWH. Conscientious objection to abortion or to the provision of EC also represents the exercise of a right to self-determination, but is often abused, with the consequence that 'self-determination matters more or less depending whether it is exercised by the doctor or the woman.'[189] The thought of Francesca Rescigno precisely caught the point: a secular – truly secular – state (and for this scholar Italy is not) is a state in which the law does not interfere with self-determination, following the principles of equality and solidarity.[190] Society must be capable, in Rescigno's view, of adopting measures of prevention, education and assistance which affirm the 'freedom not to have an abortion,' and must 'step back before the woman's self-determination and will.'[191] Similarly, Rodríguez-Ruiz has contended that 'the choice of the woman must be autonomous,' and 'this includes the possibility of saying *No* to an unexpected pregnancy but also of saying *Yes* to it unimpeded by socio-economic constraints.'[192]

Conclusions

The concept: new elements and old ones

The diagnosis has allowed us to conceptualise the new concept of VAWH, which shares many elements with that of VAW, but at the same time better encompasses the two dimensions of violence as conceived in this book. In particular, I followed the reasoning of the CEDAW Committee in its GR No. 35 when it contended that criminalising abortion, for example, is a form of VAW, and, more specifically, of gender-based violence against women. However, in state practice, and in the jurisprudence of human rights courts as well as in the quasi-jurisprudence of UN treaty bodies, VAW is generally conceived as interpersonal violence, or violence within the community, and it is harder to find clear affirmations of violence committed by the state through the adoption of laws and policies in the field of health. This is why the idea of VAWH can fill this gap. The concept of VAW can be complemented and enriched, but not replaced, by that of VAWH, to grasp the complexity of violence that derives from patterns of discrimination existing in society and in states' policies along a double dimension. VAWH is a form of discrimination against women, and a violation of their rights to health and to reproductive health, characterised by acts that produce physical and psychological harm. The element of intent is not relevant, much as it is not relevant in the definition of VAW; however, in both the horizontal and vertical dimensions it is possible to identify a 'pattern of discrimination,' which courts and UN treaty bodies have defined in different ways: as 'tolerance' to violence, but also in terms of 'repetition' of certain types of conduct. I also pointed out the importance of intersectionality in the analysis of 'patterns of discrimination,' which will prove to be helpful in theorising states' obligations, and in reflecting on reparations. Compared to the notion of VAW, I added to the notion of VAWH the element of consent, which expresses and gives strength to women's autonomy. VAWH is a limitation of women's autonomy and alters their consent.

Challenges to the public/private divide

My concept allows us to reflect on the 'public/private divide' developed, and challenged soon after its conceptualisation, by (Western) feminist scholarship. A product of the industrialisation process, this divide 'denotes the ideological division of life into apparently opposing spheres of public and private activities, and public and private responsibilities.'[193] The public/private distinction has also appeared in international law, where 'public' is the world of inter-state relations, whereas 'private' means national affairs.[194] Women have traditionally been excluded from international law and its legal structures.[195] The 'private', an author has argued, identifies what is 'free', 'the sphere in which others do not interfere,' while 'public' acquires 'a different meaning depending on the source of the interference.'[196] However, for women the 'private' sphere has been a zone of oppression, and of violation of their human rights.

Even though the distinction between public and private has been important when theorising and emphasising the unequal power relations between women and men, feminists have challenged it, considering it a myth. For example, Hilary Charlesworth, Christine Chinkin and Shelly Wright stressed 'the myth that State power is not exercised in the "private realm" allocated to women masks its control.'[197] Others have pointed out that the sphere of the 'public' and the 'private' is too indeterminate.[198] And, indeed, the state has traditionally interfered in women's decisions about their sexuality and reproductive health, but refrained from intervening in the family context. Liberal states started to regulate reproduction during the late nineteenth and early twentieth centuries when industrialisation and universal suffrage 'began to transform *laissez-faire* State into mass (welfare) societies.'[199] The regulation of sex was deemed as essential in emergent welfare states. This was – and unfortunately seems to still be[200] – the product of a patriarchal understanding of society. Why are women's bodies always considered the *prime locus* of population control policies, and not men's? The answer is related to the stereotyped roles of the women in societies.[201]

In light of these views of the public/private divide, I can argue that women's rights to health and to reproductive health have been neglected because of the *male* conception of the private sphere. In this sense, the two approaches to the public/private divide, one in favour of it, the other more critical, can be reconciled to a certain extent. DV was a private matter in as much as reproductive decisions could not be left to the woman only. In both cases, women's autonomy was set aside.

The question is then to what extent must the state interfere in the private sphere? Gavison has proposed an interesting perspective. She said that what is 'private' can support claims both of non-interference – for example, in some decisions such as the timing and spacing of children – and of interference – for example, to fight against abuses – and that 'though we must assess such conflicting arguments to reach a conclusion, the fact that the same feature (privateness) may point in both directions does not undermine its utility.'[202]

After conceptualising the notion of VAWH, I can contend that the state must interfere in private life to the extent necessary to counter violence, without interfering with the exercise of women's autonomy in all instances related to their sexual and reproductive health. In other words, when we talk about violence and health, the state must interfere where there is an episode of violence that occurs within the community or within the family, but its intervention must stop when women's autonomy comes into play. To propose a clear example, rape must be prevented, and punished when it occurs, and it requires a clear intervention by the state both through laws and through specific actions ad hoc measured in relation to the situation of the victim. However, if the rape causes a pregnancy, then the state must refrain from interfering in whatever autonomous decision is taken by the woman relating to her reproductive health. Its intervention would in turn cause another form of violence against her health, perpetuating a patriarchal mechanism that the evolution of human rights law is progressively trying to dismantle. The state must intervene in cases of DV to protect the woman, and prosecute the perpetrator. In this example, it is clear how the divide is dismantled, and how DV comes into the public sphere. The protection of a woman who suffers violence, as Friedman has argued, 'comes with a price': loss of control over the legal consequences that follow DV.[203] However, under my paradigm, the state must stop when its action causes VAWH in turn, for example in cases of secondary victimisation, provoking psychological violence. In that sense, the law should be 'more sensitive to the needs of crime victims.'[204] It is also possible to argue that states do not cause VAWH when they interfere with a woman's autonomy in ways 'required and justifiable to preserve individuals' human rights,' an example being the definition of a legal minimum age for marriage in order to save young women from the health risks of premature childbearing.[205]

To propose another example, to phase out OV the state – which acts through healthcare services and health personnel – must not interfere with a woman's free choice, and must always wait for her free and informed consent, unless it is a matter of urgency which leaves the practitioner no choice. Cases of OV analysed by national courts have proved to focus on malpractice rather than on the violation of the woman's human rights. This is not *per se* negative, because malpractice litigation can lead to a form of reparation for the suffering caused to the woman, but it does not take into account the violation of her rights to health and to reproductive health.

The example of FGM/C is more complex. The state must interfere to suppress this form of violence against girls' bodily integrity – irrespective, as I argued, of the 'intensity' of the harm, given the impact on physical and mental health – but must also pay attention to a woman's consent when she is capable of expressing her free consent without manipulation. I analysed this aspect in detail in 'Consent and autonomy in the horizontal dimension: FGM/C'. It was surprising to note that cases of FGM/C have mainly been decided at national level, especially in Europe and in the United States, rather than in front of regional human rights courts, and that they mainly concerned the recognition of refugee status of women escaping violence. This is less surprising when we consider the paternalistic attitude with which some courts have approached the problem, considering the girls and the women subjected to the practice as victims in need of protection from the 'brutality' of a traditional practice that comes from another 'culture'.[206] If I limit my analysis to FGM/C only, then my paradigm can be challenged, and sharply criticised because it is based only on a particular perspective of human rights which does not take into consideration cultural differences; however, if I develop my argument a bit further, as I did in 'Consent and autonomy in the horizontal dimension: FGM/C', and consider other practices, then the analysis is much more in line with my paradigm, and I can support my main argument on the presence of VAWH when consent to a practice, such as cosmetic genital surgery, is not free and genuine. I agree with the affirmation that 'culture is much more frequently invoked in the context of women's rights than in any other area,'[207] and that culture has been invoked in order to justify violations of women's rights. Here, indeed, I am not challenging this argument, but rather turning it into a reflection on women's autonomy and consent, considering that VAWH is a cultural phenomenon in every society. As Susan Deller Ross has argued:

No ethical defense can be made for preserving a cultural practice that damages women's health and interferes with their sexuality. It is important, however, that those who are alien to the culture make themselves familiar with the causes and meanings of cultural practices and relate them to ideas of sex roles in their own societies.[208]

Victims/survivors and perpetrators

The notion of VAWH does not define a specific gender for the perpetrator. Men and women cause VAWH. Not prescribing a gender for the perpetrator does not diminish the understanding of VAWH as discrimination based on gender and characterised by unequal power relations between women and men. When a female obstetrician commits violence against women's health, she probably does not *intend* to commit violence. She might have experienced and internalised, or better, 'normalised,' the stereotype of the woman as mother, this way reproducing patterns of discrimination.

The woman who was subjected to a form of VAWH has been called, in the judgments and decisions I analysed in chapter 1, a victim, the applicant, the patient, occasionally the survivor, which is the language used (positively) in GR No. 35 adopted by the CEDAW Committee in 2017. From a legal perspective, one might argue that calling a woman 'survivor' instead of 'victim' does not change the substance of the complaint. Probably not, but it changes the lens through which the woman is seen during proceedings: not as a human being who cannot defend herself, always in need of help, but rather as an active agent of change.

Notes

1 S.H. Miles, 'The art of medicine: Hippocrates and informed consent', *Lancet* 374 (2009) 1322.
2 C.F. Kleisiaris, C. Sfakianakis and I.V. Papathanasiou, 'Health care practices in ancient Greece: the Hippocratic ideal', *Journal of Medical Ethics and the History of Medicine* 7 (2014) 6.
3 I. Scobbie, 'Thinking about international law', in Evans, *International Law*, p. 77, referring to C. Perelman and L. Olbrechts-Tyteca, *La nouvelle rhétorique: traité de l'argumentation* (Paris: University of Notre Dame Press, 1958).
4 Charles, 'Obstetricians and violence against women'.
5 See in that respect, S. De Vido, 'The prohibition of violence against women as customary international law? Remarks on the CEDAW General Recommendation No. 35', *Diritti umani diritto internazionale* 2 (2018) 379.
6 See also the Istanbul Convention, where the only reference to states' policies in the field of health causing VAW could be forced abortion and forced sterilisation.
7 J.S. Mill, *On Liberty* (1859) (Kitchener, Ontario: Batoche Books, 2001), p. 13.
8 J. Feinberg, *Harm to Others* (New York: Oxford University Press, 1984).

9 Eriksson, *Defining Rape*, p. 55.
10 Eriksson, *Defining Rape*, p. 67.
11 R. Rubio-Marín and C. Sandoval, 'Engendering the reparations jurisprudence of the Inter-American Court of Human Rights: the promise of the *Cotton Field* judgment', *Human Rights Quarterly* 33 (2011) 1062, p. 1068.
12 *Valiulienė*, para. 69.
13 Dissenting opinion of Judge Jŏcienė, paras 11 and 12.
14 Sifris, *Reproductive Freedom*, p. 67.
15 Sifris, *Reproductive Freedom*, p. 67.
16 Sifris, *Reproductive Freedom*, pp. 77–8.
17 Eriksson, *Defining Rape*, p. 60.
18 See, for example, the Italian legislation until 1996 (chapter 1, 'Rape').
19 See, with specific regard to rape, R. Whisnant, 'Feminist perspectives on rape', in E.N. Zalta (ed.), *The Stanford Encyclopedia of Philosophy* (Fall 2017 edn), available at https://plato.stanford.edu/archives/fall2017/entries/feminism-rape/.
20 R. Rubio-Marín, 'The gender of reparations in transitional societies', in R. Rubio-Marín (ed.), *The Gender of Reparations* (Cambridge: Cambridge University Press, 2009), 63 p. 91.
21 Istanbul Convention, preamble.
22 Fredman, *Discrimination Law*, p. 41.
23 See, in that respect, CEDAW Convention, Article 5.
24 GC No. 20, ESCR Committee, para. 12.
25 *Da Penha*, paras 55 and 56.
26 *Gonzáles*, para. 170. C. Bettinger-Lopez, 'Introduction: *Jessica Lenahan (Gonzáles) v. United States of America*: Implementation, litigation, and mobilization strategies', *American University Journal of Gender, Social Policy, and Law* 21 (2012) 207.
27 *López Soto* (IACommHR), para. 224.
28 *López Soto* (IACHR), para. 223.
29 'Access to justice for women victims of sexual violence in Mesoamerica' (IACommHR), OEA/Ser.L/V/II. Doc. 63, 9 December 2011, para. 17.
30 *Opuz*, para. 192.
31 *Opuz*, para. 198. See P. Londono, 'Developing human rights principles in cases of gender-based violence: *Opuz v. Turkey* in the European Court of Human Rights', *Human Rights Law Review* 9 (2009) 657, p. 665.
32 *Talpis*, para. 145.
33 Judgment of 27 May 2014, Appl. No. 72964/10, *Rumor v. Italy*.
34 *Talpis*, paras 146–7. See also judgment of 28 May 2013, Appl. No. 3564/11, *Eremia and others v. Moldova* (ECtHR), paras 87 and 89.
35 Dissenting opinion of Judge Eicke, *Talpis*, para. 22.
36 This argument is presented in De Vido, 'States' due diligence obligations', and it is supported by a reference to the Istanbul Convention.
37 *González Carreño*, para. 7.5.
38 *Equality Now*, para. 125.
39 *CGIL v. Italy*, para. 190.
40 Sifris, *Reproductive Freedom*, p. 129. See also Greasley, *Arguments*, p. 88.
41 Sifris, *Reproductive Freedom*, pp. 130–1.

42 CEDAW Committee, Concluding observations on Japan, CEDAW/C/JPN/CO/7–8, 7 March 2016, para. 24.
43 Rubio-Marín and Möschel, 'Racial and gender-based violence', p. 193.
44 *I.G. and others*, para. 165.
45 CEDAW Committee, Concluding observations on Slovakia, CEDAW/C/SVK/CO/5–6, 25 November 2015, para. 32.
46 UN Committee on the Elimination of Racial Discrimination in Slovakia (CERD), Concluding observations on Slovakia, CERD/C/SVK/CO/11–12, 8 December 2017, para. 23.
47 CERD, Concluding observations, Slovakia.
48 Cook and Cusack, *Gender Stereotyping*, p. 85.
49 Sifris, *Reproductive Freedom*, p. 135.
50 S. Laurel Weldon, 'Intersectionality', in G. Goertz and A.G. Mazur (eds), *Politics, Gender, and Concepts* (Cambridge: Cambridge University Press, 2008) 193, p. 195.
51 J.C. Nash, 'Re-thinking intersectionality', *Feminist Review* 89 (2008) 1.
52 L.P.A. Sosa, *Intersectionality in the Human Rights Legal Framework on Violence Against Women* (Cambridge: Cambridge University Press, 2017), p. 15.
53 Sosa, *Intersectionality*, p. 16.
54 See the analysis of legal instruments in Sosa, *Intersectionality*.
55 Sosa, *Intersectionality*, p. 33, referring to the work by Margaret Satterthwaite, 'Women migrants' rights under international human rights law', *Feminist Review Labour Migrations: Women on the Move* 77 (2004) 167, p. 170.
56 Bettinger-Lopez, 'Introduction', p. 219.
57 *Gonzáles*, para. 113.
58 See 'Consent and autonomy in the concept of VAWH' below.
59 See *Whole Woman's Health*, for example.
60 *CGIL v. Italy*, for example. For a comparative analysis (covering the United States, Europe, Latin America and South Africa) see A. O'Rourke, L. De Crespigny and A. Pyman, 'Abortion and conscientious objection: The new battleground', *Monash University Law Rev*iew 38 (2012) 87.
61 See the Indian case, *Lakshmi Dhikta*.
62 See the Irish casesdiscussed in 'Abortion: Who is the applicant?' in chapter 1.
63 CERD, Concluding observations, Slovakia, para. 23.
64 GR No. 35 (CEDAW), para. 12.
65 GR No. 35 (CEDAW), para. 9.
66 L. Peroni and A. Timmer, 'Gender stereotyping in domestic violence cases', in E. Brems and A. Timmer (eds), *Stereotypes and Human Rights Law* (Cambridge: Intersentia, 2016) 39, p. 45.
67 Explanatory report to the Istanbul Convention, para. 44.
68 Cook and Cusack, *Gender Stereotyping*, p. 9.
69 B. Bianchi, 'La violenza domestica nella riflessione femminista (1833–1917)', in S. De Vido and L. Candiotto (eds), *Home-Made Violence* (Milan: Mimesis, 2016) 17, p. 18.
70 Cook and Cusack, *Gender Stereotyping*, p. 36.
71 *A.T.*, para. 9.4. See Peroni and Timmer, 'Gender stereotyping', p. 43.
72 *Karen Tayag Vertido v. The Philippines*, Communication No. 18/2008, 16 July 2010 (CEDAW), para. 8.4. Emphasis added.

73 *Vertido*, para. 8.5.
74 *Vertido*, para. 8.4.
75 *Law and Advocacy for Women*, see chapter 1, note 236 and text to which it relates.
76 Sjöholm, *Gender-Sensitive Interpretation*, p. 515.
77 S. Cusack, 'Building momentum towards change', in Brems and Timmer, *Stereotypes*, 11, p. 16.
78 The Administrative Tribunal in Lazio (TAR Lazio, sez. IIIQ, Judgment of 2 August 2016, n. 8990) refused to accept the exercise of conscientious objection by health personnel in public dispensing where it prevented (or vitiated) the prescription of contraceptive pills, including EC.
79 See the US cases on forced caesarean sections in T. Morris and J.H. Robinson, 'Forced and coerced cesarean sections in the United States', *Contexts* 16 (2017) 24.
80 L. Purdy, 'Medicalization, medical necessity, and feminist medicine', *Bioethics* 15:3 (2001) 248, p. 249 and p. 257. See also S. Sherwin, *No Longer Patient: Feminist Ethics and Health Care* (Philadelphia, PA: Temple University Press, 1992), p. 179. On the ways in which medical science has shaped ideas of the female body, see M. McDougal, H.D. Lasswell and L.-C. Chen, 'Human rights for women and world public order: the outlawing of sex-based discrimination', *American Journal of International Law* (1975) 497; S.E. Moore, 'Is the healthy body gendered? Toward a feminist critique of the new paradigm of health', *Body Society* 16 (2010) 295; E. Annandale, *The Sociology of Health and Medicine: A Critical Introduction* (Cambridge: Polity Press, 1998); M. Bass and J. Howes, 'Women's health: the making of a powerful new public issue', *Women's Health Issues* 2 (1992) 3.
81 See also *Bălşan* and *Talpis,* for example.
82 *Opuz*, para. 161.
83 *Opuz*, para. 138. See in that respect C. Hanna, 'Health, human rights, and violence against women and girls: Broadly redefining affirmative State duties after *Opuz v. Turkey*', *Hastings International & Comparative Law Review* 34 (2011) 127, p. 146.
84 *López Soto*, IACommHR, para. 225.
85 *Laxmi Mandal*, see chapter 1, note 562 and related text.
86 Hanna, 'Health, human rights', p. 146.
87 This argument was taken from the draft protocol on the right to a healthy environment discussed by the Parliamentary assembly of the Council of Europe in 2009. An additional protocol to the European Convention on Human Rights was drafted, concerning the right to a healthy environment, Doc. 12003, 2009, para. 6.
88 Except in the most recent case *López Soto*; see chapter 1, notes 137–8 and related text.
89 Article 2, Inter-American Convention to Prevent and Punish Torture, 9 December 1985, Organization of American States Treaty Series No. 67.
90 *R.R.,* see chapter 1, notes 365 and 389 and related text.
91 J.H. and S.P. Levison, 'Women's health and human rights', in M. Agosín (ed.), *Women, Gender, and Human Rights* (New Brunswick, New Jersey and London: Rutgers University Press, 2001) 125, p. 136.
92 G. Donoghue (ed.), *Women's Health in the Curriculum: A Resource Guide for Faculty* (Philadelphia, PA: National Academy of Women's Health, 1996), p. 10.
93 See, in more detail, De Vido, *Donne, Violenza*, p. 49.

94 Sheila Dauer has noted the existence of 'patterns of violence committed against women both by public and private actors ('Indivisible or invisible. Women's human rights in the public and private sphere', in Agosín, *Women, Gender, and Human Rights*, 66, pp. 79–80).

95 A comparative analysis of *mens rea* in different criminal law traditions and in international criminal law can be found in M. Elewa Badar, *The Concept of Mens Rea in International Criminal Law. The Case for a Unified Approach* (Oxford and Portland: Hart, 2013).

96 See Lord Goddard in *Brend v. Wood* [1946] 62 TLR 462 (Divisional court) at 463. Case reviewed in *Cambridge Law Journal*, 1947, p. 376*ff.*

97 Sifris, *Reproductive Freedom*, p. 97.

98 Copelon, 'Recognizing the egregious in everyday', p. 325.

99 Sifris, *Reproductive Freedom*, p. 106.

100 See, with regard to genocide, S. De Vido, 'On the specific intent of the crime of genocide. Beyond individual criminal responsibility', in L. Candiotto and L. Zagato (eds), *Il genocidio. Declinazioni e risposte di inizio secolo* (Turin: Giappichelli, 2018), and references therein.

101 B. Conforti, *Diritto internazionale* (Naples: Editoriale Scientifica, 10th edn, 2014), p. 393.

102 De Vido, 'On the specific intent'.

103 This is not the purpose of the analysis in these pages, because it would require a comparative analysis of different national criminal law systems. See, among others, P. Cane, '*Mens rea* in tort law', in N. Naffine, R. Owens and J. Williams (eds), *Intention in Law and Philosophy* (Aldershot: Ashgate, 2001) 129; and, concerning the US system, B. Furrow, 'Medical malpractice liability: of modest expansions and tightening standards,' in I.G. Cohen, A.K. Hoffman and W.M. Sage (eds), *The Oxford Handbook of US Health Law* (Oxford: Oxford University Press, 2016), p. 421.

104 *Opuz*, para. 191.

105 *Opuz*, para. 197.

106 See, for example, *Rumor*.

107 R. Pollack Petchensky, 'Abortion and women's choice: the state, sexuality and reproductive freedom', 1984, rev. 1990, republished in C. Grant, L.A. Rosenbury, D.T. Verkheimer and K.A. Yuracko, *Feminist Jurisprudence* (St Paul, MN: Thomson Reuters, 2011), p. 414.

108 M. Nowak and E. McArthur, *The United Nations Convention against Torture: A Commentary* (Oxford: Oxford University Press, 2008), p. 73. Reflecting on states legally restricting access to abortion and torture, see Sifris, *Reproductive Freedom,* p. 98. This problem echoes the doctrinal debate on negligence (*culpa*) in assessing international state responsibility, which started at the beginning of the twentieth century. See, without pretending to encompass a long and complex debate, the 'objective' conception of the act giving rise to international responsibility elaborated by Anzilotti, who argued against considering negligence as an element of an internationally wrongful act (D. Anzilotti, *Corso di diritto internazionale* (Rome: Atheneum, 1912–14), vol. I, pp. 251–2), and the position of scholars, such as Morelli, who have contended that state responsibility arises when state organs act with negligence, in particular in cases of due diligence obligations (G. Morelli, *Nozioni di diritto internazionale* (Padua: Cedam, 1967), p. 346).

109 *Opuz*, para. 197.
110 M. Friedman, *Autonomy, Gender, Politics* (Oxford: Oxford University Press, 2003), p. 3.
111 F. Rescigno, 'L'autodeterminazione della persona: il faticoso cammino del diritto positivo', *Rivista critica del diritto privato* 36 (2018) 13, p. 17.
112 GC No. 22, ESCR Committee, para. 25.
113 Nelson, *Law, Policy*, p. 2.
114 S.A.M. McLean, *Autonomy, Consent, and the Law* (Abingdon: Routledge, 2010), p. 6.
115 Friedman, *Autonomy, Gender, Politics*, p. 4.
116 See references in Nelson, *Law, Policy*. According to Sjöholm (*Gender-Sensitive Interpretation*, p. 517), procedural autonomy 'raises the question as to whether women can make autonomous decisions with regard to motherhood when they, as a group, are strongly socialised into motherhood,' whereas substantive autonomy is linked to ethics and reflects on 'which reproductive decisions should be considered to be human rights norms, such as whether it involves choosing the gender or physical appearance of the foetus, but also access to abortion or *in vitro* fertilisation.'
117 See McLean, *Autonomy, Consent*, pp. 13–14, referring to works by Kant, Mill and Kluge.
118 Friedman, *Autonomy, Gender, Politics*, p. 81.
119 McLean, *Autonomy, Consent*, p. 6. See N. Stoljar, 'Feminist perspectives on autonomy', in *The Stanford Encyclopedia of Philosophy* (2015), available at https://plato.stanford.edu/archives/fall2015/entries/feminism-autonomy/.
120 C. Gilligan, *In a Different Voice* (Cambridge, MA: Harvard University Press, 1982). Commenting on her work, Friedman, *Autonomy, Gender, Politics*, p. 83; S. Dodds, 'Choice and control in feminist bioethics', in C. Mackenzie and N. Stoljar (eds), *Relational Autonomy* (Oxford: Oxford University Press, 2000), 213 p. 221; G.P. McDonough, 'Moral maturity and autonomy: appreciating the significance of Lawrence Kolhberg's Just Community', *Journal of Moral Education* 34 (2005) 199, p. 204.
121 S. Sherwin, 'A relational approach to autonomy in healthcare', in S. Sherwin (ed.), *The Politics of Women's Health: Exploring Agency and Autonomy* (Philadelphia, PA: Temple University Press, 1998), p. 19. On relational autonomy, see also the contribution of A. Donchin, 'Understanding autonomy relationally: toward a reconfiguration of bioethical principles', *The Journal of Medicine and Philosophy: A Forum for Bioethics and Philosophy of Medicine* 26 (2001) 365.
122 Sherwin, 'A relational approach', p. 35.
123 Sherwin, 'A relational approach', p. 36.
124 S. de Beauvoir, *The Second Sex* (London: New English Library, 1969), p. 338.
125 A. Philipps, *Gender and Culture* (Cambridge: Polity, 2010), p. 108.
126 Dodds, 'Choice and control', p. 226.
127 Dodds, 'Choice and control', p. 231. She also refers to D.T. Meyers, *Self, Society, and Personal Choice* (New York: Columbia University Press, 1989), p. 170.
128 Dodds, 'Choice and control', p. 231.
129 Nelson, *Law, Policy*, p. 29.
130 Nelson, *Law, Policy*, p. 29.
131 Nelson, *Law, Policy*, p. 31.
132 McLean, *Autonomy, Consent*, p. 41.

133 Report of the International Bioethics Committee of UNESCO (IBC) on consent, Paris, 2008, para. 12.
134 McLean, *Autonomy, Consent*, p. 91.
135 Friedman, *Autonomy, Gender, Politics*, p. 141.
136 Friedman, *Autonomy, Gender, Politics*, p. 142*ff*. 'Why men rape' is one of the questions of feminist critique of rape law: is rape motivated by sex or power? The different views on the issue are reported in Grant *et al.*, *Feminist Jurisprudence*, p. 329*ff*.
137 Friedman, *Autonomy, Gender, Politics*, p. 147.
138 Friedman, *Autonomy, Gender, Politics*, p. 149.
139 See, in that respect, Article 49(2) of the Istanbul Convention: '[p]arties shall take the necessary legislative or other measures, in conformity with the fundamental principles of human rights and having regard to the gendered understanding of violence, to ensure the effective investigation and prosecution of offences established in accordance with this Convention.'
140 Friedman, *Autonomy, Gender, Politics*, p. 151.
141 Meyersfeld, *Domestic Violence*, p. 246.
142 See, from a philosophical point of view, A. Wertheimer, *Consent to Sexual Relations* (Cambridge: Cambridge University Press, 2010).
143 Article 7(1)(g)–(1).
144 Eriksson, *Defining Rape,* p. 502, and references therein. See also Londras, 'Prosecuting sexual violence in Rwanda and the former Yugoslavia', p. 295.
145 *Brown v. State,* 106 N.W. 536 (Wisconsin 1906). See J. McGregor, 'The legal heritage of the crime of rape', in J.M. Brown and S.L. Walklate (eds), *Handbook on Sexual Violence* (London, New York: Routledge, 2012) 69, p. 73.
146 Eriksson, *Defining Rape,* p. 102.
147 *Contra*, referring to 'cultural imperialism' of Western countries, A.A. Oba, 'Female circumcision as female genital mutilation: human rights or cultural imperialism', *Global Jurist* 8 (2008) 1.
148 The news was published in the *Guardian* in 2015. See https://www.theguardian.com/society/2015/feb/04/doctor-not-guilty-fgm-dhanuson-dharmasena.
149 One author would have called this approach 'soft paternalism': S. Hopgood, 'Modernity at the cutting edge: Human rights meets FGM', in M.N. Barnett (ed.), *Paternalism Beyond Borders* (Cambridge: Cambridge University Press, 2017), pp. 256, 270. He explains that 'those who perpetuate the practice are mothers, grandmothers, and other village women who do it from an ethic of care and concern for their daughters,' and criticises scholars that consider the practice a form of patriarchy. Nonetheless, when I apply my paradigm to the analysis, FGM/C does constitute VAWH, because it affects women's and girls' reproductive health. Furthermore, my analysis does not preclude perpetrators being women, because who matters in the relationship is the victim/survivor, affected because she is a woman (or a girl).
150 Phillips, *Gender and Culture*, p. 63.
151 Phillips, *Gender and Culture,* p. 64.
152 See the website of the UK NHS, which stresses how the procedure differs from FGM: https://www.nhs.uk/conditions/cosmetic-treatments/labiaplasty/.
153 Except for intersex new-borns, who will be the subjects of future research. See, *inter alia,* the report by Human Rights Watch and InterAct, *I want to be like nature made me*, 2017.

154 See the declaration of a paediatrician, reported on 3 July 2017 on the BBC. The practitioner compared the surgery, where it is not necessary, to FGM: https://www.bbc.com/news/health-40410459. See also L. Avalos, 'Female genital mutilation and designer vaginas in Britain: crafting an effective legal and policy framework', *Vanderbilt Journal of Transnational Law* 48 (2015) 621, p. 694, referring to UK legislation, arguing that 'in keeping with the principle of nondiscrimination, GCS and FGM should be treated similarly under the law. This means that any non-medically necessary procedure carried out in contravention of the (UK) FGM Act should be prosecuted, regardless of whether the procedure is considered FGM or GCS by those involved.'

155 See also D.J. Baker, 'Should unnecessary harmful non-therapeutic cosmetic surgery be criminalised?', *New Criminal Law Review* 17 (2014) 587.

156 Cook and Cusack, *Gender Stereotyping*, p. 11.

157 McLean, *Autonomy, Consent*, p. 128. With regard to 'wrongful' decisions, see the US Supreme Court judgment *Gonzales v. Carhart*, 127 S. Ct. 1610, 1633 (2007), which found the Partial-Birth Abortion Ban Act constitutional. As put by one author (M.K. Plante, 'Protecting women's health: How *Gonzales v. Carhart* endangers women's health and women's equal right to personhood under the Constitution', *American University Journal of Gender, Social Policy, &* Law 16 (2008) 387, 402), '*Carhart* essentially and wrongly implies that it is unreasonable for a woman's health ever to be a priority over foetal life.'

158 P. Laufer-Ukeles, 'Reproductive choice and informed consent: Fetal interests, women's identity, and relational autonomy', *American Journal of Law and Medicine* 37 (2011) 567, p. 595.

159 Laufer-Ukeles, 'Reproductive choice', p. 570.

160 Laufer-Ukeles, 'Reproductive choice', p. 593.

161 Nelson, *Law, Policy*, p. 123.

162 B. Rodríguez-Ruiz, 'Gender in constitutional discourses on abortion: looking at Spain from a comparative perspective', *Social & Legal Studies* 25 (2016) 699, p. 700.

163 J. Hendricks, 'Body and soul: equality, pregnancy and the unitary right to abortion', *Harvard Civil Rights-Civil Liberties Law Review* 45 (2010) 329, p. 366.

164 S. Martin, 'A woman-centered approach to laws on human reproduction', in K-E. and P. Mahoney (eds), *Human Rights in the Twenty-First Century: A Global Challenge* (Dordrecht: Martinus Nijhoff Publishers, 1993) 905, p. 915.

165 Laufer-Ukeles, 'Reproductive choice', pp. 614–15.

166 P. Laufer-Ukeles, 'The disembodied womb: Pregnancy, informed consent and surrogate motherhood', *North Carolina Journal of International Law and Commercial Regulation* 43 (2018) 1, pp. 14–15.

167 Laufer-Ukeles, 'The disembodied womb', p. 17.

168 Greasley, *Arguments*, p. 197.

169 McLean, *Autonomy, Consent*, p. 151.

170 McLean, *Autonomy, Consent*, p. 152.

171 McLean, *Autonomy, Consent*, p. 153.

172 I. Karpin and R. Mykitiuk, 'Feminist legal theory as embodied justice', in Albertson Fineman, *Transcending the Boundaries of Law* 115, p. 119.

173 Rodríguez-Ruiz, 'Gender in constitutional discourses', p. 700.

174 On the gradualist approach, see M.O. Little, 'Abortion and the margin of personhood', *Rutgers Law Journal* 8 (2007) 331, p. 332.

175 Laufer-Ukeles, 'The disembodied womb', p. 4.
176 Cmnd 9314/1984.
177 Greasley, *Arguments*, p. 199.
178 Martin, 'A woman-centered approach', p. 913.
179 *I.V.,* para. 166.
180 Laufer-Ukeles, 'Reproductive choice', p. 602.
181 See in that respect Nelson, *Law, Policy*, p. 186*ff.*, and I.L. Feitshans, 'Legislating to preserve women's autonomy during pregnancy', *Medicine and Law* 14 (1995) 397, p. 404.
182 Nelson, *Law, Policy*, p. 164.
183 *Ternovszky,* joint concurring opinion of Sajó and Tulkens.
184 McLean, *Autonomy, Consent*, p. 31.
185 McLean, *Autonomy, Consent*, p. 31, referring also to E.D. Pellegrino and D.C. Thomasma, 'The conflict between autonomy and beneficence in medical ethics: proposal for a resolution', *Journal of Contemporary Health Law and Policy* 23 (1987) 23, p. 24.
186 McLean, *Autonomy, Consent*, p. 32.
187 Judgment of 29 April 2002, Appl. No. 2346/02, *Pretty v. UK,* para. 61.
188 Judgment of 17 February 2005, Appls No. 42758/98 and 45558/99, *K.A. and A.D. v. Belgium,* para. 61.
189 Rescigno, 'L'autodeterminazione della persona', p. 26.
190 Rescigno, 'L'autodeterminazione della persona', p. 27.
191 Rescigno, 'L'autodeterminazione della persona', p. 24.
192 Rodríguez-Ruiz, 'Gender in constitutional discourses', p. 712.
193 S.B. Boyd, 'Challenging the public/private divide: an overview', in S.B. Boyd, *Challenging the Public/Private Divide* (Toronto: University of Toronto Press, 1997) 3, p. 8, and references on the scholarship related to the public/private divide.
194 Chinkin and Charlesworth, *The Boundaries of International Law*, p. 31.
195 Charlesworth, Chinkin and Wright, 'Feminist approaches to international law,' pp. 621–2. On international law studies of the public/private divide, see D.E. Buss, 'Going global: feminist theory, international law, and the public/private divide', in Boyd, *Challenging*, 360, p. 364*ff.*
196 R. Gavison, 'Feminism and the public/private distinction,' *Stanford Law Review* 45 (1992) 1, p. 6.
197 Charlesworth, Chinkin and Wright, 'Feminist approaches to international law,' p. 627. See also Sifris, *Reproductive Freedom*, p. 158.
198 Boyd, 'Challenging the public/private divide', p. 15.
199 D.E. Chunn, 'A little sex can be a dangerous thing: regulating sexuality, venereal disease, and reproduction in British Columbia, 1919–1945', in Boyd, *Challenging*, 62, p. 63.
200 The attempts by some states to 'regulate' reproduction have increased in the years since the financial crisis of 2008.
201 B. Hartmann, *Reproductive Rights and Wrongs: the global politics of population control* (rev. edn, New York: Harper and Row, 1995), p. 170.
202 Gavison, 'Feminism and the public/private distinction', p. 12.
203 Friedman, *Autonomy, Gender, Politics*, p. 151.
204 Friedman, *Autonomy, Gender, Politics*, p. 151.

205 R.J. Cook and M. Fathalla, 'Duties to implement reproductive rights', *Nordic Journal of International Law* 67 (1998) 1, p. 5.

206 The applicant is seen as 'the cultural other'. See G. Firth and B. Mauthe, 'Refugee law, gender and the concept of personhood', *International Journal of Refugee Law* 25 (2013) 470, p. 481.

207 Chinkin and Charlesworth, *The Boundaries of International Law,* p. 222.

208 S. Deller Ross, *Women's Human Rights Book. The International and Comparative Law Casebook* (Philadelphia: University of Pennsylvania Press, 2008), p. 470.

3

The treatment: re-conceptualising states' obligations in countering VAWH

Starting from the beginning: the nature of state obligations

This chapter consists in the treatment, and it attempts to find an answer to the question which obligations states must abide by with regard to VAWH? There is often no univocal response – and hence a treatment – to a disease. However, the current legal instruments underestimate – to the point of not even mentioning women's rights to health and to reproductive health – the point that focusing on health is a way, in considering states' obligations as in other discussions, to counter VAW committed, whether by private or public actors (or both), in interpersonal relations, or perpetrated through policies, laws and, as underlined in chapter 2, accepted practices in the public or private health sector, in the field of health and reproductive health.

In the analysis of VAWH as conceived in this book, I will reconceptualise states' obligations including both dimensions. In the horizontal dimension, interpersonal violence, it is easier to find elaborations of states' positive obligations, expressed as 'prevention, protection, prosecution and policies,' to use the pillars of the Council of Europe Istanbul Convention – and jurisprudence is quite abundant in that respect. In the vertical dimension, as Rebecca Cook has argued, 'the challenge remains of requiring States to satisfy the positive duty of providing qualified services where women have no access to them on their own.'[1] This is especially true, for example, in the field of access to contraceptives, since this 'may depend on governments' financial resources and the political will to allocate them to the service of such rights.'[2] If, on one hand, 'the right to reproductive choice as a negative right has been successfully asserted in many countries by judicial decisions restricting governmental intervention,' the right to such choice 'has not been as successfully advanced as a positive right, since courts are less willing and able to direct governmental discretion on resource allocation.'[3]

My paradigm will allow us to put the two dimensions 'under the same umbrella' in terms of states' obligations, and to find that states' obligations 'specialise' along one or other of the dimensions. In this section, I will elaborate further the intuition of the CEDAW in GR No. 35 of 2017, which stressed that states have obligations stemming from actions committed by state and non-state actors and, with regard to the former, to ensure that laws, policies, programmes and procedures do not discriminate against women.[4] The recommendation does not refer, however, or only partly, to cases in which it is the state that, through its policies in the field of health, causes violence against women. The GR then refers to due diligence obligations under the paragraph on 'responsibility for acts or omissions of non-State actors,'[5] missing the opportunity to clarify the concept better and to conceive due diligence obligations in terms of the vertical dimension of violence as conceptualised in this book, as well as the horizontal dimension.

It is necessary to start, although briefly, from states' obligations and state responsibility. In exploring the literature, the different ways in which states' obligations have been 'categorised' have not always been clear. In particular, the framework used in international human rights law – to respect, to protect and to fulfil human rights – was confused with other 'categories,' such as obligations of conduct and of result. There might be some overlap, but distinctions should be made. After analysing possible ways to pigeonhole states' obligations, I will find the category within which my paradigm works, in order to proceed with the legal analysis of states' obligations in countering VAWH, as conceived in its double dimension. The concept of due diligence, despite being criticised and put to the test by legal scholarship, will also play a pivotal role, and cannot be neglected, given the fact that it has been elaborated by jurisprudence,[6] by UN bodies including the Special Rapporteurs on State Responsibility,[7] and scholars alike. A categorisation of states' obligations with regard to VAWH is not devoid of meaning and cannot be considered merely descriptive, because, as has been pointed out, 'la différente nature et la différente structure de l'obligation internationale a nécessairement une influence sur la nature et la forme de la responsabilité en cas de violation de cette obligation.'[8]

To discuss state responsibility it is worth starting from a key text, the Draft Articles on Responsibility of States for Internationally Wrongful Acts of 2001, whose Article 2 reads as follows: 'there is an internationally wrongful act of a State when conduct consisting of an action or omission: (a) is attributable to the State under international law; and (b) constitutes a breach of an international obligation of the State.'[9] The text does not provide a definition of international obligation, except that it can consist in an action or an omission, and can derive from any legal instrument, not necessarily a treaty. As outlined by the then UN SR on State Responsibility James Crawford:

> One notable feature of this provision consists in the absence of any requirement concerning fault or a wrongful intent on the part of the State in order to ascertain the existence of an internationally wrongful act ... it reflects the consideration that different primary rules on international responsibility may impose different standards of fault, ranging from 'due diligence' to strict liability.[10]

A major objection can be raised here from a feminist point of view. In their pioneer work, Christine Chinkin and Hilary Charlesworth argued that 'the traditional rules of State responsibility have provided a number of obstacles to the recognition of women's concerns as issues of international law.'[11] That was attributable to the distinction between 'public' actions and 'private' ones, the latter not triggering state responsibility, until the disruption of the public/private divide in the 1990s. Hence, the question could be posed this way: why is it plausible to rely on traditional concepts of international law to counter VAW, and in particular VAWH? Why, in other words, use categories that have proved to be guided by a patriarchal view of international law?

The answer will find its way in this chapter. What is indisputable is that it is not worth creating a parallel system of states' obligations, and a parallel regime of state responsibility in case of breach of these obligations, but better to challenge the traditional categories of international law from a feminist law perspective. The recognition of state responsibility for acts or omissions that originate in actions of non-state actors 'eliminates distinctions between public and private sector conduct in a way that feminist analysis endorses,'[12] for example, and its development has started with the traditional rules on the protection of foreigners. The concept of due diligence, which is not unknown to international law,[13] is another illustrative example. Despite being criticised and considered too vague, it is the key concept for the identification of the content of states' obligations and the determination of the responsibility of states for violations of women's rights. Some remarks on the long-standing debate in international law seem therefore unavoidable.

Obligations of conduct and of result

The first coherent structure for the rules on state responsibility was conceived by the then SR Roberto Ago, whose mandate lasted from 1969 to 1972. He argued in favour of a distinction between obligations of conduct and obligations of result, or rather, between 'obligations that call categorically for the use of specific means' (conduct), and those that leave the state free to choose among various means (result).[14] This is the first category that I will analyse, to see whether or not it is suitable for my paradigm. In the fifth report elaborated by Ago, Article 20 of the Draft Articles on State Responsibility referred to obligations 'calling for the State to adopt a specific conduct,'[15] and the specific conduct of the state required by the international obligation could be 'a course of action,' such as enacting laws, or an 'act of omission,' meaning not adopting particular laws or regulations.[16] In terms of state responsibility, an action or omission not in conformity with the 'specifically required' conduct constituted 'an immediate breach of the obligation in question.'[17] Applying the two dimensions elaborated in this book, both the failure to adopt laws on preventing and suppressing DV, for example, and the adoption of laws criminalising abortion without exceptions, would constitute violations of an obligation of conduct. This approach is not devoid of interest, even though, as I found in chapter 1, it is far from what the jurisprudence means by 'conduct', which is linked more to the standard of 'due diligence.' Article 21 of the Draft Articles proposed by SR Ago concerned violations of an 'obligation requiring the

State to achieve a particular result.' Obligations of result require a state to ensure a particular outcome, leaving the state a free choice of means to achieve it.[18] More problematic was the article on obligations of prevention (Article 23). Two conditions *sine qua non* were required:[19] 'the event to be prevented must have occurred,' and, secondly, it must have been 'made possible by a lack of vigilance on the part of State organs.'[20] Lack of vigilance and occurrence of the event had to be in a causal relation.

These definitions prompted criticism among international scholars. The distinction between obligations of conduct and obligations of result is indeed known to civil law countries, but has a meaning different to the one elaborated by Ago. Special Rapporteur Crawford, in his second report of 1999, argued concerning the basic distinctions between conduct, result, and prevention, that 'there is a strong case to simply delet[e] them,' and that 'means and ends can be combined in various ways,' being that the distinction is a 'spectrum' rather than a dichotomy.[21] Dupuy explains that Ago's position created confusion, since he meant the obligation of conduct in a sense that was opposite to the classic civil law tradition.[22] According to the latter, the obligation of conduct is an obligation of endeavour, a 'best efforts' obligation, whereas the obligation of result is aimed at achieving a precise result, with the consequence that 'lack of due diligence is a breach of the obligation of conduct.'[23] The debate on the obligation of prevention surrounded the question whether it was an obligation of conduct or of result, and it was not clear at the time which position Ago had taken in that respect.[24] The International Law Commission departed from the notion elaborated by the Special Rapporteur, and approved at a first reading this version of Article 23:

> When the result required of a State by an international obligation is the prevention, by means of its own choice, of the occurrence of a given event, there is a breach of that obligation only if, by the conduct adopted, the State does not achieve that result.[25]

What determined breach of the obligation was the failure to achieve a result and not the actual conduct of the state. *Contra*, Dupuy clearly argued that it was necessary to 'get rid of the idea that obligations of prevention are obligations of result.'[26]

The distinction between obligations of conduct and obligations of result has rarely been mentioned by UN Treaty bodies, except in some soft law acts, such as General Comment No. 3 on Article 2 of the ICESCR, elaborated by the ESCR Committee in 1990. The Committee considered that Article 2 encompassed both obligations of conduct and obligations of result.[27] As for the latter, they referred to the basic commitment by the parties to the 'full realisation' of the rights enshrined in the Covenant, whereas obligations of conduct consisted in the adoption of measures, 'including legislative measures.' The Committee was extremely clear, however, in contending that 'the adoption of legislative measures, as specifically foreseen by the Covenant, is by no means exhaustive of the obligations of States parties.'[28] In 1994, Rebecca Cook considered obligations of means and of result with regard to the CEDAW, contending that an example of the latter was to embody the principle of equality between women and men, whereas an obligation of means was provided in Article 2(c), 'to establish the legal protection of women,' which, in Cook's view, 'leaves to State parties choice of means.'[29] Her position departs from the framework elaborated by Ago, and adheres to the version of obligation of means as a 'best efforts' obligation. In GR No. 28, the CEDAW Committee argued that Article 2 CEDAW entails both obligations of means or conduct and obligations of results.[30]

The distinction, which led to some confusion, was soon abandoned. As anticipated, the categorisation was not eventually included in the final Draft elaborated in 2001. The debate around it never stopped, though. In Italian scholarship, for example, Antonio Marchesi proposed a tripartite structure of international obligations, in order to reconcile the different approaches that had emerged over time: obligations of conduct as elaborated by the International Law Commission at the time of Ago's mandate; obligations of conduct according to the 'French' traditional understanding of it (due diligence); obligations of result.[31]

Positive and negative obligations

Positive and negative obligations have become, write Dinah Shelton and Ariel Gould, 'a major part of human rights law,' to the extent of expanding in some cases 'both rights and obligations beyond the strict textual confines of international instruments.'[32] This opinion is mirrored in Pisillo Mazzeschi's complete study for the Hague Academy of International Law, where he affirmed that positive obligations have become more and more of interest in international law, especially after the development of international human rights law.[33] This does not come as a surprise, given the fact that, to use Alston's words, 'the world is much more poly-centric than it was in 1945,' and that 'non-State actors are looming even larger on the horizons of international and human rights law.'[34] If the obligation to prevent was conceived at Ago's time as referring to the protection of foreign nationals, and in particular foreign states' ambassadors – and hence, to a certain extent, his definition as obligation of result was understandable – in today's world the state is required by international human rights law to prevent private parties, under specific circumstances, from committing actions such as DV, for example by a person against his/her partner or a former partner.

UN treaty bodies and regional human rights courts often refer to positive obligations as a unique category of obligations, under which several obligations can be included, from obligations towards an individual who has suffered a specific violation to more general obligations. The distinction between negative and positive obligations seems adamant: the former are conceived as obligations to abstain from interfering in the sphere of rights and individual freedoms, the latter require the state to perform certain actions, to intervene, and they are meant to promote the 'realisation of individual rights and freedoms.'[35] The two types of obligation are not so neat as this; they may overlap, and the state may be able to abide by both in a particular sector. Even though the debate on negative and positive obligations gained momentum with the affirmation of human rights law, Pisillo Mazzeschi warned against the separation of this branch of international law from international law itself. The category of obligations developed in international human rights law must be brought under the general umbrella of international law, because the principles underpinning it were drawn 'from the more traditional doctrines of the law of State responsibility.'[36] It is interesting to note that, despite being relevant for the affirmation of women's human rights, from a feminist point of view positive obligations have rarely been explored; much more attention has been devoted to a specific aspect of positive obligations, namely due diligence obligations.

Pisillo Mazzeschi explained the notion of positive obligations having horizontal effects, which can be compared to the responsibility to protect elaborated at UN level.[37] It refers to the responsibility of the state for the acts of individuals. Despite considering the category negative/positive obligations relevant, he identified three sub-categories to better grasp the consequences in terms of state responsibility for the violation of a specific obligation: positive obligations of result, positive obligations of *due diligence*, positive obligations of progressive realisation.[38] The former can include legislation which respects and protects human rights; the positive obligation of due diligence encompasses concrete activities and measures of prevention which are however subject to *alea* (risk) in relation to the result;[39] the third type of obligation consists in the progressive adoption of measures with the aim of guaranteeing the effective exercise of particular rights. To go back to the previous categorisation, due diligence can be conceived as an obligation of conduct,[40] and a positive obligation. If it is correct to argue that all due diligence obligations are positive obligations, it cannot be said that all positive obligations are due diligence obligations.[41]

... in particular the positive obligation of due diligence

Literature on due diligence is significant, and it is not the purpose here either to provide the entire history of the evolution of this concept or to challenge its use in the field of VAW. The purpose is rather to stress the importance of due diligence in the protection of women's rights. Due diligence can be conceived as a standard, a tool, an approach, a process, to measure whether the state has undertaken all necessary steps to, for example, prevent a violation of women's rights, or to protect a female victim of violence, or to investigate a violent act. Condorelli defined due diligence as a 'basic principle of international law.'[42] Due diligence stems from the law of neutrality, and has developed in specific areas of law: the security of aliens and representatives of foreign states, the security of foreign states, the conservation of the environment[43] and, more recently, the protection of human rights, investment law[44] and security in cyberspace.[45]

In the field of human rights law, Sarkin points out that due diligence 'means that states take reasonable steps to stop human rights abuses from occurring, and use the means they have to adequately investigate abuses committed to determine who was responsible, to take appropriate steps against such individuals, and to guarantee victim redress and reparations.'[46] As clearly outlined by the African Commission on human and people rights in the case *Zimbabwe Human Rights NGO Forum* v. *Zimbabwe*:

> [an] act by a private individual and therefore not directly imputable to a State can generate responsibility of the State, not because of the act itself, but because of the lack of *due diligence* to prevent the violation or for not taking the necessary steps to provide the victims with reparation ... The established standard of *due diligence* ... provides a way to measure whether a State has acted with sufficient effort and political will to fulfil its human rights obligations. Under this obligation, States must prevent, investigate and punish acts which impair any of the rights recognised under international human rights law ... The doctrine of *due diligence* is therefore a way to describe the threshold of action and effort which a State must demonstrate to fulfil its responsibility to protect individuals from abuses of their rights.[47]

It can be said that the obligation of due diligence corresponds to the duty to protect, as I will see further elaborated at UN level, but unlike that duty, due diligence is a standard that already existed in international law, has been investigated by scholars,[48] was later included in legal instruments and has been used over time by courts in their decisions. Legally, it is a 'long-standing concept in international law,'[49] despite its vagueness, on which a significant jurisprudence has been elaborated over the years. Its vagueness should not necessarily be considered a point of weakness, but rather as expressing flexibility and adaptation to the context of different violations. Flexibility should be appreciated, indeed, in terms of 'variability', as pointed out by Karine Bannelier in her work on 'cyber due diligence':

> La due diligence n'est pas une norme indéterminée mais une obligation objective de comportement qui implique certains 'facteurs de variabilité.'[50]

These factors of variability consist in the state 'knowledge' of what is happening in its own territory, which is subject to a standard of reasonableness applied by international and regional courts;[51] in the state's capacity to prevent the use of its territory by non-state actors or, as in the case of women's rights, to prevent violations of human rights by private individuals; in the risk that a harm may materialise; and in the harm itself.[52] The degree of diligence varies 'in relation to the different standard of behaviour required by international law in each of the areas in which this concept is at issue.'[53]

Due diligence has been sometimes misinterpreted in the field of women's rights. Not every obligation to protect women's rights can be identified as a due diligence obligation. In her preliminary report of 1994, the then SR on VAW, Radhika Coomaraswamy, strongly argued that 'a State that does not act against crimes of violence against women is as guilty as the perpetrator.'[54] This affirmation anticipates the reasoning on due diligence obligations in the protection of women's rights.

In her outstanding report, a later SR on VAW, Yakin Ertürk, described the evolution of the due diligence standard as 'a tool for the elimination of violence against women.'[55] She did an excellent job of analysis, and the application of the standard in different contexts of violence is remarkable. However, some pivotal affirmations seem to depart from a rigorous international legal approach. For example, when she mentioned measures of protection, she stated that 'many measures undertaken by States in terms of their due diligence obligation to protect ... consist mainly of provision of services to women, such as telephone hotlines, health care, counselling centres, legal assistance, shelters, restraining orders and financial aid to victims of violence.'[56] In these cases, however, it is hard to see obligations of due diligence; they are rather obligations either of result – to establish certain services – or of progressive realisation (therefore to guarantee the effective exercise of the rights). There is no indeterminate result, as conceived by Pisillo Mazzeschi in his work, in the adoption of laws that allow the establishment of shelters: they are a purpose, which the state can achieve progressively if it does not have the means to achieve it immediately.[57] Ertürk was right to argue that not much effort is required to analyse 'the more general obligation of preventing violence from occurring, including by supporting women's empowerment and engaging in transformative change at the community and societal level,'[58] but this does not necessarily correspond *in toto* to due diligence obligations; it might be a form of progressive realisation or, more likely, a combination of different obligations. The standard of due diligence is, according to Joanna Bourke-Martignoni, a 'yardstick against which the efforts of States to prevent and respond to violence against women must be measured.'[59] She correctly argues that the concept is not new – it is quite old, indeed, and was applied by arbitral tribunals during the nineteenth century;[60] it was mentioned in the judgment by the IACHR, *Velásquez Rodríguez v. Honduras*, in which the Court posited that the state is responsible when an action is performed by individuals 'because of the lack of due diligence to prevent the violation.'[61] In this case, security agents acting on behalf of the state abducted, tortured and murdered Manfredo Velásquez, so their behaviour was directly attributable to the state. Nonetheless, the more general reasoning followed by the Court paved the way for further regional human rights courts' jurisprudence. The standard of due diligence must be applied case-by-case, considering the context,[62] and, as the ECtHR explained with regard to DV, also taking into account the specific circumstances of the violation of women's rights.[63]

Due diligence is also included in several soft law and hard law legal instruments regarding women's rights. The 1993 Declaration on the Elimination of Violence against Women urged states to exercise due diligence to prevent VAW committed by private individuals.[64] GR No. 19, adopted by the CEDAW Committee in 1992, stressed that states are responsible for acts committed by individuals 'if they fail to act with due diligence to prevent violations of rights or to investigate and punish acts of violence, and for providing compensation.'[65] The recent GR No. 35 on VAW does not follow the tripartite structure to respect, to protect and to fulfil human rights, and connects due diligence to the obligation of 'taking all appropriate measures to eliminate discrimination against women' under Article 2(e) CEDAW:

> Due diligence obligations for acts and omissions of non-State actors ... This obligation, frequently referred to as an obligation of due diligence, underpins the Convention as a whole and accordingly States parties will be responsible if they fail to take all appropriate measures to prevent as well as to investigate, prosecute, punish and provide reparation for acts or omissions by non-State actors which result in gender-based violence against women.[66]

One passage might appear misleading, but only at first sight. When the Committee states that 'under the obligation of due diligence, States parties have to adopt and implement diverse measures to tackle gender-based violence against women committed by non-State actors,' followed by, after a full stop, 'they are required to have laws, institutions and a system in place to address such violence,' this does not mean that the *adoption* of laws is a due diligence obligation. It seems to me that where the Recommendation reads 'in place,' it precisely means that it requires a precise outcome. The due diligence obligation rather arises in the *implementation* of laws, as stressed by the Committee: '[a]lso, States parties are obliged to ensure that these [laws] function effectively in practice and are supported and diligently enforced by all State agents and bodies.'[67]

Most importantly, echoing the jurisprudence of the ECtHR:

> The failure of a State party to take all appropriate measures to prevent acts of gender-based violence against women when its authorities know or should know of the danger of violence, or a failure to investigate, prosecute and punish, and to provide reparation to victims/survivors of such acts, provides tacit permission or encouragement to acts of gender-based violence against women. These failures or omissions constitute human rights violations.[68]

In GR No. 28 on core obligations of 2010, the CEDAW Committee explained that Article 2 CEDAW 'imposes a due diligence obligation on States parties to prevent discrimination by private actors;' it then adds that in some cases, 'a private actor's acts or omission of acts may be attributed to the State under international law.'[69]

The Council of Europe Istanbul Convention enshrines the standard of due diligence in its Article 5(2), according to which states must take 'the necessary legislative and other measures to exercise due diligence' in order to 'prevent, investigate, punish and provide reparation for acts of violence' covered by the Convention that are perpetrated by non-state actors.[70] The text here is fundamental. The Convention does not establish all the obligations it encompasses as due diligence obligations, but rather requires that due diligence must be exercised to prevent, protect, prosecute and provide reparations for acts committed by non-state actors. When it comes to the obligation on states to criminalise certain types of conduct, this is an obligation of immediate result, if I follow the distinction explained in the previous paragraph. The application of the law that criminalises rape, for example, must be then assessed under the standard of due diligence. In the explanatory report, due diligence obligations are (correctly) conceived as obligations of means, which allow state responsibility for breach of these obligations to be determined for what otherwise are acts of private persons. In the words of the explanatory report, 'parties have the obligation to take the legislative and other measures' – as I understand it, with the aim of achieving a result in the short or long term – 'necessary to exercise due diligence,' and that 'failure to do so violates and impairs or nullifies the enjoyment of their human rights and fundamental freedoms.'[71] It is true that the Convention or the explanatory report (or both) could have been more precise in distinguishing the different obligations, but it is also true that in no article or part of the explanatory report is it written that the standard should be applied to the adoption of laws, for example, which of course does not require a due diligence standard. In the first state evaluations, the Council of Europe's Group of Experts on Action against Violence against Women and Domestic Violence (GREVIO) has shown great knowledge and competence in distinguishing legal obligations. In its report on Austria, for example, the Group does not apply the standard of due diligence throughout, but only in some chapters. In particular, the Group argued that 'if a State agency, institution or individual official has failed diligently to prevent, investigate, and punish acts of violence … victims and/or their relatives must be able to hold them accountable.'[72] This can be achieved by means of appropriate laws, which, in the case of Austria, were already in force.[73]

The obligation to respect, to protect and to fulfil human rights, and the meaning of core obligations

In international human rights law, three different types – 'layers' – of states' obligations have been elaborated: obligations to respect, to protect and to fulfil human rights. In 1983 the then Rapporteur to the UN Sub-Commission on prevention of discrimination of minorities, Asbjorn Eide, proposed four 'layers' of state obligations, namely obligations to respect, to protect, to ensure and to promote, later reduced to the three categories in his report on the right to adequate food as a human right, adopted in 1987.[74] From a philosophical point of view, it was Henry Shue in 1980 who showed that there is no distinction between rights and that the distinction can be only made in terms of duties, dividing them into the duty to avoid depriving, the duty to protect people from deprivation by other people and the duty to provide for security.[75]

While the obligation to respect human rights can be defined as a negative one – the state must abstain from various behaviours – the obligations to protect and to fulfil them are positive ones, because they require states to take steps to implement human rights. Taking one relevant General Comment for my analysis, No. 22 of the ESCR Committee, the obligation to respect human rights means that states must refrain from 'directly or indirectly interfering with the exercise by individuals of the right to sexual and reproductive health.'[76] The obligation to protect human rights consists in 'tak[ing] measures to prevent third parties from directly or indirectly interfering with the enjoyment of the right to sexual and reproductive health.'[77] Even though it can easily be said that this obligation resembles the obligation of due diligence, this is only partly correct, since the duty to protect also requires 'States to put in place and implement laws and policies prohibiting conduct by third parties that causes harm to physical and mental integrity,' which seems to me to define a specific result, rather than an obligation to make best efforts. Finally, there is the obligation to fulfil human rights, requiring states to 'adopt appropriate legislative, administrative, budgetary, judicial, promotional and other measures to ensure the full realization of the right to sexual and reproductive health.'[78]

The three layers of obligation aim at guaranteeing the implementation of economic, social and cultural rights, which have been considered the 'least justiciable' among human rights, precisely because their character means they must be realised progressively. However, as can be seen, the different layers can be referred to one or more of the traditional categories of state obligations conceived in international law. The difference is probably in the capacity of these three layers to encompass the complexity of human rights in their implementation, in particular states' responsibility for acts of non-state actors.

To further counter the risk that rights will be implemented weakly, in particular economic, social and cultural rights, the notion of core obligations, or minimum core obligations, was introduced in the 1980s. One of the 1986 Limburg Principles on the Implementation of the ICESCR obliges states 'regardless of their level of economic development, to ensure respect for minimum subsistence rights.'[79] It was then that Philip Alston, once appointed as Rapporteur of the ESCR Committee in 1987, mentioned that corresponding to each right there must be an 'absolute minimum entitlement.'[80] In an interesting analysis conducted by four scholars, including Lisa Forman and Audrey Chapman, the notion of 'minimum core obligations' is explored in depth, with specific regard to the right to health. They point out the many unresolved questions surrounding the concept, such as, for example, 'is the core fixed or moveable, non-derogable or restrictable, universal or country-specific?,' and 'what are acceptable methods to further develop the content of these entitlements and duties?'[81] The positions in legal scholarship range from denial of the concept to detailed accounts of minimum core obligations.[82] Minimum core obligations, as elaborated by the ESCR Committee, have four consequences: immediate effect, immunity from the excuse of 'insufficient resources,' not being retrogressive and being directly applicable.[83] As argued by Martin Scheinin, 'the ICESCR contains no underlying "deep theory" or positive law basis for the approach.'[84] He considered the 'minimum core obligation' 'a methodology.'[85] In GC No. 14 on the right to health, the Committee listed core obligations, which should include as a minimum the non-discriminatory access to health services; access to food, basic shelter, housing, sanitation and water; the provision of essential drugs; the equitable distribution of all health facilities, goods and services; and the adoption of a national public health strategy.[86] Obligations defined of 'comparable priority' were, among others, to ensure reproductive, maternal and child health care. As clearly emphasised by Forman and the other co-authors, the debate surrounding the core is still open, and focuses on the question whether the core is a floor or a ceiling, and whether core obligations are obligations of conduct or of result.[87] The authors concluded that the concept is essential, but that greater clarity is required 'about its intended role in concretising, clarifying, enforcing and realising the right to health.'[88]

In GC No. 22, the ESCR Committee defined core obligations more precisely, contending that they 'should be guided by contemporary human rights instruments and jurisprudence, as well as the most current international guidelines and protocols established by United Nations agencies, in particular WHO and the United Nations Population Fund (UNFPA),' and should include 'at least' the following elements, which are worth reproducing *in extenso:*

> (a) To repeal or eliminate laws, policies and practices that criminalize, obstruct or undermine access by individuals or a particular group to sexual and reproductive health facilities, services, goods and information;
> (b) To adopt and implement a national strategy and action plan, with adequate budget allocation, on sexual and reproductive health, which is devised, periodically reviewed and monitored through a participatory and transparent process, disaggregated by prohibited ground of discrimination;
> (c) To guarantee universal and equitable access to affordable, acceptable and quality sexual and reproductive health services, goods and facilities, in particular for women and disadvantaged and marginalized groups;
> (d) To enact and enforce the legal prohibition of harmful practices and gender-based violence, including female genital mutilation, child and forced marriage and domestic and sexual violence, including marital rape, while ensuring privacy confidentiality and free, informed and responsible decision-making, without coercion, discrimination or fear of violence, in relation to the sexual and reproductive needs and behaviours of individuals; (e) To take measures to prevent unsafe abortions and to provide post-abortion care and counselling for those in need;
> (f) To ensure all individuals and groups have access to comprehensive education and information on sexual and reproductive health that are non-discriminatory, non-biased, evidence-based, and that take into account the evolving capacities of children and adolescents;
> (g) To provide medicines, equipment and technologies essential to sexual and reproductive health, including based on the WHO Model List of Essential Medicines;
> (h) To ensure access to effective and transparent remedies and redress, including administrative and judicial ones, for violations of the right to sexual and reproductive health.[89]

It is clear that these are all positive obligations, and include obligations of due diligence, of result and of progressive realisation, following the categorisation set out in 'Positive and negative obligations'. An important aspect of this list is the emphasis put on the need for positive measures in fields where the state usually had a duty not to interfere. Core obligations are taken from the paragraphs of the GC related to the duty to respect, to protect and to fulfil. Nonetheless, the negative duty on the state 'to refrain from directly or indirectly interfering with the exercise by individuals of the right to sexual and reproductive health' is not included in the core. Does this mean that core obligations only consist in positive obligations requiring an action by the state? It is hard to argue that this is so. In GR No. 28 of the CEDAW, on core obligations, the adjective 'core' is included in the title only, and therefore it seems that all the obligations included in the document must be considered to be 'core obligations'; they include negative obligations to 'refrain from making laws, policies, regulations, programmes, administrative procedures and institutional structures that directly or indirectly result in the denial of the equal enjoyment of women of rights.'[90] Non-retrogression, for example, can be considered as an element of a minimum core obligation, and it is negative in nature.[91]

The point is to consider how useful this category of core obligations is, in terms of state responsibility. In the part of GC No. 22 of the ESCR Committee relating to 'violations' (Part V), core obligations are not mentioned; the duties to respect, to protect and to fulfil may be violated. Similarly, GR No. 28 of the CEDAW does not refer to violation of core obligations. A second point is: to what extent are core obligations reflected in the views and concluding observations of the CEDAW and other UN treaty bodies? If we have a look at recent practice in CEDAW concluding observations, the analysis has been thematic rather than examining types of obligation separately.[92] Accordingly, for example, in its concluding observations on Saudi Arabia, the CEDAW Committee does not refer to 'core obligations,' but rather recommends and encourages the state to adopt measures that will allow the rights included in the Convention to be achieved.[93] Even though it refers to preceding general recommendations, the Committee does not structure the analysis to follow the three well-known layers (to respect, to protect, to fulfil human rights). In an interesting paragraph in the concluding observations, the Committee recommends the state not only to adopt provisions to legalise abortion, but also to provide 'comprehensive health services, in particular sexual and reproductive health services,' and 'ensure the availability and accessibility of affordable modern forms of contraception.'[94] Are these core obligations, or (merely) obligations to respect, to protect and to fulfil human rights? Similar detailed recommendations relating to the rights to health and to reproductive health are included in the concluding observations on Chile, where a verb recurrently used is 'to ensure.'[95] The recent concluding observations adopted by the ESCR Committee are also divided into thematic paragraphs, containing recommendations that combine, for example, the obligation to protect and the obligation to fulfil. In one of its observations, the Committee recommended that Niger 'take steps to outlaw and prevent child marriages contracted under customary law, including by adopting legislative and administrative measures and conducting culturally sensitive awareness-raising campaigns to encourage the abandonment of the practice.'[96]

Neither are core obligations included in the legal reasoning of regional human rights judicial bodies, although in a few cases courts and commissions have referred to the three layers of obligations and to the distinction positive/negative obligations. The ECtHR mentioned the 'positive obligation to protect life' in *Osman v. United Kingdom*, for example,[97] and the African Commission referred, in *Equality Now*, to the obligations to respect, to protect and to fulfil the rights included in the African Charter.[98] The IACHR touched on the three layers in several judgments, including *Velásquez Rodríguez*.[99]

The tripartite structure and the theory of core obligations possess a lot of merit, despite being quite descriptive, in highlighting how each human right creates a wide spectrum of legal obligations, against which states' actions must be assessed.[100] A possible solution to the *impasse* could be to conceive core obligations as obligations that have consolidated as customary international law, thereby binding all states without requiring ratification of a specific treaty, but it is not my purpose here to dwell on their nature; rather to reflect on the most suitable 'type' to apply to my analysis.

A more practical perspective: the pillars of the Council of Europe Istanbul Convention

A more practical approach to the issue of states' obligations could be to refer to already existing legal instruments dealing with VAW. The Council of Europe Istanbul Convention is quite innovative in its structure, being at the same time a human rights law *and* a criminal law convention. It mirrors the 3Ps (plus 1) paradigm of state obligations that was elaborated in countering human trafficking: prevention, protection, prosecution and partnerships. The 2000 Protocol against Human Trafficking to the UN Convention against Transnational Organized Crime is precisely focused on 'prevention, suppression and punishment,'[101] and the Council of Europe Convention on Action against Trafficking in Human Beings of 2005 contains chapters on prevention, protection and prosecution.[102]

The four pillars of the Council of Europe Istanbul Convention are prevention, protection, prosecution and policies.[103] As I wrote earlier, even though Article 5 of the Convention provides due diligence obligations, this does not mean that all the obligations included in the Convention are of this nature. The value that the Convention adds to previous legal instruments is precisely to address VAW from multiple angles and provide a spectrum of obligations states must abide by. As for prevention, the Convention elaborates a general obligation in its Article 12 to 'adopt measures necessary to promote changes in the social and cultural patterns of behaviours of women and men with a view to eradicating prejudices, customs, traditions, and all other practices which are based on the idea of the inferiority of women.' Being a general obligation, 'this paragraph does not go into detail as to propose specific measures to take, leaving it within the discretion of the party.'[104] Article 12 is followed by more precise measures, such as awareness raising, education, training of professionals, preventive intervention and treatment programmes, and participation by the private sector and the media (Articles 13 to 17). The GREVIO Committee, established by the Convention, is competent to assess whether the measures adopted by states are sufficient to guarantee the scope of the Convention, through mutual evaluation reports. Prevention also means ensuring that legislation is in force: Chapter V of the Convention is dedicated to substantive law, and requires states to have laws which criminalise certain behaviours (Articles 33 to 39), treat forced marriages as null and void (Article 32), subject sexual harassment to criminal or other legal sanctions (Article 40), provide grounds of jurisdiction (Article 44) and decide sanctions, measures and aggravating circumstances (Articles 45–6).

Under the second pillar, protection, the Convention provides a general obligation 'to take the necessary legislative or other measures to protect all victims from any further acts of violence,' and to 'ensure effective cooperation' among different actors, both public and private (Article 18). It then clarifies which measures it regards as protective, namely general support services, assistance in individual/collective complaints, the provision of shelters, telephone helplines and support for victims of sexual violence, and protection for children witnessing violence (Articles 20 to 26). Prosecution is based on Chapter VI of the Convention. It includes general obligations in Article 49, such as the obligation to adopt measures necessary to ensure that investigations are carried out 'without undue delay,' respecting the victim's rights. It then lays down more specific obligations, such as providing legislation on emergency barring orders, and on restraining or protection orders, and to ensure that investigations do not wholly depend on the victim filing a report or complaint (Articles 52, 53, 55). Specific measures are conceived for migrant women (Chapter VII). In effect, the policies pillar surrounds and supplements the other three, since it requires the activation of 'effective, comprehensive and coordinated policies encompassing all relevant measures to prevent and combat all forms of violence' (Article 7). Measures include the allocation of appropriate resources, partnership with different actors, data collection and research (Articles 7 to 11).

It is difficult to pigeonhole the measures states are obliged to adopt under the Convention into specific categories. It is possible to say that the obligations included in the Convention are positive obligations, of different – and sometimes intersecting – nature. The obligation to adopt measures to 'change attitudes' in society, it seems to me, confers a positive obligation to 'take steps,' which can be categorised as an obligation of 'progressive implementation' or, in the language of UN treaty bodies, 'to fulfil.' It means that, in assessing state compliance with the Convention, the GREVIO Committee will examine whether the state has taken steps towards this outcome. Conversely, the obligation to criminalise a specific behaviour is an obligation of result. The adoption of certain measures can amount to an obligation of conduct or an obligation of result, or both as intersecting. Christian Tomuschat has stressed that 'not infrequently obligations of conduct and obligations of result are intertwined to such a degree that the different component[s] can hardly be separated from one another.'[105] For example, adopting a measure could be a result, leaving discretion to the state on how to proceed (for instance, whether to provide a criminal or other sanction in response to a specific violent behaviour); at the same time, however, the Convention defines the result in detail, recommends the means and guides the state in achieving the desired outcome. In light of the principle of effectiveness, the state has an obligation to choose its means diligently.[106] As highlighted in GR No. 28, to 'pursue by all appropriate means' a specific policy means to use 'means' or a particular course of conduct, which gives a state party 'a great deal of flexibility,' but, at the same time, 'each State party must be able to justify the appropriateness of the particular means it has chosen and demonstrate whether it will achieve the intended effect and result.'[107] Compensation, to take another example, can be an obligation of result but might also be a due diligence obligation, to create the conditions necessary to provide individuals access to compensation.

This very practical approach suits the Convention, and will easily guide the work of the GREVIO Committee in evaluating situation reports from states that have ratified the Convention.

Methodology for treatment: reconceptualising state obligations in countering VAWH

Having analysed the structure of state obligations under international law, I will now turn to apply one of these categorisations, or, better, elaborate one of them to fit my paradigm. As showed in chapter 2, VAWH is an innovative concept capable of encompassing two dimensions of violence against women as related to the rights to health and to reproductive health: on one hand VAW as a cause of violating a woman's right to health and to reproductive health; and on the other hand, health policies and laws, or the practices of actors having public functions (hospitals, for example), that cause VAW or contribute to causing it. In this section of this chapter, I will bring the two dimensions under the same umbrella, in order to outline which state obligations exist in countering VAWH as it emerges in state practice and in the jurisprudence and quasi-jurisprudence of judicial and quasi-judicial bodies.

I first need to choose one of the categories proposed. I could have developed the analysis conducted by the CEDAW Committee in its GR No. 35, distinguishing acts or omissions by state organs from acts or omissions of non-state actors, stressing how the actions of private bodies providing public services must be attributable to the state.[108] Nonetheless, the idea of VAWH is more elaborate than that of VAW as known at the international level, and encompasses two dimensions of violence which do not correspond to the nature of the actor (state or non-state) committing violence, but rather to the nature of the violence itself, which is represented in its horizontal dimension by forms of interpersonal violence and in its vertical dimension by state policies in the health field that cause violence against women. Furthermore, due diligence obligations are only mentioned in the paragraph of GR No. 35 that covers acts or omissions of non-state actors. My purpose is to find a structure that better describes states' obligations to counter VAWH as I conceive it in this book.

At first, I was fascinated by the elaboration of 'core obligations' in the ESCR Committee's GC No. 22. It was clear that it was the beginning of the evolution of positive 'core' obligations in fields such as the right of access to health services in cases, for example, of abortion. Nonetheless, the *anamnesis* and the diagnosis have led me away from this initial purpose. Despite being interesting and having scope to react to the 'vagueness' of the rights to health and to reproductive health, the concept of core obligations has rarely been invoked by courts and human rights bodies.

The layers 'respect', 'protect' and 'fulfil' human rights are of interest from a legal perspective, but they are limited to the sphere of human rights, and do not allow me to clearly distinguish between obligations of means and of result.[109] Furthermore, they tend to be merely descriptive, and to reduce the system of protection of human rights to a *self-contained* regime.[110] The structure of the Istanbul Convention has its appeal and has proved to guide the work of the GREVIO Committee, at the beginning, anyway. Nonetheless, it is too far linked to the specificity of a Convention, which, despite having potential to become universal, remains anchored to the European context.

Each categorisation I have previously discussed has some merit in systematising state obligations in the field of VAWH. I found however that the structure proposed by Pisillo Mazzeschi worked best for my analysis. It allows me to consider the two dimensions of VAWH together, and to elaborate states' obligations in a more coherent and rational way, contributing to the debate on due diligence in the protection of women's rights to health and to reproductive health. It also brings the feminist human-rights-law analysis of VAWH back to the general theories of the international law of state responsibility. It means, in other words, providing a gender perspective on already well-established categories of international law and challenging them, while at the same time contributing to establishing feminist legal scholarship within the international legal mainstream.

It especially provides more guidance in the elaboration of due diligence obligations, which I consider the cornerstone of my reflection. Accordingly, in the following sub-paragraphs and taking into account the *anamnesis* (analysis of some of the cases decided at the international, regional and domestic levels) and the diagnosis (the elaboration of the concept of VAWH), I will differentiate the following types of obligation: positive obligations of result, positive obligations of due diligence and positive obligations to progressively take steps. I will consider the negative obligation not to interfere when positive obligations intersect, to emphasise in particular that respect for women's autonomy is pivotal in the protection of women's rights to health and to reproductive health.

A positive obligation of result consists, in the words of Pisillo Mazzeschi, in requiring 'an enactment (in the broad sense of the term) which respects and protects human rights.'[111] This obligation derives from international treaties, 'but also from international human rights law as a whole, given that it is an obligation with the function of achieving the general scope of protection of these rights.'[112] In his view, it cannot be considered a due diligence obligation, because the state is obliged to enact, amend or repeal laws, not just to make 'best efforts' in this direction, the outcome not being subject to any form of *alea*.[113] In the context of VAWH, it means that states must enact laws on DV, for example, or amend existing laws on rape to introduce lack of consent as an element of the offence, or decriminalise abortion, or repeal laws on forced sterilisation. To this list I will add the adoption of laws providing measures to grant women access to health services, as a preventive measure, and I will discuss the room for manoeuvre given to states in some cases (or margin of appreciation as the ECtHR puts it).

The second type is the positive obligation of due diligence, which (usually) includes the majority of obligations to prevent. However, as Pisillo Mazzeschi has pointed out, creating the apparatus to prevent violations of human rights is an obligation of result, whereas 'the concrete activities and the measures of prevention required of State authorities ... are subject to uncertainty (*alea*) in their results.'[114] The justification of the distinction between obligations of conduct and obligations of result 'rests ... on the objectively different content of two categories of obligations of the State, differing by how probable it is that the obliged State will achieve the result wanted by law.'[115] This argument is supported in my *anamnesis* by *V.K. v. Bulgaria*, in which the CEDAW Committee acknowledged the hiatus between the provisions of a legal instrument and its implementation by state organs. It argued:

> The Committee notes that the State party has *taken measures* to provide protection against domestic violence by adopting the Law on Protection against Domestic Violence, which includes a fast-track procedure for issuing immediate protection orders. However, in order for the author to enjoy the *practical* realization ... the political will that is expressed in such specific legislation must be supported by all State actors, including the courts, which are bound by the obligations of the State party. The issue before the Committee is therefore whether the refusal of the Plovdiv courts to issue a permanent protection order against the author's husband, as well as the unavailability of shelters, violated the State party's obligation to *effectively* protect the author against domestic violence.[116]

To enact laws and to exercise due diligence in their implementation are both legal obligations; the difference lies in the consequences of violation: breach of a due diligence obligation mainly affects an individual's ability to obtain monetary compensation, and redress for the violation he/she has suffered, while failure to enact laws (and also of the obligation to progressively take steps) causes general recommendations to be raised in UN treaty bodies and the IACommHR, and references to what a state is required to do in the jurisprudence of the European and the Inter-American Courts of Human Rights.

Indeed, if I go back to my analysis, the cases in which the performance of due diligence has been assessed concerned *specific* activities by the authorities in *specific* individual cases ('procedural' due diligence). Hence, for example, in *Talpis*, the ECtHR found the Italian authorities responsible because they had not acted with the diligence necessary to prevent Talpis's son being murdered by her husband. In the *Cotton Field* case, the IACHR found that Mexico had not exercised due diligence in investigating the abduction, sexual violence against and murder of women in Ciudad Juarez. In the sub-section below entitled 'Positive obligations of due diligence in specific cases – or "procedural" due diligence', I will reflect on the 'particular' due diligence necessary to counter, for example, DV, and on whether due diligence pertains to both the dimensions I have conceptualised in my book or only to the interpersonal one.

Finally, I will explore what Pisillo Mazzeschi called positive obligations 'à réalisation progressive' (of progressive realisation), which I call obligations to 'progressively take steps'. They impose on states an obligation to 'take steps,' 'through a series of measures of different nature, with the purpose of gradually and over time ensuring the effective exercise of these rights.'[117] They do not require an immediate, or at least reasonably immediate, result. An example will be the obligation to disrupt patterns of discrimination common to both dimensions. Decisions of human rights bodies and judicial bodies have shown that states can be held responsible for violating the norm prohibiting discrimination because they have 'condoned' or 'tolerated' violence against women. It is evident that to disrupt patterns of discrimination requires time – especially when we consider this pattern at the state *and* at the societal level – but this does not preclude state responsibility. In obligations of this type the requirement of diligence has a role to play, which is different, as I can prove by reference to the *anamnesis*, from ensuring due diligence in specific cases. When assessing respect for the obligation to take steps, monitoring bodies must consider whether the state has shown *diligence* in working to disrupt patterns of discrimination. I will discuss how and to what extent. As observed by Rebecca Cook:

> States can never guarantee that discrimination against women will not occur; they cannot be held liable simply because an act of discrimination is observed. States parties are liable only for failures to implement means the drafters considered reasonably achievable.[118]

In GR No. 28, the CEDAW Committee clarified that 'each State party must be able to justify the appropriateness of the particular means it has chosen and demonstrate whether it will achieve the intended effect and result.'[119]

The trend that I will show in state obligations is generated by state practice, jurisprudence and interpretation of the provisions of binding instruments. I will also show how, directly or indirectly, the right to health and the right to reproductive health permeate all state obligations.

Positive obligations of result

To enact, amend or repeal laws to counter VAWH

An obligation of result consists in the adoption, amendment or repeal of laws. These obligations can derive directly from a legal instrument, such as the Council of Europe Istanbul Convention, or indirectly from human rights law, since legislation is the essential prerequisite to counter VAWH and guarantee to women the enjoyment of their human rights and the exercise of their autonomy. Hence, for example, in *A.T. v. Hungary*, the CEDAW Committee recommended that 'a specific law be introduced prohibiting domestic violence against women, which would provide for protection and exclusion orders as well as support services, including shelters.'[120] In *Bevacqua and S. v. Bulgaria*, to take another example, the ECtHR acknowledged that, at the time of the facts in the case, 'Bulgarian law did not provide for specific administrative and policing measures,' which were later added by the 2005 Domestic Violence Act.[121]

Which provisions must a law on DV include? States have *room for manoeuvre* in that respect. A law should at least establish the administrative and police apparatus capable of effectively investigating cases of DV, and prosecuting the alleged perpetrators; it should provide at least a minimal range of services for victims/survivors including shelters, notwithstanding the resources available at state level. In light of the impact of DV on women's health, laws must provide free medical and psychological treatment for the victim. A law need not necessarily – or the state or the authorities could be obliged to progressively take steps to – include the establishment of special courts on domestic violence,[122] or grant leave of absence to victims/survivors of DV.[123] Two possible provisions are worth mentioning, both included in the Istanbul Convention. One (Article 55) is for formal investigation or proceedings to continue even if the report of abuse is withdrawn by the victim; the other (Article 8) covers allocation of resources. In chapter 2, 'Challenges to the public/private divide', I showed that the state *must* intervene in cases of DV, and disrupting the public/private divide has proved fundamental when considering DV in terms of violation of human rights by states. The autonomy of the woman, who can decide to return to her home even if her partner is violent, is not infringed when the authorities intervene, not even if they do so after withdrawal of the complaint, provided that this intervention is gender-sensitive and does not cause another form of violence to her; it could include, for example, issuing victims of domestic violence with a bracelet or waistband as 'life-savers', to use if they approach a women's shelter but are reluctant to formally report to the authorities.[124] With regard to the second type of provision, the Istanbul Convention (Article 8) requires states to allocate resources to counter the violent behaviours it prohibits, such as DV. Resources are clearly fundamental in support of laws on DV, but it does not appear from the cases examined in the *anamnesis* that an obligation exists to define a specific budget heading, although this would clearly be desirable.

Identifying the elements of the offence has proved to be complex in criminalising rape. Chapter 1 showed that lack of consent is an essential element of the offence.[125] The CEDAW Committee, in its concluding observations and views, has repeatedly clarified this aspect.[126] In 2003 the ECtHR analysed state practice and concluded in the same way in *M.C. v. Bulgaria*. However, the Court did not exclude seeking 'the prosecution of non-consensual sexual acts in all circumstances … in practice by means of interpretation of the relevant statutory terms ("coercion", "violence", "duress", "threat", "ruse", "surprise" or others) and through a context-sensitive assessment of the evidence.'[127] There must be no need to prove physical resistance to demonstrate lack of consent.

Many countries in the world do not criminalise marital rape.[128] Nonetheless, marital rape does constitute a form of VAWH, and criminalising it is encouraged at the international level.[129] With regard to specific cultural practices, the African Commission on Human and Peoples' rights, in *Equality Now*, recommended the state adopt measures 'to specifically deal with marriage by abduction and rape.'[130]

The trend at the international level, also confirmed by regional and national courts, as I showed in the *anamnesis*, is to adopt laws prohibiting FGM/C. The content of the legislation varies a lot from country to country, and can include extraterritorial application of the law to prosecute individuals performing the practice abroad on girls resident or domiciled in the home state.[131] As I argued in chapter 2, the element of lack of consent should be added to the definition of the offence. The Istanbul Convention provides, in Article 38, that 'coercing' a woman to undergo the practice must be made an offence. In light of the reasoning relating to rape, it seems likely that adding lack of consent – and presuming, also by law, that girls below a certain age are unable to give consent[132] – could better guarantee the protection of a woman's rights, and her autonomy. It could also be established by law that, upon women's genuine consent as assessed in courts, only re-infibulation will be permitted.[133] This legislation could inspire legislation on GCS, a practice that, as I pointed out in the chapter 2, has become widespread in European countries.

Turning to the vertical dimension, decisions of human rights courts and UN treaty bodies demonstrate that states must decriminalise abortion at least where it follows rape, sexual violence and/or incest,[134] and in cases of severe malformation of the foetus and risks to the life or health (including mental health) of the pregnant woman. States could still retain *room to manoeuvre*, the 'margin of appreciation' in the jurisprudence of the ECtHR, in deciding to what extent abortion can be limited, provided that, as I argue in this book, denial of abortion does not cause VAWH, in terms of intense suffering, and what the HRC has called a 'high level of mental anguish,' connected to an 'intense stigma and loss of dignity' for the pregnant woman.[135] In terms of negative obligations, states must also refrain from adopting laws that oblige practitioners to give 'false, misleading, and irrelevant' information to a woman seeking access to abortion.[136] Informed consent is a 'process … intended to ensure that a patient is left alone to make decisions based on a set of medical facts free from direct coercion.'[137] Laws must ensure appropriate and objective counselling, in order to allow women to make free decisions, without coercion, and ensure confidentiality. In *L.C. v. Peru*, the CEDAW Committee argued that, when it comes to state intervention in a personal decision, 'such intervention should be legal and regulated in such a way that, following due process, the person affected has the right to be heard,' and added that 'the contrary situation constitutes a violation of the right of protection from arbitrary interventions in decisions that, in general, are based in the intimacy and autonomy of each human being.'[138]

In cases of involuntary sterilisation, it is an obligation well established at the international level that states must repeal eugenic laws. The issue is no longer whether or not such laws are in force – states have gradually repealed eugenic laws over recent decades – but whether sterilisation occurs *de facto* in public or private health structures and the state does not prevent it; and whether the state is capable of providing reparation for the harm caused by eugenic laws applied in the past.

In terms of state obligations, maternal health is the field in which the major steps have been taken, especially with regard to the obligation to provide access to health services. For what concerns the adoption of laws, an obligation that I consider as confirmed at the international level is the prohibition of perinatal shackling of women in prison.

One might wonder whether states are obliged to adopt a law on OV. For the time being, state practice is not sufficient to elaborate an obligation in that respect. Such an obligation might evolve in the years to come and might require states to enact laws that compel practitioners to obtain the objective and informed consent of a woman before performing a practice during childbirth, in order to avoid VAWH. Laws on malpractice, which are in place in many states, only address episodes of OV that have the severest consequences and fail to recognise the psychological and emotional harm caused by practices that sometimes are common in the maternity ward. A counter-argument might be that legislation risks 'freezing' the activity of practitioners, who might fear sanctions should they fail to comply with the will of their patient. If such a risk is faced, one might wonder whether a form of collective responsibility vested in the hospital, rather than in the individual practitioner, could be of any help.

To provide access to health services

The positive obligation to provide access to health services belongs to the category obligations of result, because it is not subject to the *alea* in the outcome that characterises due diligence obligations; it is not even an obligation to progressively take steps, because it requires the state to immediately provide, at minimum, an essential level of health care.[139] Since the provision of health services requires financial resources, one might ask what kind of services must be granted in cases related to the two dimensions of VAWH. It is clear that this minimum level has risen over time as the activity of human rights bodies, and the jurisprudence of domestic and human rights courts, have implemented the rights to health and to reproductive health of women who survive violence.

It means the state must have in place facilities that can respond to the needs of a woman exposed to DV (and her children). So, for example, shelters must be able to host disabled children, health personnel must provide immediate support to victims of domestic violence in a non-judgemental way and psychological support must be available.[140] In *Aydin v. Turkey*, the ECtHR contended that, when the examination of a rape victim/survivor is necessary for an effective investigation to be conducted, this must be done 'with all appropriate sensitivity, by medical professionals with particular competence in this area and whose independence is not circumscribed by instructions given by the prosecuting authority as to the scope of the examination.'[141] Along the same line of reasoning, the IACHR, in the well-known *Ortega v. Mexico* judgment, explained that 'the psychological or psychiatric treatment must be provided by State personnel and institutions specialized in attending to victims of acts of violence,' and that, 'if the State does not have this type of service available, it must have recourse to specialized private or civil society institutions.'[142] The Court also made some suggestions concerning the characteristics of the service that must be provided: it must be designed to respond to the specific needs of the individual, and it must be provided, so far as possible, in the institutions nearest to the victims'/survivors' place of residence.[143]

In the vertical dimension, the evolution of the jurisprudence, and the quasi-jurisprudence of regional human rights courts and UN treaty bodies, have marked the most significant steps. The landmark *L.C. v Peru* decision, handed down by the CEDAW Committee in 2011, paves the way for an in-depth consideration of what positive obligations to provide access to health services entail in the context of abortion. The Committee acknowledged that L.C. had been the victim of 'exclusions and restrictions in access to health services based on a gender stereotype that understands the exercise of a woman's reproductive capacity as a duty rather than a right.'[144] On the nature of the obligation as one of result, the Committee considered that, 'since the State party has legalized therapeutic abortion,' it must establish 'an appropriate legal framework that allows women to exercise their right to it under conditions that guarantee the necessary legal security, both for those who have recourse to abortion and for the health professionals that must perform it.'[145] Furthermore, in some general recommendations, the Committee required the state to:

> [r]eview its laws with a view to establish[ing] a mechanism for effective access to therapeutic abortion under conditions that protect women's physical and mental health and prevent further occurrences in the future of violations similar to the ones in the present case.[146]

Access to abortion services must also include post-abortion services, including counselling, medical care and psychological support.[147] In Ireland, at the time of *Mellet*, women could get access to abortion abroad, but no protection and coverage from the public healthcare system, no paid leave of absence, no support from public or private insurance; once back in Ireland, Amanda Mellet could obtain medical care, but no form of public-funded post-abortion counselling, which was eventually granted by an association. When denial of access to abortion causes VAWH, there is an obligation on the state not only to abstain from certain behaviours – in this case abstain from interfering if the woman decided to travel abroad to get access to the service – but also to provide services in order to avoid physical and psychological consequences for the woman. The jurisprudence of the ECtHR, in similar cases, focused more on the lack of access to effective remedies, and of provision of objective and appropriate information to pregnant women. Developments in the Inter-American jurisprudence, awaited in the case *Manuela y familia v. El Salvador*, might be relevant in defining what a positive obligation to provide access to health services means. One can object that this positive obligation only stems from the quasi-jurisprudence of UN treaty bodies, whose outcome is not binding. However, when denial of access to abortion services causes VAWH, there is a violation of the woman's rights to health and to reproductive health which the ECtHR might regard as a violation of the prohibition of torture, inhuman or degrading treatment or punishment. This trend towards the recognition of positive obligations in the provision of health services still needs to be developed, but the path has been traced, both directly, through the views of UN human rights treaty bodies, and indirectly, through the jurisprudence of regional human rights courts that take health concerns into consideration in their decisions. The HRC's GC No. 36 on the right to life clearly construes a 'duty to ensure that women and girls *do not have* to undertake unsafe abortions,' and acknowledges that 'States parties should ensure the availability of, and effective access to, quality prenatal and post-abortion health care for women and girls, in *all circumstances*.'[148]

It is well established that, in operating abortion services, practitioners can exercise conscientious objection, but the state must ensure that the law obliges conscientious objectors to refer their patients to other practitioners, and hospitals to provide an adequate number of doctors performing abortion.[149] Related to this aspect is physical accessibility of abortion services: access can be impaired by the exercise of conscientious objection and the absence of practitioners within a reasonable distance from the woman's habitual residence, or by provisions that impose requirements on service providers, justified by a declared purpose to protect the woman's health, which are not easy to meet and therefore reduce the number of the providers available.[150] This obligation might intersect with a due diligence obligation, when, for example, a woman reports to the authorities difficulties in gaining access to abortion and the authorities do not act with due diligence in monitoring whether the law is being correctly applied in a specific hospital.

One question could be whether abortion services must be free of charge. In other words, does the obligation to provide access to abortion services include the provision of free services? In GC No. 22 the ESCR Committee stressed that 'publicly or privately provided sexual and reproductive health services must be affordable for all,' and that 'essential goods and services, including those related to the underlying determinants of sexual and reproductive health, must be provided at no cost or based on the principle of equality to ensure that individuals and families are not disproportionately burdened with health expenses.'[151] Are these services essential? One might argue that these services are essential in all cases in which abortion is legitimate under national law, and they must be free. However, what about abortion when performed abroad? Must health insurance cover it? There is no definite answer to these questions in light of state practice. Nonetheless, from the analysis in the *anamnesis* and from GC No. 22 it is possible to propose some reflections. In the latter, the ESCR Committee stressed that 'States parties [to the ICESCR] should … ensure that all individuals and groups have equal access to the full range of sexual and reproductive health information, goods and services, including by removing all barriers that particular groups may face.'[152] Furthermore, it is suggested that 'laws or policies revoking public health funding for sexual and reproductive health service' should be avoided.[153] As well as an interesting case at the national level, *Lakshmi Dhikta v. Nepal*, decided by the Supreme Court of Nepal, the economic issue has been addressed by the HRC in the *Mellet* and *Whelan* cases. The Committee stressed that discrimination based on social and economic conditions had occurred, because to gain access to abortion both Mellet and Whelan had to go abroad without any form of support:

> The differential treatment to which the author was subjected in relation to other women who decided to carry to term their unviable pregnancy created a legal distinction between similarly-situated women which failed to adequately take into account her medical needs and socioeconomic circumstances and did not meet the requirements of reasonableness, objectivity and legitimacy of purpose. Accordingly, the Committee concludes that the failure of the State party to provide the author with the services that she required constituted discrimination.[154]

Discrimination was therefore within the same gender, between women that miscarried and those who sought abortion abroad. Nonetheless, as argued by two members of the Committee in their concurring opinions, there had also been discrimination on the basis of gender because the prohibition of access to abortion services 'par son effet contraignant, indirectement punitif et stigmatisant, vise les femmes *en tant que telles* et les place dans une situation spécifique de vulnérabilité, discriminatoire par rapport aux personnes de sexe masculine.'[155] Another expert, Sarah Cleveland, added that state regulations must 'accommodate the fundamental biological differences between men and women in reproduction and … not *directly or indirectly* discriminate on the basis of sex,' hence they require states to protect 'on an equal basis, in law and in practice, the unique needs of each sex.'[156] Accordingly, I argue that, when this practice is allowed by law, abortion services must be free of charge, or at least affordable, to the extent that reproductive health services for men are free or affordable, and must respond to the specific needs of the different genders. The same can be said for post-abortion services, which the state must provide for free in all cases of abortion, even when abortion is illegal in one country and women undergo the procedure abroad before going back to their country of origin.[157] The lack of affordable access to these services would entail causing VAWH. It could also be argued that a possible future development of positive obligations consists not only in providing access to abortion and post-abortion services, but also in creating the economic and social conditions for the autonomous and uncoerced decision of a pregnant woman 'where pregnancy and motherhood are meaningful options.'[158]

The jurisprudence of some national courts, combined with the practice of UN treaty bodies, seems to support the argument that states bear the obligation to provide medically indicated health services to HIV-positive women, and pregnant HIV-positive women in particular; and that sterilisation is a failure to meet this obligation.[159]

It can be acknowledged that maternal health has been increasingly protected at the international level. It is striking to see how law has provided 'little significance to pregnancy as a source of rights worthy of consideration or as a special status needing of protection. In recent jurisprudence and quasi-jurisprudence, however, State obligations have evolved.'[160] An obligation to adopt laws that supply a legal framework for the provision of services to which women can have access can be identified, though: for example, a law that allows free access for poor women to prenatal, natal and post-natal services. An Indian Court required the state to provide access to hospital to women in labour, so they would not be obliged to give birth in the streets.[161] There is no coherent state practice or jurisprudence on home birth, regulation of which is left within the state's margin of appreciation, as emerged in the *Dubská and Krejzova v. Czech Republic* case decided by the ECtHR. It is worth mentioning, however, the opinion of five dissenting judges in *Dubská* who, although recognising that states have a wide margin of appreciation in regulating home births, concluded that the interference in Dubská's right to respect for private and family life had been unnecessary in a democratic society.[162] The dissenting judges explained that the single-option birth model, which stemmed from a regulation imposing strict requirements on maternity clinics, was *per se* problematic as regards Article 8 ECHR. In cases of low-risk pregnancies in women who were not first-time mothers, the interference was not considered to be justified.[163]

In *Xákmok Kásek Indigenous Community v. Paraguay*, the IACHR contended that 'States must *design* appropriate health-care policies that permit assistance to be provided by personnel who are adequately trained to attend to births, policies to prevent maternal mortality with adequate prenatal and post-partum care, and legal and administrative instruments for health-care policies that permit cases of maternal mortality to be documented adequately,' and added that 'pregnant women require special measures of protection.'[164] Moreover, the Court decided that the state must adopt general measures, obligations of result, since it was extremely clear in saying: 'The obligations indicated in the preceding paragraph must be complied with immediately.'[165] The list of measures that might concern pregnant or lactating women is worth mentioning here, because it is precisely the answer to my re-conceptualisation of states' obligations:

> (a) provision of sufficient potable water for the consumption and personal hygiene
> …
> (c) specialized medical care for pregnant women, both pre- and post-natal and during the first months of the baby's life;
> (d) delivery of food of sufficient quality and quantity to ensure an adequate diet;
> (e) installation of latrines or any other adequate type of sanitation system …[166]

In the ground-breaking decision *Alyne da Silva Pimentel Teixeira*, concerning the death of the applicant's daughter as a consequence of complications during childbirth, the CEDAW Committee presented several recommendations to the state, which can be considered as falling within all three types of obligation I have mentioned here. For example, it is possible to consider the obligations of the state to ensure that pregnant women have access to 'safe motherhood and affordable access for all women to adequate emergency obstetric care,' and 'that adequate sanctions are imposed on health professionals who violate women's reproductive health rights' as obligations of result.[167] The service must be affordable. This can be read in terms of intersectional discrimination: poor women are the ones that suffer the most from the lack of financial means to pay for health services. 'Affordable' might mean, in certain circumstances such as emergency maternal care, that the service, at least a minimum service, must be provided free of charge. This 'minimum level' was evoked by the High Court of Delhi, which, in *Laxmi Mandal*, reflected on the 'minimum standard of treatment and care in public health facilities, and in particular the reproductive rights of the mother.'[168] In a further judgment started *motu proprio*, the High Court obliged the state – and this is an obligation of result, not subject to any *alea* and not progressive – 'to demarcate or hire or create at least two shelter centres meant for destitute pregnant women and lactating women so that proper care can be taken to see that no destitute woman is compelled to give birth to a child on the footpath.'[169]

As for access to EC, the reasoning is similar to that on abortion. When limited access to EC is a cause of VAWH, an obligation falls on the state to establish the legal and regulatory framework to provide emergency contraception free of charge, and without obstacles attributable to conscientious objection. So, for example, in Latin American countries lack of, or limited access to, EC is an example of VAWH, because it is associated with high rates of clandestine abortion and of teen pregnancies, which are often the result of sexual violence. The debate on conscientious objection is also relevant when considering the case of EC: may a pharmacist or a hospital refuse to provide EC on the grounds of personal religious and cultural belief? One author has interestingly argued that, even though the general view in bioethics is that pharmacists should be allowed the right to refuse to provide EC in areas where pharmacies are numerous and EC can be obtained another way, there should be strong public policy requiring that *all* pharmacists dispense EC to customers who request it, notwithstanding moral or religious belief.[170] In countries where conscientious objection by pharmacists is permitted, a practitioner who does not provide EC on grounds of conscience must refer eligible women to an alternative pharmacist or hospital. Refusal to do so should constitute legally actionable negligence.[171]

What about public hospitals? Public hospitals might claim to have a moral identity, which is enshrined in their mission, or statute. This mirrors the right to conscience of individuals, although a hospital does not have a 'conscience'. Hospitals, however, have obligations to prevent harm to their patients, and are indeed the institutions that must deal as a matter of urgency with women who, for example, have been raped. In the analysis that I am conducting in this book, concerning the vertical dimension of VAW, since states are responsible for the actions of health services providers, hospitals should ensure that rape victims have access to EC and the opportunity to receive information, no matter how old they are, or be taken, at the expense of any hospital that does not want to dispense the medicine, to the closest centre for rape victims.[172]

To provide effective remedies for violations of a woman's right to health and reproductive health

The obligation to provide remedies for violations of human rights is present in many international and regional legal instruments.[173] To reflect on the evolution of this obligation through the centuries, and to highlight the passage from a state-centred to a human rights-based approach to the provision of remedies, is not the purpose of this book.[174] Accordingly, I will only provide a few remarks on this issue, before dealing with state obligations to provide effective remedies in cases of VAWH. As outlined by M. Cherif Bassiouni, 'the existence of State duties to provide a remedy and reparations forms the cornerstone of establishing accountability for violations and achieving justice for victims.'[175] Dinah Shelton sees this obligation as composed of a procedural obligation (to afford remedies – complaints relating to the violation of human rights must be heard and decided by a competent judicial body) and a substantive obligation (to provide reparation, strictly speaking), related to the outcome of the proceedings and to its capacity to provide relief to the victim/survivor of the violation.[176] Redress consists in both 'the substance of the relief' and the procedures through which relief may be obtained.[177]

Starting from the procedural aspect, the state must have in place 'un appareil adéquat d'administration de la justice pour ce qui est des droits de l'homme.'[178] This is an obligation of result. For example, the CEDAW Committee found that Hungary had violated A.T.'s human rights because the state lacked specific legislation on DV and sexual harassment providing sanctions against perpetrators of violence, and also lacked provisions for protection orders.[179] In cases of DV and rape, the obligation to provide access to remedies is strictly related to other obligations on the state. For example, in *M.C. v. Bulgaria*, decided by the ECtHR, the Bulgarian prosecutor had refused to start a criminal proceeding against alleged rapists because 'in the absence of proof of resistance, it could not be concluded that the perpetrators had understood that the applicant had not consented.'[180] In *Equality Now v. Ethiopia*, the system was in place, but insufficient: even though the actions of a prosecutor and a judge led to the acquittal of the perpetrators, there was no mechanism capable of granting retrial of the perpetrators and punishment for the acts committed.[181]

Turning to the vertical dimension, a judicial remedy is fundamental in cases of abortion, to avoid the exercise of a completely discretionary power by medical personnel. In the landmark *L.C. v. Peru* case, the CEDAW Committee acknowledged that the medical decision – to delay spinal surgery and deny abortion – had been guided by 'sociocultural pattern based on a stereotypical function of a woman and her reproductive capacity.'[182] L.C. had been at the mercy of the medical personnel, because of the lack of legislative measures regulating access to abortion, and her right to be heard, following due process, had ben violated.[183] Not all judicial procedures are suitable for granting an effective legal remedy. In the case at issue, *amparo*, a procedure that works as an extraordinary legal remedy against violations of constitutional rights by state organs, was not considered to have been adequate given the time frame.[184] According to the Committee, which analysed the issue for admissibility, the *amparo* procedure 'was too long and unsatisfactory,' and it had not been reasonable for the applicant to initiate 'a proceeding of an unpredictable duration.'[185]

In *Tysiac v. Poland*, the ECtHR found that an ordinance issued in 1997 governing access to therapeutic abortion did not provide any mechanism to solve disagreements arising between the pregnant woman and her doctors, or between the doctors themselves, therefore 'Polish law as applied to the applicant's case [did not contain] any effective mechanisms capable of determining whether the conditions for obtaining a lawful abortion had been met in her case. It created for the applicant a situation of prolonged uncertainty.' The law, in this case, caused 'severe distress and anguish' to Tysiac.[186]

In cases of involuntary sterilisation, the IACHR clearly contended that a system ought to have been in place capable of 'criminalising certain violations,' and that it must allow the possibility for the patient to report to relevant authorities cases in which physician(s) have not complied with the ethical and legal requirements of medical practice, in order to establish responsibilities and have access to compensation.[187] The obligation on the state to provide access to remedies exists even where, at the time of the procedure, the law admitted the practices complained of for eugenic purposes. These proceedings can only start when the victims/survivors of the practice are capable of speaking out and of reporting cases, even though many years may have passed.[188]

Providing access to remedies is also fundamental in cases where violations relate to maternal health.[189]

Turning to the substantive aspect, the analysis will be conducted both here and in the next sub-section of this book, on due diligence obligations.[190] The obligation to provide reparations must aim not only at providing monetary compensation, but also, and most importantly, at 're-humanising' victims, 'restoring' them as 'functioning members of the society.'[191] My reasoning aims to understand how to 'gender' reparations, in terms both of obligations of result and of due diligence obligations. To 'gender' reparations means to rely on the 'transformative potential of reparations,' which seeks to disrupt the domino effect that condemns victims/survivors to continue suffering.[192] As Margaret Urban Walker has argued, the project of gendering reparations does not aim to disregard men's suffering, but rather to examine how, with women, 'the original violation is extended, ramified, and augmented in multiple ways.'[193] Ruth Rubio-Marín, though discussing large-scale reparation programmes in transitional societies, has identified some elements that 'gender' reparations.[194] She observes that due recognition to victims should include recognition of the wrongful violation of the victim's rights, acknowledgement of state responsibility, recognition of the most serious harms resulting from the violation and a serious attempt to help victims cope with some of the effects of the violation, and to subvert, even though minimally, the structures of subordination.[195] These elements are scattered across the analysis of the jurisprudence and quasi-jurisprudence that I proposed in the *anamnesis* and discussed in the diagnosis.

Reparations can consist in the acknowledgement of state responsibility, plus monetary compensation. The obligation to provide the amount of compensation fixed in the judgment is meant to be an obligation of result. As UN treaty bodies require the state to provide 'appropriate' compensation, in that sense I might suggest that the obligation to provide reparations is an obligation of result, whereas the definition of the amount of financial compensation is an obligation of due diligence, subject to the *alea*, the uncertainty how the courts will decide the case. Where it finds that a state party violated one or more rights of the applicant, the ECtHR decides the amount of 'just satisfaction' in the victim's favour. Determination of reparations is not usually gendered, and the victim's rights to health and to reproductive health are only indirectly mentioned in the text of the judgment.

The jurisprudence of the IACHR has proved, quite to the contrary, to have broadened the scope of reparations, following a 'holistic gender approach.'[196] In *da Penha*, the state was required to adopt measures 'to grant the victim appropriate symbolic and actual compensation for the violence …, in particular for its failure to provide rapid and effective remedies, for the impunity that has surrounded the case for more than 15 years,' but also 'for making it impossible, as a result of that delay, to institute timely proceedings for redress and compensation in the civil sphere.'[197] The violation of the rights to health and to reproductive health is not only an essential element in determining the amount of compensation, but also leads to the inclusion, among reparation measures, of free medical and psychological treatment for the victim. For example, in *I.V. v. Bolivia*, which relates to the vertical dimension of my analysis, the IACHR required the state to 'immediately' provide I.V., at no expense to her, through its specialised institutions, medical treatment relating to her sexual and reproductive health, 'as well as psychological and/or psychiatric treatment,' including all medicines that might be necessary.[198] The Court also recommended the state to provide such treatment, whether necessary or not, for other members of the family. In a previous judgment on VAW, *Cotton Field*, which relates to the horizontal dimension of my analysis, the Court required the state to 'provide appropriate and effective medical, psychological or psychiatric treatment, immediately and free of charge, through specialized state health institutions to all the next of kin considered victims by this tribunal.'[199] In *Cotton Field* the women had been abducted, sexually violated and murdered, and the case was brought by their relatives, who were therefore entitled to receive compensation. The Court also ordered, as a measure of satisfaction, which is clearly an obligation of result, the judgment to be published in the official journal of the state, and a public act acknowledging international responsibility to be organised.[200] (A similar order was made in *I.V. v. Bolivia.*)[201] In *Cotton Field*, the Court also required the state to create a legal mechanism 'for transferring cases from the civil courts to the federal jurisdiction when impunity exists or when serious irregularities are proven in the preliminary investigations.'[202]

Turning back to the vertical dimension of my analysis, in *I.V. v. Bolivia* the Court ordered the state, 'within a year', to adopt education and permanent training programmes for medical students and health personnel on informed consent, discrimination based on gender and stereotypes, and gender-based violence.[203] I consider this an obligation of result, because the Court clearly set a time frame within which the goal must be attained,[204] although it could be considered an obligation to progressively take steps. Despite the innovative legal reasoning in terms of reparations, however, in *I.V.* the element of discrimination against I.V. as a refugee, although mentioned in the merits, was not taken into account in determining the amount of compensation.[205] In comparison, the reasoning in *Cotton Field* was more advanced, since it considered that measures of reparation must be 'designed to identify and eliminate the factors that cause discrimination,' and be adopted 'from a gender perspective, bearing in mind the different impact that violence has on men and on women.'[206] This perspective on reparations, which contemplates a 'transformative redress' beyond mere restitution, should guide the legal reasoning of every court and UN treaty body.[207]

Positive obligations of due diligence in specific cases – or 'procedural' due diligence

To investigate without delay

The decisions that I put forward in the *anamnesis* show that it is well established that acts that constitute VAWH under the definition I propose must be investigated by national authorities with due diligence. This obligation is linked to the duty to prosecute the alleged perpetrator, which can be considered as standing at the intersection of the three forms of obligation: it can be seen as an obligation of result, because the outcome is to prosecute the alleged perpetrator and assess his criminal responsibility; of due diligence in the manner in which both the investigation and prosecution are conducted, without undue delay and in a gender-sensitive way;[208] and an obligation to progressively take steps, since it requires a process of training the authorities, including the judiciary, and a complex change of attitude in a given society.

It should be stressed that the state might be responsible for violating human rights, even where the victim obtained justice (arrest and conviction of the perpetrator, for example).[209] Due diligence means, in practice, ensuring that authorities act without 'undue delay,' and avoid any form of secondary victimisation which would place unbearable stress on injured party, with the consequence of causing her another form of gender-based violence. This aspect was evident in particular in the decisions rendered on DV, and it is now enshrined as legal obligation in the Council of Europe Istanbul Convention (Article 49(1)). So, for example, in *Yildirim v. Turkey*, the CEDAW Committee recommended the state prosecute the alleged perpetrators promptly, and give due consideration to Fatma Yildirim's safety.[210] In *Opuz v. Turkey*, the ECtHR was not convinced that 'the local authorities displayed the required diligence to prevent the recurrence of violent attacks against the applicant,' and the proof was that 'the applicant's husband perpetrated them without hindrance and with impunity to the detriment of the rights recognised by the Convention.'[211] How may we clearly define the due diligence obligation to act without undue delay? It means to act when the authorities 'know or should know' the risk of harm for the victim, or, to borrow an expression used by the ECtHR, in the 'immediacy' of the risk.[212] Harm, as seen in chapter 2, consists in both physical and psychological suffering for the victim. In that respect, the rights to health and to reproductive health, despite being seldom invoked even by the CEDAW Committee in cases of DV, play a pivotal role. In *V.K. v. Bulgaria*, the CEDAW Committee argued that the risk does not manifest as 'a direct and immediate threat to the life or health of the victim,' because DV 'is not limited to acts that inflict physical harm, but also covers acts that inflict mental or sexual harm or suffering, threats of any such acts, coercion and other deprivations of liberty.'[213] In other words, the immediacy of the harm was determined by the consequences of DV for V.K.'s health. The argument elaborated by the ECtHR in *Talpis v. Italy* is of utmost interest, even though not yet consolidated by further decisions of the Court. As I have argued elsewhere,[214] in *Talpis* a revised '*Osman* test' – envisaging positive obligations on the state in situations presenting imminent risk to an individual's right to life caused by a non-state actor – as suggested by Judge De Albuquerque in *Valiulienė v. Lithuania,* gradually entered the legal reasoning of the Court. The case involved DV; it caused Loreta Valiulienė minor bodily injuries; but Judge De Albuquerque acknowledged that the stage of 'immediate risk' might be too late for the state to intervene, and that 'a more rigorous standard of diligence is especially necessary' in societies where the problem of domestic violence is widespread. Seeming to refer to a 'collective' harm caused by DV, which affects women in a given society *because* they are women, he reformulated the test as follows:

> If a State knows or ought to know that a segment of its population, such as women, is subject to repeated violence and fails to prevent harm from befalling the members of that group of people when they face a present (but not yet imminent) risk, the State can be found responsible by omission for the resulting human rights violations. The constructive anticipated duty to prevent and protect is the reverse side of the context of widespread abuse and violence already known to the State authorities.

The ECtHR, in *Talpis v. Italy*, followed the way paved by Judge De Albuquerque, in stressing the 'particular context' of domestic violence, and the aspect of repetition of violent acts.[215] The judges also used the expression 'particular due diligence,' which refers to the context of DV: a very interesting perspective, although quite unique at the moment, which can be reinforced in future judgments by some considerations on the right to health of the woman who has survived violence. As outlined by the CEDAW Committee in *A.T. v. Hungary*, a general obligation on the state is to 'assure victims of domestic violence the maximum protection of the law by acting with due diligence to prevent and respond to such violence against women.'[216] To borrow the expression used by Karine Bannelier on due diligence in cyberspace, '*qui peut et n'empêche, pèche*,' the state is responsible for violating a woman's rights to health and reproductive health if it knew or should have known (constructive diligence) that she risked a form of violence, had the means to prevent this and did not do anything.[217] Of course this might sound easy in theory and difficult *in concreto*; nonetheless, the jurisprudence has started to identify what a 'diligent' prevention of violence against women means.

In femicide and rape cases investigations are fundamental. In *Cotton Field,* despite Mexico admitting responsibility for the first stage of investigations, the Court found that the state had not displayed due diligence in the second stage of investigations, owing to the 'ineffective responses and the indifferent attitudes that have been documented in relation to the investigation of these crimes.'[218] In the *López Soto* report, the IACommHR concluded that, 'taking into account the extreme risk to which a woman who was reported missing is exposed' – López Soto had been abducted and raped – the state had failed to comply with 'its duty to prevent and protect once it became aware or should have known about the situation of risk she faced.'[219] The Court, to which the case was referred, highlighted how state responsibility stemmed from the 'insufficient and negligent reaction of the public servants who … did not adopt the measures that one could have reasonably expected to comply with the due diligence required to prevent and interrupt the concatenation of events.'[220] Interestingly, it also argued that an alleged episode of VAW requires 'a reinforced due diligence,'[221] evoking the 'particular due diligence' in the European jurisprudence. Judges then identified how stereotypes prevent appropriate investigations. This means, in other words, that states have due diligence obligations to investigate actual cases of gender-based VAW in an efficient and timely way, without being misled by stereotypes.

Investigation without delay must also characterise cases belonging to the vertical dimension. Here, for example, in *Andrea Szijjarto v. Hungary* the CEDAW Committee considered the complaint admissible even though the domestic remedies had not been exhausted, and the reason was the 'unreasonably prolonged' delay of more than three years from the dates of the incidents, 'particularly considering that the author has been at risk of irreparable harm and threats to her life during that period.'[222] Even though rarely stressed by the doctrine, investigation is also relevant in cases of abortion. In *Mellet v. Ireland*, the HRC found that a petition to a domestic court 'would have been ineffective and inadequate,' and that 'in the extremely unlikely event that a court found that she had a legal right to access abortion in Ireland, the author would have been unable to terminate her pregnancy there.'[223] Furthermore, the mechanisms available were insufficient and inadequate because they would have caused 'mental suffering by forcing [Amanda Mellet] to undergo public litigation.'[224] In other words, states must provide an expeditious and confidential way to decide cases in which a woman may challenge a decision by physicians to deny her access to abortion. She must also be protected from interference by third parties, so her case must be anonymous and adjudicated without delay. This aspect emerged in *P. and S. v. Poland*, where the ECtHR found that the provisions of the civil law 'as applied by the Polish courts did not make available a procedural instrument by which a pregnant woman seeking an abortion could fully vindicate her right to respect for her private life,' and that, furthermore, the civil law remedy was 'retroactive' and 'compensatory' only.[225] When involuntary sterilisations are performed, according to the jurisprudence of the Inter-American Court of Human Rights, the investigation that follows must respond to an 'urgent and careful scrutiny of the circumstances of the case.'[226]

To provide access to health services and to information

As I investigated in chapter 1, the jurisprudence of regional human rights courts and the quasi-jurisprudence of UN treaty bodies has determined a significant development in the elaboration of an obligation to provide access to health services and to information, which is an obligation of result. Are there elements of due diligence? The answer is positive. In cases of DV and rape, for example, this means that real access must be provided to health services capable of providing support to a specific victim/survivor of violence. In other words, it must be possible for any woman to gain access to the forms of protection and support envisaged by the law. If the obligation of result consists in having in place adequate shelters and services to respond to victims of DV, the due diligence obligation means providing health services and information in actual cases, doing whatever is needed to grant protection to the victim/survivor and her children.

Since the vertical dimension includes state laws and policies in the field of health, it does not seem possible to find margin for the application of the due diligence standard. Nonetheless, I contend that there is margin. My conclusion in chapter 2 was that the vertical dimension is also characterised by policies and practices adopted by public or private bodies dealing with public services, such as the health service. Therefore, even though it may have put laws in place, the state is responsible when it does not exercise due diligence to prevent practices that cause VAWH in individual cases. In a case involving an entire indigenous community, including its women, the IACHR declared that Paraguay had 'failed to take the required positive measures, within its powers, that could reasonably be expected to prevent or to avoid the risk to the right to life.'[227] The death of many women before, during or after bearing children had been caused by the lack of an adequate state apparatus to provide minimum health services (an obligation of result), and because of the lack of due diligence in providing access to health services in the specific case.

The passage from obligations of result to due diligence obligations seems clear in the landmark *Pimentel Teixeira* decision, where the CEDAW Committee argued that 'the State is *directly* responsible for the action of private institutions when it outsources its medical services and … furthermore, the State always maintains the duty to *regulate and monitor* private health-care institutions.'[228] Indeed, among the recommendations of the Committee to the state, 'ensure that private health-care facilities comply with relevant national and international standards on reproductive health care'[229] is relevant. It entails 'the policy … [ensuring] that there are strong and focused executive bodies to implement such policies.'[230] In a similar case, when a pregnant woman had to wait too long before getting medical support, the judges of the ECtHR were convinced that the negligence attributable to the hospital staff 'went beyond a mere error or medical negligence, in so far as the doctors working there, in full awareness of the facts and in breach of their professional obligations, did not take all the emergency measures necessary to attempt to keep their patient alive.'[231] The Court found that the state had violated the procedural obligation under Article 2 ECHR, in particular because, as I will discuss in the next sub-section, it had not provided an effective remedy to Mrs Şentürk. In a broader sense, as suggested by the CEDAW Committee, it can be argued that the state also has the obligation to 'regulate and monitor' healthcare institutions, both public and private, to avoid cases of malpractice.

The issue which challenges my paradigm in its vertical dimension is the instance of a state failing to allow pharmacists to conscientiously object to EC by law, but *de facto* allowing pharmacists to exercise conscientious objection. According to the analysis conducted in this book, the state bears an obligation to establish the legal framework necessary to grant to women access to EC (a law that, while permitting conscientious objection, compels pharmacists to refer the woman to another pharmacist, for example); to adopt all necessary measures to respond to an actual case in which a woman reports to the authorities difficulties in gaining access to the medicine; and to progressively take steps to disrupt the 'male' attitude in the medical sector.

I have already argued that the obligation to provide information is an example of obligation of result, because it implies the enactment of laws obliging appropriate and objective information to be given to women. I am arguing here that it can also be a kind of due diligence obligation, when the law is in place but its application is not effective. For example, in *P. and S. v. Poland* the ECtHR considered that, despite Polish law obliging practitioners to state in writing any refusal to perform abortion, and to refer the case to another physician, 'the staff involved in the applicants' case did not consider themselves obliged to carry out the abortion expressly requested by the applicants on the strength of the certificate issued by the prosecutor,' and that the applicants 'did not receive appropriate and objective medical counselling which would have due regard to their own views and wishes.'[232]

The provision of objective and reliable information is fundamental where a woman is to be sterilised. The state violates its due diligence obligations when it does not act in order to prevent the provision of misleading information or coercion by health personnel to undergo the practice. In *Szijjarto*, the CEDAW confirmed the reasoning in its GR No. 24, and considered that Hungary 'has not ensured that the author gave her fully informed consent to be sterilised.'[233] In that respect, the Committee recommended the state 'monitor public and private health centres, including hospitals and clinics, which perform sterilization procedures so as to ensure that fully informed consent is being given by the patient before any sterilization procedure is carried out, with appropriate sanctions in place in the event of a breach.'[234] The ECtHR followed a similar reasoning in *V.C. v. Slovakia*, when it decided that the laws in force at the time of V.C.'s sterilisation had required her consent prior to medical intervention, but that '*in the applicant's case*, [they] did not provide appropriate safeguards.'[235]

The element of consent, which matters in a case of involuntary sterilisation but can be considered as a generally important element in all cases, was defined in the following terms by the IACHR in *I.V. v. Bolivia*: consent must be granted prior to the medical procedure; it must be given in a free, voluntary, autonomous way, without pressure of any kind; it must not be used as a condition for access to other procedures or benefits, and no coercion, threats or disinformation may be employed; it must be full and informed.[236] In particular, the Court argued that the obligation of 'active transparency' (*transparencia activa*) requires the state to provide information that is necessary so that individuals can 'exercise other rights;'[237] in other words, access to information is instrumental to the enjoyment of other rights. Consequently, according to the Court, the obligation of active transparency the state must abide by consists in the duty of health personnel to provide information which can contribute to the patient making free and responsible decisions regarding his/her own body and reproductive health.[238] Accordingly, the obligation of active transparency includes both an obligation of result to establish the limits to the medical action, and a due diligence obligation to guarantee that these limits are adequate and effective in practice.[239] As pointed out by the Court: 'in the implementation of the Bolivian laws which regulate access to sexual and reproductive health,' the state must adopt the necessary measures to 'ensure that in all public and private hospitals the prior, free, full, and informed consent is obtained from the woman before interventions that lead to sterilisation.'[240]

To provide access to an effective judicial remedy with due diligence

When laws are in place, states can be held responsible for violation of due process rights when a woman encounters difficulties in gaining access to judicial remedies. I list this aspect under both obligations of result and obligations of due diligence: on one hand, it is true that providing access to a judicial remedy is an obligation of result, but I contend that the way in which this access is provided is subject to an *alea* which characterises this obligation as an obligation of due diligence. So, for example, the IACommHR considered the application of Maria da Penha admissible, although she had not exhausted all domestic remedies, because of the length of the proceedings and the attitude shown to victims of DV by courts and lawyers.[241] In *V.K. v. Bulgaria*, the CEDAW Committee noted that the state party had adopted a law on protection against DV, which included a fast-track procedure for issuing immediate protection orders, but that 'the political will that is expressed in such specific legislation must be supported by all State actors, including the courts, who are bound by the obligations of the State party.'[242] Accordingly, the Committee found that when the Plovdiv courts refused to issue a permanent protection order against V.K.'s husband, the restrictive definition of DV that was applied, along with the 'very high standard of proof' required, meant that the state had violated its obligation to effectively protect V.K. against DV. In *Valiulienė*, the ECtHR found that the national law provided 'a sufficient regulatory framework to pursue the crimes,' but that in the case at hand enormous delay had occurred in the proceedings: the criminal proceedings were discontinued, and this had been the opposite of a guarantee of effective protection.[243] In *Lenahan et al.* the IACommHR, despite considering the USA responsible for not protecting Jessica Lenahan and her daughters from DV, found that the state was not internationally responsible for failures to grant her access to courts.[244] Lenahan, whose daughters were killed by her husband who then committed suicide, had been able to reach the Supreme Court, which ruled against her, without any irregularities, omissions or delays. The due diligence obligation had been met.

An effective remedy should also be characterised by gender-sensitive proceedings, in which courts are capable of 'seeing' how gender matters in the prosecution of certain offences. This aspect was highlighted by the CEDAW Committee in *V.K. v. Bulgaria*.[245]

In a case of rape committed by state organs, the IACommHR found that Mexico had not acted with due diligence in investigating the violation of Mariana Selvas Gómez and another ten women's rights: their complaint to obtain justice was not thoroughly examined by courts during more than ten years after the facts complained of.[246] Judicial ineffectiveness, as argued by the IACHR in *Cotton Field* concerning femicides committed by private parties, 'encourage[d] an environment of impunity that facilitate[d] and promote[d] the repetition of acts of violence in general and sen[t] a message that violence against women [wa]s tolerated and accepted as part of daily life.'[247]

Turning to maternal health, the ECtHR stressed the procedural element of the right to life in *Byrzykowski v. Poland*, where the state was found in violation of Article 2 ECHR for not effectively investigating after Byrzykowski died as a consequence of epidural anaesthesia. In a similar, more recent case, *Z. v. Poland*, the Court pointed out that states are required to 'set up an effective independent judicial system so that the cause of death of patients in the care of the medical profession, whether in the public or the private sector, can be determined and those responsible made accountable,' and that the obligation to determine responsibility in the case at issue was an 'obligation of means only.'[248] Such a system could have considered, on one hand, the need to have a system in place competent to deal with the deaths of patients and to assess the possibility of granting compensation – a result – and, on the other hand, the margin the state has in choosing a type of remedy. As the Court further argued, in the specific sphere of medical negligence the obligation may be satisfied through *different means*: a remedy in the criminal courts, or 'a remedy in the civil courts, either alone or in conjunction with a remedy in the criminal courts, enabling any responsibility of the doctors concerned to be established and any appropriate civil redress, such as an order for damages and/or for the publication of the decision, to be obtained.'[249] This argument is upheld in the *Şentürk v. Turkey* judgment, where the Court referred to the state's positive obligation to establish an 'effective and independent system' to decide with promptness and due diligence cases of the death of patients, and to this obligation being violated when the protection afforded by domestic law 'exist[s] only in theory:' so 'it must also operate effectively in practice, and that requires a prompt examination of the case without unnecessary delays.'[250]

Beyond the obligation on states to establish a specific mechanism to provide remedies to the victims of human rights violations, there are due diligence obligations to provide effective remedy, in the sense that they are subject to the *alea* of the outcome.[251]

For example, in *Cotton Field* the Court ordered the state to 'effectively' conduct 'the criminal proceedings that were underway and, if applicable, those that may be opened in the future, to identify, prosecute and punish the perpetrators and masterminds of the disappearance, ill-treatments and deprivation of life' of the women, whose relatives had brought the case before the Inter-American human rights bodies.[252] In identifying the elements of the obligation, the due diligence standard emerges strongly: the Court asked the state 'to use all available means to ensure that the … judicial proceedings are conducted promptly in order to avoid a repetition of the same or similar acts as those in the instant case.'[253] In *Fernández Ortega*, the IACHR, amid a long list of measures to be adopted as reparation for the rape of a young woman belonging to an indigenous minority, pointed out 'the importance of implementing reparations that have a community scope and that allow the victim to reincorporate herself into her living space and cultural identity,' which required the state in this specific case, 'to provide the necessary resources for the Me'phaa indigenous community … to be able to establish a community centre.'[254] The determination of the resources 'necessary' constitutes an obligation of due diligence, on which the IACHR wished to stay informed. In assessing compliance with the judgment in 2015, the Court required the state to present a report every six months in order to verify that it had respected the obligation to provide redress to Inés Fernández Ortega in her status within the community.[255]

Positive obligations to progressively take steps

To change patterns of discrimination that contribute to VAWH

In the diagnosis, I argued that VAWH can be seen in terms of patterns of discrimination, both in its horizontal and in its vertical dimension. I further contended that patterns of discrimination are not just social and cultural patterns rooted in society, but also the persistence of and 'tolerance' states demonstrate for VAWH.

The question now is how to disrupt these patterns of discrimination, and in what sense this can be identified as an obligation to progressively take steps. The CEDAW Committee has repeatedly considered the prohibition of discrimination as an obligation of immediate effect,[256] and so it is, particularly when it comes to pursuing non-discrimination *de jure*, in the law, or, if read in terms of reparations, obliging the state to provide public acknowledgement of its responsibility, condemnation of discrimination. An element of due diligence obligation could also be identified, if we read the prohibition of discrimination in a specific case, for example when investigations are conducted. For instance, in *I.V. v. Bolivia*, where I.V. was sterilised without prior and informed consent, the IACHR posited that consent can be extorted by forms of violence, coercion or *discrimination*,[257] and that the relationship of power between the physician and the patient can be 'exacerbated by the unequal power relations that have historically characterised men and women, as well as by gender stereotypes ... which, consciously or unconsciously constitute the basis of practices that reinforce the dependent and subordinate position of women.'[258]

The obligation to eliminate all forms of discrimination against women includes the obligation to eliminate discrimination based on gender stereotypes,[259] which can persist in society and in the attitude of organs of the state or of people working in public fields, such as health. It is an obligation to take steps progressively, which implies respecting, over time, obligations both of result and of due diligence.[260] Examples of these measures are the publication of a pamphlet on women's sexual and reproductive health that includes the requirement for informed consent.[261] This is a result, but one that requires time and an action by the state which is not immediate.

An interesting example of positive obligations to take steps to disrupt patterns of discrimination in cases of DV is found in the *Maria da Penha* case. The IACommHR acknowledged that 'the State has adopted a number of measures intended to reduce the scope of domestic violence and tolerance by the State thereof, although these measures have not yet had a significant impact on the pattern of State tolerance of violence against women, in particular as a result of ineffective police and judicial action in Brazil,' and recommended the state 'continue and expand the reform process that will put an end to the condoning by the State of domestic violence against women in Brazil and discrimination in the handling thereof.'[262] In particular, the Commission called for a change in the pattern of discrimination both within society and within the state apparatus; the former, by the 'inclusion in teaching curriculums of units aimed at providing an understanding of the importance of respecting women and their rights recognized in the Convention of Belém do Pará, as well as the handling of domestic conflict'; the latter, through 'measures to train and raise the awareness of officials of the judiciary and specialized police so that they may understand the importance of not condoning domestic violence.'[263]

In a case of rape, the IACommHR considered, in the *López Soto* report, 'the more general contexts of gender violence and impunity for violence' and recommended several mechanisms to ensure non-repetition, which can be grouped within my category of 'obligations to progressively take steps.' These include designing and implementing 'a national policy on prevention of violence against women and gender-based violence that includes effective supervision and oversight mechanisms,' and reinforcing 'the institutional capacity for responding to the structural problems identified in this case as factors of impunity in cases of violence against women.'[264] In the judgment in the same case, the Court required the state, '[with]in a reasonable time', to include in the education system a permanent programme named after López Soto with the purpose of eradicating gender-based violence.[265] In *Atenco*, the IACHR asked the state to draw up a plan addressed to police forces in order to assess respect for the standards elaborated by the court on the use of force during demonstrations, and the gender-sensitivity of their actions.[266]

In abortion cases, the CEDAW Committee, in *L.C. v. Peru*, recommended that the state should 'take measures to ensure that the relevant provisions of the Convention and the Committee's GR No. 24 with regard to reproductive rights are known and observed in all health-care facilities,' including 'education and training programmes to encourage health providers to change their attitudes and behaviour in relation to adolescent women seeking reproductive health services and [to] respond to specific health needs related to sexual violence,' and 'guidelines or protocols to ensure health services are available and accessible in public facilities.'[267] This obligation can also entail elements of due diligence, when the state, whose legislative apparatus is supposed to meet international obligations, must ensure that health services comply with laws in place. The CEDAW Committee found, in *Pimentel Teixeira*, obligations which can fall under the category of obligations to progressively take steps to protect maternal health, including the provision of 'adequate professional training for health workers, especially on women's reproductive health rights, including quality medical treatment during pregnancy and delivery, as well as timely emergency obstetric care,' training 'for the judiciary and for law enforcement personnel,' and 'the implementation of the National Pact for the Reduction of Maternal Mortality at state and municipal levels.'[268]

As highlighted in the provisions of the Istanbul Convention which, except for sterilisation and forced abortion, mainly focuses on the horizontal dimension of VAWH, it is fundamental to involve men and boys in changing patterns of discrimination (Article 12(4)). It is important to consider why perpetrators commit DV, why men rape women, why women continue to perform FGM/C on new-born girls, why a society limits women's access to abortion, why in hospital the will of the physician prevails when he/she forces a woman to be sterilised or to be subjected to damaging procedures while giving birth. An approach which combines both the dimensions of violence envisaged in this book and highlights the interconnections between the two in terms of states' obligations might prompt an evolution of state practice and of the jurisprudence of regional human rights courts and UN treaty bodies alike.

To establish mechanisms of non-repetition

The jurisprudence of the IACHR helps to identify obligations to progressively take steps by adopting mechanisms and procedures to counter gender-based VAW. So, for example, following the trend inaugurated by *Cotton Field*,[269] in *López Soto* the IACHR acknowledged that the state had already adopted a law establishing tribunals on VAW, and required Peru, 'within [a] reasonable time' to guarantee the adequate and efficient functioning of these mechanisms.[270] This obligation to take steps also entails an obligation of result – the establishment of efficient tribunals – but one which requires time, and action by the state which is not immediate. State practice would not allow me to assert that states are *obliged* to establish such tribunals; however, when they have enacted laws doing so, they must guarantee the efficient functioning of the tribunals. In *Atenco*, the Court recognised that Mexico had established mechanisms to monitor cases of sexual violence against women, but it asked the state to reinforce the system within two years, to include a process of diagnosis of the 'phenomenon of sexual torture against women,' and to draw up periodic proposals for public policies.[271]

In a case of involuntary sterilisation, the IACHR decided that the state must ensure that all hospitals adopt a document stating, 'in a concise, clear and accessible' style, women's rights with regard to their sexual and reproductive health, in conformity with the *I.V.* judgment and international obligations. This document must be available in all public and private hospitals in Bolivia, accessible to both patients and doctors.[272]

To provide data on VAWH

For similar reasons data must be collected on specific types of violence, such as DV and femicide; this has been encouraged both by the CEDAW in its GR No. 35, and by the Special Rapporteur on VAW.[273] There is an increasing trend to collect data on such practices to better counter them, but what about other forms of violence? It seems to me, but this is again *de jure condendo*, that states ought to collect and make available data covering all the types of violence I have discussed in these pages, namely DV, rape, FGM/C, abortion, involuntary sterilisation, OV and limiting access to contraception. The 'first and continuing task'[274] to collect data has preventative purposes in the fight against VAHW, but also raises awareness of the existence of a pattern of discrimination and can propel reforms or changes in society. In *López Soto* the IACHR required the state to collect and analyse data on VAW, and during the first three years to report annually on the steps taken in that direction.[275] As I mentioned in the *anamnesis*, the publication of data on OV in Italy paved the way for women to come forward and report maternity-room practices that damaged their physical and psychological health, while the recognition of a practice of forced sterilisation in Japan prompted the first case ever before a Japanese court. The EU Commission has affirmed, in its 'Strategic engagement for gender equality 2016–2019', that ending VAW entails 'ongoing actions' to improve the availability, quality and reliability of data on gender-based violence through cooperation with several actors.[276]

Conclusions on state obligations: a mutually reinforcing framework and some open issues

The strength of this chapter lies in the fact that both dimensions, the horizontal and the vertical as conceived in this book, can be unified while discussing the reconceptualisation of states' obligations. In both dimensions, I contended that, and provided examples of how, states bear legal obligations of result, due diligence obligations and obligations to progressively take steps.

At the beginning of the chapter, the first impression could have been that due diligence obligations only pertain to the horizontal dimension, because they concern interpersonal relations and the state is responsible for preventing and combating violence committed by private individuals. I showed that this is only partly true, since practices in the field of health causing VAWH can also be prevented by the state monitoring *with due diligence* the activity of health personnel operating both in the private and public sector, and responding in an efficient way to episodes of malpractice. It was perhaps tempting to argue that in the horizontal dimension positive obligations prevail, whereas negative obligations – plus some obligations of result – are present in the vertical dimension. I demonstrated that this is not the case.

The difference between the two dimensions does not lie in the 'type' of the obligations, but rather the fact that obligations 'specialise' along the line of one or the other dimension. I noticed that in cases of DV one crucial aspect of the state obligations stressed by courts and UN bodies alike is investigation. Be that as it may, DV affects women's rights to health and to reproductive health, it causes VAWH, and so the authorities must respond by providing services capable of supporting victims/survivors of DV. As for the vertical dimension, the emphasis could have been solely on repealing laws that criminalise abortion and eugenic laws, or on adopting laws relating to maternal health, because the dimension does concern state policies and laws in the health field, and practices within health services. Nonetheless, as I showed, investigation and access to justice are also fundamental. When a woman is denied proceedings that expeditiously analyse her request for reconsideration after abortion has been refused by a physician, this illustrates these aspects.

In this section I turn to consider a few issues that have been left aside or that will open the way for future research and analysis. Given the above, one might ask whether the obligations that I have reconceptualised in this chapter belong to the category of 'core obligations', in the expression used by UN treaty bodies. Considering the ambiguous nature of these obligations, it is difficult to pin down in a list what is a core obligation and what is not. Furthermore, in its GC No. 22 on the right to sexual and reproductive health the ESCR Committee has already performed the analysis. What seems clear to me is that there is a trend towards determining positive obligations, especially in fields in which it was difficult to conceptualise them, such as access to health services. This does not mean that all the obligations I have explored have been clearly established at the international level. I could see a *trend* towards conceptualising positive obligations to provide access to health services, especially in the vertical dimension; but I also notice, in the horizontal dimension, that the provision of health services, such as psychological and psychiatric assistance for example, has become pivotal.

In this chapter I also argued that a minimum level of health care relating to both the horizontal and vertical dimensions should be provided for free, or at least be affordable, taking gender particularities into account, to the extent that men's access to reproductive services is free or affordable. This obligation stems from the rights to health and to reproductive health, and from the prohibition of discrimination on the basis of gender. Such care would include abortion services when abortion is legal in a given country, and post-abortion services in states that outlaw abortion. This argument is reinforced by the decisions and judgments that I analysed in the *anamnesis*. Nonetheless, this trend cannot be said to be entirely part of state practice, especially in countries such as the United States which are characterised by 'an individualistic system based on private health care insurance for the majority.'[277] This issue cannot be thoroughly explored here. Let us mention however that, in the USA, twenty-six states have laws that prohibit insurance companies from 'offering coverage of abortion as part of a comprehensive health care plan sold in the insurance marketplaces,' and that eleven among the twenty-six 'prevent all private insurers in the state – whether in the marketplace or elsewhere – from offering coverage of abortion as part of a comprehensive health care plan.'[278] According to my paradigm, the state can be held responsible for adopting laws that cause, or contribute to causing, VAWH. Such laws might cause anguish and mental suffering. Furthermore, they demonstrate a clear discrimination within the female gender, and among genders. Abortion, pre- and post-natal services, and services during birth should be provided for free or should at least be affordable, and hence covered in health insurance plans. As I investigated in chapter 2, however, insurance companies, in Europe and elsewhere, do not cover in their travel insurances complications deriving from abortion.[279] The pattern of discrimination that considers women as 'reproductive objects' is resilient. In this connection, one author has inspiringly argued that there is an 'ethical imperative' to take public health actions to eliminate the global problem of unsafe abortions, including family planning to reduce the need of abortion, the provision of safe abortion to the full extent of the law and the provision of post-abortion care.[280]

VAWH is a form of discrimination against women, and in both dimensions I identified the existence of resilient patterns of discrimination, which manifest in society and in attitudes of tolerance shown by the state. As argued in a study by the Office of the High Commissioner for Human Rights (OHCHR), 'discrimination against women includes those differences of treatment that exist because of stereotypical expectations, attitudes and behaviours towards women.'[281] How can patterns of discrimination in the field of VAWH be disrupted? I found obligations to progressively take steps to that end, but it is true, as contended by Simone Cusack, that 'many States are … unsure about the steps they should take to implement their obligations fully, which is undermining efforts to modify or transform harmful stereotypes and eliminate wrongful stereotyping.'[282] Guidelines elaborated by the OHCHR might be useful in this area, and could stem from the jurisprudence and quasi-jurisprudence analysed in the *anamnesis*. In particular, they might address 'taking measures to train public officials and the judiciary to ensure that stereotypical prejudices and values do not affect decision-making,' and 'adopting positive measures to expose and modify harmful gender stereotypes within the health sector.'[283] This has emerged in both dimensions under investigation in these pages.

FGM/C could be considered as atypical. It was condemned in all the judgments that I have analysed. However, no relevant cases have reached UN treaty bodies or regional human rights courts, except a few complaints citing it as persecution. In the analysis, I recommended that lack of consent be added as an element of the offence. This paved the way for some consideration of universalism and the relativism of human rights. I am convinced by the arguments in favour of universal human rights, and do not feel that reading FGM/C in relative terms would help new-born girls who are forced to undergo a procedure which impairs their reproductive health. Nonetheless, the phenomenon cannot be appreciated without considering the 'context' in which these practices are performed. If we examine context, we can understand how not only FGM/C, but also GCS, must be prohibited when a woman has not given fully informed consent. Accordingly, the perspective should not be on which culture determines the 'standard' to be respected at the international level – something that could be dangerous – but rather which lines of discrimination, in a given context, prompt the perpetrating of VAWH. This means, in other words, conceiving intersectionality as a tool for understanding VAWH. Based on which grounds is VAWH perpetrated? On the basis of sex or gender, or also on ethnicity, religious or social and economic conditions (here, for example, girls who at the age of 12 want to change their genitals because they 'do not like them' and have the money to undergo cosmetic surgery)? Intersectionality is rarely considered by legal scholars, and courts find enormous difficulty in seeing in this concept a tool not only for understanding whether discrimination has occurred, but also for determining the amount of compensation for the victim/survivor, and which measures the state must adopt to comply with its obligations.[284] Intersectionality should enter legal scholarship and the practice of courts and tribunals. For example, in *López Soto*, the IACommHR clearly found that women face enormous obstacles in gaining access to 'suitable and effective judicial remedies,' and that these obstacles were especially critical 'because victims suffer[ed] from a combination of forms of discrimination – because they are women, because of their ethnic or racial background, and/or because of their socioeconomic condition.'[285]

One final comment, *de jure condendo*, concerns reparations. States have been required by human rights courts and UN treaty bodies to adopt general measures, such as repealing or amending laws, and/or providing reparations to victims/survivors of violence. The missing point is the gender of the reparations offered, which means considering the gendered nature of reparations and envisaging measures that specifically aim to address rooted causes of VAWH. This means that reparations cannot be limited to the victim/survivor, but must be extended to relatives, for example women's children; they must include general measures aimed at disrupting patterns of discrimination that persist in society, especially in the health sector.

The obligation to provide psychological support to a victim of rape, for example, should be combined with action at societal level that involves men and boys in eradicating VAW. Gendering reparations, despite some positive attempts, has not completely permeated the jurisprudence and quasi-jurisprudence of regional (especially the European) human rights courts and UN treaty bodies. In the Council of Europe Istanbul Convention, Article 30(2) provides that:

> [a]dequate State compensation shall be awarded to those who have sustained serious bodily injury or impairment of health, to the extent that the damage is not covered by other sources such as the perpetrator, insurance or State-funded health and social provisions. This does not preclude Parties from claiming regress for compensation awarded from the perpetrator, as long as due regard is paid to the victim's safety.

Even though this article refers only to the types of violence covered by the Convention, it could provide a model for both dimensions of violence and also an answer to the concerns relating to insurance coverage.

Unfortunately, this provision has not been welcomed by many state parties to the Convention, which have appended reservations to it. It is far from being an obligation well established at the international level, at least for the time being. Nonetheless, it clarifies that state compensation is particularly necessary when violence impairs women's rights to health and to reproductive health, supporting the importance of the relationship that I theorised.

Notes

1 Cook, 'Gender, health', p. 349.
2 Cook *et al.*, *Reproductive Health and Human Rights*, pp. 152–3.
3 Cook *et al.*, *Reproductive Health and Human Rights*, pp. 152–3.
4 GR No. 35, para. 22.
5 GR No. 35, para. 24.
6 In the words of the IACommHR, 'there is a broad international consensus over the use of the due diligence principle to interpret the content of state legal obligations towards the problem of violence against women; a consensus that extends to the problem of domestic violence:' *Lenahan (Gonzáles) et al.*, para. 134.
7 See the First Report on State Responsibility by James Crawford, A/CN.4/490 (1998), para. 16.
8 R. Pisillo Mazzeschi, 'Responsabilité de l'état pour violation des obligations positives relatives aux droits de l'homme', *Recueil des Cours de l'Academie de Droit International de la Haye* 333 (2008) 175, p. 192.

9 Text adopted by the International Law Commission at its fifty-third session, in 2001, and submitted to the GA (A/56/10). J. Crawford, *The International Law Commission's Articles on State Responsibility* (Cambridge: Cambridge University Press, 2002), p. 81.

10 J. Crawford, *Articles on Responsibility of States for Internationally Wrongful Acts,* United Nations Audiovisual Library of International Law, 2012, available at www.un.org/law/avl, p. 3. Legal doctrine on state responsibility is enormous and it is not possible even to try to mention the most important texts. See, *inter alia,* D. Carreau and F. Marrella, *Diritto internazionale* (Milan: Giuffrè, 2018); B. Conforti, *Diritto internazionale* (Naples: Scientifica, 11th edn, 2018); A. Cassese, *International Law* (Oxford: Oxford University Press, 2nd edn, 2005) and the Italian version edited by M. Frulli; M.D. Evans, *International Law* (Oxford: Oxford University Press, 5th edn, 2018).

11 Chinkin and Charlesworth, *The Boundaries of International Law*, p. 148.

12 R. Cook, 'State responsibility for violations of women's human rights', *Harvard Human Rights Journal* 7 (1994) 125, p. 143.

13 See the 1872 award rendered on the Alabama claims of the United States against Great Britain (in *Reports of International Arbitral Awards*, UN, 8 May 1871, XXIX, pp. 125–34, reprinted 2012).

14 A/CN.4/302 and Add.1, 2 and 3 (1977), Sixth report on State Responsibility by Roberto Ago – the internationally wrongful act of the state, source of international responsibility, para. 4.

15 'A breach by the State of an international obligation specifically calling for it to adopt a particular course of conduct exists simply by virtue of the adoption of a course of conduct different from that specifically required.'

16 Sixth report, paras 5–6.

17 Sixth report, para. 7.

18 'A breach of an international obligation requiring the State to achieve a particular result *in concreto*, but leaving it free to choose at the outset the means of achieving that result, exists if, by the conduct adopted in exercising its freedom of choice, the State has not in fact achieved the internationally required result.'

19 The formulation of the proposal by Ago was in negative terms: '[t]here is no breach by a State of an international obligation requiring it to prevent a given event unless, following a lack of prevention on the part of the State, the event in question occurs.'

20 A/CN.4/307 and Add.1 and 2 and Corr.1 and 2 (1978), Seventh report on State Responsibility by Roberto Ago – the internationally wrongful act of the State, source of international responsibility, para. 3.

21 A/CN.4/498 and Add.1–4 Second report on State Responsibility (1999), by James Crawford, para. 79.

22 P.M. Dupuy, 'Reviewing the difficulties of codification: on Ago's classification of obligations of means and of result in relation to State responsibility', *European Journal of International Law* 10 (1999) 371; R. Pisillo Mazzeschi, 'Le chemin étrange de la due diligence: d'un concept mystérieux à un concept surévalué', in SFDI, *Le standard de due diligence et la responsabilité internationale* (Paris: Pedone, 2018) 225, p. 228.

23 Dupuy, 'Reviewing the difficulties', p. 378.

24 A. Marchesi, *Obblighi di condotta e obblighi di risultato* (Milan: Giuffrè, 2003), p. 59.

25 A/CN.4/L.271 and Add.1, Draft Articles on State Responsibility. Text adopted by the Drafting Committee: articles 23–27 and title of chapter IV of the draft – reproduced in A/CN.4/SR.1513 and SR.1524 (1978), p. 206.
26 Dupuy, 'Reviewing the difficulties', p. 380.
27 GC No. 3 (1990) on the nature of States parties' obligations (ESCR Committee), para. 1.
28 GC No. 3, para. 4. On the debate in legal scholarship, see Marchesi, *Obblighi di condotta*, pp. 163–4.
29 Cook, 'State responsibility', p. 161.
30 GR No. 28 (2010) on the core obligations of States parties under Article 2 CEDAW (CEDAW Committee), para. 9.
31 Marchesi, *Obblighi di condotta*, p. 129.
32 D. Shelton and A. Gould, 'Positive and negative obligations', in Shelton, *Oxford Handbook of International Human Rights Law*, 582. See also the pioneer work D. Shelton, 'Private violence, public wrongs, and the responsibility of States', *Fordham International Law Journal* 13 (1989) 1.
33 Pisillo Mazzeschi, 'Responsabilité de l'état', p. 187.
34 P. Alston, 'The not-a-cat syndrome: can the international human rights regime accommodate non-State actors?', in P. Alston (ed.), *Non-State Actors and Human Rights* (Oxford: Oxford University Press, 2005) 3, p. 4.
35 Pisillo Mazzeschi, 'Responsabilité de l'état', p. 187.
36 A. Byrnes, 'Women, feminism and international human rights law – methodological myopia, fundamental flaws or meaningful marginalisation? Some current issues', *Australian Year Book of International Law* 12 (1992) 205, p. 227.
37 See 'The obligation to respect, to protect and to fulfil human rights, and the meaning of core obligations' below.
38 These correspond to the titles of chapters III, IV, V of his contribution for the Hague Academy of International Law.
39 Pisillo Mazzeschi, 'Responsabilité de l'état', p. 390.
40 T. Koivurova, 'Due diligence', in *Max Planck Encyclopedia of Public International Law* (last update 2010).
41 L. Grans ('The concept of due diligence and the positive obligation to prevent honour-related violence: beyond deterrence', *International Journal of Human Rights* 22 (2018) 733, p. 734) argues that 'due diligence says something both about the efforts the state has made, that it has actually tried to fix the problem and has dedicated reasonable resources to doing so, and about its competence in doing so (i.e. that it has chosen effective measures),' and that 'it is doubtful whether just referring to positive obligations will get the same message across.' Nonetheless, positive obligations are more than due diligence obligations, they also include obligations of result.
42 L. Condorelli, 'The imputability to States of acts of international terrorism', *Israeli Yearbook on Human Rights* 19 (1989) 233, p. 240.
43 In his first works, Pisillo Mazzeschi included the first three areas, while in the later study for the Hague Academy of International Law he extensively considered the application of due diligence in human rights law. R. Pisillo Mazzeschi, *Due diligence e responsabilità internazionale degli Stati* (Padua: Cedam, 1989) and 'The due diligence rule and the nature of the international responsibility of states', *German Yearbook of International Law* 35 (1992) 9.

44 E. De Brabandere, 'Host States' due diligence obligations in international investment law', *Syracuse Journal of International Law & Commerce* 42 (2015) 319.
45 For due diligence in cyberspace see S.J. Shackelford, S. Russell and A. Kuehn, 'Unpacking the international law on cybersecurity due diligence: Lessons from the public and private sectors', *Chicago Journal of International Law* 17 (2016) 1; K. Bannelier, 'Obligations de diligence dans le cyberspace: qui a peur de la cyber-diligence?', *Revue belge de droit international* 2 (2017) 612; P.Z. Stockburger, 'From grey zone to customary international law: How adopting the precautionary principle may help crystallize the due diligence principle in cyberspace', in T. Minárik, R. Jakschis and L. Lindström (eds), *2018 10th International Conference on Cyber Conflict* (Tallinn: NATO Cooperative Cyber Defence Centre of Excellence, 2018); L. Chircop, 'A due diligence standard of attribution in cyberspace', *International & Comparative Law Quarterly* 67 (2018) 643.
46 J. Sarkin, 'A methodology to ensure that states adequately apply due diligence standards and processes to significantly impact levels of violence against women around the world', *Human Rights Quarterly* 40 (2018) 1, p. 4.
47 Views of 15 May 2006, ACHPR, Appl. No 245/2002, *Zimbabwe Human Rights NGO Forum v. Zimbabwe*, paras. 143, 146, 147; also quoted in Pisillo Mazzeschi, 'Responsabilité de l'état', p. 392.
48 In the late sixteenth century, Alberico Gentili argued that the state can be held responsible for violations of rights committed by its citizens, hence 'the state, which knows because it has been warned, and which ought to prevent the misdeeds of its citizens, and through its jurisdiction can prevent them, will be at fault and guilty of a crime if it does not do so'. *De Jure Belli Libri Tres* (John Rolfe (tr.), Oxford: Oxford University Press, 1933), p. 100.
49 Shelton and Gould, 'Positive and negative obligations', p. 578.
50 Bannelier, 'Obligations de diligence', p. 639.
51 O. Corten, *L'utilisation du 'raisonnable' par le juge international* (Brussels: Bruylant, 1997), arguing that reasonableness is determined through rational methods and criteria. Hart clearly argued that 'the open texture of law means that there are, indeed, areas of conduct where much must be left to be developed by courts or officials striking a balance, in the light of circumstances, between competing interests which vary in weight from case to case' (V.H. Hart, *The Concept of Law* (Oxford: Clarendon Press, 1961), p. 132).
52 Bannelier, 'Obligations de diligence', p. 639*ff*.
53 Pisillo Mazzeschi, 'Due diligence', p. 44.
54 UN Doc. E/CN.4/1995/42, para. 72. I would say: 'a state is as much responsible for the crime as the perpetrator is guilty (or criminally responsible).'
55 'The due diligence standard as a tool for the elimination of violence against women', Report of the SR on VAW, Yakin Ertürk, E/CN.4/2006/61, 20 January 2006.
56 Ertürk, 'The due diligence standard', para. 47.
57 Sarkin contended that the absence of state resources is not 'an excuse' for a state for not 'taking at least some measures to ensure compliance' (Sarkin, 'A methodology', p. 31).
58 Y. Ertürk, 'The due diligence standard: what does it entail for women's rights', in C. Benniger-Budel (ed.), *Due Diligence and its Application to Protect Women from Violence* (Leiden, Boston: Martinus Nijhoff, 2008) 27, p. 28.

59 J. Bourke-Martignoni, 'The history and development of the due diligence standard in international law and its role in the protection of women against violence', in Benniger-Budel, *Due Diligence,* 47.
60 See Crawford, *ILC Articles*, p. 82. On the evolution of the concept in history, see, for example, J.A. Hessbruegge, 'The historical development of the doctrines of attribution and due diligence in international law', *New York University Journal of International Law and Politics* 36 (2004) 265. For cases relevant to the history of arbitration, starting from the famous Alabama case, see Pisillo Mazzeschi, 'Due diligence', p. 34.
61 Judgment of 29 July 1988, IACHR, *Velásquez Rodríguez v. Honduras*, para. 172. See L. Hasselbacher, 'State obligations regarding domestic violence: the European Court of Human Rights, due diligence, and international legal minimums of protection', *Northwestern Journal of Human Rights* 8 (2010) 190, pp. 193–4.
62 Bourke-Martignoni, 'The history', p. 57.
63 For example DV, which requires a 'diligence particulière' (*Talpis*).
64 Article 4(c).
65 GR No. 19, para. 9.
66 GR No. 35, para. 24(b).
67 GR No. 35, para. 24(b).
68 GR No. 35, para. 24(b).
69 GR No. 28, para. 13.
70 On the due diligence standard in the Istanbul Convention, see C. Chinkin, 'The duty of due diligence', 21 May 2010, available at https://rm.coe.int/CoERMPublicCommonSearchServices/DisplayDCTMContent?documentId=0900001680593fc8. Criticising Article 5, V. Stoyanova, 'Critical reflections on the due diligence standard under Council of Europe Convention on violence against women', in J. Niemi, L. Peroni and V. Stoyanova (eds), *Violence against Women: Transformations and Legal Challenges after the Istanbul Convention* (London: Routledge, 2020, forthcoming).
71 Explanatory report to the Istanbul Convention, para. 59.
72 Council of Europe's Group of Experts on Action against Violence against Women and Domestic Violence (GREVIO), 'Baseline evaluation report', Austria, 27 September 2017, para. 123.
73 GREVIO, 'Baseline evaluation report'. Even though already in force, these laws established a 'very high threshold,' which was difficult to cross in individual cases.
74 Report E.CN.4/Sub.2/1987/23. See the evolution in O. De Schutter, *International Human Rights Law* (Cambridge: Cambridge University Press, 2014) p. 280.
75 H. Shue, *Basic Rights, Subsistence, Affluence, and US Foreign Policy* (Princeton, NJ: Princeton University Press, 1980) p. 52.
76 GC No. 22, para. 40.
77 GC No. 22, para. 42.
78 GC No. 22, para. 45.
79 Limburg Principles on the Implementation of the International Covenant on Economic, Social, and Cultural Rights, Maastricht, 2–6 June 1986, UN doc. E/CN.4/1987/17, Annex, para. 25; also at *Human Rights Quarterly* 9 (1987) 122.
80 P. Alston, 'Out of the abyss: the challenges confronting the new UN Committee on economic social and cultural rights', *Human Rights Quarterly* 9 (1987) 332, p. 352.
81 Forman *et al.*, 'Conceptualising minimum core obligations', p. 532.

82 Forman *et al.*, 'Conceptualising minimum core obligations', p. 534.
83 M. Scheinin, 'Core rights and obligations', in Shelton, *Oxford Handbook of International Human Rights Law*, p. 538.
84 Scheinin, 'Core rights and obligations', p. 538.
85 Scheinin, 'Core rights and obligations', p. 538.
86 GC No. 14, para. 43.
87 The authors clearly investigate the existing literature on the topic, and I do not reproduce their summary here. See Forman *et al.*, 'Conceptualising minimum core obligations', p. 535*ff*.
88 Forman *et al.*, 'Conceptualising minimum core obligations', p. 543.
89 GC No. 22, para. 49.
90 GR No. 28, para. 9.
91 See Scheinin, 'Core rights and obligations', p. 538.
92 In the views of the CEDAW Committee, it is possible to find a general recommendation to the state to 'respect, protect, promote and fulfil women's human rights, including their right to be free from all forms of domestic violence, including intimidation and threats of violence,' without these three layers being explicitly affirmed. See, for example, *A.T. v. Hungary*, para. 9.6.II(a).
93 Concluding observations on the combined third and fourth periodic reports of Saudi Arabia, CEDAW Committee, 19 February–9 March 2018.
94 Concluding observations, Saudi Arabia, para. 48.
95 Concluding observations on the seventh periodic report of Chile, CEDAW Committee, 19 February–9 March 2018, para. 39.
96 Concluding observations on the initial report of the Niger, ESCR Committee, E/C.12/NER/CO/1, 4 June 2018, para 44.
97 *Osman,* para. 116.
98 *Equality Now*, para. 114.
99 Shelton and Gould, 'Positive and negative obligations', p. 578*ff*.
100 Pisillo Mazzeschi, 'Responsabilité de l'état', p. 247.
101 UN Protocol to Prevent, Suppress and Punish Trafficking in Persons Especially Women and Children, supplementing the United Nations Convention against Transnational Organized Crime, 15 November 2000, 2237 UNTS 319.
102 CoE Treaty Series No. 197. Sarkin proposed a 7P response: prevention, protection against, promoting awareness, probing, prosecuting, punishing, providing redress ('A methodology', p. 2).
103 See Explanatory report to the Istanbul Convention, para. 63.
104 Explanatory report to the Istanbul Convention, para. 85.
105 C. Tomuschat, 'What is a breach of the ECHR?', in R. Lawson and H. De Blois (eds), *The Dynamics of the Protection of Human Rights in Europe: Essays in Honour of Henry G. Schermers* (Dordrecht: Martinus Nijoff, 1994) 315, p. 324.
106 Cook, 'State obligation', p. 161.
107 GR No. 28, para. 23.
108 GR No. 35, paras 22 and 24.
109 See the important intuition, as early as 1995, of D. Sullivan, 'The nature and scope of human rights obligations concerning women's right to health', *Health and Human Rights* (1995) 368, p. 389, applying the three layers of obligation as elaborated at the UN level.

110 In that sense, Pisillo Mazzeschi, 'Le chemin', p. 230.
111 Pisillo Mazzeschi, 'Responsabilité de l'état', p. 311. The translation is mine.
112 Pisillo Mazzeschi, 'Responsabilité de l'état', p. 311.
113 Pisillo Mazzeschi, 'Responsabilité de l'état', p. 313.
114 Pisillo Mazzeschi, 'Responsabilité de l'état', p. 390.
115 Pisillo Mazzeschi, 'Due diligence', p. 48.
116 *V.K.*, para. 9.4. Emphasis added.
117 Pisillo Mazzeschi, 'Responsabilité de l'état', p. 434.
118 Cook, 'State responsibility', p. 159.
119 GR No. 28, para. 23.
120 *A.T.*, para. 9.6.II(e).
121 *Bevacqua,* para. 83.
122 The provisions of the Maria da Penha law (Federal Law No. 11340), which was adopted in Brazil after the case of that name before the IACommHR, established special courts.
123 The Italian provisions in Article 24 of the Legislative Decree No. 80/2015 do this.
124 See chapter 2, 'Consent and autonomy in the horizontal dimension: Domestic violence'.
125 See above, the reflection on autonomy and consent in chapter 2, 'Consent and autonomy in the horizontal dimension: Rape' and also chapter 1, 'The horizontal, "interpersonal" dimension: Rape'.
126 See, for example, Views of 16 July 2010, *Vertido,* para. 8.7.
127 *M.C.*, para. 161.
128 See chapter 1, 'The horizontal, "interpersonal" dimension: Rape: Judgments and decisions'.
129 See, for example, the CEDAW concluding observations on Mauritius, CEDAW/C/MUS/CO/6–7, 21 October 2011, para. 22; and the concluding observations on Indonesia, CEDAW/C/IDN/CO/6–7, 27 July 2012, para. 25, observing the lack of criminalisation of marital rape in domestic law.
130 *Equality Now,* para. 160(d).
131 See, for example, the UK Female Genital Mutilation Act 2003, as amended by the Serious Crime Act 2015 (Section 70); also Istanbul Convention, Article 44 on jurisdiction.
132 In chapter 2, 'Consent and autonomy in the horizontal dimension: FGM/C', I mentioned the age of 18, in conformity with Article 1 Convention of the Rights of the Child. It should be borne in mind that in some countries majority is attained with puberty, which can be as early as 9 years old. This opens a debate that it is not my purpose here to analyse in depth.
133 This is not devoid of risks. In Uganda, for example, the trend has changed in favour of performing FGM/C on married women. Married women who are not circumcised receive a lot of pressure from their husbands and society. See www.monitor.co.ug/News/National/Married-women-now-undergoing-circumcision-FGM/688334–4269400-k8b075/index.html.
134 See, for example, *L.C.*, para. 8.18. See also GC No. 36 (HRC), para. 8.
135 *Mellet*, and GC No. 36 (HRC), para. 8.
136 See, in that respect, the US jurisprudence in chapter 1, 'The vertical, 'state policies' dimension: Abortion'.

137 Laufer-Ukeles, 'Reproductive choices', p. 378.
138 *L.C.,* para. 7.13.
139 See, in that respect, Pisillo Mazzeschi, 'Responsibilité de l'état', p. 342.
140 *A.T.* could not find support because the local shelters were not equipped to host her disabled child.
141 *Aydin*, para. 107.
142 *Fernández Ortega,* para. 252.
143 *Fernández Ortega,* para. 252. See also 'Access to justice for women victims of sexual violence in Mesoamerica', p. 98.
144 *L.C.,* para. 7.7.
145 *L.C.,* para. 8.17.
146 *L.C.,* para. 9(b)(i).
147 *Mellet*, para. 9.
148 GC No. 36, para. 8. Emphasis added.
149 See in that respect, for example, *CGIL v. Italy.*
150 *Whole Woman's Health*, for example. See, also GC No. 22, para. 16.
151 GC No. 22, para. 17.
152 GC No. 22, para. 34.
153 GC No. 22, para. 38.
154 *Whelan*, para. 7.12, and *Mellet*, para. 7.11.
155 Opinion individuelle (concurrente) du membre du Comité Yadh Ben Achour, in *Mellet*, para. 4.
156 Individual opinion of Committee member Sarah Cleveland (concurring), in *Mellet,* para. 7.
157 Erin Nelson supports the argument that abortion must be state-funded in *Law, Policy,* p. 238.
158 Rodríguez-Ruiz, 'Gender in constitutional discourses', p. 712.
159 In this sense, see R.J. Cook and B.M. Dickens, 'Human rights and HIV-positive women', *International Journal of Gynecology & Obstetrics* 77: 1 (2002) 55, p. 56.
160 Laufer-Ukeles, 'The disembodied womb', p. 4.
161 *Court of its own motion v. India.*
162 Dissenting opinion of judges Sajó, Karakaş, Nicolaou, Laffranque and Keller, para. 25.
163 Dissenting opinion, para. 35.
164 *Xákmok Kásek Community,* para. 233. Emphasis added.
165 *Xákmok Kásek Community,* para. 302.
166 *Xákmok Kásek Community,* para. 301.
167 *Pimentel Teixeira*, para. 8.
168 *Mandal*, para. 2.
169 See above, chapter 1, note 589 and related text.
170 J.P. Kelleher, 'Emergency contraception and conscientious objection', *Journal of Applied Philosophy 27* (2010) 290.
171 Cook *et al.*, *Reproductive Rights*, p. 292.
172 M.R. Wicclair, 'Conscientious refusals by hospitals and emergency contraception', *Cambridge Quarterly of Healthcare Ethics* 20 (2011) 130, p. 138.
173 See the evolution of victims' rights in M.C. Bassiouni, 'International recognition of victims' rights', *Human Rights Law Review* 6 (2006) 203.

174 See the whole work by D. Shelton, *Remedies in International Human Rights Law* (Oxford: Oxford University Press, 2015).
175 Bassiouni, 'International recognition', p. 231.
176 Shelton, *Remedies,* p. 16.
177 Shelton, *Remedies*, p. 17.
178 Pisillo Mazzeschi, 'Responsabilité de l'état', p. 368.
179 *A.T.*, para. 9.3.
180 *M.C.,* para. 180.
181 *Equality Now,* para. 138.
182 *L.C.*, para. 7.12.
183 *L.C.,* para. 7.13.
184 *L.C.,* para. 8.16.
185 *L.C.,* para. 8.4.
186 *Tysiac*, para. 124.
187 *I.V.,* paras 300 and 310. On damage and redress in the IACHR system, see V. Madrigal-Borloz, 'Damage and redress in the jurisprudence of the Inter-American Court of Human Rights (1979–2001)', in G. Ulrich and L. Krabbe Boserup (eds), *Human Rights in Development Yearbook 2001. Reparations: Redressing Past Wrongs* (The Hague: Kluwer, 2001) 213.
188 See, in chapter 1, 'The vertical, "state policies" dimension, Involuntary sterilisation', the Japanese law on involuntary sterilisation.
189 See, in that respect, *Pimentel Teixeira*, para. 8.
190 Pisillo Mazzeschi ('Responsabilité de l'état', p. 369) considered the provision of compensation an obligation of result, whereas the adoption of specific measures could be either an obligation of result or an obligation of means.
191 Bassiouni, 'International recognition of victims' rights', p. 231.
192 C. Duggan and R. Jacobson, 'Reparation of sexual and reproductive violence. Moving from codification to implementation', in Rubio-Marín, *The Gender of Reparations* 121, p. 148.
193 M. Urban Walker, 'Gender and violence in focus: A background for gender justice in reparations', in Rubio-Marín, *The Gender of Reparations*, 18, pp. 50 and 53.
194 R. Rubio-Marín, 'The gender of reparations in transitional societies', in Rubio-Marin, *The Gender of Reparations,* 63.
195 Rubio-Marin, 'The gender of reparations', p. 71.
196 Rubio-Marín and Sandoval, 'Engendering the reparations', p. 1076. See also 'Access to justice for women victims of sexual violence in Mesoamerica', para. 106.
197 *Da Penha*, para. 23.
198 *I.V.*, para. 332. The translation is mine.
199 *Cotton Field*, para. 549.
200 *Cotton Field*, paras 468–9.
201 *I.V.,* paras 334, 336.
202 *Cotton Field*, para. 519.
203 *I.V.,* para. 342.
204 See also below, 'Methodology for treatment, Positive obligations to progressively take steps, To change patterns of discrimination'.
205 The Commission addressed this aspect, as reported in the judgment of the Court, at para. 337.

206 *Cotton Field*, para. 451.
207 Rubio-Marín and Sandoval, 'Engendering the reparations', p. 1088. See also below, 'Conclusions on state obligations'.
208 'S'efforcer de capturer les personnes coupables de la violation': Pisillo-Mazzeschi, 'Le chemin', p. 231.
209 See for example *Yildirim*, and *Talpis.*
210 *Yildirim,* para. 12.3(b).
211 *Opuz*, para. 169.
212 The '*Osman* test' applied, for example, by the Court in *Talpis*.
213 *V.K.*, para. 9.8.
214 De Vido, 'States' positive obligations'.
215 *Talpis,* para. 130.
216 *A.T.*, para. 9.6.II(b).
217 Bannelier, 'Obligation de diligence', pp. 641 and 664.
218 *Cotton Field,* para. 164.
219 *López Soto* (IACHR), para. 224.
220 *López Soto* (IACHR), para. 169.
221 *López Soto* (IACHR), para. 136.
222 *Szijjarto,* para. 8.4.
223 *Mellet*, para. 3.27.
224 *Mellet*, para. 3.27.
225 *P. and S.,* para. 110.
226 *I.V.,* para. 300.
227 *Xákmok Kásek Community*, para. 234.
228 *Pimentel Teixeira*, para. 7.7. Emphasis added.
229 *Pimentel Teixeira,* para. 8.
230 Fredman, *Comparative Human Rights*, p. 256.
231 *Şentürk,* paras 104–5.
232 *P. and S.*, para. 108.
233 *Szijjarto,* para. 11.3.
234 *Szijjarto,* para. 11.5.
235 *V.C.,* para. 152. Emphasis added.
236 *I.V.,* paras 176, 181. See also 'Access to information on reproductive health from a human rights perspective' (IACHR), OEA/Ser.L/V/II. Doc. 61, 22 November 2011.
237 *I.V.,* para. 156.
238 *I.V.,* para. 158.
239 *I.V.,* para. 163.
240 *I.V.,* para. 341.
241 *Da Penha*, para. 32.
242 *V.K.*, para. 9.4.
243 *Valiulienė*, paras 78 and 85.
244 *Lenahan (Gonzáles) et al.*, para. 197.
245 *V.K.,* para. 9.12.
246 As confirmed by the IACHR, *Mujeres Víctimas (Atenco),* para. 338.
247 *Cotton Field*, para. 388.
248 *Z. v. Poland,* para. 93.

249 *Z. v. Poland,* para. 94.
250 *Şentürk,* paras 81, 82.
251 Pisillo Mazzeschi, 'Responsabilité de l'état', p. 422.
252 *Cotton Field,* para. 455.
253 *Cotton Field,* para. 455.
254 *Fernández Ortega,* para. 267.
255 Resolución de la Corte Interamericana de derechos humanos, *Fernández Ortega y otros y Rosendo Cantú y otra v. México*, supervisión de cumplimiento de sentencia, 17 April 2015, p. 14.
256 GR No. 28, para. 15.
257 *I.V.,* para. 161.
258 *I.V.,* para. 186.
259 *I.V.,* para. 186.
260 Pisillo Mazzeschi, 'Le chemin', p. 231.
261 *I.V.,* para. 372.
262 *Da Penha*, paras 60 and 61.4.
263 *Da Penha*, paras 60 and 61.4.
264 *López Soto* (IACHR), para. 291(5).
265 *López Soto* (IACHR), para. 345.
266 *Mujeres Víctimas (Atenco)*, para. 355.
267 *L.C.,* para. 9(b)(ii).
268 *Pimentel Teixeira*, para. 8.
269 Mexico was required to launch long-term programmes aimed at periodically reporting information on the efforts to discover the truth. *Cotton Field*, para. 475.
270 *López Soto* (IACHR), para. 324.
271 *Mujeres Víctimas (Atenco),* para. 360.
272 *I.V.,* para. 341.
273 38th session of the Human Rights Council, Statement by Dubravka Šimonović, SR on VAW, Geneva, 21 June 2018.
274 C. Chinkin, 'Violence against women: The international legal response', *Gender and Development* 3 (1995) 23, p. 24.
275 *López Soto* (IACHR), para. 349.
276 'EU Strategic engagement for gender equality 2016–2019', 22 January 2016, p. 15.
277 See L.O. Gostin and P. Fennell, 'Health: the health care system, therapeutic relationships, and public health', in M. Tushnet and P. Cane (eds), *The Oxford Handbook of Legal Studies* (Oxford: Oxford University Press, 2005), p. 439.
278 Data provided by the National Women's Law Center, 2017, available at https://nwlc-ciw49tixgw5lbab.stackpathdns.com/wp-content/uploads/2017/12/50-State-Insurance-Coverage-of-Abortion.pdf.
279 See chapter 2, 'Why is intersectionality appropriate for conceptualising the idea of VAWH?'.
280 M.F. Fathalla, 'Abortion and public health ethics', in A.C. Mastroianni, J.P. Kahn and N.E. Kass (eds), *The Oxford Handbook of Public Health Ethics* (Oxford: Oxford University Press, 2019).
281 'Gender stereotypes and stereotyping and women's rights', September 2014. Available at www.ohchr.org/Documents/Issues/Women/WRGS/OnePagers/Gender_stereotyping.pdf.

282 S. Cusack, 'Building momentum towards change', in Brems and Timmer, *Stereotypes and Human Rights Law*, 11, p. 34.
283 'Gender stereotypes and stereotyping and women's rights', p. 2.
284 See also, with specific regard to the Inter-American system, L.P.A. Sosa, 'Inter-American case law on femicide. Obscuring intersections?', *Netherlands Quarterly of Human Rights* 35 (2017) 85.
285 *López Soto* (IACommHR), para. 267.

Conclusion: the prognosis

Prognosis: what we achieved – the dimensions intersect

The prognosis is the final step in Hippocratic medicine. It consists in 'the prediction of the outcome of the disease, as well as its fluctuations and transmutations.'[1] In my book, the prognosis will include some final thoughts on the main findings of the analysis. Predictions are not part of a lawyer's work, but it is possible to reflect on the impact that law, in particular international human rights law, has on the eradication of VAWH.

The paradigm composed of *anamnesis*, diagnosis, treatment *and* prognosis has provided a sufficient descriptive framework for systematising my argument and has encouraged a reflection which has led me to the elaboration of a new concept in international law around which to construe states' obligations.

I started my analysis from the conviction that VAW always relates to the right to health and the right to reproductive health. I contended that the relationship is not merely a causal one, however, in the sense that VAW causes a violation of the rights to health and to reproductive health (what I called the horizontal dimension, characterised by interpersonal violence). I also argued that state laws and policies in the field of health cause or contribute to causing VAW (my vertical dimension). I found confirmation of this bi-dimensional relationship in the *anamnesis*, through the investigation of judgments and decisions of regional human rights and domestic courts, and the views of UN treaty bodies. The idea of VAWH, which I constructed in the diagnosis, has proved to be capable of grasping the intersections between VAW on one hand, and the rights to health and to reproductive health on the other. The idea is not aimed at replacing that of VAW, but rather at enriching it by encompassing a further, vertical, dimension, which is not sufficiently explored under the generally accepted definition of VAW. Despite the efforts of the CEDAW Committee in GR No. 35, which theorised the existence of an international custom prohibiting all forms of gender-based violence against women, the notion of VAW is generally conceived as mainly enshrining forms of interpersonal violence. One only has to look at the list of behaviours that states are required to criminalise under the Council of Europe Istanbul Convention to find confirmation of that.[2] I regard denial of access to abortion, denial of access to emergency contraception, obstetric violence and involuntary sterilisation as forms of VAWH in their vertical dimension, because they are the product of policies or laws in the field of health. I also characterise the notion of VAWH as having an additional element: the limitation of women's autonomy. This element has proved particularly useful in reflecting on the prohibition of FGM/C and in broadening my view in order to include genital cosmetic surgery in the analysis.

The descriptive function of the concept of VAWH is not limited, but capable of embracing two dimensions of violence. It was indeed fundamental when I came to reconceptualise states' obligations. In the treatment, therefore, I placed both the horizontal and the vertical dimensions beneath the same 'umbrella' in terms of obligations, without departing from the well-established categories of international law. I reflected on which categorisation of states' obligations could be more useful for my paradigm. To this end, I chose the tripartite structure composed of positive obligations of result, of due diligence and to progressively take steps. I demonstrated how all three types of obligation are present in both dimensions. The decisions I have analysed demonstrated a trend towards the affirmation of a positive obligation to provide access to health services, which is especially relevant for, but not limited to, the vertical dimension. The difference between the two dimensions does not lie in the 'type' of the obligations, but rather the fact that obligations 'specialise' along one or other of the explored dimensions.

When talking about interpersonal violence, one of the most relevant aspects of state obligations stressed by courts and UN bodies alike is investigation. Needless to say, this aspect is fundamental. Nonetheless, since interpersonal violence severely affects women's rights to health and to reproductive health, the response of the authorities must be to provide services that are capable of supporting the victim/survivor of interpersonal violence. This response must be efficient, timely, gender-sensitive and avoid forms of secondary victimisation. In the vertical dimension, it was tempting to say simply that the state ought to be prevented from interfering in women's autonomy. The network characterising this dimension, however, is composed of obligations of result (to repeal laws that criminalise abortion, to enact laws relating to maternal health, to adopt measures to guarantee the provision of health services), obligations of due diligence in actual cases (to respond to cases of malpractice in the health sector causing VAWH, to efficiently investigate episodes of violence) and obligations to progressively take steps, which embrace, in a longer perspective, obligations both of means and of result (drawing up documents for health personnel explaining what is meant by women's rights to health and to reproductive health). In both dimensions lack of interference is not enough, because what is needed is to eradicate the root causes of violence, to disrupt the patterns of discrimination at societal and state level, and to subvert the dominant patriarchal nature of the state and the health sector. Using republican theory, this would mean 'freedom as non-domination,' rather than a mere 'freedom from interference.' In Pettit's words, 'freedom as non-domination comes about only by design: only because there are legal and social arrangements in place which ensure that the other people who are about cannot interfere with you on an arbitrary basis.'[3] Despite being neglected by feminist scholarship,[4] a modern view of freedom as non-domination can be useful in the eradication of VAW, and, in my case, of VAWH: 'the ideal for women is precisely that of being secured against arbitrary interference: being given freedom in the sense in which it connotes, not just an absence of interference, but an absence of domination.'[5] It means to emphasise positive rather than negative legal obligations, where positive obligations also aim at dismantling the 'unequal power relations between women and men, which have led to domination over, and discrimination against, women by men and to the prevention of the full advancement of women.'[6]

My paradigm led me to conceptualise states' obligations in both dimensions and can be used to transfer aspects of one dimension to the other. For example, a femicide watch to collect aggregated data on gender-related killings of women, which was proposed by the SR on VAW Dubravka Šimonović, could be considered as a model for the collection of data in both the horizontal and the vertical dimension. In the latter, for instance, it would be useful to monitor cases of involuntary sterilisation and raise awareness of situations characterised by silence for decades. Furthermore, the paradigm can respond to the challenge posed by some countries that, on one hand, condemn DV and have taken steps to prevent and suppress it, but on the other hand are reluctant to recognise women's reproductive autonomy. What I mean can be explained using an example that dates back to 2016 in Italy. On 31 August, the then Italian Minister of Health launched a campaign called 'Fertility Day', in which women were encouraged in dubious advertisements to become mothers 'while they are still young' and warned that the biological clock can run quickly. Italian women have perceived it as an aggression, an interference in their private lives, a shocking way to blame women for not bearing children.[7] The government has stayed aloof from the minister, who in turn said that she would have changed the campaign. At the same time, the government professed to be worried about VAW and its consequences on women and committed to take further actions to counter it. The missing step here is the link between VAW and health: violence not only implies violation of the rights to health and sexual and reproductive rights, but also can be provoked by health policies which strongly and arbitrarily interfere with women's reproductive autonomy and reproduce patterns of discrimination.[8] Not being aware of that connection means perpetuating discrimination against women, and the unequal power relations between women and men.

The analysis also confirmed the approach that I adopted with regard to VAW: the absence of the element of intent in its definition. It was interesting to find 'patterns of discrimination' which I found in this book to encompass forms of 'tolerance' of violence by the state, state 'policies' in the health field and 'societal' patterns of discrimination which require a response in the long term.

The reconceptualisation of states' obligations as I conceived it in these pages can inspire the jurisprudence of regional human rights courts and the quasi-jurisprudence of UN treaty bodies, and, at the same time, reinforce the interpretation of existing legal instruments on VAW. It would also support the gradual consolidation of the prohibition of VAW as an international custom, confirming the proposal of the CEDAW Committee in GR No. 35 of 2017.

Women's rights to health and to reproductive health have underpinned the assessment: even though often not applied directly, these rights have played a role in determining the consequences of violence (horizontal dimension), the causes of violence (vertical dimension), state responsibility, how to decide reparations and the general measures states must adopt. This way, the content of the right to health and of the right to reproductive health has been clarified, reinforced and seen from a gender-based perspective. The rights to health and to reproductive health can play a pivotal role in defining, for example, the 'immediacy of the risk' in cases of DV, and the forms of support a victim of DV must receive, but also in identifying and 'gendering' reparations in order to consider women's specific needs and to respond to all forms of VAWH as conceived in this book.

Prognosis: what we did not achieve – international law as a cause of violence?

Even so, my analysis can be criticised because, despite the framework provided in these pages, VAWH can be said to persist in all societies. What is the point in elaborating new legal frameworks if they do not work, if they do not bring change for many women in the world? States have adopted contradictory behaviours in recent years: on one hand criminalising obstetric violence, on the other hand restricting women's access to abortion or putting into question women's autonomy.[9] Other governments have launched strategies against DV, advertising in populist ways the utmost commitment to fighting such a scourge for society, and at the same time emphasised episodes of DV only when they are committed by refugees or immigrants, 'others'. 'Let us save the women and the children only' was said by one politician in the first days of January 2019, about a ship that had not been allowed to enter any European port, perpetuating the male structure of a state that 'allows' pity to save the vulnerable, the weak, (women and children) and considers men as 'others', 'beasts' that could hurt society.

My paradigm can be challenged by those who have raised doubts about the potential of human rights and international law. 'Human rights remedies, even when successful, treat the symptoms rather than the illness, and this allows the illness not only to fester, but to seem like health itself,' posited David Kennedy, where he stressed the contradictions of human rights movements and their 'dark sides.'[10] He also pointed out that the result of initiatives which aim at reframing emancipatory objectives in human rights terms is 'more often growth for the field – more conferences, documents, legal analysis, opposition and response – than decrease in violence against women, poverty, mass slaughter and so forth.'[11] Viewed in this light, my paradigm and my reconceptualisation of states' obligations will not help reduce VAWH. Furthermore, as Chinkin and Wright argued in 1993 with regard to the right to food – which shares with the right to health its (weak) position among social, economic and cultural rights – there is a gap 'between legal provisions and realities of life for women,' and that 'the primacy accorded to the protection of individual rights does not correspond to the reality of most women's experience.'[12] We might acknowledge that states do ratify treaties without implementing them. The Council of Europe Istanbul Convention has been ratified by states that have strongly violated human rights. Does this mean that its existence is a paradox? That international human rights law is not effective? As international lawyers, we know how the system works, and as feminist lawyers we know how weak, to the point of sometimes being non-existent, are gender issues in international and human rights law. The state has been revealed to be a 'male' actor throughout my analysis. Nonetheless, my analysis has focused on international law, has relied on the international law on state responsibility, in the belief that we cannot challenge a system by looking at it from the outside, but can do so better when we know it from within.

One provocative conclusion can be drawn from the analysis contained in this book: international law, international human rights law more specifically, constitutes in itself a form of VAWH. The reason is not the absence of international legal instruments protecting women's rights – at least not after some very recent developments – but the weakness of its monitoring mechanisms, and the intrinsic limits of law, namely the competence of UN treaty bodies and regional human rights courts, the fact that the human rights to health and to reproductive health cannot be applied because they are missing from the legal instruments establishing the monitoring mechanism. Is this not a form of discrimination against women in itself, considering that redress for violations of women's rights to health and to reproductive health depends on the ratification by states of international human rights law instruments that provide for those rights? In other words, is it not the system itself that has insurmountable limits?

A question then spontaneously follows: 'should we abandon law altogether?'[13] Should we say that the international legal framework is insufficient, gender-biased, useless? My answer is No, and this book has hopefully demonstrated this conclusion. Legal requirements are essential because they define the rules states must abide by. Beth Simmons, in her remarkable book, posited that 'rather than viewing international law as reinforcing patriarchal and other power structures, the evidence suggests that it works against these structures in sometimes surprising ways,' and that 'legal commitments potentially stimulate political change[s] that rearrange the national legislative agenda, bolster civil rights litigation, fuel social and other forms of mobilization.'[14]

Legal provisions, which might bind or not bind, are not enough, though. They must be accompanied by judicial action that interprets the law in a gender-sensitive way. The judiciary is itself biased, full of myths and stereotypes, but it is also the state organ that has contributed over time to the affirmation of women's rights to health and to reproductive health. Another key role is played by groups (feminist groups, but not only them) which are not subjected to the legal obligations stemming from the treaties, but which know the provisions of international treaties and can work to put pressure on states to convince them to change legislation and to put women's rights to health and to reproductive health at the centre of policies and strategies at national level (and by individuals working to the same end).

An affirmation of states' obligations concerning the two dimensions of violence explored in this book through legal instruments and the interpretations given by the judiciary will not eradicate VAWH, unless combined with action that must start from society. Society is the actor that, through its individuals and groups, has filed complaints with international and regional bodies for the protection of human rights, and with national courts, participated in the elaboration of strategies and codes of conduct, stimulated the adoption of laws and promoted referenda to mark constitutional changes. The Istanbul Convention is very clear when stressing the importance of the involvement of society, including boys and men, in eradicating rooted and resilient stereotypes.

Law can help in making a change, but the international legal order must overcome its 'blindness' – which manifests through 'false dichotomies between categories of rights' – and its focus on 'men's needs and fears,' through 'priorities of rights that put women last rather than first.'[15] If international law is the cause of violence, then we must go back to international law to find in the system itself an answer to the challenge: law as the cause *and* the cure; law that stems from society and in society finds its nourishment and its improvement. Civil society has 'strong incentives to use law … to enhance the legitimacy of [its] claims and the prospects for realizing [its] interests.'[16] Judicial and quasi-judicial bodies have the enormous responsibility to promote an interpretation that, needless to say, conforms with the law, but is capable, as I could show from many cases examined in the *anamnesis*, of taking up the challenge of recent times.

The prognosis is not of complete cure from the disease, but of long convalescence, with eyes wide open against attempts to undermine a fragile 'health' that has been achieved through the complex and not always straightforward development of human rights law and through a mobilisation that comes from society.

Notes

1 Edelstein, 'Hippocratic prognosis', and see Introduction.
2 Except for forced abortion and forced sterilisation, which belong to the vertical dimension, all the other behaviours that are criminalised consist in interpersonal violence.
3 P. Pettit, *Republicanism. A Theory of Freedom and Government* (Oxford: Clarendon Press, 1997), p. 122.
4 Pettit (*Republicanism*, p. 48) recalls in his work Mary Astell's words in the seventeenth century: 'if all Men are born free, how is it that all Women are born Slaves?'
5 Pettit, *Republicanism,* p. 139.
6 Istanbul Convention, preamble.
7 The campaign was reported by major international newspapers. See, for example, www.nytimes.com/2016/09/14/world/europe/italy-births-fertility-europe.html.

8 The complex dimensions of the organisation and delivery of healthcare are underestimated. E. Kuhlmann and E. Annandale, 'Introduction,' in Kuhlmann and Annandale (eds), *The Palgrave Handbook of Gender and Healthcare* (Basingstoke: Palgrave Macmillan, 2010), p. 1.
9 In Italy, between the end of 2018 and the beginning of 2019, the law which decriminalised abortion (No. 194/1978, adopted on 22 May 1978) was challenged by the Minister of the Family, who called for greater restriction.
10 D. Kennedy, *The Dark Sides of Virtue* (Princeton, NJ: Princeton University Press, 2004), p. 24.
11 Kennedy, *Dark Sides of Virtue*, p. 24.
12 Chinkin and Wright, 'The hunger trap', pp. 262 and 298.
13 Chinkin and Wright, 'The hunger trap', p. 312.
14 B. Simmons, *Mobilizing for Human Rights* (Cambridge: Cambridge University Press, 2009), p. 7.
15 Chinkin and Wright, 'The right to food', p. 320.
16 Simmons, *Mobilizing*, p. 380.

Select bibliography

(See the complete bibliography, with further updates, on vawh.wordpress.com.)

Bannelier, K., 'Obligations de diligence dans le cyberspace: qui a peur de la cyber-diligence?', *Revue belge de droit international* 2 (2017) 612.

Benninger-Budel, C. (ed.), *Due Diligence and its Application to Protect Women from Violence* (The Hague: Brill, Nijhoff, 2008).

Brems, E. and Timmer, A. (eds), *Stereotypes and Human Rights Law* (Cambridge: Intersentia, 2016).

Brownmiller, S., *Against our Will. Men, Women and Rape* (New York: Fawcett Columbine, 1975).

Bunch, C., 'Transforming human rights from a feminist perspective', in Peters, J.S. and Wolper, A. (eds), *Women's Rights, Human Rights, International Feminist Perspectives* (New York, London: Routledge, 1995) 11.

Cahn, C., *Human Rights, State Sovereignty and Medical Ethics* (Leiden, Boston: Brill, 2015).

Carreau, D. and Marrella, F., *Diritto internazionale* (Milano: Giuffrè, 2018).

Cassese, A. and Gaeta, P., *Cassese's International Criminal Law* (Oxford: Oxford University Press, 2013).

Chapman, A.R., *Global Health, Human Rights and the Challenge of Neoliberal Policies* (Cambridge: Cambridge University Press, 2016).

Charlesworth, H., Chinkin C. and Wright, S., 'Feminist approaches to international law', *The American Journal of International Law* 85 (1991) 613.

Chinkin, C., 'Violence against women', in Freeman, M.A., Chinkin C. and Rudolf B. (eds), *The UN Convention on the Elimination of All Forms of Discrimination against Women* (Oxford: Oxford University Press, 2012) 443.

Chinkin, C. and Wright, S., 'The hunger trap: women, food and self-determination', *Michigan Journal of International Law* 14 (1992–3) 262.

Chinkin, C. and Charlesworth, H., *The Boundaries of International Law: A Feminist Analysis* (Manchester: Manchester University Press, 2000).

Clapham, A. and Robinson, M. (eds), *Realizing the Right to Health* (Zurich: rüffer and rub, 2009).

Cook, R.J., *Women's Health and Human Rights* (Geneva: World Health Organization, 1994).

Cook, R.J. and Dickens, B.M., *Advancing Safe Motherhood through Human Rights* (Geneva: World Health Organization, 2001).

Cook, R.J. and Cusack, S., *Gender Stereotyping: Transnational Legal Perspectives* (Philadelphia, PA: University of Pennsylvania Press, 2011).
Cook, R.J., Dickens, B.M. and Fathalla, M.F. (eds), *Reproductive Health and Human Rights: Integrating Medicine, Ethics, and Law* (Oxford: Oxford University Press, 2003).
Cook, R.J., Erdman J.N. and Dickens B.M. (eds), *Abortion Law in Transnational Perspective: Cases and Controversies* (Philadelphia, PA: University of Pennsylvania Press, 2014).
Cusack, S., 'Eliminating judicial stereotyping: Equal access to justice for women in gender-based violence cases', submitted to the Office of the High Commissioner for Human Rights on 9 June 2014, available online at https://rm.coe.int/1680597b20.
De Vido, S., *Donne, violenza e diritto internazionale. La Convenzione di Istanbul del Consiglio d'Europa del 2011* (Udine, Milan: Mimesis, 2016).
De Vido, S., 'States' positive obligations to eradicate domestic violence: the politics of relevance in the interpretation of the European Convention on Human Rights', *ESIL Reflection* 6:6 (2017), available at https://esil-sedi.eu/post_name-119/.
De Vido, S., 'The prohibition of violence against women as customary international law? Remarks on the CEDAW General Recommendation No. 35', *Diritti umani diritto internazionale* 2 (2018) 379.
Edwards, A., *Violence Against Women under International Human Rights Law* (Cambridge: Cambridge University Press, 2011).
Engle Merry, S., *Human Rights and Gender Violence: Translating International Law into Local Justice* (Chicago and London: University of Chicago Press, 2006).
Eriksson, M., *Defining Rape: Emerging Obligations for States under International Law?* (Leiden, Boston, MA: Martinus Nijhoff, 2011).
Evans, M.D. (ed.), *International Law* (Oxford: Oxford University Press, 2018).
Feinberg, J., *Harm to Others* (New York: Oxford University Press, 1984).
Forman, L., Caraoshi, L., Chapman, A.R. and Lamprea, E., 'Conceptualizing minimum core obligations under the right to health: how should we define and implements the "morality of the depths"?', *The International Journal of Human Rights* 20:4 (2016) 531.
Fredman, S., *Discrimination Law* (Oxford: Oxford University Press, 2011).
Fredman, S., *Comparative Human Rights Law* (Oxford: Oxford University Press, 2018).
Freeman, M., Chinkin, C. and Rudolf, B. (eds), *The UN Convention on the Elimination of All Forms of Discrimination against Women* (Oxford: Oxford University Press, 2012).
Friedman, M., *Autonomy, Gender, Politics* (Oxford: Oxford University Press, 2003).
Galtung, J., *Peace by Peaceful Means* (London: Sage, 1996).
Greasley K., *Arguments about Abortion. Personhood, Morality, and Law* (Oxford: Oxford University Press, 2017).
Hendriks, A., 'The right to health', *European Journal of Health Law* 1 (1994) 187.
Herrera Vacaflor, C., 'Obstetric violence: a new framework for identifying challenges to maternal healthcare in Argentina', *Reproductive Health Matters* 24:47 (2016) 65.
Kennedy D., *The Dark Sides of Virtue* (Princeton, NJ: Princeton University Press, 2004).
Kulczycki A. (ed.), *Critical Issues in Reproductive Health* (Dordrecht, Heidelberg, New York, London: Springer, 2014).
Leary, V.A., 'The right to health in international human rights law', *Health and Human Rights* 1:1 (1994) 24.

MacKinnon, C.A., *Are Women Human? and Other International Dialogues* (Cambridge, MA: Harvard University Press, 2006).
McLean, S.A.M., *Autonomy, Consent, and the Law* (Abingdon: Routledge, 2010).
McQuigg, R., *The Istanbul Convention, Domestic Violence and Human Rights* (Abingdon: Routledge, 2017).
Mégret, F., 'International human rights law theory', in Orakhelashvili, A., *Research Handbook on the Theory and History of International Law* (Cheltenham: Elgar, 2011) 199.
Meyersfeld, B., *Domestic Violence and International Law* (Oxford: Hart Publishing, 2012).
Minna Stern, A., *Eugenic Nation* (Oakland: California University Press, 2015).
Moeckli D., S. Shah and S. Sivakumaran (eds), *International Human Rights Law* (Oxford: Oxford University Press, 3rd edn, 2018).
Murphy, T., *Health and Human Rights* (Oxford and Portland, OR: Hart Publishing, 2013).
Nelson, E., *Law, Policy, and Reproductive Autonomy* (Oxford and Portland, OR: Hart Publishing, 2013).
Ngwena, C.G., 'Inscribing abortion as a human right: significance of the protocol on the rights of women in Africa', *Human Rights Quarterly* 32:4 (2010) 783.
Nowak, M., *UN Covenant on Civil and Political Rights – CCPR Commentary* (Kehl: Engel, 2005).
Nussbaum, M.C., *Frontiers of Justice* (Cambridge: Belknap Press, 2006).
Nussbaum, M.C., *The Therapy of Desire* (Princeton, NJ : Princeton University Press, 2009).
Otto, D., 'Gender and sexual diversity: A question of humanity?' *Melbourne Journal of International Law* 17 (2016) 477.
Otto D. (ed.), *Queering International Law. Possibilities, Alliances, Complicities, Risks* (London : Routledge, 2017).
Philipps, A., *Gender and Culture* (Cambridge : Polity, 2010).
Pisillo Mazzeschi, R., 'Le chemin étrange de la due diligence : d'un concept mystérieux à un concept surévalué', in Société Française pour le Droit International (SFDI), *Le standard de due diligence et la responsabilité internationale* (Paris: Pedone, 2018) 225.
Pisillo Mazzeschi, R., 'Responsabilité de l'état pour violation des obligations positives relatives aux droits de l'homme', *Recueil des Cours de l'Academie de Droit International de la Haye* 333 (2008) 175.
Purdy, L., 'Medicalization, medical necessity, and feminist medicine', *Bioethics* 15:3 (2001) 248.
Rescigno, F., 'L'autodeterminazione della persona: il faticoso cammino del diritto positivo', *Rivista critica del diritto privato* 36 (2018) 13.
Rubio-Marín, R. (ed.), *The Gender of Reparations* (Cambridge: Cambridge University Press, 2009).
Rubio-Marín, R. and Sandoval, C., 'Engendering the reparations jurisprudence of the Inter-American Court of Human Rights: the promise of the *Cotton Field* judgment', *Human Rights Quarterly* 33 (2011) 1062.
Russell, D., *Rape in Marriage* (New York: MacMillan Publishing, 1982).
Saul, B., Kinley, D. and Mowbray, J., *The International Covenant on Economic, Social and Cultural Rights. Commentary, Cases and Materials* (Oxford: Oxford University Press, 2014).

Scheinin, M., 'Core rights and obligations', in Shelton, D. (ed.), *The Oxford Handbook of International Human Rights Law* (Oxford: Oxford University Press, 2013) 527.
Schneider, E. and Wildman, S.M. (eds), *Women and the Law Stories* (New York: Foundation Press, 2011).
Shelton, D., *Remedies in International Human Rights Law* (Oxford: Oxford University Press, 2015).
Sherwin, S., *No Longer Patient: Feminist Ethics and Health Care* (Philadelphia, PA: Temple University Press, 1992).
Siegel, R.B., 'A short history of sexual harassment', in MacKinnon, C.A. and Siegel, R.B. (eds), *Directions in Sexual Harassment Law* (New Haven, CT: Yale University Press, 2004) 1.
Sifris, R., *Reproductive Freedom, Torture and International Human Rights* (London: Routledge, 2014).
Simmons, B., *Mobilizing for Human Rights* (Cambridge: Cambridge University Press, 2009).
Sjöholm, M., *Gender-Sensitive Norm Interpretation by Regional Human Rights Law Systems* (Leiden, Boston, MA : Brill, 2018).
Solinger, R. and Nakachi, M. (eds), *Reproductive States* (Oxford: Oxford University Press, 2016).
Sosa, L.P.A., *Intersectionality in the Human Rights Legal Framework on Violence Against Women* (Cambridge: Cambridge University Press, 2017).
Tasioulas, J., 'The minimum core of the human right to health' (Washington DC: World Bank, 2017), available online at https://openknowledge.worldbank.org/handle/10986/29143.
Tobin, J., *The Right to Health in International Law* (Oxford: Oxford University Press, 2012).
Wertheimer, A., *Consent to Sexual Relations* (Cambridge: Cambridge University Press, 2010).
West, C. and Fenstermaker, S. (eds), *Doing Gender, Doing Difference* (New York, London: Routledge, 2002).
Wicks, E., *The State and the Body* (Oxford and Portland: Hart, 2016).
Yllö, K. and Torres, M.G. (eds), *Marital Rape: Consent, Marriage and Social Change in Global Context* (Oxford: Oxford University Press, 2016).

Table of treaties

(In chronological order – updated 30 June 2019 – see the table of other legal instruments and documents on vawh.wordpress.com.)

1945 Charter of the United Nations and Statute of the International Court of Justice, 26 June 1945, 1 UNTS XVI.

1950 Council of Europe, European Convention for the Protection of Human Rights and Fundamental Freedoms, 4 November 1950, ETS No. 5.

1966 International Covenant on Civil and Political Rights, 16 December 1966, 999 UNTS 171 (and Optional Protocol).

International Covenant on Economic, Social and Cultural Rights, 16 December 1966, 993 UNTS 3.

1969 American Convention on Human Rights, Pact of San José, Costa Rica, 22 November 1969, available at www.oas.org/dil/access_to_information_American_Convention_on_Human_Rights.pdf.

Vienna Convention on the Law of Treaties, 23 May 1969, 1155 UNTS 331.

1979 UN Convention on the Elimination of All Forms of Discrimination Against Women, 18 December 1979, 1249 UNTS 13.

1981 African Charter on Human and Peoples' Rights, Banjul, 27 June 1981, CAB/LEG/67/3 rev. 5, 21 ILM 58 (1982).

1984 UN Convention against Torture and Other Cruel, Inhuman or Degrading Treatment or Punishment, 10 December 1984, 1465 UNTS 85.

1985 Inter-American Convention to Prevent and Punish Torture, 9 December 1985, Organization of American States Treaty Series No. 67.

1989 UN Convention on the Rights of the Child, 20 November 1989, 1577 UNTS 3.

1994 Inter-American Convention on the Prevention, Punishment and Eradication of Violence against Women, Belém do Parà, 9 June 1994, available at www.oas.org/juridico/english/treaties/a-61.html.

League of Arab States, Arab Charter on Human Rights, 15 September 1994, updated version, available at http://amitiecode.eu/sites/default/files/uploads/las_arab_charter_on_human_rights_2004_en.pdf.

1997 Convention for the Protection of Human Rights and Dignity of the Human Being with regard to the Application of Biology and Medicine, Oviedo, 4 April 1997, ETS No 164.

1998 Rome Statute for the International Criminal Court, 17 July 1998, UN Doc. A/CONF. 183/9.

1999 Optional Protocol to the Convention on the Elimination of All Forms of Discrimination against Women, 6 October 1999, 2131 UNTS 83.

2000 Council of Europe, Protocol 12 to the European Convention on Human Rights and Fundamental Freedoms on the Prohibition of Discrimination, 4 November 2000, ETS No. 177.

Explanatory Report to Protocol No. 12 to the European Convention for the Protection of Human Rights and Fundamental Freedoms.

UN Protocol to Prevent, Suppress and Punish Trafficking in Persons Especially Women and Children, supplementing the United Nations Convention against Transnational Organized Crime, 15 November 2000, 2237 UNTS 319.

2003 Protocol to the African Charter on Human and People's Rights on the Rights of Women in Africa (Maputo Protocol), 11 July 2003, available at https://au.int/en/treaties/protocol-african-charter-human-and-peoples-rights-rights-women-africa.

2005 Council of Europe Convention on Action Against Trafficking in Human Beings, Warsaw, 16 May 2005, CETS No. 197.

2008 Optional Protocol to the International Covenant on Economic, Social and Cultural Rights, 10 December 2008, Doc. A/63/435, C.N. 869.2009, available at https://treaties.un.org/doc/Publication/CN/2009/CN.869.2009-Eng.pdf.

2011 Council of Europe Convention on preventing and combating violence against women and domestic violence, Istanbul, 2011, CETS No. 210.

Explanatory Report to the Council of Europe Convention on preventing and combating violence against women and domestic violence, CETS 210.

Table of cases

(Last updated on 30 June 2019 – see also vawh.wordpress.com for national jurisprudence and further updates.)

Views of UN treaty-based bodies

Alyne da Silva Pimentel Teixeira (deceased) v. Brazil, CEDAW/C/49/D/17/2008 (2011), Communication No. 17/2008.

Amanda Jane Mellet v. Ireland, CCPR/C/116/D/2324/2013 (2016), Communication No. 2324/2013.

Andrea Szijjarto v. Hungary, CEDAW/C/36/D/4/2004 (2006), Communication No. 4/2004.

Angela González Carreño v. Spain, CEDAW/C/58/D/47/2012 (2014), Communication No. 47/2012.

A.T. v. Hungary, CEDAW/C/32/D/2/2003 (2005), Communication No. 2/2003.

Fatma Yildirim v. Austria, CEDAW/C/39/D/6/2005 (2007), Communication No. 6/2005.

Karen Noelia Llantoy Huamán (K.N.L.H.) v. Peru, CCPR/C/85/D/1153/2003 (2005), Communication No. 1153/2003.

Karen Tayag Vertido v. The Philippines, CEDAW/C/46/D/18/2008 (2010), Communication No. 18/2008.

K.L. v. Peru, CCPR/C/85/D/1153/2003 (2005), Communication No. 1153/2003.

L.C. v. Peru, CEDAW/C/50/D/22/2009 (2011), Communication No. 22/2009.

M.N.N. v. Denmark, CEDAW/C/55/D/33/2011 (2013), Communication No. 33/2011.

Şahide Goekce v. Austria, CEDAW/C/39/D/5/2005 (2007), Communication No. 6/2005.

Siobhán Whelan v. Ireland, CCPR/C/119/D/2425/2014 (2017), Communication No. 2425/2014.

S.V.P. v. Bulgaria, CEDAW/C/53/D/31/2011 (2012), Communication No. 31/2011.

V.K. v. Bulgaria, CEDAW/C/49/D/20/2008 (2011), Communication No. 20/2008.

European Court of Human Rights (and previous European Commission)

Alicja Tysiac v. Poland, Appl. No. 5410/03, ECtHR, 20 March 2007.

Angelica Camelia Bălşan v. Romania, Appl. No. 49645/09, ECtHR, 23 May 2017.

Anna Ternovszky v. Hungary, Appl. No. 67545/09, ECtHR, 14 December 2010.

A., B., C. v. Ireland, Appl. No. 25579/05, ECtHR, 16 December 2010.

Bruno Pichon and Marie-Line Sajous v. France, Appl. No. 49853/99, 2 October 2001.

C.R. v. United Kingdom, Appl. No. 20190/92, ECtHR, 22 November 1995.

Elisaveta Talpis v. Italy, Appl. No. 41237/14, ECtHR, 2 March 2017.
Emily Collins and Ashley Akaziebie v. Sweden, Appl. No. 23994/05, ECtHR, Decision on admissibility of 8 March 2007.
Enitan Pamela Izevbekhai and others v. Ireland, Appl. No. 43408/08, ECtHR, Decision on admissibility of 17 May 2011.
Giulia Rumor v. Italy, Appl. No. 72964/10, ECtHR, 27 May 2014.
G.H. v. Hungary, Appl. No. 54041/14, ECtHR, 9 June 2015.
Hayriye Pinar Civek, Rabia Merve Civek and Yaşar Civek v. Turkey, Appl. No. 55354/11, ECtHR, 23 February 2016.
I.G., M.K. and R.H. v. Slovakia (*I.G. and others*), Appl. No. 15966/04, ECtHR, 13 November 2012.
Jorgen Olof Nylund v. Finland, Appl. No. 27110/95 ECtHR, 29 June 1999.
K.A. and A.D. v. Belgium, Appls No. 42758/98 and 45558/99, ECtHR, 17 February 2005.
Lilia Eremia and others v. The Republic of Moldova, Appl. No. 3564/11, ECtHR, 28 May 2013.
Loreta Valiulienė v. Lithuania, Appl. No. 33234/07, ECtHR, 26 March 2013.
Mary Magdalene Omeredo v. Austria, Appl. No. 8969/10, ECtHR, Decision on admissibility of 20 September 2011.
Mehmet and Bekir Şentürk v. Turkey, Appl. No. 13423/09, ECtHR, 9 April 2013.
Mulkiye and Ahmet Osman v. United Kingdom, Appl. No. 23452/94, ECtHR, 28 October 1998.
M.C. v. Bulgaria, Appl. No. 39272/98, ECtHR, 4 December 2003.
Nahide Opuz v. Turkey, Appl. No. 33401/02, ECtHR, 9 June 2009.
Necati Zontul v. Greece, Appl. No. 12294/07, ECtHR, 17 January 2012.
N.B. v. Slovakia, Appl. No. 29518/10, ECtHR, 12 June 2012.
Oumou Fadil Sow v. Belgium, Appl. No. 27081/13, ECtHR, 19 January 2016.
Pretty v. United Kingdom, Appl. No. 2346/02, ECtHR, 29 April 2002.
P. and S. v. Poland, Appl. No. 57375/08, ECtHR, 30 October 2012.
R.B.A.B. and others v. The Netherlands, Appl. No. 7211/06, ECtHR, 7 June 2016.
R.R. v. Poland, Appl. No. 27617/04, ECtHR, 26 May 2011.
Sarka Dubská and Alexandra Krejzová v. Czech Republic, Appls No. 28859/11 and 28473/12, ECtHR, 15 November 2016.
Şükran Aydin v. Turkey, 57/1996/676/866, ECtHR, 25 September 1997.
S.W. v. United Kingdom, Appl. No. 20166/92, ECtHR, 22 November 1995.
Thi-Nho Vo v. France, Appl. No. 53924/00, ECtHR, 8 July 2007.
Valentina Bevacqua B. and S. v. Bulgaria, Appl. No. 71127/01, ECtHR, 12 June 2008.
V.C. v. Slovakia, Appl. No. 18968/07, ECtHR, 8 November 2011.
Wojciech Byrzykowski v. Poland, Appl. No. 11562/05, ECtHR, 27 June 2006.
Z v. Poland, Appl. No. 46132/08, ECtHR, 13 November 2012.

Court of Justice of the Europe Union

Joined Cases C-71/11 and C-99/11, *Federal Republic of Germany v. Y* (C-71/11), *Z* (C-99/11) (CJEU), ECLI:EU:C:2012:518.

Inter-American Commission and Inter-American Court of Human Rights

Ana, Beatriz and Celia González Pérez v. Mexico, Case No. 11.565, Report No. 53/01, IACommHR (2001).

Angel Manfredo Velásquez Rodríguez v. Honduras, IACHR, 29 July 1988.

Brisa Liliana De Angulo Losada v. Bolivia, Case No. 86/12, Report No. 25/17, IACommHR (2017).

Claudia Ivette González et al. ('Cotton Field') v. Mexico, IACHR, 16 November 2009.

F.S. v. Chile, Case No. 112-09, Report on admissibility No. 52/14, IACommHR (2014).

Gladys Carol Espinoza Gonzáles v. Peru, IACHR, 20 November 2014.

Inés Fernández Ortega et al. v. Mexico, IACHR, 30 August 2010.

I.V. v. Bolivia, Case No. 12.655, Report No. 72/14, IACommHR (2014).

I.V. v. Bolivia, IACHR, 30 November 2016.

Jessica Lenahan (Gonzáles) et al. v. US, Case No. 12.626, Report No. 80/11, IACommHR (2011).

Las Dos Erres Massacre v. Guatemala, IACHR, 24 November 2009.

Linda Loaiza López Soto and relatives v. Venezuela, Case No. 12.797, Report No. 33/16, IACommHR (2016).

Linda Loaiza López Soto and others v. Venezuela, IACHR, 26 September 2018.

Manuela y Familia v. El Salvador, Case No. 424/12, Report No. 29/17, IACommHR (2017).

Maria da Penha Maia Fernandes v. Brazil, Case No. 12.051, Report No. 54/01, IACommHR (2001).

María Mamérita Mestanza Chávez v. Peru, Case No. 12.191, Report No. 71/03, IACommHR (2003).

Mariana Selvas Gomez and others v. Mexico (Atenco), Case No. 12.846, Report No. 158/11, admissibility, IACommHR (2011).

Matter of B., IACHR, order, provisional measures, of 29 May 2013.

Mujeres Víctimas de Tortura Sexual en Atenco v. Mexico (Atenco), IACHR, 28 November 2018.

Paulina del Carmen Ramírez Jacinto v. Mexico, Report No. 21/07, friendly settlement agreement, IACommHR (2007).

Plan de Sánchez Massacre v. Guatemala, IACHR, 19 November 2004.

Raquel Martín de Mejía v. Peru, Case No. 10.970, Report No. 5/96, IACommHR (1996).

Xákmok Kásek Indigenous Community v. Paraguay, IACHR, 24 August 2010.

European Committee of Social Rights

CGIL v. Italy, decision of 12 October 2015, published on 11 April 2016, complaint No. 91/2013, cc-91-2013-dadmissandmerits-en.

International Planned Parenthood Federation – European Network (IPPF EN) v. Italy, decision of 10 September 2013, published on 10 March 2014, complaint No. 87/2012, cc-87-2012-dmerits-en.

African Commission on Human and People's Rights

Equality Now and Ethiopian Women Lawyers Association (EWLA) v. Federal Republic of Ethiopia, Communication 341/2007, adopted by the African Commission on Human and Peoples' Rights during the 19th Extra-Ordinary Session, from 16 to 25 February 2016, Banjul, Gambia, available at www.achpr.org/sessions.

Zimbabwe Human Rights NGO Forum v. *Zimbabwe,* Communication No 245/ 2002, adopted by the African Commission on Human and Peoples' Rights during the 39th

Ordinary Session, from 11 to 25 May 2006, Banjul, Gambia, available at www.escr-net.org/sites/default/files/caselaw/equality_now_ethiopian_w_omen_lawyers_association_decision_2007_0.pdf.

National courts

Argentina

Judgment of 5 September 2014, *G., M. C. Y v. Hospital Luis Lagomaggiore s/ d y p*, 2014, RCyS2015-III, 137 (Cámara 3ra de Apelaciones en lo Civil, Comercial, Minas, de Paz y Tributaria de Mendoza).

Judgment of 5 March 2002, *Portal de Belén Asociación Civil sin Fines de Lucro v. Ministerio de Salud de la Nación/ANMAT* (Supreme Court of Argentina).

Judgment of 26 December 2000, *T., S. v. Gobierno de la Ciudad de Buenos Aires* (Tribunal Superior de la Ciudad Autónoma de Buenos Aires).

Australia

R v. A2; R v. K.M.; R v. Vaziri (No. 2) [2015] NSWSC 1221 (27 August 2015).

R v. A2; R v. K.M.; R v Vaziri (No. 23) [2016] NSWSC 282 (18 March 2016).

Brazil

Supremo Tribunal Federal, ADPF 54, 12 April 2012.

Supremo Tribunal Federal, *Habeas Corpus* 124.306, Rio de Janeiro, 29 November 2016.

Colombia

C-355/2006, 10 May 2006, expedientes D- 6122, 6123 y 6124 Demandas de inconstitucionalidad contra los Arts. 122, 123 (parcial), 124, modificados por el Art. 14 de la Ley 890 de 2004, y 32, numeral 7, de la ley 599 de 2000 Código Penal.

Emberá-Chamí Community FGM Case, Juzgado Promiscuo Municipal [Municipal Jurisdiction Court], 24 July 2008, Radicación No. 66572–40–89–001–2008–00005–00 (Colom.).

State Council, Chamber of Administrative dispute, Ref.: Expediente núm. 200200251 01, Actor: Carlos Humberto Gómez Arambula, 5 June 2008.

T-388/09, 28 May 2009, Colombian Constitutional Court, *En el proceso de revisión del fallo proferido por el Juzgado Segundo Penal del Circuito de la ciudad de Santa Marta*.

T-627/12, Colombian Constitutional Court.

France

Cour de Cassation, chambre criminelle, No. de pourvoi: 83-92616, 20 August 1983.

India

Court of its own motion v. Union of India, W.P. (C) 5913/2010 (High Court in Delhi).

Independent Thought v. Union of India, Writ Petition (Civil) No. 382 of 2013, 11 October 2017 (SC)– summary and comment at https://reproductiverights.org/sites/default/files/documents/Independent-Thought-Factsheet-0118.pdf.

Laxmi Mandal v. Deen Dayal Harinagar Hospital (2010) 172 D.L.T. 9 (High Court in Delhi).

R/Criminal Misc., Application No. 26957 of 2017, 2 April 2018 (High Court of Gujarat at Ahmedabad) – summary and comment at https://indiankanoon.org/doc/185050052/.

Sandesh Bansal v. Union of India and others, W.P. no. 9061/2008; W.P. no. 11860/2013 (High Court in Delhi).

Italy

Administrative Tribunal in Lazio (TAR Lazio), sez. IIIQ, judgment of 2 August 2016, n. 8990.

Cassazione sez. civile, sez. III, judgment of 17 May 2010, n. 11958.

Cassazione sez. penale, judgment of 16 February 1976, n. 12855.

Cassazione sez. penale, sez IV, judgment of 24 January 2013, n. 11493.

Corte d'appello di Catania, sez. della Famiglia della Persona e dei Minori, *A.F. v. Ministro dell'Interno*, judgment of 17 December 2012.

Tribunale di Verona, judgment of 14 April 2010, n. 279, and Court of Appeal in Venice, judgment of 23 November 2012, n. 1485.

Kenya

J.O.O. (also known as J.M.) v. The Attorney-General & 4 others [2017] eKRL, Petition No.5 of 2014 (High Court in Bungoma).

Namibia

L.M. and Others v Government of the Republic of Namibia (I 1603/2008, I 3518/2008, I 3007/2008) [2012] NAHC 211 (30 July 2012).

Nepal

Supreme Court Special Bench, Order Writ No. 55 of the year 2058 BS (2001–2), *on behalf of the Forum for Women, Law and Development, Thapathali, ward No. 11 of Kathmandu Municipal Corporation and on her own, Advocate Meera Dhungana, 33 v. His Majesty's Government, Ministry of Law, Justice and Parliamentary Affairs, The House of Representatives, The National Assembly.*

Lakshmi Dhikta v. Government of Nepal, Writ No. 0757, 2067 (2009), Supreme Court of Nepal, 2009 (translation available at www.reproductiverights.org/sites/crr.civicactions.net/files/documents/Lakshmi%20Dhikta%20-%20English%20translation.pdf).

South Korea

2017 *Hun-Ba* 127, 11 April 2019. English translation at http://search.ccourt.go.kr/ths/ep/selectThsEp0101List.do.

Spain

STS (Contencioso-Administrativo) de 17 de julio 2018, Rec. de Casación núm. 1002/2017.

Uganda

Law and Advocacy for Women in Uganda v. Attorney-General [2010] UGCC 4; Constitutional Petition No. 8 of 2007, 28 July 2010 (Constitutional Court).

United Kingdom

Brend v. Wood [1946] 62 TLR 462 (Divisional court).

Doogan v. Greater Glasgow and Clyde Health Board [2015] UKSC 68.

Janaway v. Salford Area Health Authority [1988] 3 All ER 1079 (UKHL).

K (F.C.), Fornah (F.C.) v. Secretary of State for the Home Department, [2006] UKHL 46, 18 October 2006.

R v. R [1991] 2 WLR 1065, 1074 B–C (UKHL).

Zainab Esther Fornah v. Secretary of State for the Home Department, [2005] EWCA Civ 680, 9 June 2005 (Court of Appeal).

USA

Brown v. State, 106 N.W. 536 (Wisconsin 1906).

Buck v. Bell, 274 US 200 (1927).

Gonzales v. Carhart, 127 S. Ct. 1610, 1633 (2007).

Mohamed v. R. Gonzales [2005] USCA9 150; 400 F.3d 785 (10 March 2005).

Planned Parenthood of Indiana v. Commissioner of Indiana State Department of Health, Nos 11/2464 and 17/1883 (United States Court of Appeals for the Seventh Circuit), argued 20 October 2011, decided 23 October 2012.

Planned Parenthood of Indiana and Kentucky, Inc. v. Commissioner of Indiana State Department of Health, No. 17/1883 (United States Court of Appeals for the Seventh Circuit), argued 6 November 2017, decided 25 July 2018.

Planned Parenthood of Southeast Pennsylvania v. Casey, 505 US 833 (1992), 91/744, *certiorari* to the United States Court of Appeals for the Third Circuit, argued 22 April 1992, decided 29 June 1992.

Roe v. Wade, 410 US 113 (1973).

Shawanna Nelson v. Correctional Medical Services, 583 F.3d 522 (8th Cir. 2009).

Whole Woman's Health et al. v. Hellerstedt, Commissioner, Texas Department of State Health Services, et al., Certiorari to the United States Court of Appeals for the Fifth Circuit No. 15–274, argued 2 March 2016, decided 27 June 2016.

Women Prisoners of DC Departmentt of Corrections v. District of Columbia, 877 F. Supp. 634, 668–69 (D.D.C. 1994), 899 F. Supp. 659 (D.D.C. 1995), 93 F.3d 910 (DC Cir. 1996).

Index

EU authorised representative for GPSR:
Easy Access System Europe, Mustamäe tee 50,
10621 Tallinn, Estonia
gpsr.requests@easproject.com

www.ingramcontent.com/pod-product-compliance
Ingram Content Group UK Ltd.
Pitfield, Milton Keynes, MK11 3LW, UK
UKHW021840100926
8556IPUK00004B/458

* 9 7 8 1 5 2 6 1 2 4 9 7 5 *